VAULT GUIDE TO THE

# TOP 50 MANAGEMENT AND STRATEGY CONSULTING FIRMS

VAULT GUIDE TO THE

# TOP 50 MANAGEMENT AND STRATEGY CONSULTING FIRMS

MARCY LERNER
AND THE STAFF OF VAULT

# ACKNOWLEDGMENTS

Thanks to everyone who had a hand in making this book possible, especially Todd Kuhlman, Marshall Lager, Stephanie Clifford, Kelly Shore and Laurie Pasiuk. We are also extremely grateful to Vault's entire staff of writers, editors and interns for all their help in the editorial and production processes.

Vault also would like to acknowledge the support of Matt Doull, Ahmad Al-Khaled, Lee Black, Eric Ober, Hollinger Ventures, Tekbanc, New York City Investment Fund, Globix, Hoover's, Glenn Fischer, Mark Hernandez, Ravi Mhatre, Carter Weiss, Ken Cron, Ed Somekh, Isidore Mayrock, Zahi Khouri, Sana Sabbagh, and other Vault investors, as well as our family and friends.

In order to ensure that our research was thorough and accurate, we relied on a number of people within the consulting firms that we profiled. A special thanks to all of the recruiting managers, public relations executives, marketing professionals and consultants who graciously provided feedback whenever we needed it.

To the 1,700-plus consultants who took the time to be interviewed or to complete our survey, we could never thank you enough. Your insights about life inside the top consulting firms were invaluable, and your willingness to speak candidly will be a great service to job seekers and career changers for years to come.

5

You may not know us, but our
**clients** certainly do

MONITOR GROUP was named one of the top 5 strategy
consulting firms by Vault.com. Visit our website to find out what
our Fortune 500 clients and Vault.com already know…

Monitor is one of the better kept "secrets" in consulting.

www.monitor.com

# Table of Contents

## THE BEST OF THE REST                        369

# CONSULTING EMPLOYER DIRECTORY 489

# APPENDIX 501

# How many consulting job boards have you visited lately?

## (Thought so.)

Use the Internet's most targeted job search tools for consulting professionals.

## Vault Consulting Job Board

The most comprehensive and convenient job board for consulting professionals. Target your search by area of consulting, function, and experience level, and find the job openings that you want. No surfing required.

## VaultMatch Resume Database

Vault takes match-making to the next level: post your resume and customize your search by area of consulting, experience and more. We'll match job listings with your interests and criteria and e-mail them directly to your inbox.

> VAULT
> the most trusted name in career information™

# Introduction

To help you in your quest for the perfect consulting position, this year we've focused this guide, the *Vault Guide to the Top 50 Management and Strategy Consulting Firms*, on, yes, management and strategy consulting firms. We have also included specialized consulting firms – economic consulting, financial consulting, human resources consulting, energy consulting, operations consulting and business research.

This year is the third year we've ranked consulting firms for prestige to create our Top 50 list. 2004 marks the first year, however, that we've ranked the Top 50 Management and Strategy consulting firms. Vault surveyed over 1,700 practicing consultants to bring you this ranking – chosen by the consultants themselves.

The 76 company profiles in this book are based on painstaking research and detailed feedback from current consultants. The companies range from gigantic ex-Big Four juggernauts to specialized consulting boutiques with fewer than 50 consultants.

If you know you want a job in consulting, of course, you've got your work cut out for you. Even in the boom years of the 1990s, there were far more candidates for plum consulting opportunities than open positions. Now, in the third year of tough economic times in the consulting industry, consulting jobs are scarcer and more sought after than ever. To find a job, you need to do your research – and to cast your net wider, learning about as many possible employers as you can. Prestige is one way to choose an employer, and it's a good one. Prestigious consulting firms often attract a higher caliber of clients and projects, and a recognizable name looks great on any resume. Still, there are other reasons to choose a consulting firm – specialty, location, perks – and you'll learn about all of them in the *Vault Guide to the Top 50 Management and Strategy Consulting Firms*.

Good luck in your consulting career!

The Editors

Vault, Inc.

# A Guide to this Guide

If you're wondering how our entries are organized, read on. Here's a handy guide to the information you'll find packed into each firm profile in this book.

## Firm Facts

- **Locations:** A listing of the firm's offices, with the city of its headquarters bolded. For firms with a relatively small number of offices, all cities are included. Countries for international offices are typically not specified unless the location is uncommon.

- **Practices Areas:** Official departments that employ a significant portion of the firm's consultants. Practice areas are listed in alphabetical order regradless of their size and prominence.

- **Uppers and Downers:** Good points and bad points of the firm, as derived from associate interviews and surveys, as well as other research. Uppers and downers are perceptions based on surveys and are not based on statistics.

- **Employment Contact:** The person, address or web site that the firm identifies as the best place to send resumes or the appropriate contact to answer questions about the recruitment process. Sometimes more than one contact is given.

## The Buzz

When it comes to other consulting firms, our respondents are full of opinions! We asked them to detail their opinions and observations about firms other than their own, and collected a sampling of these comments in The Buzz.

When selecting The Buzz, we included quotes most representative of the common outside perceptions of the firms, even if in our opinion the quotes did not accurately or completely describe the firm. Please keep in mind when reading The Buzz that it's often more fun for outsiders to trash than praise a competing consulting firm. Nonetheless, The Buzz can be a valuable means to gauge a firm's reputation in the consulting industry, or at least to detect common misperceptions. We typically included two to four Buzz comments. In some rare instances we opted not to include The Buzz if we did not receive a diversity of comments.

## The Stats

- **Employer Type:** The firm's classification as a publicly traded company, privately held company or subsidiary.
- **Stock Symbol:** The stock ticker symbol for a public company.
- **Stock Exchange:** The exchange on which a public company's stock is traded.
- **Chairman, CEO, etc.:** The name and title of the leader of the firm. Sometimes more than one name, or the name of the head of the firm's consulting business, may be provided.
- **No. of Employees:** The total number of employees, including consultants and other staff, at a firm in all offices (unless otherwise specified). Some firms do not disclose this information; numbers for the most recent year the information is available (if at all) is included.
- **Revenue:** The gross sales (in U.S. dollars) the firm generated in the specified fiscal year(s). Some firms do not disclose this information; numbers for the most recent year the information is available (if at all) is included. In some cases, revenue is given in Euros (EUR).

## The Profiles

The profiles are divided into three sections: The Scoop, Getting Hired and Our Survey Says.

- **The Scoop:** The firm's history, clients, recent firm developments and other points of interest.
- **Getting Hired:** Qualifications the firm looks for in new associates, tips on getting hired and other notable aspects of the hiring process.
- **Our Survey Says:** Actual quotes from surveys and interviews with current consultants of the firm on topics such as the firm's culture, feedback, hours, travel requirements, pay, training and more. Profiles of some firms do not include an Our Survey Says section.

## Best of the Rest

Even though the name of this book is the Vault Guide to the Top 50 Management and Strategy Consulting Firms, we didn't stop there, including 26 other firms we thought notable and/or interesting enough for inclusion. These firms are listed alphabetically.

# THE VAULT
# PRESTIGE
# RANKINGS

# Ranking Methodology

The Vault consulting survey keeps getting bigger and better. This year, for the 2004 edition of the *Vault Guide to the Top 50 Management and Strategy Consulting Firms*, we selected a list of top management, strategy and specialist consulting firms to include on the Vault survey. These firms were selected because of their prominence in the consulting industry and their interest to job seekers.

The Vault survey was distributed through the firms on Vault's list in the spring and summer of 2003. In some cases, Vault contacted practicing consultants directly. Survey respondents were asked to do several things. They were asked to rate each consulting firm on the survey on a scale of one to 10 based on prestige, with 10 being the most prestigious. (Consultants were unable to rate their own firm. They were asked only to rate firms with which they were familiar.)

Vault collected the survey results and averaged the score for each firm. The firms were then ranked, with the highest score No. 1, all the way to No. 50.

We also asked survey respondents to give their perceptions of other consulting firms besides their own. A selection of those comments is featured on each firm profile as "The Buzz." We typically included two to four Buzz comments. In a few isolated cases, we opted not to include the Buzz on a profile.

Remember that Vault's Top 50 Management and Strategy Consulting Firms are chosen by practicing consultants at top consulting firms. Vault does not choose or influence the rankings. The rankings measure perceived prestige (as judged by consulting professionals) and not revenue, size or lifestyle.

# The Vault 50 • 2004

[The 50 most prestigious consulting firms]

| RANK | FIRM | SCORE | RANK 2003 | HEADQUARTERS |
|------|------|-------|-----------|--------------|
| 1 | McKinsey & Company | 8.249 | 1 | New York, NY |
| 2 | Boston Consulting Group | 7.848 | 2 | Boston, MA |
| 3 | Bain & Company | 7.371 | 3 | Boston, MA |
| 4 | Booz Allen Hamilton | 6.432 | 4 | McLean, VA |
| 5 | Monitor Group | 6.060 | 5 | Cambridge, MA |
| 6 | Mercer Management Consulting | 5.801 | 6 | New York, NY |
| 7 | Gartner | 5.552 | 10 | Stamford, CT |
| 8 | A.T. Kearney | 5.528 | 11 | Plano, TX |
| 9 | Mercer Oliver Wyman | 5.524 | 25 | New York, NY |
| 10 | Roland Berger Strategy Consultants | 5.314 | 21 | Munich, Germany |
| 11 | Deloitte Consulting | 5.292 | 8 | New York, NY |
| 12 | Accenture | 5.180 | 9 | New York, NY |
| 13 | Mercer Human Resource Consulting | 5.099 | 17 | New York, NY |
| 14 | Marakon Associates | 5.067 | 15 | New York, NY |
| 15 | Parthenon Group, The | 5.065 | 20 | Boston, MA |
| 16 | IBM BCS | 5.009 | 12 | Somers, NY |
| 17 | L.E.K. Consulting | 4.987 | 22 | Boston, MA |
| 18 | Cap Gemini Ernst & Young | 4.910 | 14 | New York, NY |
| 19 | Towers Perrin | 4.580 | 18 | New York, NY |
| 20 | BearingPoint | 4.550 | 13 | McLean, VA |
| 21 | DiamondCluster International | 4.266 | 23 | Chicago, IL |
| 22 | Charles River Associates | 4.211 | 34 | Boston, MA |
| 23 | Hewitt Associates | 4.205 | 16 | Lincolnshire, IL |
| 24 | Stern Stewart & Co. | 4.203 | 30 | New York, NY |
| 25 | NERA Economic Consulting | 4.175 | NA | White Plains, NY |

| RANK | FIRM | SCORE | RANK 2003 | HEADQUARTERS |
|---|---|---|---|---|
| 26 | Mars & Company | 4.017 | 31 | Greenwich, CT |
| 27 | Hay Group | 4.013 | 32 | Philadelphia, PA |
| 28 | OC&C Strategy Consultants | 3.975 | NA | New York, NY |
| 29 | First Manhattan Consulting Group | 3.896 | 42 | New York, NY |
| 30 | Watson Wyatt Worldwide | 3.850 | 26 | Washington, DC |
| 31 | Grant Thornton | 3.659 | 33 | Chicago, IL |
| 32 | Kurt Salmon Associates | 3.588 | 29 | Atlanta, GA |
| 33 | ZS Associates | 3.444 | 35 | Evanston, IL |
| 34 | PRTM | 3.412 | 39 | Waltham, MA/ Mountain View, CA |
| 35 | The Brattle Group | 3.407 | NA | Cambridge, MA |
| 36 | Strategic Decisions Group | 3.316 | NA | Menlo Park, CA |
| 37 | PA Consulting | 3.292 | 40 | London, UK |
| 38 | Corporate Executive Board | 3.152 | 44 | Washington, DC |
| 39 | Dean & Comp. | 3.089 | 37 | Vienna, VA |
| 40 | Giuliani Partners | 3.077 | NA | New York, NY |
| 41 | Droege & Company | 3.038 | NA | Düsseldorf, Germany |
| 42 | Aon Consulting | 3.020 | 47 | Chicago, IL |
| 43 (tie) | LECG | 3.000 | NA | Emeryville, CA |
| 43 (tie) | Value Partners | 3.000 | 49 | Milan, Italy |
| 45 | Braun Consulting | 2.984 | NA | Chicago, IL |
| 46 | Navigant | 2.980 | NA | Chicago, IL |
| 47 | Analysis Group | 2.919 | NA | Boston, MA |
| 48 | Corporate Value Associates | 2.788 | NA | Paris, France |
| 49 | Putnam Associates | 2.774 | NA | Burlington, MA |
| 50 | Buck Consultants | 2.682 | NA | New York, NY |

# How many consulting job boards have you visited lately?

## (Thought so.)

---

Use the Internet's most targeted

job search tools for consulting

professionals.

## Vault Consulting Job Board

The most comprehensive and convenient job board for consulting professionals. Target your search by area of consulting, function, and experience level, and find the job openings that you want. No surfing required.

## VaultMatch Resume Database

Vault takes match-making to the next level: post your resume and customize your search by area of consulting, experience and more. We'll match job listings with your interests and criteria and e-mail them directly to your inbox.

# Practice Area Ranking Methodology

Vault also asked consultants to rank the best firms in several areas of business focus: operations and implementation; economic consulting; energy consulting; financial consulting, health care/pharma consulting and human resource consulting. Consultants were allowed to vote for up to three firms as the best in each area.

The following charts indicate the rankings in each practice area, along with the total percentage of votes cast in favor of each firm. (If at least one consultant voted for more than one firm, no firm could get 100 percent of the votes; if every consultant had voted for the same three firms, for example, the maximum score would be 33.3 percent.)

## Strategy Consulting

| RANK | FIRM | % | RANK 2002 |
|------|------|-----|-----------|
| 1 | McKinsey & Company | 30.68 | 1 |
| 2 | Boston Consulting Group | 23.84 | 2 |
| 3 | Bain & Company | 14.18 | 3 |
| 4 | Booz Allen Hamilton | 8.25 | 4 |
| 5 | A.T. Kearney | 3.32 | 6 |
| 6 | Accenture | 2.9 | 5 |
| 7 | Monitor Group | 2.87 | 7 |
| 8 | Deloitte Consulting | 1.76 | 8 |
| 9 | Mercer Management Consulting | 1.34 | 7 |
| 10 | BearingPoint | 1.18 | 11 |

# HR Consulting

| RANK | FIRM | % | RANK 2003 |
|------|------|-----|-----------|
| 1 | Mercer Human Resource Consulting | 27.99 | 5 |
| 2 | Towers Perrin | 16.73 | 1 |
| 3 | Hewitt Associates | 11.97 | 2 |
| 4 | Hay Group | 11.09 | NR |
| 5 | Watson Wyatt Worldwide | 8.8 | 4 |
| 6 | Cap Gemini Ernst & Young | 2.11 | 10 |
| 7 (tie) | Accenture | 1.94 | 8 |
| 7 (tie) | Deloitte Consulting | 1.94 | 7 |
| 8 | A.T. Kearney | 1.41 | NR |
| 9 | IBM BCS | 1.23 | 9 |
| 10 (tie) | Boston Consulting Group | 1.06 | NR |
| 10 (tie) | Booz Allen Hamilton | 1.06 | NR |
| 10 (tie) | Bain & Company | 1.06 | NR |

# Operations

| RANK | FIRM | % |
|------|------|---|
| 1 | Accenture | 19.19 |
| 2 | A.T. Kearney | 18.95 |
| 3 | Cap Gemini Ernst & Young | 8.17 |
| 4 | Deloitte Consulting | 7.69 |
| 5 | McKinsey & Company | 7.22 |
| 6 | IBM BCS | 6.82 |
| 7 | Booz Allen Hamilton | 5.95 |
| 8 | Bain & Company | 3.97 |
| 9 | Boston Consulting Group | 3.81 |
| 10 | BearingPoint | 3.65 |

# Pharmaceuticals/Health Care

| RANK | FIRM | % |
|---|---|---|
| 1 | McKinsey & Company | 17.28 |
| 2 | Boston Consulting Group | 15.23 |
| 3 | ZS Associates | 6.38 |
| 4 (tie) | Accenture | 5.14 |
| 4 (tie) | Cap Gemini Ernst & Young | 5.14 |
| 5 | Bain & Company | 4.73 |
| 6 | IMS Health | 4.53 |
| 7 | Deloitte Consulting | 3.7 |
| 8 | Health Advances | 3.09 |
| 9 (tie) | IBM BCS | 2.26 |
| 9 (tie) | Monitor Group | 2.26 |
| 10 | A.T. Kearney | 2.06 |

# Energy

| RANK | FIRM | % |
|------|------|---|
| 1 | McKinsey & Company | 21.55 |
| 2 | A.T. Kearney | 10.5 |
| 3 | Accenture | 6.91 |
| 4 | Charles River Associates | 6.63 |
| 5 | Booz Allen Hamilton | 6.08 |
| 6 | Boston Consulting Group | 5.8 |
| 7 | Cap Gemini Ernst & Young | 4.97 |
| 8 | Deloitte Consulting | 3.87 |
| 9 | Bain & Company | 3.04 |
| 10 | LECG | 2.49 |

# Economic Consulting

| RANK | FIRM | % |
|------|------|---|
| 1 | McKinsey & Company | 14.6 |
| 2 | NERA Economic Consulting | 12.03 |
| 3 | Boston Consulting Group | 10.45 |
| 4 | Charles River Associates | 8.09 |
| 5 | Bain & Company | 5.92 |
| 6 (tie) | Accenture | 3.75 |
| 6 (tie) | LECG | 3.75 |
| 7 | Cap Gemini Ernst & Young | 2.96 |
| 8 (tie) | Marakon Associates | 2.76 |
| 8 (tie) | Stern Stewart & Co. | 2.76 |
| 9 (tie) | Deloitte Consulting | 2.56 |
| 9 (tie) | Monitor Group | 2.56 |
| 10 (tie) | A.T. Kearney | 2.17 |
| 10 (tie) | Lexecon Inc. | 2.17 |

# Financial Sector

| RANK | FIRM | % |
|---|---|---|
| 1 | McKinsey & Company | 24.56 |
| 2 | Mercer Oliver Wyman | 12.72 |
| 3 | Boston Consulting Group | 11.31 |
| 4 | Bain & Company | 7.95 |
| 5 | First Manhattan Consulting Group | 4.42 |
| 6 | Accenture | 3.89 |
| 7 tie) | Cap Gemini Ernst & Young | 3.18 |
| 7 (tie) | Deloitte Consulting | 3.18 |
| 8 | A.T. Kearney | 2.83 |
| 9 | Booz Allen Hamilton | 2.65 |
| 10 (tie) | BearingPoint | 2.12 |
| 10 (tie) | IBM BCS | 2.12 |

# OVERVIEW OF THE CONSULTING INDUSTRY

# The State of Consulting

## Shorter engagements, tighter budgets

It's been a tough few years for management and strategy consulting firms. Traditionally, engagments for huge Fortune 500 companies have been the mainstay of the consulting industry. At one point in the 1990s, for example, AT&T was estimated to employ 300 management and strategy consultants at any one time, running up bills of up to $1 billion – yes, billion – a year.

Those salad days are long gone. With economic times tough, former fat cat clients are taking a hard look at consulting budgets – and slashing left and right. Some former clients, like investment banks Credit Suisse First Boston and Lehman Brothers, have imposed a moratorium on hiring management consultants altogether. Other firms have placed their hiring under much tighter scrutiny, which tends to affect management and strategy consultants disproportionately – it's easier to get approval for a technology installation than a big picture analysis of future markets. Other big corporations, like American Express and AOL Time Warner, have created their own internal consulting units, further decreasing the need to hire outsiders.

Engagements have been getting shorter as clients seek to cut costs. The average engagement length, according to seasoned industry analyst Tom Rodenhauser, has plummeted to 90 days from a high of six to 18 months in the mid-1990s. Strategy consultants are typically given more direction – a specific analysis of a competitor, for example, instead of a wide-ranging exploration of strategic possibilities. In November 2002, Ken Favaro of Marakon Associates estimated to *The Economist* that the consulting industry was still at 30 percent overcapacity. Another estimate by *The Economist* holds that revenues at the top strategy firms are shrinking by 10 percent a year.

Of course, dire predictions of ill times ahead for consulting firms were rampant in the late 1980s and early 1990s – and were followed by a rebound of great robustness. Will the same hold true for management and strategy consulting in years to come? The next few years will tell whether the consulting business model is sound.

## Coping mechanisms

What are management and strategy consulting firms doing to find clients? Going after different clients, and broadening their mix of services. Booz Allen Hamilton, for example, has traditionally served both "commercial" clients (i.e., private employers and corporations) and government clients. While the commercial side of its business has suffered, its government contracts continue to enjoy strong growth as the appetite of the United States government for consulting services increases. McKinsey, traditionally the purest of strategy plays, has been beefing up its technology strategy services, creating a worldwide practice specifically for such assignments.

At the same time, larger, more technology-oriented firms like Accenture and IBM are crowding into the strategy space. In October 2002, for example, IBM completed its acquisition of PwC Consulting, allowing it greater entrée into the strategy and management consulting space. Accenture has also capitalized on the inroads made by its technology consulting practice to gobble up integrated strategy and management consulting work as well. In years to come, perhaps the distinction between strategy and technology will fade as technology becomes integrated into the strategy of company operations.

## Outsourcing

Perhaps one of the greatest areas of growth for management consulting firms has been in outsourcing – an operational specialty. Outsourcing involves helping clients find cheaper ways to get essential operations done – everything from human resources to printing brochures. Sometimes consulting firms may undertake the function themselves – Hewitt, for example, is a human resources consulting firm that manages the pensions and payroll functions for clients. In other cases, the consulting firm acts as the intermediary, helping the client find the most cost-effective vendors and locations to outsource its business. Many companies, even management and strategy consulting firms, anticipate that outsourcing will come to represent a third, a half or more of all engagements in years to come.

## Boutiques

One change reflected in this year's edition of the *Top 50 Management and Strategy Consulting Firms* is the increased importance of boutique consulting firms, which are usually small and focused on a few core competencies. Oftentimes, refugees from top consulting firms such as McKinsey and BCG establish these firms. Clients use boutiques because of their deep niche expertise, and because they are more likely to work with senior consultants at such a small firm. While boutique consulting firms do not hire new consultants in the same numbers as larger consulting firms, many of them are actively growing.

## Sarbanes-Oxley's fallout

In 2002, Congress passed the Sarbanes-Oxley act in response to the accounting scandals rocking the United States, such as the spectacular Enron and WorldCom bankruptcies and the related collapse of Big Five stalwart Arthur Andersen. The Sarbanes-Oxley act, intended to increase the reliability of corporate reporting and accounting, requires accountants to maintain much stricter internal controls. Limitations are placed on the ability of firms to perform outside consulting services to audit clients. In response, most of the remaining Big Four firms completed or took steps to complete the spin-off or sale of their consulting arms – PricewaterhouseCoopers, for example, after planning to spin off its consulting business under the much-derided name Monday, abruptly sold it to IBM in October 2002. The sole exception? Deloitte Consulting. Deloitte & Touche had planned to spin off Deloitte Consulting under the Braxton name. (Braxton Associates is a smaller consulting firm previously acquired by Deloitte.) However, in March 2003, Deloitte abruptly shelved those plans. The firm says it will still abide by Sarbanes-Oxley.

## De-incentivizing the leverage of value-added knowledge capital

If there's one thing consulting firms are known for, it's impenetrable jargon. Why provide help to a client when you can offer "solutions to maximize value?" Why "do" something when you can instead both "implement" and "execute" it? Do you really need to "incentivize" employees? Fortunately, Deloitte Consulting has come to the rescue. In June 2003, Deloitte Consulting began to distribute a program it cheekily calls "Bullfighter," which flags documents that are too jargon-heavy. "We've had it with repurposable, value-added knowledge capital and robust, leverageable mindshare," said Deloitte Consulting parter Brian Fugere. Fugere noted that tests of the software showed that companies tended to use more jargon as their financial performance deteriorated.

# Practice Areas

## Operations and implementation

Operations is the difference between strategy (making a plan) and putting that plan into action. Operations consultants examine a client's internal workings, such as production processes, distribution, order fulfillment and customer service. While strategy involves setting a client's goals, operations ensures that clients reach these goals. Operations consultants may investigate customer service response times, cut operating costs, assist with outsourcing, or look into the allocation of client resources. Operations consulting normally includes the implementation of these findings and processes.

Typical engagements may include:

- Streamlining the equipment purchasing processes of a major manufacturer

- Outsourcing customer call centers to India

- Working with a newly-merged commercial bank to increase customer response efficiency

## Human resources consulting

The best business strategies and finest operational processes mean nothing without the people to put them in place. HR consulting addresses the issue of maximizing the value of employees and placing the right people in the right roles. HR consulting firms are also hired for organizational restructuring, systems implementation and ongoing studies and initiatives.

An important corollary to HR consulting is HR outsourcing. Increasingly, clients are turning to HR consulting firms to manage their internal HR systems. Hewitt Associates, for example, now earns 65 percent of its revenue from HR outsourcing.

Examples of typical human resources consulting engagements include:

• Creating or updating a client's compensation structure

• Counseling and processing laid off (or downsized, "rightsized," etc.) employees and assisting them with outplacement

• Helping to blend the cultures and processes of merged companies

## Health care/pharmaceuticals consulting

This practice area is one of the growth areas in the consulting world. As the population of the United States and of other industrialized countries around the world ages, and as scientists steadily unlock the mysteries of genetic engineering, the health care industry continues to thrive at a time when so many sectors of the economy are faltering. The United States health care market was worth nearly $1.4 trillion as of 2002, and the European market $700 million. Yet just because the market is large doesn't mean it is easy to profit from it. That's where health care and pharmaceuticals consulting firms come in – helping clients like hospitals, HMOs, drug companies and supply distributors cope with an increasingly complicated maze of legislation, competition with other health care providers, cutting costs on vendors and equipment and managing new technology.

Examples of typical health care/pharmaceuticals engagements include:

• Creating a strategy to help a hospital become competitive in new markets

• Helping drug companies speed up the R&D and marketing process for products

• Promoting usage of a fertility center

## Economic consulting

As the global economy becomes increasingly interconnected and complex, clients often turn to think tank-like economic consulting firms for guidance. These firms are typically loaded with economics PhDs and MBAs, as well as industry experts, and investigate economic factors in order to give clients the ability to resolve problems caused by competition, antitrust issues, public policy and regulations. These consultancies are prized for their independence and ability to give candid counsel to clients buffeted by the vagaries of the economy.

Examples of typical economic consulting engagements include:

• Assessing the impact of deregulation of the utilities industry in Hungary for a client

• Helping to create rules for more efficient government auctions

• Creating a sophisticated economic model to improve the bundling of services

### Financial consulting

Financial consulting firms tend to be one of two animals: either they work with financial services firms to enhance their strategies and performance, or they have a specific financial model they use with clients to enhance their performance. In either case, the focus is typically on enhancing shareholder value.

Examples of typical financial consulting engagements include:

• Applying a proprietary framework to enhance market performance and value

• Presenting market position analysis to a CEO

• Refining online strategies for a commercial bank

---

• For more detail about consulting careers, including days in the life, career paths, and compensation, get the *Vault Career Guide to Consulting*

• prepare for case interviews for consulting firms, get the *Vault Guide to the Case Interview* and the *Vault Case Interviews Practice Guide.*

# http://consulting.vault.com

---

# THE VAULT 50

# McKinsey & Company

55 East 52nd Street
New York, NY 10022
Phone: (212) 446-7000
Fax: (212) 446-8575
www.mckinsey.com

## LOCATIONS

**New York, NY**
82 offices worldwide

## PRACTICE AREAS

Automotive & Assembly • Banking
& Securities • Business Technology
Office • Chemicals •
Consumer/Packaged Goods •
Corporate Finance & Strategy •
Electric Power/Natural Gas • High
Tech • Insurance • Marketing •
Media & Entertainment • Metals &
Mining • Nonprofit • Organization &
Leadership • Operations Strategy &
Effectiveness • Payor/Provider •
Petroleum • Pharmaceuticals and
Medical Products • Private Equity •
Pulp & Paper • Retail/Apparel and
Hospitality • Strategy •
Telecommunications • Travel &
Logistics Services

## THE STATS

**Employer Type:** Private Company
**Managing Director:** Ian Davis
**2002 Employees:** 11,000
**2001 Employees:** 13,000

## UPPERS

- Excellent brand recognition
- Alumni network
- Generous treatment of counsel-
  outs

## DOWNERS

- Relentlessly increasing
  expectations
- Rigid, constant review process
- Limited mobility without advanced
  degree

## KEY COMPETITORS

Accenture
A.T. Kearney
Bain & Company
Booz Allen Hamilton
Boston Consulting Group

## EMPLOYMENT CONTACT

E-mail:
career_information@mckinsey.com

## THE BUZZ
WHAT CONSULTANTS AT OTHER FIRMS ARE SAYING

- "Yardstick for other consultancies"
- "Started to believe their own myth"
- "Robotic. Intense. Top notch.
  Snooty"

# THE SCOOP

## An MBA's dream come true

Consultants who want the satisfaction of having a real and lasting impact on the workings of giant corporations should take a look at McKinsey & Company. The consulting industry leader counts such notable entities as Hewlett-Packard, IBM and General Motors among its clients. In a 2003 Universum survey, McKinsey was rated the company where MBAs would most like to work for the seventh year in a row.

Founded by James O. McKinsey in 1926, the firm currently operates 82 offices in 44 countries with about 6,000 professional employees. McKinsey is not the world's largest consultancy, but then again size isn't everything. Overall, McKinsey has served more than 70 percent of the Fortune Global 500 and 85 percent of the U.S. Fortune 100. Besides working with these high-visibility entities, McKinsey also offers pro bono assistance to educational, social, environmental and cultural organizations. In fact, most of the firm's consultants work on a pro bono engagement at some time during their careers.

## The ultra-international consulting firm

McKinsey has a better claim than most firms to being truly global. Its consultants are citizens of 90 countries, and McKinsey consultants provide their expertise to clients around the world. During the 1990s, McKinsey opened 20 new locations and doubled its professional staff; in 1999 alone, the firm opened offices in Antwerp, Dubai, Manila and Rio de Janeiro.

In March 2000 McKinsey opens a new office in Tel Aviv. (Previously, McKinsey had performed client work for Israeli companies via other satellite offices.) The new office in Israel offers consulting services to large Israeli industrial companies and startups. In February 2000, McKinsey enhanced its presence in India with the launch of India Venture 2000, which was created to help Indian entrepreneurs establish and grow new IT or e-commerce businesses. In India, the firm has advised liquor company Shaw Wallace on an operational restructuring, engineering and construction firm Larsen & Toubro on strategy matters and Prime Minister Atal Behari Vajpayee on foreign investment issues. In January 2001 McKinsey took a stake in India's Aptech Internet in exchange for providing consulting services.

In March 2001, McKinsey implemented a plan to significantly strengthen its corporate finance and strategy practice in Singapore. (Launched just three years earlier, the Singapore office has counseled some of the country's most prominent clients, including Singapore Airlines and the chewing gum-banning national government.)

McKinsey's expansion has slowed considerably since the 1990s, but the always-in-demand firm will keep opening new offices when the need presents itself. The newest McKinsey office is in Zagreb, Croatia, and opened in early 2003.

## Dot-com delirium

During the Internet craze of the late 1990s, McKinsey's revenues, like that of most consulting firms, soared. During 1999 and 2000, the heyday of the dot-coms, McKinsey worked on more than 1,000 Web-related assignments. The firm's revenues reached an all-time high of $3.4 billion in 2000. But when the bubble burst, many of McKinsey's previously high-flying e-commerce clients were unable to pay for the cost of a phone call, let alone an expensive monthly consulting fee. And while McKinsey, unlike many other consulting firms, avoided taking large equity stakes in clients that couldn't pay in cash, the firm did take some small ownership chunks, some of which lost value and affected McKinsey's bottom line.

During the tech boom, many of McKinsey's best consultants jumped ship to latch onto alluring Web-related ventures. In 1999, the firm's San Francisco office saw a third (150 members) of its staff walk out the door. One year later, though, as the dot-coms sputtered, McKinsey had more employees than it knew what to do with. Out of the 3,100 recruits who were extended offers in 2000, McKinsey expected a significant number of acceptances (of course), but the firm received more than it had anticipated – 2,400. "We honored every offer and didn't push people out," then-CEO Rajit Gupta told *BusinessWeek* in July 2002, "and we had no professional layoffs other than our traditional up-or-out stuff."

## Not recession-proof

McKinsey may have avoided much of the turmoil that hit lesser consulting firms, but it has not proved totally immune to the recession that began in 2001. In November 2001, the firm determined that it would cut five to seven percent of its 3,000 support staff in the United States and Canada. Though no consultants have been officially laid off, increasing numbers have been found lacking and asked to leave as part of the firm's up-or-out policy (which may have been relaxed somewhat in the booming 1990s). In 2001, the "up-or-out stuff" amounted to 9 percent of all analysts and associates in 2001, compared with 3 percent a year earlier, according to a June 2002

*New York Times* article quoting a webcast by Gupta. (The firm's voluntary attrition rate has dropped precipitously as a result of the recession.) In some offices, new hires have been asked to defer their start dates. McKinsey has looked to cut other costs as well. According to *The New York Times,* McKinsey "cut travel and canceled or scaled back training retreats – even the Reese's Peanut Butter Cups at the firm's New York reception desk were eliminated."

## Challenging times

Recently, the golden child of consulting has faced its share of setbacks. Insiders wonder whether the massive growth in the past decade – not to mention a stalled economy – might necessitate a less collegial management approach. With major McKinsey clients such as Enron, Swissair and Kmart all filing for bankruptcy in 2001 and 2002, McKinsey's expertise has also been questioned – not a common occurrence for this overwhelmingly competent company.

Still, the increasing pressures and competition of the new economy have induced more corporations to turn to McKinsey to get a jump on the competition. And McKinsey's global orientation ensures that the firm, in serving clients, should be able to continue to draw upon a deep reservoir of talent and information worldwide.

## Unfriendly business conditions

The Enron situation is well known to aficionados of executive malfeasance. Former McKinseyite Jeff Skilling, who became CEO of the energy company in early 2001, developed a transaction- and services-based, minimal asset approach to corporate operations. McKinsey touted Enron's structure as a model for businesses to follow. Unfortunately, the transactions and services on which Enron grew its numbers were largely illusory, the result of exchanges between Enron subsidiaries. When the model could no longer sustain itself, Enron collapsed, taking much of the stock market with it. In the meantime, McKinsey consultants working out of Enron's Houston offices had racked up millions in fees – topping out at more than $10 million during one year – for dispensing strategy advice. This engagement, along with McKinsey's ties to Enron's executives (who perpetrated a shady and ultimately unworkable financial strategy), proved something of an embarrassment to McKinsey.

Fortunately for McKinsey, none of its engagements for Enron touched on the business practices that led to Enron's precipitious ruin. "In serving Enron, McKinsey was not retained to provide advice to Enron or any Enron-affiliated entity with respect to the company's financial reporting strategy, methods of financing, methods of disclosure, investment partnerships or off-balance-sheet financing vehicles," a firm spokesperson told *The Wall Street Journal.*

Enron wasn't McKinsey's only blue chip client to go bankrupt in 2001. Kmart and Swissair also filed Chapter 11 during the year. Kmart was a McKinsey client from 1994 to 2000, during which time Kmart lost market share in a devastating price war with Wal-Mart. (On the other hand, McKinsey reportedly did not recommend the retailer's "every day low price" strategy that contributed to its failure.) McKinsey advised Swissair on a strategy shift that led to Swissair paying $2 billion for stakes in other airlines. The large outlays played a major role in Swissair's bankruptcy. (An independent report commisioned by the Swiss government, however, found that Swissair had not followed McKinsey's recommended strategy. McKinsey had recommended that Swissair take stakes in airlines in growth markets such as Ireland and Hungary; Swissair instead invested in mature markets like France, Italy and Germany.)

United Airlines, another bankrupt airline, has turned to McKinsey for advice. Not everyone is pleased with the arrangement, however. United's creditors challenged allegedly excessive restructuring-advice payments, including a $1 million-a-month flat fee for McKinsey, in January 2003, feeling such expenses were unwarranted for a company unable to pay its current debts. (Those unsecured creditors, according to McKinsey, have since come around and now support McKinsey's involvement.)

## Strife amidst the cranberries

A comparatively minor shakeup with client Ocean Spray also made headlines. In a surprise move in February 2003, rival Northland Cranberries Inc. made an $800 million bid to acquire Ocean Spray's brand name and beverage business. McKinsey, an advisor to Ocean Spray since late 2002, had provided the cooperative's management a strategy for deciding when – and if – to sell any of its businesses. Ocean Spray's growers, who had been struggling with low cranberry prices since 2001, had previously pushed the company to explore a sale. The collective set up a separate meeting in advance of its 2003 annual meeting. In the end, the pro-sale growers won a vote to replace Ocean Spray's board of governors with a new, smaller panel.

## Growing pains

Excellence-obsessed McKinsey has a term, "100 percent cubed," which means that the firm seeks to bring 100 percent of firm capabilities to bear on 100 percent of

McKinsey clients, 100 percent of the time. But an internal report from 2001, quoted in a May 2002 *Wall Street Journal* article, highlights this area as one of the possible failings of McKinsey's aggressive growth policy. In the article, "Growth at McKinsey Hindered Use of Data," the study, whimsicaly referred to internally as Project Coolkat, concludes that rapid expansion hindered the firm's ability to keep track of its own information, leading to poor client performance. "It takes much too long to find the right knowledge," the report states, "and in many cases, the best existing knowledge is not identified and brought to the client." Furthermore, the report calls the work satisfaction and professional development of McKinsey research staff "unsatisfactory," and concludes, "Moving forward, this is not acceptable."

The practical upshot of the reports findings is a new initiative to improve researcher training and a major budget increase for McKinsey's knowledge-management processes and systems, $35.8 million in 2002 versus just $8.3 million in 1999. However, Senior Partner Lowell Bryan, one of the Coolkat researchers and head of the global industries practice, added, "There is no demonstrable link – in fact there's no link whatsoever – between our decision to invest in upgrading our knowledge-management systems and any specific client." According to Bryan, the key to achieving this goal will be to further increase electronic exchange of information within and outside the firm.

## The illuminati? No, just McKinsey

McKinsey & Co. does not advertise its engagements or discuss them directly, being publicity-shy by design; working for the firm has been compared to entering a secret society. McKinsey rebuts this view of the firm: "Only after many years have passed and if our clients themselves publicly refer to our involvement, do we acknowledge that we have served a company," the firm contends. "This policy is not the result of some cultivated secrecy or mystique. It is what we believe is professional behavior and the appropriate posture given our conviction that we supplement our clients' leadership, but never replace it." Of course, McKinsey consultants do often rise to lead client firms – many C-level executives have McKinsey on their resume.

McKinsey hires the cream of the crop. Its roster of consultants is studded with Rhodes Scholars, law review editors, PhDs and nuclear physicists. This network of high-quality brains continues for life; every year, McKinsey publishes an online directory listing every living person who has ever worked for the firm, where they live and their current occupation.

The firm announces the names and backgrounds of new partners after its semi-annual elections. In addition, some hires just can't be hidden. In February 2003, Chelsea Clinton, former First Daughter and impending graduate of the Oxford international relations masters program, got a $100,000 offer to join McKinsey as an analyst. Clinton held out for an assignment in New York, (to be closer to her well-known parents) and got the job in her preferred location in March 2003.

## All over the map

McKinsey's web of insiders and alumni springs from its decentralized structure, a network of offices that operates as a unified firm. McKinsey is reluctant to admit it has a global headquarters at all (though it runs its backbone administrative work from New York City). McKinsey is a corporation, but operates as a partnership. The ownership and management of the firm is vested entirely in nearly 900 active directors and principals (which roughly correspond to senior and junior partners). The managing director (the firm's chief) is elected every three years by McKinsey's directors. Rajat Gupta, the outgoing managing director, served the company's maximum of three 3-year terms. Gupta is McKinsey's first non-Western managing director, and his rise is just one more indication of McKinsey's increasing internationalization. After 30 years of aggressive global expansion, a non-American majority controls its governing shareholder committee. A full 60 percent of McKinsey revenues come from overseas, with further growth expected from new markets in Russia, Eastern Europe, Korea and China. McKinsey's work in India has exploded in recent years and the office in New Delhi is among the firm's fastest growing.

## Doing its homework

McKinsey publishes an impressive number of booklets, documents, papers and magazines, including the well-regarded *McKinsey Quarterly* (now available in an online version, with more than 300,000 subscribers). The *McKinsey Quarterly* runs articles on e-commerce, telecommunications, strategy and other fields. McKinsey partners are notorious for writing books independently. In addition to *In Search of Excellence*, recent books penned by McKinsey alums include 2000's *Measuring and Managing the Value of Companies* by Tom Copeland, Tim Koller and Jack Murrin. Titles from 2001 include *The War for Talent* by Ed Michaels, Helen Handfield-Jones and Beth Axelrod; *20/20 Foresight: Crafting Strategy in an Uncertain World* by Hugh Courtney; and the must-read *Creative Destruction,* by Richard Foster and Sarah Kaplan. The big book in 2002 was *Dangerous Markets: Managing in*

*Financial Crises* by Dominic Barton, Roberto Newell and Gregory Wilson. China-based partner Jonathan Woetzel added a new book, *Capitalist China*, to the McKinsey oeuvre in 2003.

## Clout

McKinsey is known as a preeminent information source on globalization, governance, organizational performance and corporate strategy. Over the past few years, McKinsey has been building a significant practice that focuses on the intersection of IT and strategy (i.e, IT strategy). Known as the Business Technology Office, the BTO has 48 partners and 355 associates; it's really a worldwide practice.

The McKinsey Global Institute, established in 1990, combines the disciplines of economics and management as an independent research group under the aegis of McKinsey. The Institute researches a variety of topics with a bent toward the global economy and publishes its findings in reports. The Global Institute, located just steps from the White House in Washington, D.C., has been estimated to spend more than $100 million a year on its information gathering and internal research. In 2001, the firm launched The McKinsey Institute on the Nonprofit Sector, and former Senator Bill Bradley joined as chairman of its advisory board.

## No profit required

McKinsey maintains a strong nonprofit practice, which coordinates the firm's community and pro bono activities. Though McKinsey has worked in many nonprofit areas, it has been particularly involved in global public health and education. Each office devotes five to 10 percent of its consultants' time to work for nonprofit operations. The firm served more than 200 nonprofit and/or public sector clients in 2002, representing an in-kind contribution of well over $100 million. The New York office, for example, has performed pro bono work for the United Way, the World Economic Forum and the New York City Opera, in addition to several 9/11 relief-related engagements. In fact, in the wake of September 11, McKinsey's Big Apple office worked on nine separate pro bono assignments, including serving the Lower Manhattan Development Corporation, overseeing the development of a victim database for New York State Attorney General Elliot Spitzer and studying how New York Police Department and Fire Department members reacted during the World Trade Center attacks.

## Loss of a consulting legend

McKinsey & Company paused to mourn the death of Marvin Bower on January 22, 2003. Bower, who died at the age of 99, joined James McKinsey's firm in 1933 and resurrected it in 1939 after McKinsey's death. From that point on, Bower guided and shaped McKinsey, serving as managing director from 1950 through 1967, during which time firm revenue grew from $2 million to $20 million. After his retirement in 1992, he retained close ties with McKinsey and occasionally addressed the company. Many consultants consider Bower to be the father of management consulting, due to his emphasis of valuing education over experience, providing impartial counsel, working with top management and putting the client's needs before the consultancy's.

## Meet the new boss

Rajat Gupta, McKinsey's managing director since 1994, reached the end of his third and final three-year term in March 2003. Elected to replace him in the top spot was Ian Davis, head of the firm's U.K. office. Davis, a holder of undergraduate degrees in politics, philosophy and economics from Oxford University, has been with McKinsey since 1979. His new job starts July 1, 2003, but Davis has already stated his intention to return the firm to closer alignment with its core values. These values, as excerpted on McKinsey's site a from a talk by Rajat Gupta, include taking "an impact-driven professional approach"; "being and delivering the best"; and remaining a "caring meritocracy, committed to people" and a "self-governing, one-firm partnership."

# GETTING HIRED

## Becoming the best

McKinsey is one of the premier consulting firms in the world - and getting in is brutally tough. Only 2 percent of its approximately 150,000 applicants per year get offers; approximately half of those are made outside the United States.

Every McKinsey office has its own recruiting schedule and, ultimately, control over the offers made at the office. Depending on the school, candidates either apply centrally to a McKinsey school team or to the office of their choice. Candidates at non-targeted schools should start the application process online.

The process consists of either two or three rounds of interviews, the first of which is usually held on campus. If there is an intermediary round, it may be held at a local McKinsey branch. The final round of interviews takes place at the McKinsey office to which the candidate has applied. Most interviews are conducted by current McKinsey consultants, and tend to include a combination of cases, resume/personal questions and some behavioral questions. The interview process "has changed since the boom," according to one insider. "Now there's a much bigger structure -- cases, group interviews and presentations." A third calls the screening "fair and objective." He notes, "You'll take some tests that are like part of the GMAT – in fact, we used to use old GMAT exams as our tests." (The initial test is multiple choice and simulates the sort of problem-solving McKinsey consultants do in client work. Not all candidates take the test.) If your heart is set on working at McKinsey, you should "ace the interview and know where you want to be stationed"; an insider let us know about an informal hiring policy: "If you apply to one region, you can't apply to another for one year."

Insiders tell us there is "no internship program for analysts," though the firm, of course, offers MBA-level internships. Undergrads who join the firm as analysts are "retained for 18-24 months," according to sources; after that, the entire class is cut loose to go back to school or seek employment at another firm. A return trip to the mother ship is quite possible. "If they like you and want you back, they pay for grad school," says one source. One insider thinks the company could improve by "adjusting the promotion system to promote high-performing analysts without an MBA." In the past, there have been instances of analysts being promoted straight into the associate ranks, but more than one insider describes these instances as "extremely rare."

# OUR SURVEY SAYS

## The McKinsey lifestyle

What's a company full of brilliant type A personalities like? One source assesses, "Whenever you stick overachievers together, it's competitive. But there's no backstabbing." Another consultant says it's "tough to generalize about the company; it's a work-based culture. [It's] fairly formal and uniform, but we appreciate differences." An insider infers, "To outsiders, we must look extremely competitive. We're told we should never feel comfortable doing what we're doing, that we should always be reaching to do more. But the people who come here thrive on challenge, and you're only competing with yourself."

Despite this surfeit of competitive spirit, McKinseyites rely on one another. One insider says that colleagues are "very cooperative." One associate says, "I can call colleagues in any office, any practice group, for anything and I can trust them to return my call and do whatever they can to help me." A colleague agrees, noting the difference when dealing with non-McKinseyites: "When I work with students, interns, some clients or even some other consultants from other firms and ask them to do something, I'm surprised – sometimes shocked and appalled – at the lack of response and initiative. McKinsey people go out of their way to deliver more than you ask for."

## Handling the workload

One McKinseyite warns that at McKinsey, "The work hours are very long, and it's difficult to find a balance. Even if you don't want to live this lifestyle, you will." He notes, however, "Some professional activities are half social, and company-sponsored events and retreats are coming back." Another, from New York, believes the hours are "a function of which manager you get. Some managers focus on efficiency, others focus on being thorough."

A McKinseyite notes that McKinsey isn't the place for homebodies: "There's a lot of travel, which does not add to the happiness." Another consultant agrees, "If balance is important to you, consulting is not the place you want to be, and definitely not McKinsey. But we try to do 'sanity checks' on the workload, because all these overachievers will kill themselves with the pace." Those sanity checks "are a matter of common sense. When you work 70-75 hours per week for a while, you realize it just isn't sustainable."

## Pressure cooker

McKinsey is always pushing its associates to do more, say insiders. One source, with previous experience at other consulting firms, notes, "Among all my colleagues at other firms, I think McKinsey has the most focus on constantly evaluating you. 'Meets expectations' is a failing grade around here – you're always supposed to do more, to add value that you weren't asked for." That leads to a lot of performance pressure, which isn't always good. He continues, "The expectations are so high, you never feel that your work is good enough. Management is so used to overachievers that they don't remember the the praise you need for a job well done."

## Going deep

Though it is still decidedly a general strategy firm, McKinsey increasingly hires individuals with deep experience in an industry or functional area. The firm has upped its hiring of "specialized consultants" who mostly ply their trade in a single industry or functional area. "It's still acceptable to be a generalist, but more and more people are doing specific work. Analysts are still generalists, but more associates are now specialists, and managers are often specialists in a few areas." Another consultant says, "McKinsey is now more careful about how it builds its teams. They staff with more experts and specialists." Experts in some areas are said to be "in short supply," likely because the firm did not previously try to hire them. The firm is most actively seeking experienced hires in the insurance, financial services, health care and consumer goods industries, and functional hires in information technology, marketing (from branding to pricing), operations, corporate finance and telecom.

The engagements have changed along with the firm's makeup, says an American respondent. "The typical engagement was three or four months, but there are many shorter projects now – some lasting just a couple of weeks." He says that the company is "trying to be more creative, more flexible. We're playing roles we didn't touch before; for example we've been working with investment firms." This has changed what consultants take away from each project. "You don't get the depth of experience that you would on long projects, but you get a very broad range."

## Training days

McKinsey wants to be sure its consultants are sharp enough to handle whatever gets thrown at them. Most would agree with the insider who says, "99 percent of training is on-the-job." However, McKinsey consultants do receive detailed formal training. "If you lack an MBA when you join the firm, you get a three to four week 'Mini-MBA' training orientation. You're sent to the weeklong BCR (Basic Consulting Readiness) program. At one year, there's a two-week associate training period, and another six months later." Basically, "you receive training at each new stage of your consulting career." Though times may be tough "McKinsey isn't economizing by cutting the training budget. It hasn't decreased significantly, but we have fewer consultants to spend it on. So we've held steady, and maybe improved per capita."

## Lead or leave (or both)

A source at McKinsey comments on the "very formal and structured feedback methods" used to evaluate employees. "You meet with a partner after every project."

A twice-yearly meeting of partners in each office ranks people. "Underperformers leave, performers are invited to improve, and outperformers are loved." Consultant compensation is based on these ratings. If all goes well, consultants are advanced after two years as an associate, then two to three years as an engagement manager, then one to two years each to associate principal and partner." Consultants are pushed to succeed on a strict timetable, "It's up or out; there's the expectation that you will take on new roles and responsibilities. There's a definite timeframe in which you should move up, whether you're comfortable doing so or not."

Another source agrees, "The review process is carefully and elaborately laid out," but "not egregiously political. But being more connected helps, and it's important to have 'a partner who's willing to pound the table' for you." One of the critical factors in promotion is "mastery of the McKinsey way, doing things in line with company norms."

McKinsey has had virtually no layoffs in over a decade, though there were a few in 2001. Insiders feel that "the firm has trimmed what they're going to trim," and that the layoffs were a necessary and one-time event. Another consultant clarifies, "There have been no layoffs, but lots of counsel-outs." "The official company line," according to one insider, "is 'there have never been layoffs, ever.' But then again, nobody's ever been fired, either. Counsel-outs have increased because the opportunities that led associates to other firms don't exist anymore in this economy." One source warns, "Some people are surprised how quickly the firm judges promotions and counsel-outs. You get very early feedback."

## Better unemployment than the government

Whether you call it "up or out," "succeed or leave" or the natural workings of a pure meritocracy, the majority of consultants who start at McKinsey end up leaving along the way. On average, only one in four or five consultants who starts at McKinsey finishes the hallowed journey to principal. One source quotes the average turnover rate at 20 percent. But even when the time has come to part, he says, "The firm will continue to pay your salary until you find a job you like. Not just until you find a job, but one you like."

Then again, many leave by choice. "Promotion is a pretty competitive process," says an insider, "though lots of people don't want to make partner, so they leave." Those who jump ship may find themselves in politics (like Roger Ferguson, vice chairman and governor of the Federal Reserve Board); as best-selling authors (the authors of the enormously successful business guide *In Search of Excellence* were former

McKinsey consultants); or founders of rival consultancies (as Tom Steiner did with Mitchell Madison Group, subsumed into the failed e-consultancy marchFIRST). Many McKinsey consultants wind up in top spots in corporations: The CEOs of Delta Airlines, Polaroid, Morgan Stanley Dean Witter, Marks & Spencer, Amgen, CNBC and Levi Strauss are all alums of the firm.

## McDiversity

McKinsey is tops in diversity, according to its consultants. An insider raves, "We're extremely diverse – I've never worked in such a diverse environment." A colleague agrees, "We have a large amount of diversity, not only ethnic and gender, but international. There's an amazing range of outlooks." Part of the reason for this McKinseyian rainbow, he speculates, is McKinsey's reputation. "Even though there are fewer [women and minorities] at schools, if they can get past the interview process they're more likely to come here than anyplace else."

The firm has programs in place for women, ethnic minorities (BCSS, Black Client Service Staff, is one of the best known) and gays and lesbians (GLAM, Gays and Lesbians At McKinsey). A European source notes that BCSS is "mostly active in North America, there's little call for it in Europe." McKinsey is an annual sponsor of the Gay-Lesbian MBA conference, and is pushing to "extend domestic partner benefits to all employees in every office in a location where they are legal."

# Boston Consulting Group

Exchange Place
31st Floor
Boston, MA 02109
Phone: (617) 973-1200
Fax: (617) 973-1339
www.bcg.com

## LOCATIONS

**Boston, MA (HQ)**
Over 55 offices worldwide

## PRACTICE AREAS

Branding
Consumer
Corporate Development
Deconstruction
e-Commerce
Energy
Financial Services
Globalization
Health Care
Industrial Goods
Information Technology
Operations
Organization
Pricing
Strategy
Technology & Communications
Travel & Tourism

## THE STATS

**Employer Type:** Private Company
**President & CEO:** Carl W. Stern
**2002 Employees:** 2,600
**2001 Employees:** 2.790
**2002 Revenue:** $1.02 billion
**2001 Revenue:** $1.05 billion

## UPPERS

- "People come to us with the hardest nuts to crack"
- "Variety of engagements with large and small corporations"
- "Growth opportunities that address your personal interests"

## DOWNERS

- "Getting the best work requires living the harshest life"
- "Not enough training in selling work"
- "We work a lot harder than most would choose to"

## KEY COMPETITORS

Bain & Company
Booz Allen Hamilton
McKinsey & Company
Monitor Group

## EMPLOYMENT CONTACT

www.bcg.com/careers/careers_splash.asp

## THE BUZZ
WHAT CONSULTANTS AT OTHER FIRMS ARE SAYING

- "Classic boardroom stuff"
- "Need a cash cow"
- "Good work/life balance"
- "Well-regarded, but theoretical"

# THE SCOOP

## What is the matrix?

If you're looking for the home of modern management consulting, take a good look at the Boston Consulting Group (BCG). According to *The Boston Globe*, "Some business historians set the beginning of modern management consulting" with BCG's birth. Today, more than 2,600 consultants in 54 offices around the globe carry on the legacy of founder Bruce Henderson's intellectual work. BCG has been responsible for a number of major management consulting innovations and concepts in its 39 years, including "time-based competition," "deconstruction" and "capability-driven competitive strategies."

One of BCG's best-known contributions is the "BCG Growth-Share Matrix," which explains the relationship between a company's profitability and its market share using "star," "dog," "cash cow" and "question mark" icons in a four-quadrant layout. Basically, businesses in mature markets (cash cows) provide the funding for high-growth ventures with large expected returns (stars), while divesting of low-growth and low-return ventures (dogs) and trying to build low-return fast growers (question marks) into market leaders before they become dogs. (The famous matrix is so widely applicable, in fact, that *American Square Dance* magazine ran an article in January 2001 touting use of the matrix in square dance calling.) BCG uses tools and innovations such as this to help its clients gain a competitive advantage. The firm encourages senior executives to think beyond the status quo and embrace strategic change.

## Outlook bright

BCG sees growth in the market for its highly specialized services. CEO Carl Stern, who will step down in January 2004, believes some good will come of the highly publicized scandals and conflicts of interest that have shaken the consulting industry. In an April 2002 interview with *Business Times* (Singapore), Stern said, "The immediate impact on us [of accounting firms' consulting fallout] will be slight – in most parts of the world, we don't compete terribly directly with Andersen [now gone], Accenture, PwC [now IBM BCS] and so forth." However, he continued, "There will be a general increase in interest in some fairly high-level abstractions like values, honesty and, importantly, objectivity. I think people will be more alert than they have been to conflicts of interest."

## Eurostar

BCG is loosely organized into three main geographical areas: Asia-Pacific, the Americas and Europe. In recent years, the firm has expanded its presence worldwide, opening offices in Copenhagen, Berlin, Athens and Cologne, France. The newest European office, Barcelona, opened in January 2002 to serve clients in financial services, consumer goods and retailing, technology and communications, energy, industrial goods and media.

BCG has an excellent reputation in Europe; in *Universum*'s June 2002 survey, the firm was ranked as the second-most ideal employer (in any industry) among European graduate students. (Rival McKinsey & Company was No.1.) The company gets almost half of its revenues from consulting engagements in Europe and one-third from the Americas. Europe has also provided the firm with a new leader: Hans-Paul Burkner, founder of the Frankfurt office, was elected in April 2003 to replace outgoing president and CEO Carl Stern. Burkner, a BCG employee since 1981, will be the first European to head the firm. He will take the reins in January 2004.

## BCG East

BCG is particularly strong in Asia. While some consultancies derive most of their international business from American firms conducting operations overseas, BCG gets roughly half of its business in Asia from local entities: private companies, governments and state-run businesses. The firm's clientele includes five of Asia's biggest non-Japanese companies, three of the top five business conglomerates in Korea and eight of the biggest local commercial banks in Hong Kong, Indonesia, Malaysia, Thailand and Korea.

In 1966, founder Bruce Henderson opened his company's first branch office in Tokyo (the first consulting firm to do so), anticipating that country's economic boom. Henderson took his company independent in 1974, calling it the Boston Consulting Group. The firm was one of the first to hire business school graduates right out of school, believing students have the ability and fresh perspective to solve complex business problems. BCG is also believed to be the first company to have offered an employee stock ownership plan (ESOP); Henderson launched his firm's ESOP in 1974, just after the Employee Retirement Income Security Act of 1974 made such plans possible.

BCG added offices in Beijing and New Delhi to the firm during 2001, the latest Aisa openings in a string of expansions that began in 1995. "We're growing faster in Asia than elsewhere," commented Stern in April 2002, "and I expect that trend will continue. We probably averaged, throughout the 1990s, growth of around 20 to 23 percent in constant currency terms, and in Europe and the Americas, that would have been in the high teens."

## The bite of layoffs

Despite its perch at the pinnacle of the consulting industry, BCG was bitten by the layoff bug in February 2002. Its hand forced by the decline of voluntary attrition the fall of revenues from the boom era of a few years earlier, the firm announced that it would cut about 12 percent of its North and South American consulting and support staff. Staffers at all levels of the organization got the ax. The firm did assert at the time that it planned to continue campus recruiting and other hiring, albeit on a smaller scale than in the past. Insider comments suggest that a new round of hiring is possible in 2003, as the firm is quite busy.

## Pro choice, or no choice

BCG's practice is organized into select areas of expertise – with worldwide networks of consultants working collaboratively. The networks themselves are structured around industrial sectors and business functions. One of BCG's more attractive qualities is its willingness to let consultants choose their area or areas of expertise. In fact, consultants aren't required to choose a specialty at all if they so desire. The policy is designed to ensure consultants are passionate about their work.

BCG's other pro bono engagements have included a comprehensive environmental plan for eastern Germany, an evaluation of the economics of child sponsorship for Save the Children, a major study on retail opportunities in American inner cities (in conjunction with the Initiative for a Competitive Inner City), and strategy projects for the American Red Cross and Children's Television Workshop. These projects are more than great publicity for BCG and a boon for pro bono clients. They also allow beginning associates and consultants to gain experience and make an immediate impact.

## Strategy advice

As a strategy firm, BCG specializes in helping clients overcome their most difficult obstacles. In her 2001 book, *The Change Monster: The Human Forces that Fuel or Foil Corporate Change*, BCG Senior VP Jeanie Daniel Duck targets one of these problems, the "Change Curve" – the predictable yet quite frustrating cycle of changes that cripple organizations. The book explores a new way of looking at change strategy for senior executives.

BCG has also developed what it terms a "Strategy Institute" to research and foster discussion on innovation. Founded by BCG Senior Vice President Bolko von Oetinger, the Institute gathers insights from leaders in various academic disciplines and attempts to distill them into coherent strategy ideas. BCG consultants with academic leanings may work at the Strategy Institute as counselors, and others can access articles and participate in discussion groups through the Institute's online "Strategy Gallery."

## Strategy nouveau

BCG is always looking to develop compelling new strategies, of course. A July 2002 article in *The Boston Globe* described how the firm is advocating "competitive advantage through pricing," a means for consumer companies to increase revenue through price segmentation. This could tie in nicely with a study published by BCG in November 2002. "New Luxury: Why the Middle Market American Consumer Wants Premium Goods and How Companies Create Them" details the phenomenon of the middle class "escaping the extraordinary stresses of modern life by carefully choosing high-quality, high-performance, emotionally satisfying goods and services" as well as how companies can take full advantage of this craving. It also discusses the hazards of this growing market. This concept will be explored further in a book called *Trading Up*, due to be published in the fall of 2003. In addition, the firm promoted a new concept called Workonomics, a means of addressing shareholder value through better assessment of employee productivity.

## Dust off those patents

In October 2002, BCG hired Kevin Rivette, an intellectual property expert and author of *Rembrandts in the Attic* (which explains how companies can create more value from underused patents) to be the firm's executive advisor on the subject. The firm is hoping to build a practice around Rivette and his ability to "take IP [intellectual property] into the realm of strategic analyses and actions that create sustainable advantage," according to Mark Blaxill, a senior VP. Rivette will be based in San Francisco.

## In the community

BCG encourages its employees to participate in the company's efforts to support economic development in America's inner cities. BCG's consulting efforts in this arena are geared towards providing jobs and creating wealth. In 2001, CEO Carl Stern made a commitment of $3.5 million per year to inner city economic development projects.

BCG has for the past several years been involved with another community initiative, business@school. Created in 1998 by consultants in the firm's Düsseldorf office, the program teaches business, economic and workplace skills to German high school kids. Students undergo six to seven sessions a year, analyzing companies and creating a business plan under the tutelage of BCG volunteers. The program grew to include nearly 60 schools during the 2001-2002 school year. In December 2002, BCG and the business@school program received Germany's National Corporate Citizenship Freedom and Responsibility award from the nation's federal president, Johannes Rau.

## Ambassadors abroad

BCG encourages an international approach in other ways as well. The firm offers an "ambassador" program, which allows consultants to transfer to another office for six months or longer (though the typical period is 12-18 months). Overseas consultants may also transfer to American offices. Consultants may also work on international cases (normally for multinationals). Sometimes, consultants are required to relocate to a foreign office for the duration of a case. These relocations, however, are normally kept within BCG's geographic groups. Consultants in Washington, D.C., for example, might relocate to Monterrey (like D.C., another office in the Americas).

## Change management

The shape of the consulting industry is changing, and BCG is changing with it. BCG has always been known as a pure strategy shop, and indeed, most of its engagements are still strategy based. However, the classic BCG "50/50" model – under which a consultant would spend 50 percent of his or her time on each of two strategy cases – is slowly but ever so surely falling by the wayside. BCG has been increasing the number of reengineering and process assignments that it takes. Insiders say that while "the strong majority of cases BCG takes are still strategy" that is no longer universally true. "Some strategy cases aren't just a 50 percent commitment, but a 100 percent commitment," points out one consultant. Another consultant says, "Process and reengineering cases tend to take up 100 percent of your time."

There may be some changes afoot with BCG strategy. "At BCG, we are trying to move much more toward long-term relationships with clients, as opposed to stopping in, doing our three-month project and taking off," opine consultants. "We aren't Accenture. We don't move in, but we do try to maintain that relationship." The VP on the case is usually in charge. "That allows us to find out other areas where the company needs help and where we can help. Then, of course, we try to leverage what we can. But people at all levels keep in touch. You do a lot of follow up and building deeper relationships. We call and ask how things are going."

## Riding the bear

A June 2002 article in *The Financial Times* noted that BCG had its first-ever year of declining revenues in 2001, losing 4 percent from the previous year in constant currency value. CEO Stern said the loss was worse in U.S. dollars, but predicted a return to revenue growth in 2002 and beyond. Stern (and business journalists everywhere) blamed losses such as BCG's on the downturn in the economy, with the reduction in spending it has caused among consultancies' traditional clients. (Scandals such as the well-publicized Andersen debacle have only worsened matters. In addition, now that the merger fever of the late 1990s is over, there is less work on post-merger integration.)

## Award-winning

Just as BCG's work has impressed clients and industry insiders, its workplace has also won acclaim. *Consulting* magazine, the self-appointed arbiter of success in the industry, ranked BCG No.1 in its May 2001 list of The Best Consulting Firms to Work For. The publication praised BCG's "open and honest" culture and "lack of political infighting." Six months later, the Greater Boston Business Council (GBBC) echoed the former point when it presented BCG with a Corporate Recognition Award for the efforts of the firm's Gay and Lesbian Network (GLN).

In June 2002, *Consulting* named two BCG staffers, Jeanie Daniel Duck and George Stalk, to the magazine's list of the 25 most influential consultants. Duck, a senior vice president based in Atlanta who, as noted earlier, authored the business bestseller *The Change Monster*, is a newcomer to the list. George Stalk, a senior vice president in Toronto, has made the list each of the four years *Consulting* has published it –

including the first year, in which the list only named the top 10 most influential consultants. Stalk is the author of five books, including *Competing Against Time.*

# GETTING HIRED

## Undergraduate hiring

The undergraduate interview process typically consists of two rounds. Applicants at BCG-visited schools spend the first round on campus; others do both rounds in BCG offices. In either case, the first round consists of two interviews with 15 minutes spent discussing resume and background and 30 minutes on a case.

First-round interviews for undergraduate applicants are conducted by a local office, but the second round is at the applicant s desired location (offers are office-specific, so it s ultimately up to that office to decide whether or not to hire someone). The second round, conducted by more senior staff, consists of three or four interviews; all but the last follow the format of those in the first round. The final interview, with the head of the office, is for debriefing, and respondents tell us that by the tone of the conversation is usually revealing.

## The MBA process

MBAs spend both interview rounds at the nearest BCG office, to which they are invited after dropping their resumes at their career centers. The first round consists of two interviews, both heavy on cases. The second round involves four or five interviews with managers and vice presidents; two of these are explicitly fit interviews. BCG case interviews, we hear, are harder than all competitors. They are looking for you to outline the case (like the other firms), but then dive deeply into one aspect of it, show that you understand (mathematically) how all the levers fit together, that of the 10 things on the table you can figure out which two to work on.

Insiders tell us that BCG uses a "franchise model" for hiring, meaning that each office handles its own recruitment needs. "You won't be reassigned to Guam," quips one source. In each office, we're told, "everybody gets involved" with the hiring process and "consultants do the first-round interviews." One person recommends, "Take some practice cases before your interview. It's obvious if you have experience or if you tackle it cold." Another advises, "Always listen to the interviewer – they give clues. And remember to think aloud."

# OUR SURVEY SAYS

## Building the better consultant

People at BCG say they enjoy a culture that is "humane" and "supportive, with respect for the individual." One insider says, "It's become clear that individual success equals firm success." Another notes the "growth opportunities that address your personal interests." A third notes, "The first half year you're here is devoted to training." "Culture is one of our strengths," opines a Boston insider. "It plays out day to day. We do what's right for the client, but there is significant focus on the individual."

Beyond mere personal development, many sources describe BCG as personable. A San Francisco insider calls it "warm and friendly, laid-back even while the work is intense. We maintain a sense of humor, and remember that nobody's perfect." One person in Chicago provided an anecdote about an "all-office day last summer when we built a playground. Attendance was mandatory – and it was raining. It was a great time, a big bonding experience."

## Living with BCG, not at BCG

Insiders point out that work/life balance can be tough at BCG, since it's "an inherently demanding firm" in "a demanding industry." One consultant notes that BCG "has a reputation for traveling less than we actually do." However, says another consultant, "Most people have more control over the balance than they realize." Another insider agrees that hours "depend on the individual. Those with high priority for work/life balance achieve it with full support of the firm." One of the ways BCG "does a good job of making it livable," as one source puts it, is the use of time sheets and hourly billing. "If you work more than 55 to 60 hours average over four weeks, the manager will re-assess the project to see what needs to be fixed. Overwork is flagged so it can be prevented, but some people will habitually spend too much time at the office."

## An eye on promotion

Insiders say the promotion track is "definitely up-or-out, since if you're not performing, keeping you isn't doing anybody any favors." Consultants aren't always pushed out the door, of course. Says one consultant, "More commonly, though, moves are voluntary if it is clear no promotion will be offered since after working at

BCG for a while, one can often jump into corporations and make as much or more money than the current salary level. In practice, there are very few involuntary attritions." Despite the ever-looming presence of up-or-out policies, we hear that the focus of the review process "is on improvement and support" and that "BCG hires with an eye for long-term stays." Sources describe a "fairly set career path" with "windows for promotion every two years."

## Leaving with dignity

There were layoffs at BCG's U.S. offices during 2002, a fact that the company doesn't shy away from discussing. Most sources say their offices "lost 10-12 percent" of consultants. Most current BCG consultants also feel those layoffs were "the right decision to make," and that the company was very upfront about them. "There was no accelerated up-or-out in the evaluations. We had honest layoffs of people we wanted to keep." However, one insider feels "communication was not handled as well as possible," though he admits that the outplacement of those unfortunates was kind. "They were allowed to use an office, and given the option of a few months of salary – either two months of full pay or four months of half. [The firm notes that this is the lowest level of severance, and that such packages actually vary by tenure.] Our clients and alumni serve as a network of job leads." One person, defending his firm, says, "Don't let any firm tell you they didn't [have layoffs]. BCG always gets hurt because they were forthright, admitted that there were layoffs and gave a great severance package."

## Leveling the playing field

Consultants feel the firm is strongly committed to gender and ethnic diversity. "We always look for other experiences," notes one of the firm's recruiters. "It's important to make sure the playing field is level." One person describes the gender balance as "OK, but not phenomenal," noting that the mix is "about 35 percent, about like the biz schools." Another feels the company "does a good job [promoting and retaining women] at the consultant and project leader levels, but struggles at the VP level."

In regard to minorities in the U.S., a San Franciscan says the BCG is "insanely international. The San Francisco office has Brits, Russians, Singaporeans, French, Spanish and people from South America." He continues, "The minority initiative is ongoing – it's our most challenging area. The networks, infrastructure and outreach are all in place. Now we have to try harder for retention." Another source feels the company "does better with African-Americans than with Latinos, for example."

The solution in all cases, our sources say, is achieving a "critical mass" of minority and female consultants. "People look for similarity and mentors. If they believe they can find it here, they will join and stay, which will have a snowball effect." One person suggests, "we can have a greater impact at the undergrad level, get these people before they self-select out of the consulting track."

"Overwork is flagged so it can be prevented, but some people will habitually spend too much time at the office."

— *BCG consultant*

# Bain & Company

Two Copley Place
Boston, MA 02116
Phone: (617) 572-2000
Fax: (617) 572-2427
www.bain.com

## LOCATIONS

**Boston, MA (HQ)**
27 offices worldwide

## PRACTICE AREAS

Customers
E-Commerce Strategy Growth
Mergers & Acquisitions
Operations
Organizational Change
Management
Private Equity
Strategy
Supply Chain Management

## THE STATS

**Employer Type:** Private Company
**Chairman:** Orit Gadiesh
**Managing Director:** John Donahoe
**2002 Employees:** 2,800
**2001 Employees:** 2,800

## UPPERS

- Fun, bright, sociable employees
- In-depth, recurring training
- Two-case model means lots of diverse experience

## DOWNERS

- Unpredictable workload
- Promotion probability in flux due to economic factors
- No profit sharing below manager level

## KEY COMPETITORS

Boston Consulting Group
McKinsey & Company

## EMPLOYMENT CONTACT

**Online application:**
www.bain.com/HCR/onlineapp/
asp/app1.asp

**Recruiting contacts by location:**
www.bain.com/bainweb/join/
profiles_places/places.asp

## THE BUZZ
### WHAT CONSULTANTS AT OTHER FIRMS ARE SAYING

- "Strong culture, carefully maintained"
- "Creative and insightful"
- "High-performing nerds"

# THE SCOOP

## The Bain of your existence

Bill Bain had one paltry phone line and three employees when he started a consultancy out of his Beacon Hill apartment in 1973. Today, Bain is a presence in San Francisco and Seoul, São Paulo and Stockholm. It's advised Starbucks on its muffin strategy, told Kroger to add more self-checkout aisles and helped DeBeers make its diamond business sparkle. No wonder Bain's considered one of the world's top consultancies.

The firm's client base consists primarily of diversified, international corporations in all sectors of business and industry, such as financial services, e-commerce, retail, health care, consumer products and technology. According to the company, its clients have historically outperformed the stock market by three to one. For its private-equity ventures, the returns are in the top quartile of similar investments.

Bain covers almost every industry and almost every management consulting area. Depending on the office, consultants might be working primarily with technology companies (in the San Francisco office) or financial companies (in the New York office). About half the clients are small or midsize firms, a quarter are Fortune 500 firms, and a quarter are in private equity.

## Bain's babies

In 1994, Bain became the first consulting firm to establish a private equity group. The work is intense. Engagements usually include due diligence, deal structuring and predictive modeling with private equity and LBO firms. Bain seems to invest confidence in its private equity clients, too, as it accepts stocks instead of cash payments, and frequently invests in client companies.

Bain's strength in the private equity market is augmented by the very successful Bain Capital, founded in 1984 by Bain partners. The venture capital firm now has $12 billion in assets under management. It functions as a separate company; candidates with interest in Bain Capital should apply directly to that firm (www.baincapital.com).

Bain claims yet another spinoff, the Bridgespan Group, a nonprofit that aids other nonprofits by using Bain consulting stratagems. Bridgespan is a separate entity; Bain consultants can apply for a six-month stint at Bridgespan – though they take a large pay cut to do so. The Boston- and San Francisco-based Bridgespan staff of 40 serves up to 10 clients per year and is continuing to build its roster.

Bain takes on a host of other pro bono projects and heavily supports many charitable organizations, including the United Way, Habitat for Humanity and Junior Achievement. Additionally, Bain sponsors a "Community Impact Day," when entire Bain offices will close for one day so employees can participate in local community service projects.

## A launching pad

Many Bain consultants stay at the firm for a few years , then begin entrepreneurial ventures of their own. Insiders testify that the firm is not only aware of this pioneer spirit among its staff, it even encourages it. (Take the case of Intuit Inc., a California software firm started by Scott D. Cook, a former Bain employee, or of eBay, which ex-Bain consultant Meg Whitman helped found.) Where else do former Bain consultants wind up? According to the firm, approximately 55 percent of those who have left in the past five years have joined small companies or private equity firms. Another 20 percent have joined medium-sized firms, while most of the rest have landed positions in Fortune 500 firms.

## Loving Bain

Bain prides itself on being an innovator in the field of customer loyalty. Longtime customers, Bain has found, buy more, take up less customer service time, are less price-sensitive and recruit other customers. In fact, Bain asserts that, reducing customer attrition by a mere five percentage points a year can double profits in the long run. Recent research by the firm showed that such a five percent improvement in customer retention led to a 125 percent increase in profit for a credit card company. Bain's focus on customer loyalty may help explain why clients such as Continental Airlines, Dell and DeBeers have stayed loyal in return.

## Counsel!

Bain was busy in the courtroom in 2002. The firm lost a $10 million lawsuit wherein a São Paulo consulting firm alleged Bain had usurped its consultants to start its Brazil office. The suit concluded in December 2002. In January 2003, Bain was pleased to see the dismissal by a judge of a suit a former Club Med CEO had brought against the firm asking $70 million; the exec charged that Bain had conspired with Club Med board members to oust him.

# The way things work at Bain

In some offices, consultants are staffed on two projects at a time, depending on their interests and skills; Bain consultants don't specialize in one industry. Associate consultants (the entry level post-undergrad position) get assigned to case teams right away, and perform research and data analysis and make presentations for the client. Full-time consultants, who usually have MBAs or graduate degrees, look at clients' big-picture problems, studying market dynamics, financial returns, or how competitors are performing. They make and hone a recommendation, and get the client's buy-in.

Every six months, a performance evaluation is conducted, and all the upper-level people on the consulting team give feedback about consultant's work. If a consultant is heading up a case team, he also gets monthly feedback surveys from his team members.

Bain has several international offices, and encourages transfers for its best people. Usually, about 10 percent of its consultants transfer to another office. There are three types of transfers: short-term (six months), case-driven and permanent.

# Extensive training in exotic locales

Bain is known for its intensive training. All associate consultants start with two weeks' training at their local office, and are then shipped off to a 10-day training course in Cape Cod. Follow-up training occurs at least once a year, usually in exotic locales like Cancun or Hawaii. New consultants can expect one week of training in the office, five days in Miami and annual follow-ups in enticing locations such as San Francisco or Barcelona.

Trainers are usually Bain's own consultants, strategy and industry experts. Training may focus on analytical tools (valuation strategies, business research strategies), managerial skills (case team management, work planning) or business skills (making presentations).

# GETTING HIRED

Bainies concur that the hiring process is "rigorous." "This year we reviewed over 250 resumes and made seven offers for summer associate, for example," says one insider. Bain recruits at top schools, and wants candidates who've done well academically and on standardized tests; who've had leadership roles on campus or in their community; and who have solid business experience. Typically, Bainies join just out of school – undergrad for associate consultants, graduate for consultants. While applicants can be of any major, economics coursework is a big plus.

## Narrow but heavy focus

Bain recruits heavily, though somewhat narrowly. Sources say, "Although we entertain resumes from non-core schools," the focus is very much on "strong candidates at target schools." There are "very few industry hires." Top schools for undergrad recruiting include Princeton, Harvard, Stanford, Duke, Dartmouth and Berkeley. Each office also recruits from locally prominent schools – for example, the L.A. office looks at UCLA, USC and the Claremont Colleges, while the Atlanta office visits UVA, Emory, Georgia Tech and UNC-Chapel Hill. Canadian targets include University of Western Ontario, University of Toronto, and Queens. For business schools, the list includes Harvard, Wharton, Stanford, Tuck, Kellogg, INSEAD, Fuqua, Kenan-Flagler and Darden, among others. The top international schools are also a source of some interest to Bain.

The interview process differs slightly depending on the office. One European insider relates his experience: after being selected for an initial interview based on his cover letter, resume, high school and college grades, he had "a single day with four case interviews and a review after every two rounds. If you successfully pass all four rounds, you get an interview with a partner to discuss more general stuff and to receive an offer, all on the same day." A Latin America-based source describes a similar process. After the graduates of each top MBA schools – current Bain employees – screened the resumes from their alma maters, there were "interviews in two rounds of two interviews each (case interviews). The first round was with managers, generally, and second round with partners. Some other specific interviews can take more than four interviews."

The interview includes several case questions (some examples are thoughtfully included at www.bain.com/bainweb/join/interview/practice_overview.asp) but are said to be devoid of brainteasers or theoretical problems. The interviewers are looking for a "thoughtful, energetic discussion of business," and ask that you don't churn out current events, memorized business terms or generic problem-solving frameworks. "You ought to be structured in solving the case," advises one insider. "First, introduce the problem and break it down. Then, prioritize which areas to investigate. Discuss relevant facts, based on assumptions, math and logic. Pull your conclusions together. Finally, make an actual recommendation and discuss what the results (real, not theoretical) ought to be."

## The case of cases

Here are some case questions that have been used at Bain in the past. "Estimate the market for contact lenses in Canada." "Should a company switch their current logistics chain, based on highway transportation, to railway based?" "What is the opportunity for a gym in a certain city? What would be the profitability?" In one set of case questions, the candidate was looking at a map-maker client focusing on the road-atlas market. "In order to maintain viability, the company must sell $200 million in annual atlas sales. Is this reasonable? What do you see as the biggest threats to the company on meeting its goals? Where should the company look for growth?" "There's a global pet food company in financial distress; what would you consider doing first?

## Summer loving

Bain is the happy host to summer interns every year, though it only considers undergraduate juniors and first-year MBA students for these coveted positions. Recruiting for interns occurs in winter/early spring, and takes place through schools. There are two rounds of case interviews, just as there are for full-time hires. In the 10-week paid program, interns work on real cases. It's nice work if you can get it, say our insiders. "I was staffed on a real case, with a critical piece of analysis – the summer turned out quite well. There was tremendous support, formal training, great social activities and opportunities to present my work to senior clients," says one. Another reveals, "It was a great opportunity to get to know the firm and to be able to add value for a client. The internship made taking a full time offer an easy decision." Echoes a third, "The firm made sure that I was staffed with good coaches/mentors and I was given a discrete piece of the project. My good summer convinced me to accept my full-time offer to return."

Though "selectivity is [quite] visible in the hiring process, where not even two percent of applicants are invited for an interview," the hirers are looking for more than academic brainpower. "There is an effort to hire people that are not only extremely smart, but have great people skills and can contribute socially," says an insider.

# OUR SURVEY SAYS

## Company men (and women)

Bain consultants just love, love, love to talk about the company's "open-minded," "fun" atmosphere. So many of them used the phrase "work hard, play hard" to describe Bain, in fact, that we had to repeat it here (clichéd though it is). Making the culture strong are both the company's policies and its people. "It's the best atmosphere you can imagine," says a source. "The open-door policy is not just a phrase but an actual fact of life, and it's a bunch of people that all just want to have as much fun as possible while taking their job seriously." "We have fun together as a team," says another source; adds another, "your colleagues will be smart, dynamic and outgoing." That attitude seems genuine enough, for, in fact, people do report hanging out outside of work. "People are friendly and fun; over the past two years, many of my colleagues have become good friends – recently, I went on a cruise with over 20 of them," says a source. Another calls his co-workers "incredibly intelligent people who know how to have fun – the 'cool nerds' – there's never a dull moment."

This cheeriness seems to be reflected in the atmosphere at work, where "client results are taken seriously, but the in-office atmosphere is pretty light." Though the company is "results oriented: we care a lot about making things happen and making sure that our strategy work gets implemented," "there is always time for fun" and "the social atmosphere makes the workday enjoyable." Sums up one employee, "Bain's culture is what differentiates it from other consulting firms, and is a large part of why I enjoy my job."

## Life, or something like it

Despite the happy camper-ish attitude toward Bain's culture, consultants are not quite as enthused about the work/life balance – but hey, that's consulting for you. "[Work/life balance] is not poorer than other top strategy consulting firms, but it's not the best around," sighs one consultant. "You can expect to work long hours at Bain (as you would at any other firm), but there is an emphasis on focusing on those issues which are most important and not 'boiling the ocean.'" In that vein, there are "no requirements for face time," which seems to please Bainies.

Bain's also been active in monitoring work/life balance – "This is a high-profile issue right now," says an insider. "There are many mechanisms in place to ensure that hours are not excessive. For example, both average hours worked and individuals' satisfaction are tracked for each case team every month, and presented in summarized format at our monthly office meeting, with the manager and VP's names. In addition, managers' compensation is tied materially to case team satisfaction scores," reveals a New York-based source. In Los Angeles, the situation is similar. "Monthly hours are reported to the office by position, and there is much attention paid to team members who are consistently working long hours."

## Nine to five ... a.m.

Employees report logging at least 55 to 60 hours a week, and long hours during the days or occasional weekends "can create a problem sometimes." "I can't handle 80-hour workweeks for the rest of my life. I am young, and wasting away in the office," kvetches one employee. Says a São Paulo consultant, "I know my office is an exception to the rule, but work hours can drive you nuts. We spend at least 12 hours a day at work. It is not uncommon to be here for 14 or more. You will work at least one full weekend per month." That may be the case, but the firm is also flexible on offering part-time schedules to those who need it. "I have successfully balanced work and motherhood and have been able to work part time effectively over the last year while maintaining my status and position in the firm," says one manager – certainly a rarity in the consulting world. Still, schedules are by far the biggest complaint at Bain; some go so far as to call the lifestyle "unsustainable," while others lament the "capricious" nature of Bain schedules.

Beach time is not common at Bain – our surveyees report being on the beach only once or twice in the year. Temporarily unstaffed consultants are given the task of getting new clients, and "client development work is often just as demanding as real cases." And if you are on the beach, it's not necessarily a good thing. "Being on the beach means we are not selling projects, which is bad. I am glad I have been very little on the beach," says one business-conscious consultant.

## Bain-ifits

Salary is, according to some international Bainies, a little too low for their liking. "It's too low in continental Europe (definitely compared to the true cost of living/housing), so in balance, much higher working hours versus other professions with less pay. Pay, however, is comparable to other consultants in Europe," says one consultant. A New York-based source says there's "a lower base and higher bonus relative to other top-tier firms," which is backed up by another source, who tells us,

"In good years, we get an extra bonus that can be up to 100 percent of the original one. I got it in four years out of five."

Domestically, though, most sources agree that the pay is "very competitive," "better or equal to other consulting firms, but worse than i-banking." A few note that "compensation has been dwindling."

Those fascinated by profits will indeed be interested to know that "interesting opportunities come at the manager level, when you get access to the Bain Capital funds (average 90 percent annual returns)." Other perks include "a decent amount in our 401k, without requiring that we also invest," cell phones, laptops, snacks, insurance, gym discounts, entertainment tickets, "dinner budgets for working late" and, in some locations, dry cleaners and massages. And for lucky associate consultants, "after two years, some get offers to participate in MBA or PhD programs where they will be supported by Bain" for at least two years.

## Traveling light

The amount of travel required seems to vary greatly. "There's far more continuous travel at Bain than I expected," says a New York worker. Another remarks that the lack of travel is a "big advantage for Bain, probably under-appreciated." Since consultants are not always traveling, it seems to foster "more in-office camaraderie since we work out of our offices more often than most strategy firms" and "improves the sense of a community as people are in the office often."

Travel at Bain seems to be hugely case-dependent. "Some cases require three days a week travel, while others may require one day every other week. Average over a year is about one day per week," surmises one source. Some consultants just love travel, of course – "I travel a fair amount, but it's by choice." In any case, farflung assignments have become more common as the economy sours and Bain casts a wider net for assignments. "There's more travel lately as there has been less work in Canada," says a source; it's the same in the Midwest, where "there seems to be a trend in the Chicago office of more and more travel," and in Brazil, where "the rule is clear: you don't come to the office; you spend the whole time at the client's site. If it is in another city, it means you will be away from home from Monday morning to Friday night." Don't like to fly? Head for New York City, where "most people in the NYC office never travel, as the majority of our clients are in the city."

# Promotion in motion

One nice aspect of Bain, insiders say, is how the firm doesn't require degrees for promotion. "An MBA is not necessary or obligatory, although highly encouraged," says a source. One consultant reports: "It took me 24 months to go from fresh from university to the post-MBA level;" that source continues that three of the 50 consultants in his office also fit this impressive profile. Performance reviews occur every six months, and "one can advance very quickly based on these." Most say the basis for promotions is merit. "[Promotion] seems very fair and based on personal achievements and track records," says one consultant.

According to our sources, employees can expect three years at the MBA level position before reaching manager (a title that is, incidentally, "more senior than the same title at many other firms; probably more comparable to principal/junior partner elsewhere"), and "around four years or so to get from manager to partner. It definitely does not require a graduate degree to make it into MBA positions." "It is up-or-out, particularly at the consultant level. If you do not make it to manager in a reasonable time then it will be time to leave. I think most people understand that before they start," says a source. Another elaborates, "You do well and you'll advance quicker in the career; you do badly for a couple of quarters in a row and you will be asked to leave."

# Managing just fine, thanks

In fact, the up-or-out policy seems to hold true for both peons and upper-level managers at Bain. Consultants report they're pleased with how management "has in fact been strengthened recently (some were asked to leave, talented people were recruited)." A San Francisco consultant likes the "strong management team," and notes that the company is "still weeding out some managers who were promoted during the boom – most managers are very high quality."

The management gets high scores from the consultants we surveyed, who cited the "lack of hierarchies" and the "time and effort supervisors at Bain invest in everyone's professional development" as reasons for their satisfaction. However, one consultant suggests management focus on "better case management and clearer work planning." Another consultant likes that "upward feedback is a large part of the promotion process. People here are invested in your professional development, and there is a real sense of team."

## Developing delightfully

The training and development at Bain is widely lauded as phenomenal. The global training program, which brings together worldwide employees once every year or so is called "world-class" and "perfect." "Associate Consultant Training was one of the most intense weeks of my life – but I learned tons and had a terrific time," says one source. "Bain is committed to worldwide training programs, which gives employees the opportunity to learn in a focused environment, as well as to establish relationships with colleagues [from] all over the world," says an employee. That's supplemented by local "additional training" and "on-the-job guidance" that "happens quite often and is good as well."

Perhaps one reason for the top training is that "unlike at some firms, Bain picks its best to lead training," and it's a "huge honor to be selected as a trainer." There's also computer- and Internet-based training for all consultant levels, which is "fantastic, one of the most amazing tools I have seen" – it's "exhaustive."

## Ordinary offices

Office space seems functional and pleasant enough, judging from the mildly unenthused reports from Bain insiders. In San Francisco, there are "extraordinary views, but a fairly pedestrian space and somewhat smallish space allocations." In Holland, likewise, there's "nothing spectacular inside: pretty average cubicles etc.; however, the view is wonderful." The New York office is "new and very nice," though the "Times Square location is a bummer (too many tourists clog the sidewalks and push up lunch prices), the offices are nice and the cubicle setups are comfortable, if slightly cramped." A second-year AC there reports he has "a window seat with a gorgeous view of the Hudson River." Atlanta is "comfortable without being offensive to a client." Though it's the headquarters, "Bain's Boston office is inferior to other offices. Fortunately, we are moving soon to our new space, which should improve things significantly."

## Working women

Bain earns praise from consultants for its flexibility regarding women with children. The firm is "thoroughly committed to identifying options for all women, both those with children and those without," says a source. "I am one of eight women out of 11 promoted to manager in my consultant class. We have a very strong group of women at Bain. In addition, Bain has made working part time (though these scheduels are available to all) as a new mother an effective tool to balance work/life demand," says a Boston source.

If Bain's male/female ratio isn't quite yet 50-50, it's not for lack of trying. "We just get a lot fewer female applications, which is more based on the campuses we recruit from (engineers mostly) than on a 'male stronghold' or anything. I don't feel a single bias towards men or women in this office," says a European source.

The situation is better in the United States, apparently. "Our chairman is, of course, a woman. [That would be the flamboyant Orit Gadiesh.] Speaking just for the New York office, there are a lot of women at the associate consultant, consultant and manager level. There are relatively few at the VP level, but that will change with time as the female managers get promoted." Another adds that two-thirds of his incoming class in New York were women, adding, "It is very possible to have a family and successful career here at Bain." Atlanta has a "women's group in the office that organizes monthly activities for the women in the office." Overall, "Bain's commitment and effort toward attracting women is there, and it's a great working environment for women (speaking from personal experience), but the numbers are still low in many offices," summarizes one woman consultant.

## The Bain mix

Bain's doing just fine, thank you, in terms of racial diversity, Bainies say. "It's not really an issue; we just get a lot fewer minority applications," says a source. "Our intended commitment rates a 10 (very high priority for us), but we recognize we are not where we want to be yet," says one source.

Across the board, consultants find that sexual orientation is not an issue. "I'm gay myself, and I've never felt oppressed or anything. It's an absolute non-issue, no one cares whatsoever. So there's no inclination to 'improve' the ratio of gay/straight people, it's just not important. Be whoever you want to be, you'll be hired if you're good (and fun) enough," advises one consultant.

# Booz Allen Hamilton

8283 Greensboro Drive
McLean, VA 22102
Phone: (703) 902-5000
Fax: (703) 902-3333
www.boozallen.com

## LOCATIONS

**Worldwide Technology Business &
Corporate: McLean, VA (HQ)**
**Worldwide Commercial Business:
New York, NY (HQ)**
Over 100 offices worldwide

## PRACTICE AREAS

Information Technology
Organization and Change Leadership
  Operations
Strategy
Technology Management

## THE STATS

**Employer Type:** Private Company
**Chairman & CEO:** Dr. Ralph W.
Shrader
**2003 Employees:** 12,500
**2002 Employees:** 11,500
**FY 2003 Sales:** $2.3 billion
**FY 2002 Sales:** $2.1 billion

## UPPERS

• "The rate of personal development
  is outstanding"
• Great training

## DOWNERS

• "Very political"
• "Overly competitive"

## KEY COMPETITORS

Accenture
Bain & Company
Boston Consulting Group
McKinsey & Company

## EMPLOYMENT CONTACT

www.BoozAllen.com

## THE BUZZ
WHAT CONSULTANTS AT OTHER FIRMS ARE SAYING

• "Intelligent, quantitative, analytical"
• "Gray"
• "Excellent client list, reliable"
• "Government shop"

# THE SCOOP

## Sober fellows

The name Booz Allen Hamilton make cheap jokes about the drinking habits of consultants inevitable, but that's unfair to the company (and most consultants). Booz Allen racked up more than $2.3 billion in sales during fiscal 2003, the firm's 89th year in business, and is one of the most recognizable and respected names in management consulting today. We imagine they've developed a sense of humor during that time.

Edwin Booz, who founded his eponymous firm shortly after graduating from Northwestern University in 1914, probably had no idea that his firm would be among the most prestigious consultancies in the world. Over the past few years, Booz Allen Hamilton has expanded its service lines – and grown to more than 12,000 staff in more than 100 offices worldwide – to include e-business, e-government and enterprise assurance. Booz Allen garners 80 percent of its revenues from previous clients.

## Making strategies stick

Booz Allen isn't a pure strategy firm. Putting an emphasis on transforming businesses rather than merely prescribing change, the firm reports spending one-third to one-half of its time helping clients execute its recommendations. Before said execution, Booz Allen works with a client to develop solutions for problems created by fundamental changes in a client's industry or company – a "strategy-based transformation" – and execute changes in its organization, operations and technology. Booz Allen involves its clients throughout the consulting and transformation process by making a point of integrating client executives and staff into the consulting team.

## The Booz Allen split

Booz Allen's operations are divided into two major business sectors, Worldwide Commercial Business (WCB), which serves private sector clients, and Worldwide Technology Business (WTB), which serves government agencies and other public sector organizations. In years past, the two sides rarely interacted. Booz Allen Hamilton, however, is now doing a significant amount of joint work, servicing commercial clients using expertise and techniques traditionally associated with the government sector and vice versa. For example, Booz Allen is working with commercial clients in the area of strategic security, a capability built with government clients such as the National Security Agency. In the summer of 2002, Booz Allen added two top names to its global strategic security team. R. James Woolsey, former director of the CIA, became a Booz Allen vice president in July. A month later, Dale Watson, former Executive Assistant FBI Director for Counterterrorism, came on board as a principal.

## The two sectors

The commercial sector, headquartered in New York, is a classic management consultancy to which (mainly) recent college grads and MBAs apply. It works in strategy, organization, leadership, change management, operations, information technology and business transformation. Booz Allen offers these and other management consulting services to clients in a range of industries. The firm expedites the consulting process for its clients by organizing its expertise into what it calls natural market teams, focusing either on an industry, region or key functional area. The industry-oriented teams are aerospace and defense, automotive, consumer, energy/utilities, financial service, health, media, telecom and transport. The regionally focused teams serve clients in the developing markets of Latin America, North Asia; Australia, New Zealand and Southeast Asia. Crossing industry and regional lines are function-focused teams: strategy, organizational change leadership, operations, and information technology.

The government sector, based in the Washington, D.C. suburb of McLean, Va., primarily caters to the U.S. public sector market – specifically, government agencies and institutions. (One of the unit's major engagements, which it undertook in conjunction with the commercial sector, involved a restructuring of the IRS' business processes.) Approximately 42 percent of revenue is defense-related, 30 percent is civilian, 20 percent is derived from national security clients, and 8 percent comes from international government work. The government sector is divided into three market-focused business segments. The firm is planning a greater emphasis on new business in the e-government area, as well as in information assurance. The government sector hires staff at all levels and seeks technical professionals with backgrounds in IT and engineering, as well as management consultants with backgrounds in business and liberal arts.

## Global growth

The 1990s could be considered the beginning of Booz Allen Hamilton's modern era. Early in the decade, the firm created its worldwide technology business (WTB) and worldwide commercial business units (WCB) and moved its headquarters to its current location in McLean, Va. Booz Allen, which had already established a strong presence in Europe, Latin American and the Asia-Pacific region back in the 1950s and 1960s, opened still more international offices in the 1990s, including Abu Dhabi, Bangkok, Bogota, Pretoria, Seoul and Shanghai. (The international openings brought the total number of Booz Allen offices to 90.) In 1998, Booz Allen made several key moves. The firm named Ralph Shrader, then president of the worldwide technology business, its chairman and CEO. Daniel Lewis became the worldwide commercial business's president, a position he still holds today. And Booz Allen began to give consulting advice to the Internal Revenue Service (IRS), which today is one of the firm's largest clients.

## Development: it's a way of life

Responding to a renewed interest in training and professional development, the firm implemented a new corporate university in 1999. The consulting alma mater, not-so-humbly named the Center for Performance Excellence, is located at Booz Allen's government HQ in Virginia. At launch time, the Center consisted of 20 staff. Amazingly, the Center was conceived, planned and constructed within a 10-month period. In 2003, four years after the Center (hastily) opened its doors, Booz Allen was proudly ranked No. 6 on *Training* magazine's Training Top 100. (The firm was No. 1 among professional services firms on the list.)

Booz Allen further expanded its global footprint in 1999, this time through acquisition. The firm purchased Carta Corporate Advisors AB, the leading consulting firm in Scandinavia. With offices in Sweden, Finland, Norway and Denmark, Carta serves major corporations and government bodies across the Nordic region. Carta's capabilities – strategy and organization, corporate finance and strategic communications – were integrated with Booz Allen's to further strengthen the firm's market reach and delivery capability in Europe.

## Flexi-firm

Other management consulting companies may be larger or better known than Booz Allen – but few are as versatile. Over the years, Booz Allen's list of clients has been notable for its breadth and diversity. From NASA to the Secretary of the Navy, to the

District of Columbia to a legion of large commercial companies, Booz Allen has seemingly helped just about everyone manage their businesses better and save more money. One of the pioneers in management consulting, Booz Allen has developed an enviable reputation on the basis of its success in change management and public policy advising, its commitment to social progress and its readiness to adapt to technology.

## Bursting bubbles

In early 2000, Booz Allen began accepting equity from selected clients in lieu of cash as part of its venture and entrepreneurial consulting program, "Businesses by Booz Allen." The program was designed to allow the firm both to reap financial rewards for working with fledgling companies and to better attract top-tier recruits. In November 2000, it spun off Aestix, a Web design and implementation company. This stand-alone company was a wholly owned Booz Allen subsidiary with 150 experts in McLean, Va., and London, England, meant to service Fortune 1000 and Internet clients, both in partnership with Booz Allen and independently.

When the Internet bubble burst, though, Booz Allen was caught in the aftermath. In fact, the firm was hit even harder than other consulting firms because it was late on investing in the dot-com arena; thus, Booz Allen's invested capital garnered little return. In addition, when the dot-coms were thriving, employees left Booz Allen (and other consulting firms) for Web-related jobs, and recent MBAs failed to accept consulting positions in the numbers they did in the past. As a result, Booz Allen invested considerable time and money in its recruiting effort. However, while Booz Allen added young consultants, business leveled off and employee attrition went way down. According to one insider, "Booz Allen thought it had scored a marketing success, but that's exactly why they [later] went through multiple rounds of layoffs and moved some [commercial] people to the [government] side." In another bursting bubble-related change, Aestix was folded back into Booz Allen Hamilton on January 1, 2002.

## Lots o' diversity accolades

The firm has received numerous awards for diversity and lifestyle issues. In 2001, *Washingtonian* magazine ranked Booz Allen among the top 50 Great Places to Work in the Washington, D.C. area and named the firm to its biannual list, Best Place to Be a Kid (though Booz Allen does not employ minors as consultants). Booz Allen also received the 2001 EVE Award for its diversity programs from the U.S. Department of Labor, and the 2001 Torchbearer Citation from the Northern Virginia Family Service for promoting a balance between employees' work and their lives. The firm was also a hit abroad, ranking as one of the top four companies to work for in German magazine *Junge Karreire*'s Attractive Employers of 2001 survey. In 2002, for the fourth straight year, Booz Allen was named to *Working Mother* magazine's list of the 100 Best Companies for Working Mothers. The magazine has praised Booz Allen for its flextime program, on-site child care facilities, paid family leave plan, and other family-friendly policies. Also in 2002, the Human Rights Campaign named Booz Allen to its list of Top 95 Gay-Friendly Employers. That same year, *Black Collegian* magazine named Booz Allen to its list of Top 50 Diversity Companies.

## Balancing act

Booz Allen is committed to pro bono work. Recent clients include The Nature Conservancy, the Children's Defense Fund, Special Olympics International, Lincoln University and the United Negro College Fund. Booz Allen consultants can keep track of their firm's charitable moves via Community Relations Online, the firm's intranet site, which reports on current and upcoming community service opportunities worldwide.

## Recent activities for hawks, doves and pigeons

In addition to the two high-level Global Security hires in mid-2002, Miriam Browning joined the firm as a principal in January 2003. Former director of enterprise integration for the U.S. Army's CIO Office, Browning will work with Booz Allen's federal unit on a number of projects affecting the United States military. That month, the firm also won a $56 million contract with the Defense Logistics Agency for continued work on an inter-service center for study of equipment vulnerability, survivability and effectiveness.

In other news, Booz Allen Hamilton announced an alliance with financial services specialist IM2 in November 2002. The partnership is intended to provide extensive support for merger and acquisition activities. The consultancy took on a $30 million engagement in January 2003 to upgrade IT systems for the Washington Metro Area Transit Authority. Also in January, the firm announced the election of seven new senior vice presidents in offices on three continents. February 2003 brought news of Booz Allen's winning bid to design and implement transport for athletes, officials and media during the 2004 Olympic games in Athens, Greece. The firm performed a similar role in Sydney, Australia during that city's 2000 Olympiad.

# GETTING HIRED

## A tale of two Booz Allens

While Booz Allen Hamilton is just one firm, its two business units – WCB and WTB – have very different hiring and promotion policies. WCB services commercial clients, and WTB services government clients. The differing approach to business has worked well externally, but some insiders feel the division causes some stress and confusion. One source from the government side suggests the company should "keep pushing the WTB/WCB integration. Having these two arms is among our most unique and valuable attributes, but better efforts to cross-pollinate ideas, processes and people will strengthen each and provide exciting and career-broadening opportunities, and produce more well-rounded staff."

## You've got a friend at Booz Allen's WTB (if you're lucky)

One place where the government sector differs from the commercial sector is the route into the company; an overwhelming number of sources told us that employee referrals were the chief means of recruitment. (Commercial consultants, on the other hand, are primarily hired through on-campus interviews.) One person says, "the most important aspect to firm policy is the very high rate of 'employee referrals.'" But it isn't a way to get your feeble-minded cousin a job; our source cautions "You don't refer duds."

One respondent says of recruitment via referral, "The process was very fast. I had one interview with individuals. I got the offer on the next day. This was the fastest hiring process I've ever been through." But another insider feels hiring on the government side is "very sporadic and unpredictable; slow and inefficient." Despite this, many sources describe the process overall as "fair and equitable." One notes that, in addition to its fairness and equity, the hiring is "very diverse. Of late, [there has been a] strong drive toward emphasizing diversity: race, gender, etc."

## Up the government ladder

Education is desirable, but isn't the key for moving up if you're an engineer, programmer or government consultant. One WTB source says promotions are based upon "several factors: entrepreneurship, leadership, consulting abilities and management expertise." He adds, "The firm expends considerable effort to addressing employees' development and utility." A colleague lauds the process: "I am pleased with my firm's promotion policy. My firm seems to promote based on ability and merit, and the promotion policy seems to be consistent across the firm." There is some disagreement within the division on promotion criteria, though; one insider claims, "business generation is the key to promotion." Another adds, "I think the company looks for and promotes 'shining stars.' Promotions are based more on individual performance rather than on contributions to or performance on a team, which I think is a mistake."

In any case, you can advance at your own pace, whether that's fast or slow. One source tells us, "There is no up-or-out in WTB; advancement potential is strictly based on performance." Another adds, "Iit is getting easier to remain at the senior technical level without the pressure to bring in business or move up." A tech PhD says, "Advancement can take as little as one year and is not required for you to stay at the firm. Positions are solely based on competency." Yet another respondent explains, "Advancement up to level three can occur fairly quickly if the individual already has years of experience prior to joining the firm. Promotion to level four and above requires corroboration from outside the immediate team, which I think is a good thing."

## Experience necessary

MBAs, PhDs and other advanced degrees are welcome at Booz Allen, but undergraduates interested in working with private companies in the commercial sector should probably consider another place to begin a career. On the other hand, Booz Allen actively recruits undergrads for its government business. It's possible to get in and even get ahead with just a bachelor's degree, though – one manager says, "consultants with no MBA are evaluated for appropriateness of promotion. It is unusual but does occur when warranted." A peer agrees, "Commercial consultants with only undergrad degrees have moved into MBA level positions, but that is rare."

Many positions are filled through the "internal HR department," a process termed "highly competitive." "Much of our hiring is done through the summer associate (MBA) process." Another source says, "Candidates' resumes are reviewed and we submit prospects to the schools' placement offices to create closed interview lists. Some places, we have open sign-up." If you do get an interview with the firm, you should expect "case interviews that focus on your ability to understand economics." The shy should be forewarned that "sometimes a presentation is required."

On the commerical side, all candidates must face a rigorous set of case interviews. In fact, the firm thoughtfully hosts "crack-a-case" sessions on business schools to acquaint students with this most arduous of interview techniques.

## Rounds and rounds of cases

Unlike the government side of the business, commercial-side hiring follows a more conventional management consulting route. The firms is said to recruit at "all top business schools," as well as top European programs such as INSEAD and LBS. Booz Allen Hamilton conducts prescreening and offers interview slots to selected students, though "some schools have open sign up."

The process is said to be case interview-heavy. There are reportedly two rounds of interviews with three separate interviews in each, though some European Booz Allen Hamiltonians indicate that their offices conduct three rounds with two case interviews apiece. "It varies by office," states one Dutch insider. Cases are reportedly based on real Booz Allen Hamilton assignments. There are "some market sizing and some calculation questions" as well as open-ended case questions, but "usually no brainteasers." Some examples of Booz Allen Hamilton questions include "Germany is planning to implement a public toll system for trucks on motorways. Is the investment economically profitable for the country?" and "How many French fries does McDonald's make in a year?"

## Selective fire

While government employees may stay at the same level for many years, the WCB career path is "strictly up-or-out." One consultant reveals, however, that "due to personal development needs and/or other personal circumstances, exceptions are being made." "Evaluations are done approximately every year or year and a half based on a fixed appraisal cycle," according to a source; the promotion milestones typically come at 24 to 36 month intervals. At those times, you can expect "Ten to 15 percent attrition (including voluntary moves) at each appraisal." An insider says, "Promotion policy is very selective. The appraisal process is probably one of the core competencies of the firm." Another is less sanguine, calling the process "an absurdity in the past couple of years when there has been an (unofficial) promotion freeze."

There were heavy layoffs in 2001 – as much as 25 percent in some offices, though usually much less – and another, smaller round in early 2002, amounting to "about 15 percent," according to sources. A manager says Booz Allen "laid off people early rather than wait until appraisals to let them go – the logic described internally was that it was better to lay people off for business conditions than it was to change the standard and tell them they weren't good enough." However, "the layoffs are behind us," says one insider. "Business is improving."

# OUR SURVEY SAYS

## The qualities of culture

Consultants can expect to find "many diverse personalities with distinct thoughts and ambitions regarding the firm's strategy and direction," according to one consultant. Insiders describe the setting as "demanding but fair," "intellectually curious" and "very challenging – not always forgiving." One insider calls it "flexible and accommodating but incredibly professional." Another says the firm is "very conservative, but dynamic." A source in McLean, Va., opines, "Overall, [Booz Allen] is fairly conservative and somewhat straitlaced, but our VP makes our group's subculture more relaxed." Apparently, he's not in the same branch as the insider who calls Booz Allen "analytical, hard-driving, very numbers-oriented, hierarchical, competitive and intense." Another person with a darker view says, "The economic downturn, culture has become less pleasant. Fear among the young consultants, hard competition among partners."

Most Booz Allen consultants seem to cherish the firm's "good local office camaraderie." A consultant points out, "Most of the people I hang out with [on] weekends are from Booz Allen – just because I like them. Having worked for [another major consulting firm], I had problems fitting in an atmosphere where arrogance is not tolerated at all." An analyst says, "I would say that there is not a 'Booz Allen type' of person – there is considerable diversity in characters and experience. The atmosphere around the office is not overly hierarchical – you can just as easily go and talk to a principal as you can another consultant." Another source calls Booz Allen culture "cosmopolitan and friendly – but also competitive and somewhat political."

## Diversity is part of the vocabulary

Booz Allen's policy is that women and minorities should have an equal shot, and indeed, insiders see visible support for diversity goals. A long-time consultant tells us, "Recently, buzzwords like 'diversity' and 'work/life balance' have become an integral part of our firm's vocabulary. These concepts haven't completely sunk in yet, but it's obvious that senior management has made them a priority – and so our firm culture is improving slowly but surely." Another insider confirms, "Commitment is high. Results are mixed but probably better than at many firms." However, some at the firm feel the results are "still not there – more lip service than true equality." Booz Allen says it has five African-American officers – more than any other major consulting firm.

Women are well represented in some parts of the firm, according to sources. "I am a male who works for three women at the principal and partner level," says one manager, who thinks the firm is "very progressive and gender-neutral." One analyst feels "there are several women in powerful leadership positions for me to model myself after." One female insider notes: "Booz Allen has consistently rated as the top consulting firm for women, but all of the benefits that they tout are only at one office (HQ in McLean, Va.) and are available mostly to the women in our [government sector]."

## A beautiful Booz Allen mosaic

An insider opines that in terms of diversity, "In the U.S., [Booz Allen is] probably the best of the strategy consulting firms, especially with regard to African-Americans. [We are] less impressive in Europe, but then all firms are." Another consultant says, "I think we do best with African-Americans; there are few Hispanics but a fair number of Asians. Lots of Indians, but most of them are the well-educated elite from India's top schools. I think we are more committed to diversity than our competitors, though." An Asian member of the firm adds, "We have various forums that one can belong to."

One dissenter says, "There are many internationals, but few domestic minorities (African-American and Latino-Americans) in our commercial business. We could do a better job recruiting minorities." He adds, "However, the firm does go to good lengths to support minorities once they are part of the firm."

## Ask, tell

Booz Allen is just as committed to promoting openness for gays, lesbians and bisexuals as any other group. One consultant elaborates, "[GLB orientation] is very accepted and there is a strong support network – we have a forum pertaining to this. It's quite an eye opener and a great learning experience." One person in the know says, "I am myself openly gay within the company and never had a single negative reaction or the feeling that this would have a negative impact on my career." He adds, "All benefits which include spouses are also open for same-sex partners." However, there's a special consideration. According to one government sector insider, "The gay issue is touchy because a large part of our client base is military, and many gay/lesbian/bisexual consultants are afraid to come out, no matter how supportive the firm might be."

## On the road again

There seem to be two sorts of consultants at this firm: those who travel and those who don't. Our sources were evenly split between claims like "Our work is where our clients are" and others like "One travel day out of five is probably excessive; it's more like two or three days a month." (In general, government consultants travel less.) A European source says, "Booz Allen's model of close collaboration at client sites is well appreciated by clients, but it makes extra challenges for consultants."

A manager in the know reveals, "Travel requirements depend on the client, project and practice. Some projects are out-of-town five days a week. Some are local, with a shorter commute than going to the office." Another person on the government side says, "The decision to travel is entirely personal, and in line with firm and individual expectations." Partners are told to keep a close eye on travel requirements. "When projects are outside of the home office, the firm strongly encourages partners and job managers to arrange [projects] so that staff work at the client [site] a maximum of four days (three nights) per week."

## Booz Allen-ifying community service

One thing nearly all employees agree on is Booz Allen's commitment to staying involved in the community. One insider cheers that the firm is "exceptional in this area. It's why I joined." A manager tells us, "The firm has strong community involvement, has a director (and, in fact, a department) devoted to that effort, and has won numerous awards." There is a "major commitment to pro bono work, charities and various drives. This has been a long-standing value of the firm back to Jim Allen."

## Treating people right

Given all that, does the firm take care of its people? The answer appears to be affirmative. For instance, in 2002, 101 Booz Allen reservists were called into active duty – many for a year or more. Booz Allen provided those individuals with full supplemental pay and benefits throughout to ease the financial burden on them and their families.

Many of our respondents mention "profit sharing" in the form of "contributions to retirement plans." Reports from United States insiders vary from 10 to 15 percent of annual salary and bonus, with a six-year vesting period. The actual amount of salary isn't discussed directly by our sources, but there are some comments. One person informs us, "salaries were lowered from dot-com-era highs. One notable fact: "Everyone in each class/cohort makes the same salary – very equitable." Another says, "Booz Allen offers very competitive salaries; however, during the tech bubble, we were able to avoid skewing our salary ranges, allowing our costs to remain competitive in the client marketplace." One fellow rationalizes, "I had the potential for a higher salary at other consulting firms, however, I have more job security, flexibility, variety of work and cultural fit at [Booz Allen]."

Non-salary compensation earns raves as well. In addition to the healthy retirement contributions from profit sharing, insiders are extremely happy with the perks and benefits. One consultant claims, "Great benefits are the reason I picked" Booz Allen. Most insiders favorably mention the tuition reimbursement program. One principal mentions the "lunch club, country club membership, $1,500 home office allowance and stock plan" as chief considerations. Another consultant explains, "Benefits tend to be individual in nature, rather than site-oriented – for example, there is no dry cleaning or tailoring."

# "[Booz Allen is] cosmopolitan and friendly – but also competitive and somewhat political."

*— Booz Allen Hamilton consultant*

# 5 Monitor Group

Two Canal Park
Cambridge, MA 02141
Phone: (617) 252-2000
Fax: (617) 252-2100
www.monitor.com

## LOCATIONS

**Cambridge, MA (HQ)**
Chicago, IL • Emeryville, CA • Los
Angeles, CA • New York, NY • Palo
Alto, CA • Amsterdam • Athens •
Beijing • Frankfurt • Hong Kong •
Johannesburg • London • Madrid •
Milan • Mumbai • Munich • Paris •
São Paulo • Seoul • Singapore •
Tokyo • Toronto • Zurich

## PRACTICE AREAS

Country Competitiveness
Financial Assessment/Evaluation
Marketing Strategy
Operations/Logistics
Organizational Effectiveness
Strategic Transactions
Strategy

## HE STATS

**Employer Type:** Private Company
**CEO:** Mark Fuller
**2002 Employees:** 850
**2001 Employees:** 1,200

## UPPERS

- Beautiful offices
- "Dedicated to community service"

## DOWNERS

- "Communication from senior
  leadership" less than adequate
- No bonuses in two years

## KEY COMPETITORS

Bain & Company
Boston Consulting Group
McKinsey & Company
Mercer
The Parthenon Group

## EMPLOYMENT CONTACT

www.monitor.com/cgi-bin/iowa/careers
E-mail: Recruiting_us@monitor.com

## THE BUZZ
WHAT CONSULTANTS AT OTHER FIRMS ARE SAYING

- "Tough as nails, but friendly"
- "Harvard-happy"
- "Scatterbrained"
- "The cool McKinsey"

# THE SCOOP

## Monitoring the world

Founded in 1983 by a group of professors and consultants, including Michael Porter (creator of popular case interview framework Porter's Five Forces and the consulting equivalent of a rock star), Monitor Group aims to put ideas created in the business and academic worlds into practice. Though only a medium-sized firm by industry standards, Monitor has developed a number of practices and expanded its client list to include everything from Fortune 500 companies and international firms to government agencies and major nonprofit organizations. With 28 offices in 23 countries, Monitor offers advisory services in areas including private equity and venture capital, e-commerce incubation, and mergers and acquisition-related transactions.

## Breaking it down

Monitor divides its operations into three groups: Action Group, which focuses on consulting practices; Monitor Merchant Banking, which is involved in capital investing and venture projects; and the Intelligent Products Group, which designs customized data and software products. (The Action Group is what most people think of when they think of Monitor; it represents Monitor's core strategy consulting business, and most consultants are hired into the Action Group.) Each group, in turn, comprises a number of companies; for example, Action Group includes such operations as the Global Business Network, which specializes in long term scenario planning, and Market2Customer, a marketing consulting operation. Merchant Banking companies, such as Monitor Clipper Partners and Monitor Ventures, have an equity stake in 20 firms and over their collective lifetime have invested more than $1 billion.

## Unified theory of everything (consulting)

Monitor bases its consulting philosophy on a "unified theory" approach. Rather than applying a single strategy to every client or leaning on set industry practices, the firm integrates its operations across industries, allowing its projects to use resources culled from the firm's various subsidiaries. Instead of relying on generic practices, Monitor consulting teams are able to draw on marketing, e-learning and software designers to customize their consulting solutions.

## It's academic

Much of Monitor's strength comes from its grounding in the academic world. One of its founding principals, Harvard Business School Professor Michael Porter, is a veritable demigod among consultants and still influences much of Monitor's structure and practices. Other principals, such as Bernie Jaworski, Mike Jensen and Tom Copeland, have strong ties to academia, retaining fellowships or adjunct professorships at some of the nation's leading business schools. In March 2001, MarketspaceU, Monitor's research and publishing unit, announced a partnership with McGraw-Hill to produce a series of written materials on e-commerce for business professionals, students and educators. The title that spawned the series, *e-Commerce* (co-authored by Jaworski and Jeffrey Rayport, another HBS professor), is an integrated print and online textbook that has already been adopted by nearly 200 business schools.

## Feeling the burn

The impact of the recent economic downturn hit Monitor in mid-2001, particularly in its North America and European offices (as well as its e-consultancy, Marketspace.) Layoffs hit Europe in July and North America in August of that year, with cuts as high as 15 percent in some offices (the deepest cuts came in satellite offices such as Los Angeles and Toronto). Nevertheless, the company continues to do well in Latin America and Asia, and both regions were spared from any staff reductions. Insiders at Monitor report that no bonuses were paid in 2001 or 2002, although the firm still enjoys positive cash flow.

## Energetic engagements

Monitor continues to work on some interesting engagements. In December 2002, Shell Oil Co. engaged Monitor to help improve its image. Consultants are surveying environmentalists and government officials in Louisiana, Shell's home turf, before expanding their study worldwide. And in February 2003, Monitor was hired to explore improving growth and foreign investments for the Brunei Economic Development Board. The project, it is hoped, will create 500 new jobs in Brunei and generate $300 million in new investments.

# GETTING HIRED

## More than a formality

Insiders at Monitor seem very proud of their interview process, describing it as "robust" and "cutting edge." A source says, "The process (resume screen, first round on campus or in the office for non-target school hires, second round in the office) is fairly typical. The content is anything but." While that consultant isn't specific about that atypical content, others are. "[Candidates] selected to interview do a first round case, which involves reading a case and discussing it with the interviewer," says one consultant. "Candidates invited back for final rounds spend about half a day at the company, including a group case interview, a role play exercise, and a values interview." Another consultant says the second round, at Monitor, includes a "group exercise which is another written case, but this one includes a facilitation component and group interaction with up to five candidates working through the case together." These cases are typically booklets of a few pages of text and perhaps five pages of charts. A different interview segment is "a roleplaying exercise to test the interviewee's ability to read into a mock-client interaction and test their ability to role-play in a dynamic situation." One insider reports a video "where you critique a video of a consultant/client interaction." The interivew process also involves a feedback segment "where you are given feedback on your performance." Don't be passive during this phase of the interview – it's "meant to test how you react to feedback and constructive criticism, something that is extremely valued in the firm."

Candidates are drawn from "several relationship schools that [Monitor targets] for undergrad and MBA candidates, but 'non-network' schools are considered as well." An insider opines that the pool "varies somewhat from year to year depending on hiring requirements."

Once you've been hired by Monitor, you're likely to keep moving up in the consulting firm. Monitor is especially fond of "hiring back Monitor alumni from business schools," according to a source. Furthermore, says another consultant, "Many consultants with only undergraduate degrees move into MBA-level positions and beyond because of strong performance." Indeed, some consultants reportedly stay with Monitor for up to five years before going back to school for an MBA.

## Internship admiration

Many of our respondents had been through Monitor's internship program, which one called "a tremendous learning experience." "My summer experience is one of the main reasons that I am here," says another consultant. "Not only because about 80 percent of summer consultants are extended offers, but also because I had a good experience."

# OUR SURVEY SAYS

## Monitoring the culture

Most comments about Monitorian culture are positive, with one insider describing the atmosphere as "quirky, caring, curious and flexible." Another consultant says, "The people are awesome, it's a social environment, and the lack of hierarchy makes it a more comfortable place to be." A third insider praises the "individuality" fostered by Monitor. "People are able to develop their own ways of delivering exceptional work to clients." A source in the Boston office says, "[Working at Monitor] like a full-time MBA program with constant learning."

## Earth to Monitor

Though it's not a huge company, Monitor is large enough that the most common complaint is "communication from the leadership." A 2003 gaffe by management regarding details about bonuses is called "inexcusable." One insider carps that Monitor's culture is "losing some of its luster given firm management's communication with the consultant base regarding firm performance and compensation." This has led, according to another source, to employees being "slightly disgruntled at the moment in some populations." What form does this gap in communication take? "Too many things (e.g., compensation) get stalled at the Chairman's office which makes the firm feel poorly managed to the junior ranks of the firm, which in turn affects morale." There's a certain irony to the communicative failures, as one consulant points out. "In some ways, given the emphasis on productive reasoning at Monitor, the lack of communication can feel hypocritical."

## Good guidance

Whatever the feelings about the firm's top-level officers, line managers are still cherished. One insider tells us, "Supervisors are great. They are almost always looking out for your development goals and usually try not to work you into the ground. All my managers have been extremely competent. I've never wondered, 'Why does he have this job?'" Another claims, "I've had some of the best managers of my working career while at Monitor. Certainly, some are better than others, but I've yet to encounter any that are truly bad." A third consultant explains, "One of the benefits of Monitor's 50/50 model is that I am exposed to twice the number of managers as I would be if staffed 100 percent on one case. I am therefore able to pick up on the best traits from a number of managers in a short period of time."

## Trying to compensate

The compensation and bonus issue appears to be on many Monitorian minds. A senior analyst explains, "Monitor pays smaller base salaries than McKinsey, Bain and BCG and most years makes up for it in bonuses, but the last two years there have essentially been no bonuses." A consultant agrees, "The firm has historically awarded incredible compensation in up years. Unfortunately, the converse is true — the past few years haven't been the best for the firm, and compensation has suffered." The firm appears to make up for this in part with a laundry list of perks and benefits, including dry cleaning (no pun intended), tuition reimbursement, tickets to local cultural and sporting events, employee lounges and cafeterias, on-site banking and exercise facilities; and plenty of other things to sweeten the pot.

Job satisfaction remains high at the firm. "Even though it has been a tough couple of years and the firm hasn't handled communication issues well, I still really like the firm and enjoy going to work every day," says one senior consultant. A second consultant tells us, "I've recently turned down other offers; that's one indicator that things are pretty good."

## Fab diversity record

Monitor consultants are thrilled with diversity at the firm. One woman says, "I think the firm is very well-intentioned here, taking extra steps to design roles and find allocations that allow working mothers to make their lives work." A male insider agrees, "Relative to the industry, I think we do pretty well – we have several extremely successful female account managers, many female senior project leaders, etc." Another male consultant says, "I have never worked in an environment with so many women. I have been on a number of case teams where the majority of members were women. However, there are not as many women at the most senior ranks (an aspect Monitor is working hard to improve upon)."

With regard to minorities at Monitor, says one senior consultant, "I see a good deal of commitment, but very limited success. Some of our lack of success is, however, mitigated by a strong global network. What we might not see in North America is balanced by the relationships we develop with foreign colleagues." Another insider says, "Monitor takes active steps to bring minorities into the recruiting process but does not have different standards for minorities than any other group. Despite this active effort, Monitor is not very diverse with respect to minorities." Another explains, "The commitment to diversity at the junior levels is very high; there is less effort made at the senior levels to ensure a diverse population, which probably explains our lack of diversity overall."

## Contemporary chic offices

Monitor employees rave about the workspace, for the most part. A person from the Cambridge headquarters says, "The building is beautiful. It would be nice if everyone had their own office, but sharing isn't too bad and even has perks." Another recalls, "The Los Angeles office is absolutely amazing – in Santa Monica overlooking the Pacific with offices and conference rooms with floor-to-ceiling windows." "I love our office," another insider tells us. "Lots of space, high ceilings, tons of natural light, great desk chairs and meeting spaces." A source provides this critique: "The space errs on the contemporary side, with funky art, colors (lime green and orange) and shapes (like elliptical pillars) throughout the office. Herman Miller chairs are everywhere. The office is nicer than most of our clients'."

## On the road - now and then

Unlike some consulting firms, where consultants might as well not rent apartments, Monitor consultants are relative homebodies. "You can often structure your travel requirements," volunteers one consultant. Elaborates another insider: "There is no four-day-at-the-client-site travel policy. Actually, there is no policy at all. We travel whenever it is necessary for meetings, presentations or research. The decision on whether or not to travel is wholly dependent on case team managers, who make travel tradeoffs based on how to best serve our clients."

## Generous hearts

Monitor employees feel the firm does a lot of community service; "Some would say that Monitor spends too many resources here," according to one person. Most others seem to think it's a good thing. A manager explains, "Monitor participates in Inspire, which provides consulting services to not-for-profit entities. Monitor also has a strong affiliation with New Profit, a venture philanthropy organization. The firm provides them office space, as well as teams to work with portfolio organizations." Other respondents mention "clothing drives," "blood drives," "Habitat for Humanity," "helping out at the local food shelter" and similar activities.

# Mercer Management Consulting

1166 Avenue of the Americas
32nd Floor
New York, NY 10036
Phone: (212) 345-8000
Fax: (212) 345-8075
www.mercermc.com

## LOCATIONS

**New York City (HQ)**
22 offices worldwide

## INDUSTRY AND FUNCTIONAL PRACTICES:

Aviation
Communications, Information, and Entertainment
General Operations
General Strategy
Retail/Value Engineering
Utilities

## THE BUZZ
### WHAT CONSULTANTS AT OTHER FIRMS ARE SAYING

- "Good reputation for great strategy"
- "Undifferentiated"
- "Cornell of strategy's Ivy League"
- "Growing in stature"

## THE STATS

**Employer Type:** Subsidiary of Marsh & McLennan Companies Inc.
**Chairman and CEO:** Peter Coster
**2002 Employees:** 1,400
**2001 Employees:** 1,200

## UPPERS

- "A lot of freedom in how you do things"
- "Opportunity to progress to partner without leaving for b-school"
- "Great exposure to clients even as an analyst"
- Supportive culture, plenty of mentoring

## DOWNERS

- "Our brand is not nearly as strong as it should be"
- Pay decreases
- "The firm lacks direction and momentum"
- Uncertainty over merger with Oliver, Wyman & Co.

## KEY COMPETITORS

Bain & Company
Booz Allen Hamilton
Boston Consulting Group
McKinsey & Company

## EMPLOYMENT CONTACT

E-mail: recruiting@mercermc.com

# THE SCOOP

## A part of the whole

New York's Mercer Management Consulting, a subsidiary of professional services titan Marsh & McLennan Companies, has made quite a name for itself in a little over a decade. Formed in 1990 by the merger of Temple, Barker & Sloane and Strategic Planning Associates, Mercer has grown rapidly, opening offices in Europe, the Pacific Rim and Latin America and acquiring a number of boutique consultancies, including Corporate Decisions, Inc. (CDI), Germany's Dr. Seebauer & Partner GmbH, Mexico's Analisis y Desarollo de Proyectos and Switzerland's St. Gallen Consulting Group. Today, Mercer Management Consulting has approximately 1,000 consultants and support personnel in 22 offices worldwide. (The number decreased in 2003 because some Mercer Management consultants made the move to newly acquired finance consulting arm Mercer Oliver Wyman.)

## From outsider to insider

When it was founded, Mercer was considered a brazen startup in a field dominated by giant, established firms like Bain and Booz Allen Hamilton. But the firm expanded its practice quickly by aggressively pursuing clients and rooting its work in a series of well-publicized books, including *The Profit Zone*, *Value Migration* and *Profit Patterns*. These books advocate a customer-focused approach to a company's competitive advantages, a philosophy that apparently has rung true with many business leaders. (Even with these achievements, several Mercer consultants still think that Mercer has a less established and prestigious brand name, despite "beating more branded firms for a lot of projects, and charging the same rates.")

But like many consulting firms in the last few years, Mercer's attempt to situate itself at the forefront of high-tech and international markets left it exposed to the dot-com implosion and economic downturn. Marsh & McLennan reported that its 2001 management consulting revenue was down 21 percent from the previous year. In November 2001, Mercer closed its Geneva and Washington offices, displacing 77 employees. Partners were given the choice to relocate, while rank-and-file employees were given severance packages. The economy has affected recruiting as well: where in the past Mercer hired in the range of 30 to 45 MBA interns and 25 to 30 summer analysts each year, the firm canceled its internship program in 2001. The program resumed in 2002.

## Profitable publications

One of Mercer's greatest strengths lies in its intellectual capital, led by strategy guru Adrian Slywotzky. A Mercer vice president, Slywotzky is credited with coining the term "value growth" in his 1996 book, *Value Migration*, and with spearheading the development of a more outwardly focused approach to competitive strategy. In October 1999, *Industry Week* named Slywotzky one of the most influential people in management, along with business world luminaries like management theorist Peter Drucker and Microsoft founder Bill Gates.

Slywotzky struck again in March 2002, publishing *The Art of Profitability*. In this volume, fictional master of management David Zhao walks an apprentice through 23 lessons on improving profitability without breaking relationships. According to Slywotzky, his work is meant to be savored, not gulped down. "Please read only one chapter per week. Think about it. Let it stew," the author recommended to *Publishers Weekly*. Mercer Management Consulting offers the work for free as a PDF download, as well as selling hard copies, audio versions and e-books of the work, for those eager to learn from the imaginary Zhao.

More recently, prolific author Slywotzy penned *How To Grow When Markets Don't* along with Mercer VP Richard Wise. The book was published in April 2003.

## Other engagements

The firm stayed active in 2001, providing strategy advice for the December merger of Hawaiian Airlines and Aloha Airgroup into Aloha Holdings, Inc. (Hawaii-based Mercer consultants have continued to work on the project in 2002.) And in January 2002, Mercer advised Sinotrans, a large China-based shipping company, in reorganization preparatory to a listing on the Hong Kong stock exchange. It also completed an exhaustive study of the success of transatlantic mergers and acquisitions, and advised a major automaker on branding strategies.

## Serious personal time

In the fall of 1999, Mercer announced the 10/11 Month Year, a program that allows consultants to take one or two months off each year (without pay) to pursue projects outside the firm. Consultants can also take advantage of an externship program that allows them to work for six to 12 months at selected firm clients or other corporate, venture capital, or start-up or non-profit companies. Additionally, Mercer offers a non-profit fellowship program that operates in a similar manner to the externship. Both were launched in spring 2001.

## Developing the core

Consultants who aren't partners are considered to be part of the Core Consulting Group (generalists), and are required to attend occasional weeklong programs to sharpen their consulting skills and to network with colleagues from other offices. Mercer also has a generous tuition sponsorship program on both continents for employees interested in going to business school. (They must commit to returning to Mercer upon completion of their MBA in order to qualify.)

In January 2003, Mercer traded several of its consultants to the branding specialty firm Lippincott & Margulies, a sibling in the MMC family of companies. The addition of these so-called "brand scientists" created a broader brand consulting group, dubbed Lippincott Mercer.

## Team building exercises

Mercer Management acquired the consultancy of James Miller & Company, a specialist in the oil, gas and chemicals industries, in March 2002. The boutique consulting firm promptly became Mercer's new Houston office, with James Miller remaining at the head.

David J. Morrison, formerly a vice chairman of the firm, was named to succeed James W. Down in November 2002 as president of worldwide operations. Down, a 21-year Mercer veteran, retired at the end of 2002. He held the post of president for five years, during which time Mercer Management Consulting grew from 13 offices to 22.

## New kid on the block

In April 2003, Oliver Wyman joined the Mercer family. The new firm, now called Mercer Oliver Wyman, will be led by Oliver Wyman's chairman John Drzik and have more than 600 employees in Asia, Europe and North America. It joins Mercer Management Consulting and Lippincott Mercer as part of MMC's Mercer Management Consulting reporting arm; the firm will specialize in consulting to financial services organizations.

# GETTING HIRED

## Going a few rounds with Mercer

While interviews vary a tad by country, undergraduates typically face three rounds of "very thorough and very selective" interviews, while MBAs receive a first-round bye. An insider says, "Each round involves up to three 45-minute case interviews and a 'fit' interview. The case interviews can be quantitative, qualitative or a mixture of the two." A consultant in the Asia-Pacific region reveals, "There are six interviews of 45 minutes – five interviews are composed of 15 minutes of self-presentation, motivation, etc., 25 minutes of case simulation and five minutes of Q&A." He adds, "The last interview is with a senior partner and without case simulation."

According to Mercer, the most typical schedule for full-time undergraduates is a 30-minute first round case interview, two 30-minute second round interviews (one fit and one case) and three 45-minute interviews in the final round (two case and one fit.) For summer intern hires, applicants face two rounds. The first round consists of one 30-minute case and one 30-minute fit interview, and the second round involves two 45-minute cases and one 45-minute fit interview. The later the round, the more senior the interviewers.

About the cases, another source says, "There are a few canned ones, but most people create their own cases based on personal experience." If you botch one, says an insider, there's still hope. "If the case is unsuccessful, we sometimes use a brain-teaser. For example: 'How long does it take to move Mount Fuji by 1km with a single truck?'"

Summer internships are fairly common – former interns accounted for about 20 percent of our respondents – and they face two rounds of interviews to get into the program. One insider relates, "I was assigned a buddy I could use as a resource for the 'stupid' questions and had an advisor who was responsible for my experience. I attended a couple of training programs with the rest of my summer class and participated in many social events organized for us." Another says, "It definitely made the decision for me in terms of joining the firm." The summer consultant program might not be what it once was during the height of consulting a few years ago, suggests one insider. He calls the internship "awesome – but that was during the 'Club Mercer' days."

# OUR SURVEY SAYS

## Close culture

Mercer consultants describe the firm as "supportive" and "team-oriented," with "great emphasis on developing others." One insider says, "Partners take responsibility in shaping the culture," which another claims is the "best part about the company." Another disagrees: "[Mercer] used to be a firm that believed in having fun in what we do. The culture of the firm has been on the decline, especially over the last two years."

One source calls the people "a little idiosyncratic – not too many cookie cutter types, lots of semi-academic, slightly odd partners." "It really seems that Mercer screens applicants heavily for personal fit," says one chirpy consultant, "and it shows – there isn't a single person in my office who I'd hate to get stuck with in an airport layover."

## Mobility

Consultants term Mercer a supportive environment. "Analysts are encouraged to stay and grow in the firm," says a source. (That's refreshing, considering some firms are "encouraging" consultants to leave firms at the present time.) "They are also given all the tools and support to pursue an MBA." "As long as you are contributing, you are not pressured to leave," says an analyst. Several insiders tell us that an MBA or other advanced degree is not necessary to move up in the firm. One manager says, "Consultants with only undergraduate degrees can not only move into MBA-level positions but move to partner as well. It may take an average undergraduate about three years to move to MBA-level positions, and move from analyst to partner in five (aggressive, but possible)." Another insider says, "Mercer has a history of promoting strong performers quickly. This has continued despite the economic downturn."

## No rest for the Mercerites

One reason for the juxtaposition of fast advancement with no advancement pressure is the rapid pace of work at Mercer. The cream naturally rises to the top. "We're at 90 percent utilization right now in North America," says one source. Few respondents reported being on the beach for more than five weeks in a given year. "Just about everyone seems staffed," observes one. Another consultant adds, "You have to be pretty removed to not at least be on active business development." A third opines, "The firm is very good at deploying beachers for business development work," which she says is "interesting and provides good visibility with partners."

The firm doesn't work its consultants too hard, though. A consultant tells us, "There are always going to be 'high-burn' cases, but most aren't. And when one gets on a high-burn case, it is recognized by the firm and that person is given a lighter case after that." Another insider says there is "great freedom in the work: one can work at the office or at home, choose his working hours." He adds there is "no pressure to stay at the office if there's no work."

Travel is "very variable between projects." A source says, "Firm average is about two days a week, but it's binary: half of us travel four days per week, half never travel." However, one consultant warns, "Increasingly, case teams are not able to return to their home offices for Fridays which used to be important from the perspective of building a strong firm culture."

## A favorite topic: cash

Consulting has been going through some tough times in the last few years, and Mercer has had its share of rough patches. "Compensation has gotten dramatically worse over the last year," says one manager, "to the point where people who joined two years ago are now making less than when they joined (despite promotions)." A consultant adds, "Mercer reduced pay between August and year end 2002 as a way to avoid more layoffs. The salaries for all (except associates) were brought nearly to their prior level effective January 2003, but associates are still suffering – my salary is now 12 percent below what it once was."

Despite sporadic complaints about pay, there seems to be a good bonus policy, at least for star consultants. A person in the Boston office gives details: "Mercer's bonus is based on how quickly one is promoted. Specifically, the year-end bonus reflects the difference between one's annualized year-end salary and what they actually made during the year. For example, a junior consultant who is promoted to associate (MBA-equivalent) might receive $110,000 – $80,000 + $30,000 bonus." In addition, there is "a stock purchase plan which has a guaranteed 15 percent return, and some years as high as 50 percent." Partners have access to profit sharing.

## Diversity "a non-issue"

Mercer consultants feel that, while "efforts continue on this front" the level of diversity among employees is "excellent." One insider gives us an earful: "This line of questioning feels a bit odd because diversity is such a non-issue. My teams at Mercer have been comprised of men, women, Muslims, Christians, Jews, Sikhs, gays, heterosexuals, Caucasians, African-Americans, Asians, Israelis and Pakistanis, but none of us thought of each other that way. We were all working towards our common goal of solving the client's problem. It did make for interesting case team dinners, as selecting a restaurant with an appropriately diverse menu could be a challenge!"

56 Top Gallant Road
Stamford, CT 06904
Phone: (203) 964-0096
www.gartner.com

## LOCATIONS

**Stamford, CT (HQ)**
90 locations worldwide

## PRACTICE AREAS

Community
Consulting
Measurement
News
Research

## THE STATS

**Employer Type:** Public Company
**Stock Symbol:** IT/ITB
**Stock Exchange:** NYSE
**CEO and Chairman:** Michael D. Fleisher
**2002 Employees:** 4,039
**2001 Employees:** 4,300
**2002 Revenue:** $907.2 million
**2001 Revenue:** $962 million

## UPPERS

- "Some of the smartest in the industry"
- "Flexible work hours, can work from home"
- "Open communication"

## DOWNERS

- "Frequent layoffs in the past two years"
- "Work can become routine if you stay in one area"
- "More training" needed

## KEY COMPETITORS

Charles River Associates
Corporate Executive Board

## EMPLOYMENT CONTACT

Human Resources
Fax: (203) 316-3445
E-mail: gartner@gartnercareers.com

## THE BUZZ
WHAT CONSULTANTS AT OTHER FIRMS ARE SAYING

- "Technical experts"
- "Rhona Barret of consulting"
- "Blue skies"
- "Great at magic quadrants"

# THE SCOOP

## The seat of IT knowledge

Gartner's expertise is information; it is one of the most recognized brands in market research, and also has made a noticeable impact on consulting, content and events – all with a technologic spin. The firm, founded by Gideon Gartner in 1979 as Gartner Group, first went public in 1986 and was publicly traded for two years until it was pulled off the market. A subsequent public offering in 1993 put the company back on the Nasdaq before it was transferred to the New York Stock Exchange in September 1998. The firm has been stable and growing since that time.

## Segmentation

Gartner is composed of five business units: Research, Consulting, Measurement, News and Community. Research is the firm's core offering, and all the other groups build on the work of the 500 professionals in this unit. Consulting focuses on strategy issues (and, increasingly, implementation) in a variety of industries. Measurement is the company's performance benchmarking operation. News is responsible for providing information to journalists, and serves as Gartner's publishing arm. Community brings executives together to compare experiences at one- to five-day conferences for business and IT professionals, such as the Gartner Symposium/ITxpos, the largest conference for the IT industry. San Diego, Orlando, Florence, Brisbane and Cannes will host versions of the event during 2003.

## Data down south

The expectation is that a firm dedicated to business and technology analysis would have a handle on when and where to expand its operations. So when Gartner announced the intent to expand in Latin America during the depths of resession, industry observers took notice. The firm, noting that its regional revenue expanded 9 percent during 2002 while its overall business contracted 7 percent, decided to invest where it saw the most return. In a March 2003 announcement, regional GM Donald Feinberg said, "[Latin America] is a development region. We need to have some investment, some risk, even before the numbers pan out." Feinberg later added, "Latin America is growing. Period. It's just a matter of degrees." Specific plans include hiring a handful of consultants and analysts for offices in Mexico and Brazil. Currently, Gartner has offices in seven Latin American countries, with regional headquarters in São Paulo.

Gartner is also expanding in Asia; in November 2002, Gartner India announced the appointment of Partha Iyengar as vice president and research director of applications development and IT services, and Sujay Chohan as vice president and research director of business process outsourcing. In April 2003, the firm hired Darren Tan as an associate director of the consulting practice in Hong Kong, and appointed Liza Tang senior business manager there.

## Making more with less

Overall in 2002, Gartner earned $907.2 million in revenue, down 4.7 percent from the $952 million it tallied the previous year. This result was short of the hoped-for $950 million to $975 million range. However, the firm's net income was $48.6 million for the year, a substantial increase over the $66 million loss of 2001. The firm was in transition through the end of 2002, as it changed its fiscal year-end from September 30 to December 31. For fiscal 2003, Gartner expects sales of $835 to $880 million.

## GETTING HIRED

The career section on Gartner's web site provides job listings for positions in all of the company's 90 offices worldwide. There are also instructions for applying either by e-mail, fax or postal service. The Gartner HR department will acknowledge receipt of all resumes within 24 hours. Qualified applicants are then reviewed and remain on file for up to six months or until a suitable position opens. A source tells us that Gartner prefers "referrals from current employees," and pays an "employee referral bonus" for successful hires.

The interview process at Gartner comprises "several interviews depending on department," though most respondents report a series of three interviews "with managers and future peers" in which they ask "questions about your experience" and "how you can contribute to the company." The firm occasionally uses standard case questions, but most of the emphasis in interviews is reportedly on fit and resume strength. An insider notes the process is "mostly interviews with supervisors and peers," but says the firm requires " writing samples for some positions."

# OUR SURVEY SAYS

## Sharing data

Insiders laud the "open communication" among peers at Gartner, and the management that is "generally very supportive" and stresses "having work/life balance." There are no real surprises in the work schedule: "In Gartner Research, a research agenda is pretty much set at the start of the year, so you can expect when your work load would spike," one insider reveals. However, "frequent changes to the organizational structure and selling process" rank as negatives. One insider thinks the firm should "do better planning and show more commitment when making policy changes."

A Gartner source notes that there's a "good orientation program" for new hires, and further training is available via "'Gartner University,' a new e-learning system." However, he thinks analysts could use "more training," and "the learning curriculum should be expanded." Training may be important to job proficiency, but your educational level isn't a factor. When asked if undergrads had a shot at MBA positions at Gartner, a consultant says, "Absolutely. The company focuses more on the employee's experience than education."

# 8 A.T. Kearney

5400 Legacy Drive
Plano, TX 75201
Phone: (972) 604-4600
Fax: (972) 543-7680
www.atkearney.com

## LOCATIONS

**Plano, TX (HQ)**
60 offices worldwide

## INDUSTRY AREAS

Aerospace and Defense
Automotive
Communications and Media
Consumer and Retail
Financial Institutions
Government
High Tech and Electronics
Pharmaceuticals/Health Care
Process Industries
Transportation
Utilities

## PRACTICE AREAS

Enterprise Services Transformation
Strategy (including Business
   Technology)
Operations

## THE BUZZ
### WHAT CONSULTANTS AT OTHER FIRMS ARE SAYING

- "Clever; strong in auto"
- "Captive consultancy past its best"
- "Leader in strategic sourcing"
- "'Eat what you kill' culture"

## THE STATS

**Employer Type:** Independent
Subsidiary of Electronic Data
Systems
**Stock Symbol:** EDS
**Stock Exchange:** NYSE
**CEO:** Dietmar Ostermann
**2002 Employees:** 4,600
**2001 Employees:** 5,000
**2002 Revenue:** $1.08 billion
**2001 Revenue:** $1.35 billion

## UPPERS

- Competitive pay
- History and prestige
- Short engagements allow broad
  experience

## DOWNERS

- Conflict with parent EDS
- Change-filled environment
- Reduced signing bonuses and hiring

## KEY COMPETITORS

Accenture
Booz Allen Hamilton
McKinsey & Company

## EMPLOYMENT CONTACT

A.T. Kearney
222 West Adams Street
Chicago, Illinois 60606
Phone: (312) 648-0111
Numerous international hiring contacts;
check A.T. Kearney's web site for
regional information.

# THE SCOOP

## Dean of the old school

A.T. Kearney is one of the first names in management consulting, and not just because it starts with an A. Since breaking away from McKinsey & Co. in 1939, A.T. Kearney has led the way in strategy and process optimization for many of the world's most influential companies and governments; the company's self-proclaimed focus is on "CEO-level concerns" such as globalization, mergers and leadership. Today, Kearney is a wholly owned independent subsidiary of Electronic Data Systems (EDS), an IT consultancy. EDS has allowed Kearney to maintain its identity and self-direction since the 1995 purchase.

A.T. Kearney is a fixture of the Chicago consulting scene, where the company was born and raised; it didn't even open a second location until 1961. The first international office was opened in 1964 in Düsseldorf, Germany, and today the company has 60 locations in 35 countries worldwide staffed by over 4,600 employees, fairly evenly split between support staff and professionals. A.T. Kearney earned revenues of $1.08 billion in 2002.

## A long and proud history

When management professor James Oscar McKinsey started a small consultancy in Chicago in 1926, one of the first partners to come on board was Andrew Thomas Kearney. Kearney had begun his marketing career in 1916 when, as a student at Pennsylvania State University, he gained statewide attention for helping local dairy farmers boost their milk sales. Kearney joined the faculty at Penn State, later serving as director of commercial research at Swift & Co. before joining with McKinsey. In these early years, the firm emphasized accounting and budgetary controls. When the firm split in 1939, Kearney retained the Chicago branch, which he renamed after himself.

A.T. Kearney quickly garnered a reputation for producing solid results. As one of its earliest assignments, the firm completed an extensive study of the organization of U.S. Steel, the first of nearly 30 projects for that company alone in the 1930s. The analysis resulted in the merger of several subsidiaries, the first step in the creation of modern-day USX. The Kroger Company, a Cincinnati-based supermarket chain, also retained A.T. Kearney early in the 1930s. A.T. Kearney's relationship with that firm began in 1930 with initial studies of operations, executive organization, accounting and budgetary control, and extended to more than 60 different assignments through the early 1980s. Other significant clients in the 1930s and early 1940s included Chicago meat packer Armour, United Parcel Service; heavy equipment service firm Allis-Chambers and Borg-Warner Corporation, a large Chicago manufacturing company.

## Thinking globally

Kearney took his firm in a civic-minded direction during World War II and the postwar period. During the war, A.T. Kearney provided consultation to the U.S. War Production Board for the fee of a dollar a year. In 1945, President Roosevelt personally asked Kearney to lead a mission to China to assist the Chinese government in improving its war efforts. Kearney and his staff spent six months in China, and Kearney himself earned a U.S. Medal of Freedom and a Chinese Victory Medal for his efforts. A few years later, he traveled to Germany to study that country's industrial recovery.

Jim Phelan succeeded Kearney in 1962 and began to expand the firm. By 1970, A.T. Kearney boasted nine offices in the United States, as well as offices in London and Düsseldorf. The Tokyo office opened in 1972. The next CEO, Kenneth Block, initiated a "Go for Growth" program, which doubled A.T. Kearney's size by 1980. Meanwhile, the firm continued its service to corporations around the country and the world, gaining a reputation for working with rank-and-file consultants and plant management as well as top executives, and for ensuring the successful implementation of its recommendations. Fred Steingraber followed as CEO for a term of 16 years. Steingraber's tenure produced annual double digit growth for most of that happy period of time.

The firm's current CEO is Dietmar Ostermann. Ostermann, a member of A.T. Kearney since 1989, served as head of the firm's North American automotive practice from 1996 to 1997, when he was promoted to managing director of Germany. He moved up to unit head for Central Europe in January 1999 and was named Managing Director of Europe in May 2000. He took over from outgoing CEO Fred Steingraber in November 2000.

## Who needs whom?

The absorption of A.T. Kearney by EDS in 1995 came about in a different way than many mergers do. Some referred to A.T. Kearney as "the canary that swallowed the cat" when, in 1995, the firm merged with Plano, Texas-based juggernaut Electronic

Data Systems (EDS), then recently detached from parent company General Motors. Industry observers were dubious, if not downright cynical. Could the entrepreneurial strategy firm and the computer giant find compromise and business-related bliss? It seems the companies have found both – with the ingested A.T. Kearney shaping consulting operations. EDS, which had created its money-hemorrhaging consulting arm in 1993, had approached A.T. Kearney to propose a joint venture. Kearney CEO Fred Steingraber informed EDS that it was approaching the consulting industry incorrectly; the right path toward success required a high-profile brand name, a clearly structured partnership among consultants and a structured reward mechanism for shareholders. But instead of slinking back to Plano, as Steingraber had anticipated, EDS made another proposal – would A.T. Kearney consider a merger instead?

## The advent of EDS

While the companies seemed somewhat incongruous, this differential was an asset in Steingraber's mind. EDS was a large company with deep pockets and experience with information technology, a growing area of interest to corporations. EDS' founder, the colorful H. Ross Perot, who often referred to consultants as money-sucking witch doctors, left the company in 1986 to pursue other interests. The post-Perot EDS started its consulting business in 1993, aggressively hiring bright business school grads and snapping up smaller firms. EDS' ambition, however, did not translate into success. Its consulting operation lost money. In 1994, the year of the merger proposal, EDS Consulting lost $22 million. A.T. Kearney, on the other hand, was in the midst of healthy expansion, having registered double-digit growth every year for the previous 12 years. Additionally, Kearney's geographic and industry reach would allow EDS to establish the high-level client relationships it needed to succeed.

Steingraber was interested in a merger for his own reasons. Working with the computer company would allow A.T. Kearney to develop in-depth information technology expertise, thus giving it the capability to follow through from technological strategy to implementation. EDS' deep pockets would also boost Kearney's infrastructure capabilities, and the merger would boost A.T. Kearney's rankings in the consulting industry, in the process making it more attractive to prospective clients.

Discussions between Steingraber and EDS Vice Chairman Tony Fernandes initially centered on the "vision" of the two companies, but soon turned to cold hard cash. The acquisition of A.T. Kearney by EDS, which was finally completed in October

1995, meant that EDS laid out approximately $112.7 million in cash and issued $162.3 million in short-and long-term notes to A.T. Kearney's principals and shareholders. The terms of the agreement also included a stock grant of around 6.6 million shares of GM stock, which will vest over a 10-year period for select A.T. Kearney personnel who remain with the EDS-owned firm.

## EDS in a nutshell

Founded in 1962, EDS now boasts approximately 143,000 employees and clients in 58 countries. The firm has three lines of business, as well as A.T. Kearney's management consulting operation (an independent subsidiary). EDS has taken on clients in a variety of industries: manufacturing, aerospace, health care, financial, insurance, food, retail, travel and transportation, energy and communications, among others. EDS also maintains numerous clients in the government sector. EDS boasts a private sector client list that includes Chevron, General Motors Corporation, Commonwealth Bank of Australia and BellSouth. Its company board consists of Michael Jordan (no, not that one), chairman of the board and CEO, Jeffrey M. Heller, vice chairman and Robert Swan, executive vice president and CFO.

## The A.T. Kearney-EDS relationship

It's hard to put a definitive label on the Kearney-EDS arrangement. Kearney trades on the strength of its name and over 75 years of history. EDS also trades on the strength of Kearney's name and its long history. EDS markets A.T. Kearney as just one of the many solutions it offers, moving the management consultancy's headquarters to the EDS Plano campus in February 2001 for emphasis.. (The same number of people still work in the old Chicago office, but it's no longer the HQ.) A.T. Kearney, however, retains its own unaltered name and is allowed to set its own strategy and methods; in general, EDS focuses on extended technology outsourcing deals while Kearney performs shorter-term engagements, relying on a repeat business rate of more than 90 percent. Dietmar Ostermann holds the title of CEO, not president – a minor point, but one that illustrates Kearney's independent nature.

Ironically, A.T. Kearney consultants published a book on the topic of industry consolidation in December 2002. *Winning the Merger Endgame: A Playbook for Profiting from Industry Consolidation*, by Graeme Deans, Fritz Kroeger and Stefan Zeisel, comfortably concludes that industry consolidation is "inevitable, predictable and manageable." The authors analyzed more than 1,300 mergers completed between 1988 and 2001 to develop the merger endgames theory detailed in the book.

## A loyal following, an impressive track record

A.T. Kearney serves companies in the Americas, Europe and around the Pacific Rim, with the typical client being a large corporation with around $2 billion in annual revenue. While the firm claims expertise in many industries, it is particularly strong in automotive, communications, high tech, consumer industries and retail. More than 70 percent of Kearney's client companies rank among the world's largest. Client companies also tend to show a remarkable degree of loyalty toward the firm – in a 1998 survey conducted by Louis Harris & Associates, more than 90 percent of A.T. Kearney's engagements are with past clients, and the firm claims to have maintained that rate.

## Industry slowdown

Revenue growth slowed in 1999 as Asian economies began to contract, causing the firm to lay off consultants and postpone start dates for a number of new MBA hires. The economic slowdown that hit the United States a few years later resulted in similar measures. Start dates for new hires were pushed back – some for a year or more, some indefinitely – at several points during 2001 and 2002. Certain regions are still experiencing hiring freezes as of 2003.

The company is looking to build growth again through alliances and acquisitions, such as the September 2002 purchase of certain assets of executive search firm Ray & Berndtson Inc. A. T. Kearney, along with snapping up those firm assets, also extended job offers to "key Ray & Berndtson Inc. partners and staff, including CEO and chairman Paul R. Ray Jr."

## New blood

Kearney announced a number of additions and changes to its leadership team in late 2002 and early 2003. In November 2002, the firm appointed Dr. C. Srinivasan and Ravi Kushan as chairman and managing director, respectively, of India operations. In January 2003, several changes came at once: Mike Moriarty became ATK executive vice president and EDS senior vice president in charge of ATK's global industry practices; Josh Chernoff replaced him as global leader of the consumer industries and retail practice; Sid Abrams was appointed leader of the U.S. East profit center; Shinji Yamamoto joined Yoshinori Ando as co-leader of the North Asia profit center; Craig Baker became head of the newly formed government practice. Bill Windle and Norbert Witterman have been named practice leaders for the global automotive and aerospace practice, while Wynn Bailey now leads the pharmaceutical/health care practice.

## Not eBay, eBreviate

EDS rolled out A.T. Kearney Procurement Solutions in December 2001, a global business-to-business (B2B) service built around Kearney's eBreviate capital sourcing utilities. Essentially, eBreviate is a toolset (delivered either as licensed software or through an ASP) that allows businesses to better manage their strategic sourcing needs; this includes B2B auctions, leveraging a company's buying power and various sourcing management tools. Prior to the launch of the service, eBreviate had operated for two years as a wholly owned EDS subsidiary. By May 2002, eBreviate had been used in more than 2,000 separate purchases totaling $20 billion, saving clients more than $3 billion in the process. In July 2002, eBreviate won the 2001 Volkswagen Group Award for its work in supplier management. The procurement solutions group is expanding in Europe, opening an office in Brussels in May 2002 and promoting eBreviate veteran Donna Kenyon to general manager for Northern Europe. In June 2002, A.T. Kearney allied with Manugistics Group to deliver services based on Manugistics' pricing and revenue optimization (PRO) solutions.

Further success for eBreviate came in early 2003. In March, technology leader NCR employed A.T. Kearney Procurement Solutions to provide a full suite of eSourcing services and products over a two-year period. And in April 2003, the Florida Power & Light Company signed an unlimited-use contract.

In other news, *The Bangkok Post* reported in April 2003 that A.T. Kearney's Thailand branch would partner with e-procurement firm Pantavanij to provide a strategic sourcing service. Pantavanij is slated to list on the Thailand stock exchange sometime in 2003.

## Lead parachute

In August 2002, parent company EDS filed a civil suit against Fred Steingraber, chairman emeritus and former CEO of A.T. Kearney, accusing the executive of embezzlement. The suit alleges he misappropriated $100,000 by submitting fraudulent expense reports and using corporate property for personal use. The firm seeks to fire Steingraber and force him to repay the $100,000 as well as court costs and attorney fees. Steingraber denies the charges, and was quoted in an October 2002 *Wall Street Journal* article calling them "a ruse and a sham" to cheat him out of salary, bonus and stock options.

The embattled exec fired back in February 2003 with his own accusations. His countersuit accuses EDS and its executives of "a campaign to manipulate the company's financial statements in order to artificially inflate" revenues and profits. The company denies the allegations; a spokesman claimed Steingraber's countersuit was "cut and pasted from class action lawsuits" against the firm.

## Only Kearney can go to China

Some A.T. Kearney consultants are getting new stamps in their passports. In October 2001, the Beijing Municipal Science and Technology Commission hired the firm to recommend strategies to transform the city's software industry. In January 2002, A.T. Kearney signed on for a project with the U.S. Department of Transportation, working for up to a year on the planning and implementation of the department's new Transportation Security Administration.

In other governmental engagements, Kearney began advising the government of India in January 2002 on ways to remove regulatory barriers to foreign investments in the country. In October 2002, the firm was hired by Portugal to restructure the company's Economy Ministry.

## Profit centers build better consultants

Kearney has organized its business into several regional profit centers – for example, the eastern or western United States. Consultants based in San Francisco are now utilized primarily on projects on the West Coast, with less cross-country or international travel than before. The result is less travel-related stress on individual consultants, better regional coverage and closer in-office relationships. "We realized there was a very important, very long-term need in the business to have people focus on developing business in the local areas where they were living and working on projects where they were living," notes one Kearney insider. Of course, travel hasn't been eliminated, and Kearney's "one-firm approach" to client service means it will pull resources from around the globe when necessary. This is especially true when management and IT needs overlap on a project, and EDS personnel work alongside Kearney consultants.

## Troubleshooters

A.T. Kearney pledges that no consultant will work on an engagement for more than nine months. But while the firm's engagements may be short, hours are typically long. To combat long workweeks, the firm has adopted "434U," a policy theoretically ensuring that consultants will spend no more than four days and three nights a week at a client site. Staffed consultants working away from the home office break early on Thursday to be home with their families, working from the regional office on Friday.

# GETTING HIRED

## Fraternal order of consultants

An insider describes the interview process as "usually very regimented, with two or three interviews with ranking officers. Much like joining a fraternity." He suggests, "Sponsorship can be a huge plus and get you around the interview process." As to the interview itself, another source says you should expect "lots of case questions. Some questions were 'What are all the costs that go into a can of Coke?' and 'How many hotel rooms are there in North America?'"

According to a source, A.T. Kearney is "not currently hiring consultants, just heavy hitters (if even that). Many with an IT focus are transitioning to EDS." The employee also notes salary changes: "Once upon a time, [sign-on bonuses] were around $20-30K for an associate with another $15K after 12 months. Some new entries still receive sign-on bonuses if they come from a reputable consulting house or have industry ties. New MBAs do not, and may even enter as business analysts."

# OUR SURVEY SAYS

## Culture clash

The tension between A.T. Kearney and parent EDS bears discussion. The two firms had, and have, different approaches to business, which has caused some unrest. One source, a recent departure from the firm, calls Kearney's outlook "since EDS took over" an "all business, no play" attitude. A current consultant describes the culture as "strict and with a strong hierarchy. The career path is very rigid, with an up-or-out process." He adds there is "lots of EDS corporate pressure as EDS reorganizes and seeks to integrate the two cultures. This is very difficult on people who expected a partner-type firm. It's corporate."

## Moving up

A source tells us, "Advancement was better before the dot-crash. Promotions come every two to three years depending on fit and improvement. Levels are business analyst [the entry-level position], associate, manager, principal, vice-president and corporate officer." For those seeking a long stay at A.T. Kearney, he warns, "Principal and above have large sales targets AND utilization targets with large variables and large stock options. Since [the] stock is EDS, it's not that great right now." The current situation allows "few promotions (two percent of consulting staff every six months). EDS now filters and approves promotions." The benefits of promotion include a"10-20 percent bonus and 10-20 percent raise."

## Cash on hand

Insiders seem to agree that A.T. Kearney pays well. While business analysts typically earn "less than $40,000 a year," associates fare better. One source provides salary details: "New associates make about $55-65K/year; experienced associates get $65-75K and a car; managers make about $75K with a nicer car."

# 9 Mercer Oliver Wyman

99 Park Avenue
Fifth Floor
New York, NY 10016
Phone: (212) 541-8100
Fax: (212) 541-8957
www.merceroliverwyman.com

## LOCATIONS

**New York, NY (HQ)**
London • Frankfurt • Madrid • Milan
• Munich • Paris • Toronto •
Singapore • Zurich • 16 other
offices

## PRACTICE AREAS

Actuarial
Capital Markets
Corporate & Commercial Banking
Finance & Risk
Insurance
Retail Financial Services

## THE STATS

**Employer Type:** Subsidiary of Marsh &
McLennan
**President:** John P. Drzik
**2003 Employees:** 650
**2002 Employees:** 425

## UPPERS

- "Discussions are very challenging
  and rewarding"
- "Getting to fly home on Thursday
  instead of Friday"
- Commitment to an average 55-hour
  week

## DOWNERS

- "We don't fly business class"
- Uncertainty about Mercer merger
- Lack of infrastructure

## KEY COMPETITORS

Booz Allen Hamilton
Boston Consulting Group
McKinsey & Company
IBM Global Services

## EMPLOYMENT CONTACT

**U.S., Canada and Emerging Markets
Recruiting**
E-mail: RecruitingNA@mow.com

**UK and Western European Recruiting**
E-mail: RecruitingWE@mow.com

**German and Central European
Recruiting**
E-mail: RecruitingCE@mow.com

**All other recruiting:**
E-mail: RecruitingOther@mow.com

 **THE BUZZ**
WHAT CONSULTANTS AT OTHER FIRMS ARE SAYING

- "Best in class financial consulting"
- "Pretentious"
- "Good rep with financial services"
- "Number crunchers"

# THE SCOOP

## A new name for Mercer Oliver Wyman

Mercer Oliver Wyman is one of the the the only major consulting firms dedicated to the financial services industry. Founded in 1984 by five consultants from Booz Allen Hamilton and The Boston Consulting Group, the firm (called at that time Oliver, Wyman & Company, or just OWC) had grown to more than 400 consulting professionals, with more than half its business and staff outside of North America. In fact, the firm estimates that more of its consultants are British (30 percent) than American (29 percent). The firm agreed to merge with Mercer Inc., the consulting arm of Marsh & McLennan, in February 2003. The deal combined OWC with two Mercer units (financial services strategy and actuarial consulting) to form Mercer Oliver Wyman. John Drzik, former chairman of OWC, will remain in place and head the new unit. The new group, now called Mercer Oliver Wyman, has more than 600 employees. The merger offically closed in April 2003.

As Mercer Oliver Wyman, the company will have main staffing hubs in New York, London and Frankfurt. Additional offices will include Madrid, Milan, Paris, Singapore, Munich, Toronto and Zurich. Overall, the firm will operate 26 offices in 11 countries.

## Innovating and expanding

The firm expects future growth, driven by the needs of the financial services sector. A January 2003 report by the firm stated that the sector's market value could triple to $15 trillion by 2013, but that the shareholder performance of high performers could be twice that of low performers. Sounds like a recipe for lots of consulting engagements – no firm will want to risk being an under performer. There may not be a rush, though; a joint report published by OWC and UBS Warburg in September 2002 predicts that profitability in asset management isn't likely to return to peak levels until 2004 (at least).

## An academic approach

Mercer Oliver Wyman operates the Oliver Wyman Institute, an organization of partners and selected academics that provides added insight to consultants and clients, organizes conferences and publishes working papers. The Institute promotes its work throughout the financial services industry through such channels as public round tables, dissertation fellowships and student prizes. The program will continue post-merger, though it may or may not be called the Mercer Oliver Wyman Institute.

## Keeping it in the family

Unlike many of its larger competitors, Mercer Oliver Wyman is devoted to internal promotion, and all new hires are viewed as potential partners. In fact, 34 of the current directors (including the firm's president, John Drzik) are home grown, having joined the firm as entry-level graduates from undergrad or graduate programs. And it doesn't take an MBA to make partner; while most of Mercer Oliver Wyman's directors have advanced degrees, according to the firm only six percent of all employees are business school graduates.

## Predictions and punditry

So what does Mercer Oliver Wyman have to say about the sorry state of business and finance in the early 21st century? Plenty. Consultants have been quoted widely in the news media on topics ranging from Chinese national banks to the dangers of having a high-profile CEO.

In July 2002, Dow Jones International News interviewed Asia Pacific practice head Clarence Koo about China's state-owned banks' difficulties in coming into line with international banking standards. Koo has advised the People's Bank of China, which exerts control over private shareholding banks. For the nation to comply with the Basel II banking accords, Koo says, "Basically the government needs to get out of directed-lending to state-owned enterprises because as long as the government forces banks to bail out SOEs, the banks will at best comply in letter but not in spirit."

## Taking another look at finance salaries

Consultants were quoted in separate November 2002 articles on the state of investment banking and its workers. Asked about compensation and bonuses, John Romeo told *The Observer,* "The bonus this year is to have a job." He adds later, "While these bonus cuts are necessary, they are not addressing the fundamental problem of how compensation works in investment banking." In *The Economist,* Davide Taliente stated that the current crisis "is a one-time opportunity for banks to realign their systems of bonuses and rewards," which were designed during "the go-go 1990s."

# GETTING HIRED

## Cream of the crop

Our sources at Mercer Oliver Wyman name a handful of highly prestigious universities as official recruiting pools. "Harvard, Yale, Princeton, Penn" was the chant we heard from U.S.-based consultants, typically in that very order. British insiders typically cite "Oxford, Cambridge and London" as the firm's preferred campuses. But even if Mercer Oliver Wyman doesn't recruit at your (non-Ivy) institution, you're not out of luck. Just be very smart. An engagement manager tells us, "We formally recruit at prestigious schools, but are not opposed to smart people from other places as well. The bottom line is smart." Another insider mentions a "GPA cutoff of 3.5" as the minimum acceptable GPA for potential employees; the firm states that 3.5 is an "average," not a minimum.

Once you get past the screening, insiders say to expect "two rounds of interviews, half fit interviews and half case interviews. About six to eight interviews in total." One consultant says, "[Interviewing] is one process the senior firm directors micro-manage given its importance for our culture and lifeblood. The keen attention of the top brass shows. "It's rigorous and can be intimidating," confesses an interview veteran, "because you might have the chairman sitting across from you."

# OUR SURVEY SAYS

## The Mercer Oliver Wyman commune

You won't hear much talk of a Big Five-ish management pyramid at Mercer Oliver Wyman. Insiders call the culture "non-hierarchical," even "anti-hierarchical" (whatever that means). One enthusiastic New Yorker tells us, "No matter how junior you are, your opinion will be listened to. The more capable you are, the more rapidly you advance, which is fantastic." A few caution that the flat nature of the firm is "occasionally chaotic." Post-merger, Mercer Oliver Wyman officials expect the culture of the company to remain the same; Oliver Wyman and Mercer partners developed a "specific understanding" that the corporate culture would not change post-merger.

Says one senior consultant, "The firm has a set of core values that define the company. You are expected to keep to the core values and your adherence to them is one of the factors when being considered for directorship." Another confirms the presence of "strong firm values taken seriously by members at all levels of the company."

## Punching the clock

Work/life balance isn't just a line in the recruiting brochure at Mercer Oliver Wyman – it's a reality. An analyst says it is "one of our top priorities," and a manager says there is "a real commitment to [an average] 55-hour week." The theme of average 55-hour weeks – a mere 11 hours a day – is a recurrent one. Because of this policy, says one highly placed insider, Mercer Oliver Wyman "is a sustainable career, not a two-year stint in consulting." A partner tells of the "clearly communicated aspiration of a balanced lifestyle, with partners penalized financially for persistent breaches." A senior consultant confirms, "Directors are penalized when consultants work excessive hours." For that matter, some weeks don't even hit 55 hours. "On the beach, people do spread out the towel and lie down," jokes one insider. In addition, "The firm tends to honor vacation time and allows for sabbatical leave if desired." The firm notes that the 55-hour week is considered a goal and an average, but not a firm maximum – if there is more work to do, consultants are expected to support their teams.

## Caution - merge ahead

If there's anything that clouds employees' vision of the future, it's the merger with Mercer. Mercer Oliver Wyman is "still a great place to work, with very enjoyable people," says one manager. "However," he continues, "there are some concerns if we can keep up this excellent culture in light of the merger with Mercer." Another says, "I expect further evolution as a result of Mercer acquiring us, although Mercer Oliver Wyman will be an independent 'ecosystem.'" There is considerable uncertainty about the merger. One cautious soul says it "seems good so far, but everyone is waiting to see how it will turn out."

It's clear that the merger will have some real benefits, though. Our sources expect to reap cash benefits from the new arrangement, and in fact many have already done so. "This year there was a special bonus for staff based on the transaction with Mercer," says one insider. The reason for this is the profit sharing policy. "We share in the profits of the firm with a yearly bonus. In the past six years, it's ranged from 52-91 percent. Due to the recent merger with Mercer, we'll also realize an additional bonus from the sale price." Another consultant, from Germany, says it is "not 100 percent clear to me how the merger with Mercer's financial services units will change the system; overall OWC's comp structure will remain, but there might be some additional benefits."

## Working for the man

According to one New Yorker, "[Mercer] Oliver Wyman has a decent proportion of women in the junior consultant classes (one to three years of experience), but not too many in the job manager and director ranks." A Londoner says flat out that the firm "has never had a woman promoted internally to directorship." (The firm says it has indeed promoted a woman to director in the past.) "Good written policies, zero female directors," adds another. A senior consultant summarizes, "Maybe a third of consultants are women, and none of the consulting partners are (the CFO is). I don't have reason to believe that there is prejudice, but rather that fewer women apply to consulting, and even fewer to financial services consulting, which is what we do." The firm points out that the CAO of Mercer Oliver Wyman is a woman, and that the firm does have a woman director in the Frankfurt office.

## Diversity is "not a recruiting criterion"

So speaks a senior consultant in regard to racial and ethnic minorities. A manager asks, "How do you define minority? Our firm is quite international so we have a range of demographics – Asian, Indian, Spanish, Turkish, etc." Another tells us there are "only a handful of African American consultants (although one of them is a senior JM)" and one is a director. In addition, the firm "is very international (only half of the New York office has a U.S. passport)." An insider claims, "The firm's employment offers and internal promotion are based purely on ability."

Most of those comments are also applied to the firm's gay and lesbian employees. The lack of emphasis on what many insiders agree is "a private issue" seems to have fostered an environment of openness. "We have and have had gay directors who are absolutely open about it, and this sets the standard," says one source. Consultants confirm, "There is no discrimination of any kind (either positive or negative) on a sexuality basis." One insider says, "We have several gay/bisexual partners (both currently and historically). There are also quite a few gays/bisexuals/lesbians in the consultant and infrastructure ranks. As a bisexual I find [the firm] to be a tolerant environment."

## Stand by your firm

Hardly any of our sources had anything bad to say about Mercer, beyond the usual quibbles about occasionally long hours and travel. "It is a privilege to work at [Mercer] Oliver Wyman," says one insider. Another agrees: "My best career choice was choosing to work at the firm." A manager beams, "I have had the opportunity to go many places and I am still in the same job as when I left university, while all my friends at the other places have shifted jobs quite a few times and not found the one for them." A parting suggestion from a happy consultant: "If you think you want to do consulting and you like finance, I think we are definitely worth a long look."

"If you think you want to do consulting and you like finance, I think we are definitely worth a look."

— *Mercer Oliver Wyman consultant*

# Roland Berger Strategy Consultants

Arabellastr. 33
81925 Munich
Germany
Phone: +49-89-92 30-0
Fax: +49-89-92 30-8202

350 Park Avenue
30th Floor
New York, NY 10022
Phone: (212) 651-9680
Fax: (212) 756-8750
www.rolandberger.com

## LOCATIONS

**Munich, Germany (HQ)**
**New York, NY (U.S. HQ)**
33 offices worldwide

## PRACTICE AREAS

Corporate Management
Corporate Strategy
Information Management
M&A
Marketing/Sales
Operations Strategy
Restructuring

## THE STATS

**Employer Type:** Private Company
**Speaker of the Executive Committee:**
Dr. Burkhard Schwenker
**2002 Employees:** 1,700
**2001 Employees:** 1,650
**2002 Revenue:** $526 million
**2001 Revenue:** $379.8 million

## UPPERS

- International opportunities
- Promotions come quickly

## DOWNERS

- Lots of travel required
- Long hours and heavy workloads

## KEY COMPETITORS

A.T. Kearney
Bain & Company
Boston Consulting Group
McKinsey & Company

## EMPLOYMENT CONTACT

www.rolandberger.com

## THE BUZZ
WHAT CONSULTANTS AT OTHER FIRMS ARE SAYING

- "The German McKinsey"
- "Rigid internal management"
- "One to watch for the future"
- "Still too local"

# THE SCOOP

## Continental manners

German giant Roland Berger Strategy Consultants is the largest consultancy of European origin. In 2002, a tough year for most consulting firms, Roland Berger grew at more than three times the consulting industry's average annual rate. To give a sense of its size, some 2001 figures prove helpful: according to Management Consultants International, the company was sixth in terms of market share worldwide (trailing McKinsey, A.T. Kearney, BCG, Bain and Booz Allen), third in Europe (behind McKinsey and BCG), and second (to McKinsey) in Germany. Americans take note – Roland Berger maintains U.S. offices in San Francisco, Detroit and New York

Home to 1,700 consultants in 23 countries worldwide, Roland Berger concentrates its efforts in a small number of industries, including automotive (hence the Detroit office), high tech, telecom, pharmaceuticals, transportation and insurance.

## The über-consultant

Roland Berger, a German businessman and former consultant at the Boston Consulting Group, founded his consulting firm out of Munich in 1967. He had just turned 30, and the company consisted of Berger and a secretary. By 1970, he had organized the growing company into a partnership, and by 1976, the firm had expanded overseas with the opening of its São Paolo office. The business world took notice, and in 1987, Deutsche Bank purchased a majority of the shares, though it left decision-making power in the hands of Berger and his partners. More than a decade later, in 1988, the partners orchestrated a buyout of Deutsche Bank's shares. Today, fiduciary and organizational control rests with them. In 1999, the company opened its first U.S. offices, in New York and Detroit. San Francisco was added to the map in 2001.

Berger himself is a powerful public figure in Germany, and a confidante of both left- and right-wing governments (he even addresses German chancellor Gerhard Schroeder with the informal "du," rather than the formal "Sie"). He sits on a number of corporate boards and was offered a position as Schroeder's finance minister (he turned it down). Berger's personal influence is so widespread that, despite his firm's success, when Germans hear "Roland Berger" they still think of the consultant, rather than the consultancy.

## When in Germany...

Roland Berger is deeply involved in consulting for the German government. Berger himself is a strong advocate for privatizing at least 10 percent of the German economy, and the firm has been involved in the privatization of a number of local, state and federal utilities and services. Roland Berger has also set aside part of its public services knowledge center to advise German states on how to run their public services more efficiently with what it terms "an approach to holistic transformation that focuses on new visions and priorities, redesigned business processes and organizational structures, and new incentive and controlling systems."

## Expert employees

Over 50 percent of Roland Berger's consultants are trained as engineers, natural scientists or doctors. And while only 16 percent of its consultants have MBAs, a full 20 percent have PhDs. In addition, 16 percent of Roland Berger consultants have two university degrees. Roland Berger has affiliations with a number of European business schools, and there are endowed Roland Berger chairs at INSEAD and Munich's Technische Universitat.

The firm is organized into so-called functional and industry competency centers, which in turn cross-reference each other to offer client services. Currently, 17 percent of the firm's revenue is derived from the high-tech industry and an additional 14 percent from its InfoCom (telecom) practice, with consumer goods and retail weighing in at 14 percent of revenue.

## Shiny happy clients

A key to Roland Berger's success is its client retention rate – 78 percent of its 2002 clients were repeat customers, and on average clients rate their satisfaction a 15 out of 16 in the firm's internal "Happy Customer Index" questionnaire. The firm even has a clever name for its approach to clients: proCLIENT, an acronym for "competence, leverage, implementation, experience, network and target."

## Euroclout

Some representative Roland Berger engagements demonstrate just how influential the firm is in Europe. In February 2003, Roland Berger engineered a meeting between Gerhard Schroeder and several of Germany's top bankers to try to bridge the gap between government and business. In the beginning of 2003, Roland Berger was working with troubled German utility company RWE, and published a proposal to restructure the company that included 10,000 job cuts and selling off several business units.

Also in 2002, Roland Berger thought up a strategy for ThyssenKrupp's executives, suggesting that the engineering company's brass meet directly with plant operators to get first-hand views of the company's problems and successes. In summer 2002, Roland Berger worked with now-defunct KirchMedia, the (former) German media giant, valuing its assets before its bankruptcy sale. Roland Berger also gained press for working with Babcock Borsig, a huge German shipbuilding company, which was teetering on the brink of extinction in early summer 2002. Roland Berger devised a plan to restructure the company through job cuts and selling sites, but the company could not find funding, and went under in July 2002.

Roland Berger branches outside Germany as well. A late 2002 engagement saw Roland Berger assessing Fiat Auto's layoff plans at the behest of the Italian government, which was trying to find a layoff alternative that would please both Fiat and trade unions.

## Staying strong

The company has undergone some recent internal changes. In February 2002, it opened an office in Amsterdam. And in December 2002, it announced a new executive committee – what the company calls its management team – would be taking over. Berger will still chair the committee. The proud new members are Dr. Burkhard Schwenker, António Bernardo, Thomas Eichelmann and Dr. Martin C. Wittig. They will assume their duties in July 2003.

# GETTING HIRED

Roland Berger maintains extensive information about its hiring practices and job vacancies on its web site at, www.rolandberger.com/career/en/html/fs3.html. The online application form is connected to most offices; those not linked to the form accept resumes via e-mail and post. Inquiries should be addressed to the appropriate recruiting contact, a list of which is available on the site. Once candidates have contacted the office, they should get a response within two weeks. The interview process may go forward from there.

Junior consultant and consultant applicants should contact Roland Berger four to nine months before graduation, while interns and summer associates should get in touch three months ahead of time. The company also recruits at "prestigious economic and technical universities," including "HBS, Kellogg, Wharton, Stanford, London Business School, INSEAD, IMD, IESE, RSM and St. Gallen." Other routes of contacting the company include "through a job hunter or introduction."

The interview process consists of "three to four interviews," plus a case study. The interviews are "with different consultants," and "the first interview is aimed mainly at 'technical' abilities, the last interview aimed mainly at personal skills and cultural fit."

# OUR SURVEY SAYS

## Responsibility and revenue

"The company emphasizes entrepreneurship and self-responsibility," says one consultant, a view that's echoed by colleagues, who note the "entrepreneurial initiative" and "responsibility" at the firm. It's "tough" and "challenging" but there's "entrepreneurial freedom, projects around the globe in diverse environments, and due to the undermanagement of the company, there exists a general openness to new ideas."

As for the people, respondents find them "competitive yet with a good sense of humor and cooperative," "nice," and "bright." Though "the culture depends somewhat on the competence center or unit you are working in," most agree that "all in all, the culture is quite pleasant and not too elitist."

## Culture clash-less

Consultants based outside the German home base say the culture clash really isn't all that bad. "The biggest challenge in working for most German firms," notes one insider, "is the attention to detail, which is sometimes not the priority of American-based firms." This source notes that with Roland Berger, it is imperative "that the product presented to the client is exactly what they ask for. That being said, the work ethic throughout Roland Berger is the same – working many hours to present the client with a quality product. The dedication, drive and ambition, etc. are characteristics of all employees from graphics to staff to accounting to consultants." Another source based outside of Germany has a similar take: "I cannot really say that we need cultural adjustments. The company is very tough on quality standards – work performance has to be at the same level regardless of the location (which is why we provide central training for consultants around the world, exchange consultants between offices and do international staffing for projects), but other than that we are a very entrepreneurial company and we adapt to the local environment in every country." The consultant adds, "I must recognize that Roland Berger is not a typical German company; it does not follow the German pattern in terms of hierarchy and bureaucracy."

## Moving up

Roland Berger says it conducts project evaluations at the end of each engagement, both top-down and bottom-up. Semi-annual company-wide evaluations provide for further scrutiny of each consultant's performance. At the end of every year, each consultant meets with a mentor to set goals for the following year. Whether or not you get promoted, sources say, "depends mostly on successful work." The firm's policy is "not strictly up-or-out, but we're on the way," reveals one consultant. Others disagree, saying the firm does in fact promote or push out consultants "up-or-out style, within three years at longest," while another finds it's "one year for up-or-out at the junior level," with "more flexibility afterward."

Degrees are not necessary for advancement, say insiders. There's "no limitation to promote with non-MBAs," says a source, though another adds, "An MBA is an advantage if know-how is transformed into practical solutions; however, promotion depends on performance rather than titles and degrees."

## Moving out

"There were some" layoffs in 2002 – it's "hard to get the 'real' numbers," and there was "high variation between the offices in different countries." Says one partner-level source, "layoffs were based on underperformance and the number was not higher than in other years." Also, "during the boom years around 2000, the firm was not exactly ultra selective. Starting about a year ago or so, [Roland] Berger has become a lot more selective."

## Boss men

There are varying reports of satisfaction with management. "Care is taken to uphold the mentor/mentee relationship and process and most people take this quite seriously," reports one satisfied customer. Another insider likes that management gives "significant freedom and independence, but also [takes] accountability and responsibility." One consultant's "German supervisor is very efficient and nice."

Another consultant, however, complains of the "lack of clear communication from the company leadership."

## Planes, trains and automobiles

Travel requirements are fairly stringent at Roland Berger, something which consultatnts don't seem too thrilled about. "In general, the firm's attention to your work/life balance is not spectacular, although I am convinced this is common in the industry. It is rather your attention to work/life balance which determines the type of balance you end up achieving," says one consultant philosophically.

Most of those we surveyed reported spending from two to five days each week traveling, "depending on the project and client location." "While on project assignment, we are usually at the client four to five days," says one source.

"Long working hours" are the norm. Consultants reported working 50 to 60 hours a week; senior consultants, around 70; managers, around 60; and partners/principals from 60 to 80.

## Offering benefits

Benefits at Roland Berger include an employee assistance program, accidental death/dismemberment coverage and long-term disability. Perks at some offices include free snacks, gym discounts, sports/theater tickets, tailors and dry cleaners, laptops, PDAs, cell phones, day care and cafeterias. "Employees in some countries get lease-car benefits," reports a source, while another notes that "benefits depend on the position and not all of the above are available for all positions."

Roland Bergerites, overall, seem mildly satisfied with their salaries. The firm offers "profit sharing for partners" which, by one estimate, resulted in a "dividend of another $200,000" at the last payout.

## Functional workspaces

"Most offices are comfortable but unspectacular," reports one source, "with the exception of some international offices, which can be in quite posh locations. Since you are not going to be there a lot, décor is not a problem." Other consultants find Roland Berger offices to be in a "good location and comfortable, without the company overspending," and "very nice."

## Improving diversity

According to Roland Berger, the average percentage of female consultants in the competence centers is 17 percent. "It is getting better and is already pretty good for a European company, but there is always room for improvement," says a source.

With regards to minorities and lesbian/gay consultants, the firm is more evenly balanced, it seems. "Globally and taking all offices together, the company's employees are ethnically pretty diverse," says a source. And while there's "no active 'commitment' to obtain diversity on this [lesbian/gay] account, there's certainly no discrimination whatsoever either."

# Deloitte Consulting

1633 Broadway
35th Floor
New York, NY 10019
Phone: (212) 492-4500
Fax: (212) 492-4743
www.dc.com

## LOCATIONS

**New York, NY (HQ)**
Offices in 34 countries

## PRACTICE AREAS

B2B
Communications
Consumer Business
e-Business
e-Learning
Energy
Financial Services
Health Care
Manufacturing
Outsourcing
Public Sector
Sell Side
Technology Integration
Wireless

## THE STATS

**Employer Type:** Unit of Deloitte Touche Tohmatsu
**CEO:** Paul Robinson
**2002 Employees:** 40,000 (now includes parts of Deloitte & Touche)
**2001 Employees:** 14,000

## UPPERS

- Emphasis on friendly, supportive culture
- Consultants can move between practices
- Clear, detailed promotion system

## DOWNERS

- Uncertainty about future
- Failed Braxton spin-off
- Salaries cut

## KEY COMPETITORS

Accenture
Bain & Company
BearingPoint
Booz Allen Hamilton
Boston Consulting Group
Cap Gemini Ernst & Young
IBM BCS
IBM Global Services
McKinsey & Company

## THE BUZZ
WHAT CONSULTANTS AT OTHER FIRMS ARE SAYING

- "Very woman friendly"
- "Not very exciting"
- "Problem with positioning"
- "A class act, best of breed"

## EMPLOYMENT CONTACT

www.dc.com/careers

# THE SCOOP

## What's in a name?

Enron's and Andersen's implosion had far-reaching consequences, as Deloitte Consulting's (DC) recent pass at restructuring indicates. That catastrophic failure in accounting oversight prompted the SEC to pass the Sarbanes-Oxley Act. which strictly regulated the ability of auditors to consulting services, among other internal controls. The gist was that auditors wouldn't have an interest in increasing profits (which is a consultant's job), and the consultants couldn't offer advice that would affect accounting procedures. The Sarbanes-Oxley act made it very attractive to firms to separate their accounting and consulting services by creating spinoff entities. In 2002, Deloitte Touche Tohmatsu decided to spin off its consulting wing, Deloitte Consulting, making it a separate, privately-owned firm. The separation would have made that the world's largest private consultancy. Deloitte planned to call this new firm Braxton, after a smaller consulting company that had been absorbed in years past. (As a bonus, Deloitte would not have had to trademark the name, as it already owned the rights.)

However, in March 2003, Deloitte shelved plans for the spin-off, citing the bad economy and a breakdown of funding. That makes it the last of the Big Four ( the others being KPMG, PricewaterhouseCoopers and Ernst & Young) to contain auditing and consulting under the same aegis. The company says it plans to avoid conflict of interest – and comply with the Sarbanes-Oxley law – by focusing on consulting just for those clients who are not using DTT's auditing services.

After the Braxton spinoff was abruptly shelved, CEO Doug McCracken handed in his resignation. By early April, DC had selected Paul Robinson as the new CEO. He had been Global Leader of DC's public sector practice, and had clocked over 20 years with the firm.

## Large and in charge

The company ranks among the world's largest consulting firms, with nearly 40,000 employees in 106 offices in 34 countries offering everything from strategy work to customer relationship management. Its clients range from automotive companies to telecom firms to governments, including large companies such as Kaiser Permanente, Hewlett-Packard, Philip Morris and Cable & Wireless.

## Research savvy

Deloitte Research is another important part of Deloitte's offerings. It conducts surveys, publishes reports and forecasts (often in conjunction with a university) and directs consultants to write up their on-the-case findings. It focuses on e-business, global strategy, economics, management techniques and public policy.

Deloitte Consulting has partnered with several firms to expand its tech offerings. SAP Public Services is collaborating with DC to make a tax program for public-sector tax agencies, and DC is putting that to work at the Florida Department of Revenue. And in conjuction with Hewlett-Packard, the company is offering customer relationship management and partner relationship management software to businesses.

## A rose is a rose

Separation anxiety aside, Deloitte Consulting has a long history of success. It was named the best generalist consultancy in North America by *Global Finance* magazine in 2002, and it is the only consulting firm with five consecutive appearances on *Fortune*'s list of 100 Best Companies to Work for in America (under the Deloitte & Touche name).

## Girl power

The company has a formal program (the "Women's Initiative") to make sure women are being hired, promoted and treated fairly. The Women's Initiative promotes networking events, career advice and mentoring. Indeed, it seems to be working: Deloitte Consulting has made *Working Mother* magazine's list of the best companies for moms to work for, eight years in a row; the gap between male and female turnover has disappeared; and 14 percent of DC's partners were women in 2000, up from 6.5 percent in 1993.

## All in the family

In response to the flight of employees to Internet startups during the dot-com boom, Deloitte established an alumni network to keep former employees in the consulting loop and to cultivate contacts in the high-tech industry. The firm invites network members to company events, enables them to keep in touch with colleagues and even serves as an informal job network. Today, the network has more than 3,000 members.

# GETTING HIRED

## A foot in the door

Deloitte Consulting, according to one source, takes "two different approaches" with regard to recruiting. First, it recruits nationally at the top schools. When these coveted candidates are given a job offer, they are allowed to choose which office they want to work from. Once Deloitte Consulting has filled several slots with top-tier students, each local Deloitte office "then goes to fill gaps based on local schools. So Chicago will look at Notre Dame, University of Chicago and Northwestern." However, one employee notes that "while DC used to do a significant amount of on-campus recruiting, it has scaled down."

Industry hires follow a different path. Experienced hires are "considered on a one-by-one basis," notes an insider. "Often, [industry candidates] identify the partner running a certain practice and say, 'I have experience in doing X, I'd like to work with you.'"

## What they're looking for

When looking at candidates' resumes, a Deloitte insider says, the point is to "see how they performed, and what does this mean. They're involved in 20 organizations – is that good? Probably, if they're active in 20, they're not good in any."

Interviews are "based on case studies." Usually, for would-be senior consultants, the company "takes a fairly difficult client we've had" and a case that usually concerns "an acquisition, or a [situation where a] company is facing significant pressure." The company will ask the candidate "to analyze what could be the problem with this company, and what could be the way to address that issue." DC will have available "all the financials and competitive information – a ton of stuff", but the candidates must ask for this information specifically. "Your first question should be, why is this company coming under competitive pressure?" confesses an insider.

For analyst applicants, the setup is similar, but "we'll lead you more. We'll tell you, 'They're facing a problem because the product is commoditized.' Say they're selling bars of soap. So we'll ask, 'Who do you think the competition is for bars of soap?' We'll say, 'Here are the major soap providers. Among these, which are the most competitive?' In sum, "we'll talk you through it more." DC does not use brainteasers, insiders say.

To evaluate the case study answers, an insider says, "we look at [candidates']
creativity, at their approach to the problem, at how structured they are in
understanding how to get the data, how to place that data in some meaningful
framework and what the conclusions are that the person derives from that analysis."

## Culture karma

Interviews for cultural "fit" are said to be just as important as case interviews. "Fit
is really important – you have to do well on the case, but connecting with the folks
here is [important] too," says one consultant. Another consultant agrees that
candidates must "fit with the culture. The partners, especially, get really excited
about the culture we used to have and we're trying to get back to – do you fit in, can
you deal with clients, are you laid back, can you speak your mind but in an eloquent
way?" DC itself says it is looking for good communicators with "an irrepressible
sense of humor", strong leadership qualities, poise, analytical skills, creativity,
energy and flexibility, who are team players.

# OUR SURVEY SAYS

## The ghost of Braxton

The purported high quality of Deloitte Consulting culture seems to retain an almost
mythical status. Nevertheless, layoffs and the shelved Braxton spin-off have
unsettled insiders. "That's a pretty easy call, right?" says one source. "[Morale is]
fairly low, though I think it's starting to come back up even now." Another consultant
points to the "tremendous uncertainty" surrounding the firm, and what the consultant
sees as the "movement toward becoming more of an IT shop; the movement away
from management, for those of us who are MBAs from top schools and like to be
intellectually [engaged]," is tough, this source said.

"Things are pretty bad," assesses one consultant. "When I started several years ago,
things were great, the economy was fantastic. Now morale is the lowest it's been
since I've been here." This consultant says the reasons seem to be recent layoffs and
"the way they did the layoffs – instead of doing them in one big chunk, they did a
trickle every month, and no one knew why they were on the list or not." This
consultant also reports that management "was not straight with people, when in the
past that had always been our culture" – giving the example of "in the very first
layoff, the leader of the Americas practice had left a message for everyone saying:

Many of your colleagues have chosen to continue their career elsewhere; when, in fact, he had been laying people off." However, this consultant continues, "things were starting to pick up a little bit as they recognized they needed to make changes, and we were looking forward to the whole Braxton thing. Now people are wondering what that means to us."

This view isn't echoed by everyone, though. One consultant says that although there's a problem "in the perception of us," "this may actually be a good deal in the near term." This source's assessment is that "morale depends [on] which area of the practice you're involved with. I can't say people are as excited as they were before [the abandonment of Braxton] announcement, but people are moving forward, and clients are still with the firm." Indeed, this source speculates that DC may have "dodged the bullet by not [becoming Braxton]."

Mystique surrounding the DC culture remains. "It's fun-loving, jokey, not your typical button-down stiff kind of culture," says one source. The people are widely described as bright and relaxed. "You get to work with smart people," notes one source. "Compared to other firms there's still generally a spirit of collegiality," says another. "I've worked with guys from other firms, and they're not as warm and loving. It's hard when things aren't that great; that culture doesn't get put on the back burner, but …" One consultant says, "After the boom went crazy and then burst, we laid off a ton of people, so there was a lot of fear, uncertainty and lack of trust in management – your job is not secure, so how can you have a culture?" But, says this source, today Deloitte has returned to its "very friendly" and "collegial" atmosphere.

## Moving around

One DC benefit that consultants seem to appreciate is the "wide variety of opportunities" regarding work engagements. Though "most of the revenue is driven by tech work," "we're trying to say we can bring both sides to the table with operational expertise." One source says, "In some firms, you're tied from the beginning to a practice. Here, people will make an effort to switch you into a practice you're no longer bored with."

## Travel diaries

Work/life balance gets high marks from Deloitte consultants. Travel "completely varies" from staying entirely in the office to traveling "80 to 100 percent of the week when on an out-of-town client." Though the "formal policy is four days a week out of town, that formal policy is sometimes not followed." One source says, "In the first two years I was here, I traveled every week, in the second two years I only traveled once or twice." Basically, assesses one consultant, "the job requires travel. You need to be ready to travel at any time and, at any point, recognize that your calendar is not yours." "On average," sums up one source, "you're out of the office 50 percent of the time." However, another reports traveling "80 to 90 percent of the time. That's pretty taxing. On the upside, you leave Monday morning and come back Thursday night, so it's four nights at home, three nights away. You still see kids and family, which is good." Traveling, notes one consultant, also "depends on what office you're in. From the New York office there's less travel, because a lot of the focus is on financial services.

## Punching out

Work hours also vary, but generally hover between 50 and 60 hours a week, with "one week out of the month usually spiking." "On the client site," says a source, "you typically work 12 hours." And we hear DC consultants "very rarely work weekends." "If you have a dentist appointment or your wife has surgery, the firm is very flexible about those kinds of things. With regard to religious holidays, you tell [supervisors] ahead of time and you're fine," a source says.

## How to get ahead

Promotion schedules have been extended at Deloitte Consulting. "The timelines are being extended to make it not as quick (the time between promotion can be two to six years, where it used to be two to three)." A typical career path for a recent college grad in 2003 would be "two years as a business analyst, then a promotion to consultant for one to two years, then you're expected to head off to business school." DC did have layoffs in the "10 to 15 percent" range in 2002.

DC has a "twice-yearly" review structure that "works very well" and "is recognized as one of the best review processes in the industry." At these meetings with "a counselor who works with you to make sure your goals are realistic" – a "partner or senior manager that you get to choose" – you set goals such as management responsibility or new industries you want to work with. These counselors also "collect feedback from internal projects and external projects to make sure you've made progress along those lines. You're rated on a scale of 1-2-3 – exceeds expectations, meets expectations, below expectations, respectively. Based on that and on how well you've progressed, you get insightful comments." Consultants are also given a coach, who is "typically one level above you and is more of an informal strategizing source."

## Salaries not super

Salaries at DC are "competitive, but not anything stellar," says a source. "Though we typically pay 10 to 20 percent above investment banking salaries, we don't have a cash bonus." Also, "salaries were cut last year by zero to 15 percent."

Benefits at DC include accidental death/dismemberment, long-term disability insurance, tuition reimbursement, an employee assistance program, an employee-referral bonus, profit sharing, laptops, cell phones, tuition reimbursement, free snacks, gym membership discounts and sports/theater tickets.

## DIY Management

DC is described as a "matrix organization, so you don't have a boss per se – it depends on the project." Indeed, "there's nobody that I directly report to," reports one consultant, "formal counseling system" aside.

With regard to higher-ups, "everybody is on a first name basis," says one source. "I can pick up the phone and call a partner, or go out and have a drink – there's not a whole lot of hierarchy." It seems that partners give underlings a great deal of autonomy. "Partners are always , like, take a stab at it and bring it to me and let's talk about it," says one source. "Management is pretty hands off unless they have to get involved – if you're incapable or you need help."

## The training cycle

Training, which "varies and is undergoing extensive restructuring," gets decent marks from DC consultants. There is reportedly an "introductory training period for three days to a week, for every level, depending on the level; the amount of ongoing training varies significantly." The introductory period includes "one week off site, typically in Arizona or Florida, and is the intro to whatever it is you're joining, like senior consultant life or analyst life. And it covers a lot of professional skills like leading a meeting." Especially at the senior consultant level, "Deloitte has a number of training classes that are practice-aligned: M&A, operations or strategy." Next, there's the "extremely convenient and really thorough computer-based training," wherein "thousands of courses" on subjects ranging from Excel to valuation to presentation skills are offered with "tests at the end." The final category is "thought leadership," where DC teaches its new theories or approaches to its consultants.

## Diversity equilibrium

Thanks in part to its Women's Initiative, DC is said to be a good place in terms of gender balance. "There are a fair amount of women partners and colleagues – overall, it seems like half and half," says a source. "We do a pretty good job in terms of promoting diversity." However, "I don't think we're doing as well from a racial diversity perspective," says one consultant. "Thinking of partners, I don't think the percentage of minorities we have as partners is where it should be." Another consultant disagrees, saying DC "is one of the best firms for diversity."

"Management is pretty hands off unless they have to get involved - if you're incapable or you need help."

— *Deloitte consultant*

1345 Avenue of the Americas
New York, NY 10105
Phone: (917) 452-4400
www.accenture.com

## LOCATIONS

More than 110 offices worldwide

## PRACTICE AREAS

**Global Service Lines:**
Customer Relationship Management
Finance & Performance
Management
Human Performance
Solutions Engineering
Solutions Operations (Outsourcing)
Strategy & Business Architecture
Supply Chain Management
Technology Research & Innovation

**Operating Groups:**
Communications & High Tech
Financial Services
Government
Products
Resources

## THE STATS

**Employer Type:** Public Company
**Stock Symbol:** ACN
**Stock Exchange:** NYSE
**Chairman & CEO:** Joe Forehand
**2002 Employees:** 75,000+
**2001 Employees:** 75,000+
**2002 Revenue:** $11.6 billion
**2001 Revenue:** $11.4 billion

## UPPERS

- "Learning worldwide methodologies and approaches"
- "The ability to transfer your knowledge to others"

## DOWNERS

- "Working on meaningless deliverables"
- "Infrastructure-heavy firm, communications can be difficult"

## KEY COMPETITORS

BearingPoint
Computer Sciences Corporation
Deloitte Consulting
IBM Global Services
McKinsey & Company

## EMPLOYMENT CONTACT

http://careers3.accenture.com/

## THE BUZZ
WHAT CONSULTANTS AT OTHER FIRMS ARE SAYING

- "Strong brand, smart"
- "Very demanding on its employees"
- "Expensive school kids"
- "Sharp, reputable"

# THE SCOOP

## Almighty Accenture

With more than 75,000 people in 47 countries, Accenture draws from a deep well of industrial and technical expertise. Consultants in its five operating groups (Communications & High Tech, Financial Services, Government, Products and Resources) and its eight service lines (Customer Relationship Management, Finance & Performance Management, Human Performance, Strategy & Business Architecture, Supply Chain Management, Technology Research & Innovation, Solutions Engineering and Solutions Operations) work together to design and deliver strategies and solutions for more than 2,000 clients worldwide, including 92 of the Fortune Global 100 and more than two thirds of the Fortune Global 500. The firm's huge staff and wide range of experience enables it to bring both focus and massive manpower to any consulting task.

## An accent on history

In December 1997, Andersen Consulting petitioned to break away from Arthur Andersen, its sibling under the Andersen Worldwide umbrella. After a lengthy arbitration process, in August 2000 the International Court of Arbitration in Paris finally granted independence to the consulting firm that would (as of January 1, 2001) come to be known as Accenture. Good move. Today, Accenture is among the leading providers of management consulting and technology services, with net revenues of $11.6 billion in fiscal year 2002.

## Global reach

When you're as big as Accenture, the United States alone won't provide all the revenue and opportunities you need to thrive. Indeed, Accenture is decidedly a global company . Nearly half of all its revenue comes from outside the Americas. The company garnered over $3.1 billion in revenue from its Communications & High Tech operating group in 2002, a fine performance in a tough year. The unit accounted for 28 percent of Accenture's total revenue for the year, the most of any of the firm's divisions. Regionally, Accenture's EMEA (Europe, Middle East and Africa) division grew 11 percent in 2002, but the Asia Pacific group, sadly, contracted 8 percent.

## Going public

In a widely anticipated move in July 2001 – following a successful IPO by competitor KPMG Consulting (a company that has since rebranded itself as BearingPoint) — Accenture raised about $1.7 billion through a public offering. The stock offered for public sale amounted to no more than 12 percent of the undiluted company. On the initial day, the firm saw its stock rise 5 percent – not dazzling compared to the wackily inflated moon shots of 1999, but extremely respectable for the IPO market at the time. Accenture sold 115 million shares, leaving partners with control of over 80 percent of the company. Goldman Sachs and Morgan Stanley served as the lead underwriters. Accenture sold approximately $93 million worth of its shares through another offering completed in May 2002.

## Taking leave

Like most of its competitors, Accenture underwent layoffs in 2001. In June 2001, 600 support personnel were cut, followed by an additional 1,500 staffers in August (1,000 of whom were consultants). All told, about 2 percent of the workforce received pink slips. The company, however, notably reduced its payroll costs through its "FlexLeave" program. In this program, consultants voluntarily took sabbaticals of six to 12 months at 20 percent of their current pay and continued benefits, with a guaranteed job at Accenture upon the conclusion of the program.. Currently, about 100 consultants are participating in FlexLeave. More than 3,000 consultants globally have already participated. While the company has (mostly) suspended the program for the time being, it plans to reopen the program from time to time to address temporary imbalances in workplace supply and demand.

## Incoming for outsourcing

Demand is growing in the services industry for outsourcing, not a traditional consulting service. As Accenture pumps up its outsourcing business (which grew 33 percent in 2002), it's mixing up its employee roster. Though the company cut 1,000 managerial positions worldwide in September 2002, it said it planned to hire several thousand additional people into its Solutions workforce, which provides tech-based solutions to clients, and would end the year with a net increase in global head count. Accenture has stated that outsourcing will account for as much as 50 percent of its business within a few years.

## Subcontinental news

Accenture opened a software development and business processing outsourcing (BPO) delivery center in Bangalore, India in October 2002, becoming one of many consultancies to expand its Indian operations in recent years. The center employs approximately 1,000 software engineers. After cutting 900 personnel in 2001, the Australia group of Accenture announced in November 2002 it would hire 100 new consultants throughout 2003. Group chief executive of Asian operations David Hunter cited 10 percent local revenue growth as cause for optimism. In fact, *Business Times* claimed in January 2003 that Accenture was on a "hiring spree" in the Asia-Pacific region, with plans to bring in 500 or more new recruits during 2003.

In February 2003, Accenture took over most client contracts, employees and operations of Zurich-based IT company Systor AG, which filed for Chapter 11 bankruptcy protection two months earlier. The acquisition, which included more than 500 personnel, was approved in March 2003.

## Forehand comes to the forefront

In November 1999, Joe W. Forehand was named successor to George Shaheen (who bolted for the ill-fated Internet grocery service Webvan) as CEO and managing partner. Less than two years into his tenure, Forehand was named the No. 1 Most Influential Consultant by *Consulting Magazine*. (The managing partner for Accenture's retail operating group, Angela Selden, ranked No. 15 on the June 2001 list.) Forehand also made *InformationWeek*'s list of the 15 most influential people in the IT industry. At the same time that its fearless leader was winning recognition, the firm as a whole scooped up its share of accolades. In 2001, *Red Herring* named Accenture to its list of the 100 companies Most Likely to Change the World.

Forehand doesn't seem to buy into the loneliness of command, creating an expanded Office of the CEO, which initially included Chief Operating Officer Stephan James as sub-leader of the company's group chief executives. The pair expanded into a threesome in March 2003 with the addition of William Green. Green assumed the title of COO – Client Services, while James' position was renamed COO – Capabilities. At the same time, Accenture announced the creation of a new position, Chief Executive – Business Process Outsourcing, which reports to Forehand. The first proud titleholder is Jackson Wilson, the firm's former corporate development officer.

## Training days

Accenture proudly boasts that it spent $434 million in fiscal 2002 to train and develop its workforce. Newly hired analysts typically spend two weeks at Accenture's main training facility in St. Charles, Ill., developing team-building and management skills. The system enables Accenture to offer standardized solutions and encourage consultants from disparate offices and backgrounds to work well together (important for a company with more than 75,000 employees). After their time at St. Charles, Accenture professionals can access the company's 4,000-plus classrooms, computer-based and Web-enabled training programs via a Web-based learning portal.

## Listening for opportunity's knock

Accenture has been busy creating new businesses where it detects opportunity. In March 2000, Accenture announced that it was teaming up with Microsoft to form Avanade, a jointly owned firm that focuses on large-scale technology integration surrounding Microsoft's enterprise platform. Initially valued at more than $1 billion, Avanade reportedly was launched in response to the growing dominance of IBM Global Services, which executives said was often the choice-by-default for many Fortune 500 companies. The venture has thrived, and now has more than 300 customers and over 1,200 employees in 9 cities in 14 countries.

Other businesses include Accenture Learning, Accenture's take on the increasingly important industry of distance learning. Accenture Learning was founded in December 2001. Accenture's also entered the field of HR consulting, forming Accenture HR Services in 2000. Today, Accenture HR Services, which provides outsourced HR functions from recruitment and pay to pensions, employs 2,000 Accenturites and serves more than 215,000 employees, as well as 374,000 pensioners.

Naviatare, which was originally formed in 1993 as PRA Solutions, provides reservations, ticketing and venue management services to more than 40 airlines worldwide. Navitaire employs more than 600 people around the world.

## Out of the VC game

Accenture had originally planned to invest as much as $500 million in emerging Internet businesses through its Accenture Technology Ventures unit, but reversed its decision when many of its investments (shockingly) yielded losses. (The company tells us what actually happened was that "the VC exit window lengthened and volatility began to impact corporate earnings.") In March 2002, Accenture announced that it would sell its entire stash of minority stakes in such companies (about 80 early and mid-stage technology companies). CIBC World Markets bought the portfolio in August 2002 for an undisclosed sum; Accenture retained a 5 percent stake.

## Thinking 'bout the government

Accenture's Government operating group earned more than $1.3 billion globally in 2002 and continues to pick up new engagements. In July 2002, New York City selected Accenture to help design, build and operate their new 311 service, an easy-to-remember (even for harried New Yorkers) phone number for city residents. 311 callers reach a service representative, who can assist them with a wide variety of New York City services in an uncharacteristically helpful and transparent manner. Accenture was also selected by NASA in 2002 to develop the space agency's Core Financial Project, the backbone of NASA's financial management program. The program aims to streamline NASA finances.

## The controversial move offshore

Accenture attracted some unwelcome – and misplaced – criticism in 2001 for incorporating in sunny Bermuda. Critics sniped that Accenture had "inverted," that is, moved its site of incorporation from the United States to Bermuda. However, Accenture had in fact not incorporated before 2001, as found by a GAO study, so, according to the GAO's director of tax issues, the company "didn't have a corporate structure to invert." Needless to say, the company pays its fair share of taxes in each of the 47 countries in which it gains income.

## More downsizing

In March 2003, the company quietly told its employees it would have to cut another 1 percent of its workforce, mostly from the pointy end of the management pyramid at U.S. offices – a comfort to the sizable pool of analysts and consultants, but a definite worry to those at the level of engagement managers and above. The job trim was to be handled by regional managers. Recruitment is actually expected to increase Accenture's total headcount by the end of 2003.

# GETTING HIRED

## Mixed accents

Accenture recruits via on-campus events and virtual/online strategies at campuses across the United States, as well as many international campuses. Prospective campus hires are generally encouraged to submit their resumes and a pre-application through their career service centers or the Accenture web site designed for that purpose (www.campusconnection.accenture.com). Candidates may have up to two interviews on campus. The first is a screening interview, while the second tends to be with Accenture employees (partners or experienced managers, though usually also a peer). These interviews can vary, according to a contact in the recruiting office: "In some cases these interviews are behavioral, and in others they're case-based." Also, "questions definitely depend on service line. Strategy gives case interviews, while [other service lines] give behavioral interviews." One insider reports that "at the second round I was asked a lot of 'tell me about a time when' questions. One was 'Tell me about a time when you had to work with someone you didn't know.'"

The interview process begins with a first-round interview, normally conducted face to face. The second round interview also almost always occurs in person, though it is possible that candidates in especially remote locations will need to interview by phone. The final step, an office visit, involves meetings with analysts and consultants as well as two executives (managers or partners). There are also presentations about Accenture during the office visit.

There are minor variations in the interview process at different offices and campuses; some candidates have had a second round with three managers or partners at an Accenture office. Consultants say, "Selectivity depends heavily on which service line you are aligned with. Strategy is extremely difficult to enter even with excellent credentials — Process, Technology and Organization & Human Performance a little less so." Office visitors should take heart: "We tend to hire most of the people who make it to the office." It's not necessary to interview where you want to work, "except in the case of San Francisco," a very popular office location. We hear that "offers are usually extended to successful candidates shortly after the office visit."

## Accenture-ate the positive

The company has identified several qualities that make a successful Accenture consultant. They include: a target GPA (which depends on the type of degree –

stricter standards are in order for you English majors), critical thinking, the ability to be a self-starter, ability to juggle multiple activities, problem-solving skills, a knack for being a team player, and a willingness to travel. One recruiter tells us, "The type of person we look for performed well academically and is well-rounded, a lifelong learner, committed to developing a career, interested in and understands what we do." The perfect candidate also has "strong written and oral communication skills." This contact also informs us, "Professionals who succeed at [Accenture] embrace the clients' needs" and "are team- and results-oriented."

Insiders say that even the strongest candidates can improve their chances of being hired by "reading through the [Accenture careers] web site" and "educating yourself on what [Accenture] does, how the company is structured, and what the various organizations and their respective career paths are." Sources also suggest that candidates "be prepared to articulate which is the best fit for you." Finally, "It's also tremendously helpful to have someone in the company to talk to, so you can get a better sense of what the many choices are."

# OUR SURVEY SAYS

## Defending your life

Maintaining a balance between work and home at Accenture is described as "challenging" by one consultant, who feels consultants at the firm have a "very hard workload, worse than most consultants." However, he adds, "The firm is open to work-from-home" and "while 4-1 is not official, it is standard practice." Another insider is less happy about her schedule, claiming there is "no work-life balance – work is first, and this replaces the need for a life." Her co-worker disagrees, saying, "HR reps make sure that you don't overextend yourself." One philosopher says, "Compared to investment banking, it's a vacation." A senior consultant offers this assessment: "Overall, the work/life balance at Accenture is not very good. However, over the past few years I have been pleasantly surprised by the firm's overall focus to improve work/life balance. There have been several occasions when management has urged me to implement flexible work arrangements and Thursday evening flybacks for the teams I was leading."

## Clouds in the atmosphere

Reports about the culture at Accenture are generally positive, though they are intermixed here and there with post-IPO blues. One person in a cross-industry functional group says the company offers a "learning atmosphere," adding that he has "never worked for a person I didn't enjoy." Another consultant says that Accenture culture "is generally relaxed, upbeat and fun," but notes that "recent layoffs and continued angst toward senior management has put a damper on the mood."

Some insiders point to the public offering and its aftereffects as a source of displeasure. "The culture has degraded significantly since the IPO in July 2001," says one dissatisfied manager. "We once had a vibrant professional culture with a sense of *esprit de corps* – now we've become a glorified sweatshop with a vicious political culture and a cutthroat 'up-or-out' ethos." A consultant agrees, though with less vitriol "Accenture culture is very collegial with a strong emphasis on team work. However, the culture has become increasingly dull since we went public as outings and other perks have virtually disappeared."

## Money matters

New hires may face an issue with compensation; according to one insider, "While current economic conditions have prompted [Accenture] and others to be much more selective, they are low-balling everyone – even the Ivies." Another claims the pay isn't so bad, saying that he gets "a good base but no bonus yet, since the company just became public two years ago." A consultant opines, "Compensation at Accenture is comparable to the IT industry, not the consulting industry." On the other hand, "If you are below management level, you can make a decent amount of overtime."

## Charming environs

At any rate, it doesn't seem like Accenture employees suffer for their surroundings. "The San Francisco office is fairly nice," says one insider, "with the top several floors of a nice building. Nothing fancy, but what a view!" Another says, "The New York office is used and battered, but the others are beautiful." However, says one source, they could use "more social events." A former consultant says, "Impressive offices. Unfortunately I was never there, as I was on the client site my entire time."

## Fine diversity

But is Accenture an equitable place to work? One consultant says, "The gender balance is pretty good – about 60/40, though it's very clustered." Another points out,

"Flexible work conditions have enhanced opportunities for working moms." A New York-based insider adds, "Accenture truly does make every possible attempt to support minorities." Gays and lesbians aren't left out, either. "I was surprised to hear about several gay partners and senior managers within the firm," says one respondent. "It's a positive sign of diversity."

## Charitable spirit

There's a spirit of philanthropy at Accenture as well. One source mentions such activities as "a 'Light the Night' walk for the Leukemia and Lymphoma Society, the 'Make a Wish' Foundation, helping the Washington, D.C., schools, etc." Another agrees that the firm is "very involved" in community activities. A Texan tells of "strong community involvement. We work with DePelchin Children's Center, as well as United Way. We have an adopt-a-school program for tutoring, and participate in the MS150 [a Texas bike tour to benefit multiple sclerosis research]." Somebody from the Asia/Australia region says, "We're very involved in charity work in the local scene." In 2003, Accenture sponsored an exhibit at New York City's Metropolitan Museum of Art, *Manet/Velazquez: The French Taste for Spanish Painting.* Accenture also created a web site to permit art lovers to explore the exhibit online.

# Mercer Human Resource Consulting

1166 Avenue of the Americas
New York, NY 10036
Phone: (212) 345-7000
Fax: (212) 345-7414
www.mercerHR.com

## LOCATIONS

**New York, NY (HQ)**
Offices in 150 cities worldwide

## PRACTICE AREAS

Adminstration
Client Management
Communication
Global Information Services
Health Care & Group Benefits
Human Resource Operations
   Consulting
International
Investment Consulting
Retirement
Performance Measurement &
   Rewards

## FUNCTIONS

Finance
Information Technology
Human Resources
Marketing and Sales

## THE STATS

**Employer Type:** Subsidiary of Marsh & McLennan Companies, Inc. and operating company of Mercer Inc.
**Chairman:** Peter E. Felton
**President and CEO:** Daniel L. McCaw
**2002 Employees:** 13,200
**2001 Employees:** 13,000
**2002 Revenue:** $1.83 billion
**2001 Revenue:** $1.7 billion

## UPPERS

• Exposure to global clients
• Not much travel

## DOWNERS

• Focus on earning, not training
• "Vague compensation policies"

## KEY COMPETITORS

Hay Group
Hewitt Associates
Towers Perrin
Watson Wyatt Worldwide

## EMPLOYMENT CONTACT

See "Joining Mercer" at
www.mercerHR.com

## THE BUZZ
### WHAT CONSULTANTS AT OTHER FIRMS ARE SAYING

• "Gray suited and sensible"
• "Staid"
• "Great at what they do"
• "Top firm in a dull space"

# THE SCOOP

## The "people" side of consulting

Mercer Human Resource Consulting is a world leader in employee benefits, compensation and communication consulting. One of several firms owned by Marsh & McLennan Companies and one of seven firms in Mercer Inc., Mercer Human Resource Consulting has more than 13,000 employees and some 150 offices in 40 countries, from the Netherlands to New Zealand.

Until April 2002, Mercer Human Resource Consulting was known as William M. Mercer; Marsh & McLennan changed the firm's name in order to brand its consulting companies more consistently. As part of the transition, the firm also launched MercerHRMetrics, a consulting framework to help clients more consistently measure the impact of their HR programs on the success of their business.

## Size matters

Thanks to its huge stable of consultants, Mercer Human Resource Consulting is able to provide a broad spectrum of HR services, from designing employee benefits programs to strategic HR program and policy development. The firm's human capital strategy group helps clients organize their various HR efforts into sustainable, value-focused activities. Its global communications practice, with 410 people worldwide, helps companies create internal web sites to communicate with their employees, shareholders and customers. The firm staffs each team with a principal, a project manager and a brace of interdisciplinary consultants, from economists to psychologists, to provide clients with the broadest view possible of their human capital landscape.

But size isn't the only distinguishing characteristic of Mercer Human Resource Consulting. The firm also does quite nicely in industry rankings, thank you very much. It consistently ranks among the top five HR consultancies in the world, and its investment consulting unit beat out rival Watson Wyatt Worldwide to be named the top such firm in Britain, according to a *Financial News* poll in March 2002. In April 2002, *Finance Asia* named Mercer Investment Consulting, Mercer Human Resource Consulting's investment practice, the best of its breed in Asia.

## Expanding opportunities

Mercer Human Resource Consulting has spent the last few years expanding its overseas operations, particularly in Europe. In May 2001, it opened offices in Istanbul and Prague, and in August of that year it bought Vienna-based Constantia Neuberger Bednar & Partner BesmbH, a benefit and retirement consulting firm. In early 2003, Mercer Human Resource Consulting purchased the actuarial consulting business of KPMG in Germany.

Mercer Human Resource Consulting has expanded domestically as well. In October 2001, it completed its purchase of SCA Consulting, a value management firm, adding 100 consultants to its offices in Chicago, Dallas, Los Angeles, New York and London. In February 2003, Mercer Inc. announced that its Mercer Management Consulting unit would merge with Oliver, Wyman & Co., a financial services consultancy. (The merger was completed later in 2003.) The new entity, Mercer Oliver Wyman, adds more than 400 professionals and staff to Mercer. Mercer Oliver Wyman chairman John Drzik remains as president of the renamed company, which operates independently in the Mercer reporting arm of Marsh & McLennan.

The firm has not weathered the recent recession unscathed, though; in June 2001, it laid off approximately 3 percent of its employees in the U.S. Another series of layoffs came in 2002; some insiders place the total at "about 8 percent in the U.S."

## More resources, human and otherwise

Despite the tragic loss of 295 Marsh colleagues in the September 11th attack on the World Trade Center and a continued slump in the worldwide economy, Mercer Human Resource Consulting continued to grow (albeit slowly) throughout 2002 and into early 2003. Overall, Mercer Inc. consulting revenue (including all its operating units) grew 2 percent in 2002, with a 4 percent improvement in net income to $1.37 billion. Most of the new developments have been overseas, with the U.K. and Europe seeing the most action.

In July 2002, Mercer Human Resource Consulting signed off on the construction plans for a new U.K. headquarters in London's St. Katherine's Dock neighborhood. Construction of the new seven-story office complex began in January 2003 and should be completed in late 2004. Along with the launch of the London construction project in January, Mercer opened a new Liverpool office to house 120 employees from a previous location.

Mercer HR increased its presence in the Netherlands with the October 2002 acquisition of Arnhem-based Schnitker en Voorman, a health care services firm that employs 42 consultants. Mercer also scored a major addition in February 2003 when it agreed to acquire KPMG's Actuarial Services division in Frankfurt. The acquisition will add 70 pension specialists to Mercer's German operations, bringing the firm's total to 180 employees in seven German cities. Terms of both deals were not disclosed.

## A new organizational chart

In addition to filling out the roster of consultants, Mercer Human Resource Consulting added or moved several key team members throughout 2002. In February, Leslie Kramerich joined the firm's Washington Resource Group as director of government relations and public policy. Kramerich served as Assistant Secretary of Labor in the Pension and Welfare Benefits Administration under President Clinton.

In July 2002, Daniel McCaw became president and CEO of Mercer Human Resource Consulting, taking over for Peter Coster. McCaw will retain his position as chairman and CEO of U.S. operations, which he has held since late 2000. Karen Greenbaum will report to McCaw as president and COO of U.S. operations.

In December 2002, Mercer Investment Consulting, part of Mercer Human Resource Consulting, named Garrie Lette global head of strategic research. Lette, based in Melbourne, Australia, adds 10 years of fund management experience to his 11 years with Mercer.

# GETTING HIRED

## Facing HR from the other side

As you might expect from a human resources consultancy, Mercer Human Resource Consulting's hiring regimen is the "typical first, second interview process." A source tells us they recruit from "all main universities" and don't use business cases – they don't really apply to HR consulting. However, another insider notes that there are "multiple in-office interviews" and the process "takes a LONG time."

Mercer Human Resource Consulting requests that interested applicants register at the company's web site and fill out a personal profile. This registration provides access to job matching, direct applications, internship opportunities, notification of new positions and more. The careers page includes personal profiles of employees, to show potential hires what sort of people they'll be working with. There's also a "Students of the Month" section, to show you what the competition is like.

# OUR SURVEY SAYS

## Steady pace

Insiders report that the workload is "consistent" and there is "always lots to do" at Mercer Human Resource Consulting; the typical week is 55-60 hours. Work schedules tend to be steady, with few spikes or stretches "on the beach." However, one source notes, "With the lousy economy, certain consulting revenue has dramatically lessened," resulting in less work in some disciplines. Travel is likewise very light for most of our respondents. One consultant explains, "I travel very little, but those who choose to might be in jobs where they travel extensively. There are opportunities for light-travel positions." This means a lot of time spent at the home office, where "junior consultants have cubes, but mid-level consultants get real offices. Principals get real offices with windows."

The focus at Mercer is on the work, not in other facets of corporate life. The attitude, one insider says, is "Go out and sell it and make money for all of us." But a "strong focus on billable hours, at the expense of building sales skills and developing sales opportunities" is the rule. One person notes, "Mercer cares about work life balance." Philanthropy receives "minimal encouragement on an office-by-office basis," according to one source.

## Lack of structure

One source decries the firm as "not very structured," with "vague compensation policies." A colleague thinks this is part of the problem with the meager diversity, and believes "better global systems and procedures" would address the issue. On the up side, says another insider, "People are treated with respect and dignity," and "poor management isn't tolerated once it becomes known to upper levels."

# "Poor management isn't tolerated once it becomes known to upper levels."

## — Mercer Human Resource consultant

# Marakon Associates

245 Park Avenue
44th Floor
New York, NY 10167
Phone: (212) 377-5000
Fax: (212) 377-6000
www.marakon.com

## LOCATIONS

**New York, NY (HQ)**
San Francisco, CA
Chicago, IL
London, UK
Singapore

## PRACTICE AREAS

Change Management
Customer Value Management
Finance
Leadership
Organization
Strategy

## THE STATS

**Employer Type:** Private Company
**CEO:** Ken Favaro
**2002 Employees:** 333
**2001 Employees:** 354
**2002 Revenue:** $133 million
**2001 Revenue:** $116 million

## UPPERS

- Considerable community involvement
- "Working on issues that are on the CEO's agenda"
- Young, small-firm environment

## DOWNERS

- Pay scale "recently cut for North American offices
- Rigid promotion policies
- Partners said to be "disengaged"

## KEY COMPETITORS

Bain & Company
Boston Consulting Group
McKinsey & Company
Mercer Management Consulting
Monitor

## EMPLOYMENT CONTACT

All applicants should fill out a form at /www.marakon.com/careers

 **THE BUZZ**
WHAT CONSULTANTS AT OTHER FIRMS ARE SAYING

- "High end, brainy"
- "Good process but too rigid"
- "True "C-suite" consulting"
- "Running out of clients?"

# THE SCOOP

## Running to win

Few people outside the corporate world have heard of Marakon; this is due in part to its size – in an industry dominated by big strategy consultancies like McKinsey & Company (13,000 employees), Marakon's complement of 250 is easily overlooked. But the firm's relative anonymity suits its partners just fine; as they are apt to say, they only need to know 500 people – the CEOs of the Fortune 500. In fact, Marakon claims most of its clients are Fortune 200 companies. Its partners are content to develop most new business through referrals, based on the firm's reputation. *The Economist* noted in July 2002 that Marakon "has advised some of the world's most consistently successful companies."

Because the firm works with only a small number of clients across many industries, its revenue by industry can vary widely from year to year. Typically, about a third of its billings come from financial services, a third from manufacturing/industrial and a third from consumer goods/retail/other. In 2002, almost 50 percent of the firm's business came from financial services, with another 20 percent from the manufacturing industry and 10 percent from pharmaceuticals, a sector where Marakon did no business in 2001. The rest of Marakon's clients hail from a variety of industries including retail/wholesale, health care, energy and utilities and media/telecommunications.

Marakon CEO Ken Favaro indicated to *Consultants News* in December 2002 that the company plans to bone up on IT skills in 2003, but won't expand into IT consulting. Favaro reasoned, "How can you impart independent advice about what [the client's] IT needs are if in fact you're also positioning yourself to meet those IT needs?"

## A well-kept secret

Marakon was founded in 1978 by three Wells Fargo executives and a business school professor who foresaw the impact that value-based strategies could have on the business world. They set up shop in San Francisco and started to spread the word through a small number of clients. A quarter of a century and two office moves later, the business world has validated their hunch – today nearly every strategy firm has a shareholder-value practice, and countless corporations have altered their management processes according to Marakon's principles.

One of those principles is measuring a firm's success through profitability, not growth. Despite expansion into Asia with the opening of a Singapore office in 2001, Marakon management seems content with its current level of activity, and does not seek to expand for expansion's sake. Total staff shrank to 333 in 2002, but revenue grew at a rate of 15 percent. Revenue per consultant jumped more than $100,000 that year, to about $586,000.

## Everybody works

Marakon consultants are concerned with helping the client find its own best answers. The client's CEO or another high-ranking officer leads most engagements. This means that Marakon doesn't usually do short projects or perform troubleshooting. Instead, the typical Marakon project runs two years or more, with the firm using its expertise to advise the client rather than dictate a solution. While this may overstate the difference between Marakon and other consultancies, it highlights the Marakon mindset.

In any given year, Marakon will have 12 to 18 engagements. Marakon consultants are rarely staffed to more than one client at a time, but the firm uses its entire personnel roster. All consultants, including partners, are expected (and required) to put in significant time on client engagements. CEO Favaro estimates that half of his time is billable. With a consultant-to-partner ratio of 6.5:1 in 2002, this means that clients get the full range of Marakon expertise, from newcomers to veterans.

## Expansion plans

In 2002, Marakon began to explore the possibility of opening an office in India, possibly in Mumbai, in anticipation of a future Asian clientele. Currently, India, Hong Kong and Southeast Asia are serviced by Marakon's 25-consultant office in Singapore, which opened in March 2001. Marakon partner Sandeep Malik told *The Economic Times* in November 2002 that an Indian location would only be opened if it could employ at least 20 people. Since Marakon measures itself by profitability and not growth, it remains to be seen if the firm will detect enough Asian demand to set up a new shop. In the near term, a new office in the region is unlikely. The firm did 8 percent of its total business in the Asia Pacific region in 2002, half as much as in 2001.

Malik was also interviewed in the September 2002 Singapore edition of *Business Times* for an article cautioning against Singapore corporations' expansionist leanings. Many foreign businesses are opening affiliates in Singapore, and local businesses are trying to grow as well. According to Malik, "Often, it [the desire to be a regional or global player] is asserted with very little thought to why, what is the competitive advantage they have in this market today and can they replicate it in other markets they venture to."

In November 2002, Marakon announced the appointment of a new external board of advisors to help guide the firm on its strategy, practice and growth opportunities. The board members are: Sir George Bull, chairman of J. Sainsbury, former chairman of Diageo and former chairman and CEO of Grand Metropolitan; Arthur Martinez, former chairman and CEO of Sears Roebuck; Sir Brian Pitman, former chairman and CEO of Lloyds TSB Group; Lewis Platt, former chairman, president and CEO of Hewlett-Packard and former CEO of Kendall-Jackson Wine Estates; and Frank Zarb, former chairman and CEO of the National Association of Securities Dealers and the Nasdaq Stock Market. "We feel extremely fortunate to have attracted such luminaries to advise Marakon, particularly since demand for prominent former CEOs has been enormous over the last few years," commented Marakon CEO Ken Favaro.

## Bigwigs on board

Another way Marakon is trying to build awareness with CEOs is through an exclusive new forum called "The Global Agenda," organized by *The Economist*. Launched in the fall of 2001, the forum is an invitation-only, off-the-record meeting led by senior editors of *The Economist* for 30 top executives from Global 500 companies. A handful of leading thinkers and policymakers also participate. In 2002, the firm signed a global agreement to sponsor four of these events in New York, London and Hong Kong. Marakon has also started working with other conference organizers, such as the World Economic Forum and Harvard Business School Publishing, on high-level events.

# GETTING HIRED

## Join from campus

A senior analyst at Marakon informs us, "Most analysts and consultants are hired through on-campus recruiting. A few are hired through referrals." An engagement manager lists the schools from which they typically recruit: "Undergrad: Princeton, Penn, Northwestern and Duke. Grad schools include HBS, Sloan, Kellogg and

Wharton." Another analyst adds, "You apply to an office" as opposed to joining the firm and being placed afterwards.

The interview process is mostly standard, involving "on-campus interviews, usually two rounds, with a mix of fit and cases." A senior analyst calls the process "very slow moving." A Europe-based consultant mentions a "role-play fit interview," which may throw the unprepared for a loop. Our insiders don't provide many examples of case studies, except this one: "How would you set the advertising budget for a distilled spirits company?"

# OUR SURVEY SAYS

## The first step to a diverse staff

Our sources have very little to say on the subject of diversity, as "diversity is an industry-wide issue." On the subject of minorities, one waggish consultant quips, "What minorities?" A more serious analyst claims, "Our office in Singapore is like the U.N. with people from the U.S., U.K., India, Malaysia and Indonesia," but that's also a fair description of the population of Singapore and thus not all that revealing. As far as gay, lesbian and bisexual employees are concerned, we hear "one of the top managing partners is openly gay," but there is "no explicit effort" to hire or retain.

There's a difference when it comes to a gender-balanced staff, however. While many employees feel "retention of women is an issue," they also mention "Marakon initiated a diversity initiative to improve along this dimension." An experienced associate says, "We are as good as a firm of our size can be, given the industry and nature of the work model."

## The levels of Marakon

"Very hierarchical." That's what some U.S.-based insiders call their company, despite its "small firm feel." European associates see a more "flat" and "laid-back" structure. A manager in the U.K. says, "People are accessible across levels. There are some differences between the London and U.S. offices though. The U.S. offices are more 'formal' with older partners – feels more hierarchical." Yet an overseas insider says, "There really is a flat structure [at Marakokon], with partners easily accessible to all levels."

A consultant in New York says the firm enjoys a "great culture among the consultants and associate consultants, but loses a bit with the partners and managers." From the Pacific, one analyst remarks on the "interesting dichotomy when you hire extroverts and senior management consists almost entirely of introverts." Insiders also say Marakon is "academic minded," "very competitive," "competitive yet collaborative," "hard working to a fault," "professional" and, several people agree, "fun."

## No face time, but not much leisure time either

There aren't many complaints about the work schedule here, though the consultants acknowledge they've picked a difficult profession. One insider calls Marakon "fairly flexible because it is a small firm, but you still have a consultant lifestyle." A manager from Europe says, "No complaints here. Absolutely no 'face time' culture." A recent addition to the firm adds, "I work hard, but I am a former investment banker, and nothing compares to those sweatshops." Another respondent tells us, "Work/life balance is actively measured through consultant surveys every quarter. While there are minor fluctuations over time in the absolute score, it is consistently above 'satisfied.'"

Not everyone agrees, of course. Several respondents mention workweeks of 70 hours or more, and there is talk of "not much down time." Hardly anybody reports significant time spent on the beach; in fact, one consultant says, "I have only been on the beach for one month in my three years here." Another consultant concurs: "No time on the beach, and firm-building work is taken seriously – marketing, recruitment etc." However, that same person says, "There is usually some downtime at project end, so you're not constantly working flat out."

For the most part, Marakonites aren't hit hard by travel requirements either. "Travel is part of the job," says one insider. "However, relative to other firms, our norm is for Mondays and Fridays to be in the home office." According to a European analyst, "If there's travel, then the norm is Monday and Friday in the home office, Tuesday through Thursday at the client site. Rarely do projects involve extended periods of time away – and this is usually covered by volunteers wanting to move away." A New Yorker points out, "Weekly travel is not bad. However, we have had a lot of international clients recently." Because of the change in client focus, says a colleague, "there will often be overseas assignments of extended duration. Although these are good learning experiences, the lifestyle hardship can be tough – and we don't use expense accounts extravagantly at all."

## What's in it for me?

Our sources don't mention exact pay figures, but one indicates, "The entire compensation structure was recently cut for North American offices. This reduced pay for future promotions and par bonuses at all levels below partner." Still, most said they were content with the "profit sharing and pension perks" they receive. The share is "typically 10 percent of salary," though one new hire adds, "You are ineligible in your first year of employment." One consultant mentions the occasional happy appearance of "mid-year cash bonuses." Marakon claims that its compensation packages are competitive with other top-tier strategy firms.

The offices reflect a desire to keep the consultants comfortable. One contact says, "Great locations (across all geographies) – relatively spacious with modern fittings." "Our offices are outstanding," agrees a California-based consultant. From Singapore we hear, "We have a beautiful office with the best view in Singapore." The only caveat? "We need more choices. All [offices] presently are in high cost of living locations. This is fine if you are a partner, but hard on the rest of us."

In addition, Marakon provides a good-size package of other benefits, including various bits of electronica (phones, PDAs, laptops), massages, gym discounts, sports and theater tickets, EAP and tuition reimbursement. One insider says, "As a summer intern, I received reimbursement for my full MBA tuition." Another claims, "The training budget is huge!"

## Training for a Marakon

Yes, there is training, and the budget is apparently as huge as the last quote claims. "Marakon is probably the best of any firm at training consultants," says one respondent. "This is because the practice is highly developed and well-defined." Another confirms, "The training program is outstanding and is continually evaluated for improvement." "This is consulting," says a third. "We train, and train, and then train more." Consultants get 200 hours of formal training in their first 15 months.

## Giving back

Marakon is involved with several community projects, varying by location. A manager in New York sums up the company's approach: "We do pro bono on an ad-hoc basis. We do community service on a quarterly basis. The community service efforts are all driven and managed by the consultant group." A consultant in Europe tells us the efforts are "driven by consultants. Not 'institutionalized.'" A New Yorker provides a few details: "We participate in Junior Achievement and Habitat for Humanity on a regular basis. Once a year, the firm organizes a day of volunteering for the entire staff." In Chicago, "We do an office volunteering event once a quarter." Marakon is now a corporate sponsor of Habitat for Humanity.

## Parting thoughts

What's best about working for Marakon? "You can really make a difference," says one person. "As an analyst your opinion is respected. Great prospects for advancement based on merit." Another enjoys "facing continuous challenges." A third appreciates the "high integrity individuals" in the firm. "You work on great issues with significant companies," adds another insider.

A highly placed source leaves us with these words: "This firm can be a great place. It has been a great place. A better market environment will help things, no doubt."

# The Parthenon Group

200 State Street
Boston, MA 02109
Phone: (617) 478-2550
Fax: (617) 478-2555
www.parthenon.com

## LOCATIONS

**Boston, MA (HQ)**
San Francisco, CA
London

## PRACTICE AREAS

Principal Investing
Strategy Consulting

## THE STATS

**Employer Type:** Private Company
**CEO:** Bill Achtmeyer
**2002 Employees:** 150
**2001 Employees:** 150

## UPPERS

- Small and super-prestigious
- Great pay

## DOWNERS

- Limited engagement
- Can be claustrophobic

## KEY COMPETITORS

Bain & Company
Boston Consulting Group
Marakon Associates
McKinsey & Company

## EMPLOYMENT CONTACT

E-mail: recruiting@parthenon.com

## THE BUZZ
WHAT CONSULTANTS AT OTHER FIRMS ARE SAYING

- "Fun place to be"
- "Long hours"
- "Cool boutique firm"
- "Yet another Bain spinoff"

# THE SCOOP

## A tight little ship

Two ex-Bain consultants, Bill Achtmeyer and John Rutherford, founded The Parthenon Group in 1991 as a boutique consulting firm. Since then, Parthenon has grown at an annual rate of roughly 30 percent. The company has intentionally stayed small, maxing out at 150 employees for the last three years, and only recruits from a handful of top schools. Despite its relatively modest size, Parthenon has attracted an impressive client roster, including Pepsi, American Express, McGraw-Hill, eBay and Kohlberg Kravis Roberts. Aside from these marquee names, Parthenon also advises entrepreneurial firms in fields including health care, real estate, the automotive industry and education. Its specialty is advising CEOs on high-level strategy.

## Risk and reward

Parthenon was one of the first firms to accept risk-based fees for its work. The firm allows executives to buy shares of client companies through its own equity program, which means consultants have a tangible stake in the effectiveness of their advice. This program has netted consultants between 50 and 100 percent more than a traditional equity program would.

Two former divisions of the Parthenon Group, IGS (Investor Group Services) and Parthenon Capital, still work closely with Parthenon consultants. IGS does due diligence research for private equity firms, while Parthenon Capital is an investment firm run along the lines of a venture capital fund.

## Community service

Parthenon gives direct donations and provides pro bono consulting to organizations in Boston, San Francisco and London. Arts, education and domestic violence are among the causes Parthenon supports in this manner. Parthenon founder Bill Achtmeyer has also helped create the William F. Achtmeyer Center for Global Leadership at Dartmouth's Tuck Business School (where he's the chairman of the board).

## A fighting chance

Parthenon Group's San Francisco office made a name for itself when it engaged in the largest proxy battle in history in 2001 and 2002. Hewlett Packard board member

Walter Hewlett (son of the technology giant's co-founders) opposed a proposed merger with Compaq, and enlisted Parthenon and San Francisco-based Friedman, Fleischer & Lowe to provide backup for his argument that the merger was disadvantageous for HP. Hewlett mounted an enormous campaign to persuade shareholders to reject the merger. Though Hewlett's side lost the shareholder vote narrowly, Parthenon nevertheless garnered media attention and respect for its role in the fight.

# GETTING HIRED

Parthenon recruits on-campus at fine institutions such as Darmouth/Tuck, Harvard/Harvard Business School, MIT/Sloan, Penn/Wharton, Stanford/Stanford Business School, INSEAD and the London Business School. Parthenon also considers those already in the workplace for principal positions. Principals can expect to spend five to seven years in that position before being promoted to partner. New consultants can expect a signing bonus, along with an annual bonus and salary.

To apply, submit a cover letter, resume, relevant test scores, and unofficial transcript to the following: Boston associates, Katy Ranere, recruiting@parthenon.com; Boston principals, Eileen McBride, recruiting@parthenon.com; London associates, Kate Nicholson, undergrad@parthenon.co.uk; London principals, Kate Nicholson, mba@parthenon.co.uk; San Francisco associates and principals, Colleen Lauerman, ColleenL@parthenon.com.

Once accepted, associates are trained in classes with Tuck and Harvard Business School professors. Parthenon covers business school tuition for associates promoted to the principal level who return to Parthenon after graduation.

"This firm can be a great place.  It has been a great place."

— *Marakon consultant*

Route 100
Somers, NY 10589
www-1.ibm.com/services/bcs/index.html

## LOCATIONS

160 offices worldwide

## PRACTICE AREAS

Business Transformation
   Outsourcing
Customer Relationship Management
   Services
e-Business Integration Solutions
Financial Management Solutions
Human Capital Solutions
Strategic Change Solutions
Supply Chain and Operations
   Solutions

## THE STATS

**Employer Type:** Business Unit of IBM
**Stock Symbol:** IBM
**Stock Exchange:** NYSE
**Managing Partner:** Virginia Rometty

## UPPERS

- Tremendous brand name and history
- Solid list of perks
- "Flexible dress code, based on client"

## DOWNERS

- Changes in pay and benefits
- Merger-induced morale dip
- Long reporting chain

## KEY COMPETITORS

Accenture
BearingPoint
Booz Allen Hamilton
Cap Gemini Ernst & Young
Deloitte Consulting
McKinsey & Company

## EMPLOYMENT CONTACT

www-1.ibm.com/employment
Phone: (800) IBM-7080, ext. BCS

## THE BUZZ
### WHAT CONSULTANTS AT OTHER FIRMS ARE SAYING

- "Keeps getting better and better"
- "Big Blue and world domination go hand in hand"
- "Pretenders to the strategy game"

# THE SCOOP

## Big Blue consulting

IBM Business Consulting Services (BCS) is the strategy consulting and integration arm of the giant tech company's Global Services consulting branch. On October 2, 2002, BCS was created when PwC Consulting was formally integrated into IBM, which had announced the $3.5 billion purchase of the consulting firm in August 2002. The move brought together more than 30,000 PwC Consulting employees with 30,000 IBM employees, many of whom were from IBM's Business Integration Services Unit.

## The split

In the summer of 2001, PricewaterhouseCoopers redubbed its consulting business PwC Consulting. The parent firm had originally planned the ultimate operational separation of its consulting arm from other business services at that time, but apparently did not feel that the move went far enough. In January 2002, PricewaterhouseCoopers announced it would file for a public offering of the consulting business. Press reports speculated that the IPO could be worth up to $9 billion, though the press was less admiring of PwC's decision to rebrand itself Monday.

## Monday, Monday

Soon after announcing its intent to separate, PwC Consulting announced a re-branding campaign under the brand name Monday. The new name was largely derided in the industry and media, so much so that it may have actually impacted the firm's efforts at independence. In any case, the firm announced in August 2002 that it would be taken over by IBM. The name Monday was tossed into the dustbin of business history.

## The new story

IBM BCS combines both PwC's management advisory capabilities and more traditional consulting legacy with IBM's tech-centric approach. At the same time, IBM Global Services has spent the last several years investing heavily in outsourcing services, and intends to use the new BCS unit to augment and expand its offerings by creating solutions that go beyond mere IT and infrastructure.

Heading up these efforts is Virginia Rometty (known to just about everybody as Ginni), an IBM veteran and rising star in the Global Services world. After the acquisition, Rometty took the bold step of naming three PwC regional directors as her immediate deputies, bypassing several senior GS people. And while more than 100 PwC partners were pushed out prior to the acquisition, more than 1,000 remain. IBM slashed salaries (by an average of 20 percent, with some executive partners losing twice that) to align them with its own compensation levels, but has also offered generous stock packages in return.

Rometty describes BCS as "a new kind of partner, one that can engage effectively with the senior business executives and the senior technology executives of an organization, and with every layer in between." The consultancy "collaborates actively with the other lines of business in IBM Global Services."

## Expansions and alliances

IBM BCS scored a big service victory in November 2002 for NSC Schlumberger, a French textile machinery manufacturer. The IBM product lifecycle management (PLM) system implemented in three factories is expected to cut product development time by 25 percent. The new processes are built around the Catia V5 and Smarteam software developed by Dassault Systemes, a French company specializing in PLM applications.

Outsourcing was big news at BCS in February 2003, when insiders leaked rumors of IBM's plans to open a business process outsourcing division in India to take advantage of the booming market in that country. According to an industry report quoted in *The Economic Times*, many notable consulting firms (including Accenture and the consulting branches of American Express and GE) realize 15 to 20 percent of their revenue from their Indian BPO operations.

That same month, IBM BCS announced an $8.8 million contract to migrate the systems and infrastructure of footwear and fashion designer Aldo Group Ltd. to a new operating environment. This was in addition to a January 2002 engagement where IBM took over the management of Aldo's IT needs.

## GETTING HIRED

Insiders at IBM BCS tell us that the hiring process is nothing out of the ordinary. "Two rounds of interviews, one with a direct manager and another senior company executive." The actual interview questions are "focused on actual achievements in previous positions and how those relate to the roles and responsibilities of the new position [at IBM]." A source says there is also considerable drilling "into character and work ethic." Another consultant describes an "all-day interview," starting with breakfast for all the interviewees. After an opening lecture, followed by interviews with four managers and a closing lunch, she "got a tentative offer via e-mail that afternoon."

# OUR SURVEY SAYS

## When worlds collide

It's clear from insider comments that things are still shaking out post-PwC merger. One source says she is "learning the culture again now that PwC is part of IBM. Just like when Price Waterhouse and Coopers & Lybrand merged." A colleague also claims to be "still learning the ropes and getting a feel for what the culture is like within IBM." One person refrains from comment, saying "I think it's hard for me to be honest since we are still in the process of merging our two cultures/firms."

The added uncertainty of a period of economic crisis appears to have bred discontent among the newly merged consultants. One source says, "Overall, [IBM BCS] is a good, solid company. However, the integration has caused culture clash, coupled with enormously challenging times." Another agrees, "The lifestyle has steadily deteriorated since the economic slowdown started in mid to late 2000. This has gone one step further with the acquisition of PwC by IBM, where they attempt to instill corporate standards in a consulting environment. For example, whereas in the PwC world you used to be able to earn four weeks of vacation in two years of service, you now have to work 10 years at IBM to achieve the same level." A third consultant says, "I think IBM BCS has done a good job of helping transition the legacy PwC consultants into the division. They are good at communicating company news via e-mail to employees."

## New forms, new supervisors

Likewise, there is still confusion and friction over the reporting chain. One source says that commenting on supervisors is "difficult since there are SO many levels of hierarchy here now." Another notes, "The red tape can be a little heavy."

More than a few respondents mentioned "a 7 percent salary cut in 2001 and no raise in 2002," putting at least two consultants at a salary level one described as "less than when I signed." Another insider says, "At PwC, lack of compensation was an issue – and I don't see it being rectified here." One insider states, "Bonuses and stock options were sold as a nice perk, but I have yet to see either in two years. Vacation used to be a perk but now, under IBM, it's a pipe dream since they installed IBM's corporate vacation calendar."

### Vaulable training

One consultant finds a lot of value in IBM's training offerings. "They offer a number of online training and information sessions about new and existing products and services on a regular basis." This is apparently a step up from what they had; a colleague says, "Limited emphasis had been placed on training resources [at PwC] over the last few years."

"The red tape can be a little heavy."

— *IBM BCS consultant*

# L.E.K. Consulting

28 State Street
16th Floor
Boston, MA 02109
Phone: (617) 951-9500
Fax: (617) 951-9392
www.lek.com

## LOCATIONS

**Boston, MA (HQ)**
15 offices worldwide

## PRACTICE AREAS

Business Strategy
Mergers and Acquisitions
Shareholder Value

## THE STATS

**Employer Type:** Private Company
**Chairman:** Iain Evans
**2002 Employees:** 505
**2001 Employees:** 450

## UPPERS

- "Coming into the same downtown office every day"
- International swap program
- "Short, fast-paced cases"

## DOWNERS

- "Banking hours at consultant pay"
- Comp time policy not so fab
- "Too much primary research"

## KEY COMPETITORS

Bain & Company
Boston Consulting Group
Marakon
McKinsey & Company

## EMPLOYMENT CONTACT

Carrie Brown
Phone: (617) 951-9500
Fax: (617) 951-9392
E-mail: boston_resumes@lek.com

## THE BUZZ
WHAT CONSULTANTS AT OTHER FIRMS ARE SAYING

- "Promotes good young people"
- "Low ball pricing"
- "Small and fragmented"
- "Excellent quality work"

# THE SCOOP

## Yesterday London, tomorrow the world

L.E.K. Consulting has expanded from a high-end boutique founded by three ex-Bain partners to one of the world's leading strategy consultancies. Founded in London in 1983, today the firm has more than 450 employees in 15 offices spread throughout Europe, North America, Australia and the Pacific Rim. L.E.K. derives 90 percent of its business from repeat clientele or client referrals.

In 1993, the firm (then known as the LEK Partnership) merged its U.S. operation with another consultancy, The Alcar Group, creating L.E.K. Consulting. Always seeking to boost its image and name recognition, L.E.K. has improved its marketing with efforts such as a self-branding study, which led to the adoption of a consistent worldwide name and logo, a comprehensive Web presence and the addition of periods in "L.E.K." ("We didn't want to be called 'lek,'" quips one insider.)

## Business lines times three

L.E.K.'s work is split along three business lines. The business strategy practice, which accounts for about 40 percent of the firm's work, assists management in developing high-level corporate and business strategies. Another 40 percent of the firm's workload is dedicated to its mergers and acquisitions practice. L.E.K. performs several services in this capacity, including acquisition strategy, acquisition screening, target due diligence and post-acquisition planning for both strategic and financial buyers. L.E.K. has been a player in more than 300 M&A transactions since 1994, with a total value of more than $300 billion. L.E.K.'s third area of expertise is shareholder value analysis, which accounts for approximately 20 percent of the firm's business. L.E.K.'s approach – founded on the principle that cash flow drives value – helps executives understand investor expectations, develop value-based corporate and business unit strategies, allocate capital and measure and reward performance.

Across these three business lines, areas of industry expertise include biotechnology, chemicals, life sciences, construction, energy, private equity, high technology, the Internet, medical devices, media and entertainment, telecommunications and utilities. Nevertheless, L.E.K. prides itself on being a firm of strategy experts, not industry experts, and places a premium on associates' ability to adapt, rather than their ability to absorb knowledge of a given industry. In all, L.E.K. claims 20 separate industry sectors as areas of expertise.

## The Boston/London axis

More than half of all L.E.K. consultants are based in the firm's Boston and London offices. The firm is known to be unusually flexible in its international assignments, and employees can switch easily between offices for either short-term "swaps" or permanent transfers, depending on preference. International swaps are typically six to 12 months in duration. More than a third of L.E.K. consultants have worked in two or more branch offices. L.E.K. consultants do travel frequently, but perhaps not as much as the industry standard. And the trips they do make tend to be short in duration – on average one day per workweek – with associates traveling even less.

The firm does not require its consultants to specialize in a particular practice area, though generally they gravitate to two or three preferred industries. Associates typically return to graduate school, while consultants – at least those with MBAs or advanced degrees – can expect to become managers within two to three years.

## It's all about image

L.E.K. has a reputation for working on the nuts-and-bolts, number-crunching level of a case, a fact it likes to emphasize when trying to differentiate itself from the competition. The company is also flexible and sensitive to clients' time requirements - L.E.K. averages significantly less time per assignment than other firms (and it expects its associates to be flexible as well). To enhance the firm's intellectual property and responsiveness to market needs, L.E.K. has established an advisory board of 12 renowned professionals from the academic and business worlds.

L.E.K. may showcase its no-nonsense image, but it knows how to recommend a more user-friendly appearance for its clients when necessary. A recent engagement included an analysis of New Zealand's sagging image and the economic consequences of failing to attract talented professionals to the city. The report, "Strategies for Building a Talented Nation," mentioned the virtues of a city-branding program (along the lines of New York's "Big Apple") to sell Auckland as a fun place to live, work and visit. Unlike consumer product advertising, L.E.K.'s Joanne Keestra noted that economic growth would fuel successful brand creation, not the other way around. Since L.E.K. has a branch office in Auckland, a successful implementation could only help the company.

## Extracurricular activities

L.E.K. publishes a quarterly newsletter, *Shareholder Value Insights*, written by VPs at the firm. It also collaborates with the *Wall Street Journal* on the annual Shareholder Scoreboard, a periodical that ranks companies by shareholder returns. L.E.K. publishes a similar scorecard in Australia, Thailand and New Zealand. The firm was a major sponsor of the winning yacht in the BT Global Challenge 2000/2001. (The boat, the LG Flatron, completed the race in June 2001.)

## Acquiring talent, not companies

In 2002, L.E.K. focused more on practice improvement than business expansion. Two notable hires joined the firm early that year. In January 2002, L.E.K. hired Ken Noonan to lead its life sciences practice in Europe and the U.K. Noonan's experience includes stints as Senior VP of Corporate Development at Applera; heading Booz Allen Hamilton's health practice in Europe; and starting a biotechnology practice for The Wilkerson Group (now owned by IBM). A month later, Kevin Mayer returned to the firm where he started in 1990. Mayer heads L.E.K.'s media and entertainment practice, a field where he gained expertise as CEO of Clear Channel Interactive and Playboy.com, as well as two executive positions at Disney.

In June 2002, Mark Kozin, president of the company's North America operation, was named to *Consulting Magazine*'s list of the Top 25 Most Influential Consultants. Kozin also runs L.E.K.'s life sciences practice in the U.S.

## Meetings of the minds

L.E.K. emphasizes the day-to-day involvement of its 68 senior partners, who spend 70 percent of their time in daily contact with the rest of the firm. L.E.K. also promotes senior and junior staff interaction through regular professional-development sessions that cover analytical concepts, management techniques and project reviews. An open-door policy at L.E.K. encourages sharing ideas and assistance, and also fosters mentor relationships between associates and consultants. (These mentors provide career support and guidance, as well as a forum for discussing "non-casework issues.")

# GETTING HIRED

## It's not all about DCF

Most L.E.K. employees describe the path to employment at the firm as "typical." According to a yearling analyst, the process includes "three rounds of interviews; one case-based, one fit, and one market sizing. As you progress through the rounds, you interview with more senior staff." A more experienced colleague notes, "Of late, there is increased pressure on personal referrals – low risk type recruits for better hits." A Chicago-based insider notes, "We recruit annually in the fall for full-time employees at a select number of prestigious undergraduate and MBA schools. We also recruit for summer positions at these same institutions in the winter." Some such schools include Dartmouth, Harvard, Wellesley, Berkeley, Northwestern and Stanford.

Former summer interns report excellent training and plenty of responsibility during their stints. A consultant from Boston tells us he was "put on a case day one. Had three days of training during the second week. There were social events throughout the summer, but the real focus of the program was giving the summer consultant the experience of a full-time consultant." A recent hire relates, "I was treated as any other full-time associate as far as workload. However, there were additional training sessions and wining and dining." Another consultant says L.E.K. was "very flexible with my return offer and I was given the option to choose my office."

One of the key things to know about getting a job or summer slot at L.E.K. is what the interviewers will want from you. A young manager warns, "Cases are strategy driven. Despite popular belief, we rarely ask [candidates] to do a DCF — this is merely a small part of what we do." A colleague says to expect "mostly quantitative cases and business judgment cases. Examples are estimations, or creating a business plan for an imaginary new business or product."

## Lingering at L.E.K.

Once you're hired, your employment isn't likely to be cut short. Unlike many firms, L.E.K. had no layoffs in 2002, and only "a handful" in 2001. Headcount is not apparently an issue; one insider says, "L.E.K. is relatively conservative about the number of people it brings in and there always seems to be enough work to go around." The general word is that there is no up-or-out policy at the firm. According to one senior analyst, "The policy is not up-or-out, but people are given hints if they don't have potential for further advancement."

But L.E.K. is no haven for slackers. One insider from Boston says, "Recently, the firm instituted what is known as the performance improvement plan (PIP). Employees who are determined to be below the class average are given three months to turn their performance around. After three months, performance is reevaluated and the decision is made to retain or fire the employee. In 2002, three or four people in the Boston office were PIPed and two were fired outright. In Los Angeles, the numbers were even greater. Eventually all of the people who were PIPed left the firm of their own volition, forced out by the stigma of being labeled an underperformer."

# OUR SURVEY SAYS

## Young, but no nursery school

A lot of our respondents from L.E.K. described the firm's culture as "young." One consultant elaborates on this vibrancy: "Most of the people at L.E.K. are very intelligent, clearly accomplished and highly motivated. This fosters a 'high output' culture, but this is buffered by a clear drive for work life balance. The U.S. offices have fewer than 100 employees each, giving each office its own sense of community." These small communities are apparently quite amicable. One consultant claims, "I can't think of one jerk at the firm."

It seems clear that those who don't fit at L.E.K. don't stay. A senior consultant tells us there is "little handholding and little institutionalized nurturing. Strong, aggressive, intellectually curious people thrive. People that do not have these attributes typically stumble along until either they give up or the firm does." A consultant says, "People realize it is time to move on if they don't get promoted within a reasonable timeframe." It's not about education; most of our insiders confirm that promotions are "based on merit." Another consultant says, "You can definitely become a consultant without an MBA and move throughout the firm."

## Pyramid talk

The love employees share at L.E.K. decreases further up the organizational pyramid, according to several sources. "There is a sharp disparity between the solid managers and poor managers," says one analyst, "and L.E.K. has a fair amount of both types."

A consultant offers this insight about supervisors: "They're generally open to suggestions and willing to chat about anything. But some of them have lackluster managerial skills." An insider from the same office calls the supervision "hit or miss. Half the consultants, managers and partners are excellent managers. A quarter are mediocre, and a quarter are notorious nightmares to work with."

Many consultants at L.E.K. have great things to say about supervisors. A consultant beams, "My immediate supervisors are amazing." "Leadership styles vary," says a California-based analyst, "but all are willing to mentor and work with younger members of the firm." A senior analyst from Chicago adds, "Although there is always the occasional bad apple, I have a lot of respect for most of my supervisors." Another insider says he is "impressed with and respects most consultants and all managers."

## A great place to train

On the job training is a reality of consulting, and many firms are reputed to rely on it to the exclusion of formal training. L.E.K. does not appear to have that problem – our contacts say they receive "excellent and ample training" in addition to learning from their work. An insider tells us, "Our training is best at the lower levels – we take professional development very seriously and have mandatory training. We have a full curriculum." Another adds, "Although most training occurs on the job, we do have a professional development program with frequent presentations, which has improved dramatically in the past few years." "L.E.K. seriously invests in professional development," claims one analyst. "You can expect one or two training seminars per month for the duration of your stay."

## A refuge for the travel-weary

Another place where L.E.K. breaks from the consulting pack is travel. One consulting insider reveals, "Travel is much less than most consulting firms. Although occasional projects are staffed at the client site, most work is done from L.E.K. offices. Therefore, travel is usually limited to meetings at client sites for presentations." A senior analyst claims, "I've traveled one day in five months." Another consultant opines, "As opposed to operational consulting where being on site might provide additional benefit, it appears that strategic and financial modeling can be completed more efficiently in the home office. This also has a very positive effect on work-life balance." A manager agrees, "Since our work is strategy-based, we can work from our offices – we don't often need to dig through client records."

But L.E.K.'s employees don't love the hours they work, 60 a week on average with two or more workload spikes every month. One seasoned consultant gripes, "Like most consulting firms, the hours here suck for many people. Too many late nights and weekends." A statistics-minded consultant outputs, "In a 21-22 day month, there are probably three to four days that exceed the average by more than one standard deviation." "It is not unusual to work 90-hour weeks at L.E.K.," adds another source. "The bittersweet thing is at least you won't be alone."

## The beach is closed

The issue of workload isn't moderated by non-staffed time spent on the beach – "There is no beach here," warns one analyst. According to another, "Even when 'on the beach,' we are actively doing client development projects for partners." She adds, "No associate ever has 'nothing to do' — we still log a 50 hour week minimum at the office." A third insider tells us, "Unstaffed professionals help out with client development projects." A senior consultant provides this advice: "At L.E.K., if you're on the beach it's because no one wants you on their case, and you should look around for another job."

## What about the pay?

One potential high point of working at L.E.K. is the profit sharing program, which is "awarded at the beginning of each year based on the firm's previous year performance. The range is 0-20 percent." In practice, of course, the benefit varies with the firm's fortunes. A Boston analyst says the share is "based on worldwide firm performance, and not individual office performance." Her colleague adds, "In 2000 profit share was 20 percent, 6.5 percent in 2001 and 5 percent of base salary in 2002." He continues, "In 2002, associate bonuses were eliminated."

A disgruntled analyst complains, "Compensation is a problem at L.E.K. They haven't bothered trying to keep up with other firms. Furthermore, they have the attitude that associates are 'lucky to have jobs.' The bonus situation is another sticking point for the L.E.K. consultants. "The compensation is very heavily weighted towards bonuses and profit sharing, both of which have been meager in recent years," claims one insider. An optimistic senior consultant believes "profit sharing probably will be 10 percent of base salary" in 2003.

# Cap Gemini Ernst & Young

Five Times Square
New York, NY 10036
Phone: (917) 934-8000
Fax: (917) 934-8001
www.cgey.com

## LOCATIONS

**New York, NY (U.S. HQ)**
**Paris (HQ)**
Offices in 30 countries

## PRACTICE AREAS

Advanced Development and
  Integration (Adaptive Security,
  Enterprise Application Integration,
  m-Commerce)
Customer Relationship Management
Extended Enterprise Applications/
  Enterprise Resource Planning
Finance and Employee Transformation
Network Infrastructure Solution
  (Adaptive Security)
Outsourcing (Applications
  Management, Business Process
  Management, and Infrastructure
  Management)
Strategy Consulting
Technology Consulting
Supply Chain

## THE STATS

**Employer Type:** Public Company
**Stock Symbol:** CAP.PA
**Stock Exchange:** Paris Bourse
**CEO:** Paul Hermelin
**Chairman:** Serge Kampf
**2002 Employees:** 53,000
**2001 Employees:** 55,000
**2002 Revenue:** 7.047 billion EUR
**2001 Revenue:** 7.0 billion EUR

## UPPERS

- Strong health care group
- Reasonable hours

## DOWNERS

- Shift in culture
- Managers IT types, not people-
  people

## KEY COMPETITORS

Accenture
A.T. Kearney
Deloitte Consulting

## EMPLOYMENT CONTACT

http://www.cgey.com/careers

## THE BUZZ
WHAT CONSULTANTS AT OTHER FIRMS ARE SAYING

- "Respected, good in health care"
- "Nice guys but no oomph"
- "Too big"
- "Good firm, workhorse"

# THE SCOOP

## Feathers in its cap

Operating from 30 countries around the world, Cap Gemini Ernst & Young (CGEY) provides IT outsourcing and consulting for some of the biggest global companies, along with governments and NGOs. Formed through the May 2000 merger of Ernst & Young's consulting unit and the French consultancy Cap Gemini, the firm employs more than 50,000 people worldwide.

## New in 2002

The firm called 2002 "a difficult year," and its financial results reflect that. Revenue dropped 16 percent, and income went from a gain of EUR 152 million to a loss of EUR 514 million. The company also shrunk its workforce between 2001 and 2002, laying off around 5,100 workers, about 9 percent of its staff.

Though the year was tough, it also underlined a shift in strategy for the firm. The company continues to pursue a major three-year restructuring plan, which it announced in June 2002. First, it will organize its business into four areas: consulting, technology, outsourcing, and local professional services. Second, it will streamline operating structures. Third, it will launch a sales assault on "the fastest-growing market segments." Fourth, it will speed up "the industrialization of its delivery capacity."

## Outsourcing looking up

Outsourcing is a growing revenue stream for CGEY. Outsourcing represented 27 percent of the company's 2002 revenue, versus 21 percent in 2001. Consulting and Systems Integration make up 73 percent of revenue, down from 79 percent the year before. The company is making a push in the Health and Public Services sector. The relatively robust health care sector contributes 26 percent of CGEY revenue, versus 16 percent in 2001. Life sciences made up 7 percent of 2002 business, versus 6 percent in 2001; Telecom dropped to 13 percent from 18 percent; and Financial Services dropped from 15 percent to 17 percent.

## Telecom tyros

In December 2000, CGEY and Cisco Systems formalized their March 2000 agreement by launching a new industry practice, Cap Gemini Ernst & Young

Telecom Media Networks. The practice works under Cap Gemini Ernst & Young auspices, providing software and other strategic telecommunications technology solutions to over 150 clients. Its work in this arena won the TeleStrategies Billing World 2002 Excellence Award for Integration Project of the Year. The specific project was for overhauling and integrating Nextel's business networks.

### Been 'round the world

A look at some of CGEY's recent projects indicates the firm's global scope. It's working on SAP outsourcing for Mölnlycke Health Care, giving IT support to government councils in five New South Wales, Australia locations; providing outsourcing for the Steilmann Group, a German company; doing software implementation for HBOS, a large UK financial-services company; making suggestions to Phoenix Children's Hospital on how to become profitable again; and is providing IT outsourcing for a number of GE's European businesses.

### Back to school (No basketweaving majors here!)

CGEY has an educational wing, called, not surprisingly, Cap Gemini Ernst & Young University. Its courses are offered to clients and employees, and include on-campus programs (the main campus is in Béhoust, France), as well as distance-learning channels. The University also publishes *Focus*, CGEY's online magazine about business and technology.

## GETTING HIRED

Cap Gemini Ernst & Young typically recruits on campus at a mere handful of top business and undergraduate schools, and also accepts applicants through "a detailed application form" through the Internet. "Selectivity depends on what service line and what industry you're interested in."

There are two rounds of interviews, first with "recently promoted graduates from the development community and then a Vice President," says one source; another consultant says his interviews were "with managers or above and at least one VP in the second round."

Insiders suggest highlighting technical skills during interviews: "The hiring focus is now on technical skills (as announced in February 2003). Interview content can vary – one source says, "The main questions I remember are what university you were at, and do you mind travel." Some report having been given case studies, while others say they did not-"these are at the discretion of the interviewer and are typically real world scenarios that the individual has experienced," notes one CGEY-er.

After the interview, "interviewers complete a detailed form regarding the interviewee, and a group discussion is made over each candidate. Many times, a decision is made at that time."

# OUR SURVEY SAYS

## Identity mix

With offices all over the world, different practices and a recent merger, Cap Gemini Ernst & Young's culture is hardly uniform, our sources say. "The original Cap Gemini culture harnesses smart casual dress and an eight-hour workday in a very male-dominated culture," notes one source. Another consultant says, "After the merger with Cap Gemini, the organization became obsessed with internal functions and placed its best people on these functions rather than client or market-facing opportunities. The level of this internal focus and lack of risk taking meant that senior executives are unable to make decisions with 'approval' from elsewhere. This slows down the organization's ability to respond to the market."

There seems to be a move toward pure IT offerings, which traditional management consultants don't seem to be too thrilled about. "The corporate culture is that of an IT integrator, which is very difficult to bear when you are a management consultant," says one consultant. "Assignments are more and more IT-oriented." Especially in France, notes one source, "CGEY is essentially an IT integrator, so the culture and the organization is not the culture of a consultancy."

While there seems to be a sense of "insecurity" around CGEY these days, some find it "friendly and competitive." One U.S.-based source remarks, "Being a French-owned company has been a challenge this year." In general, though, insiders seem to agree that there is no defined culture – as one consultant says, it's "still trying to find an identity post-acquisition." The layoffs of about 5,000 employees probably didn't help matters much. However, the health care group is growing, and, says an insider, managed to avoid layoffs: " Most layoffs were in telecom and financial services. Health care appears to be very strong, with only the typical fat cutting."

## La vie en France

The "several offices in Paris" will "soon be together in the same tower." The neighborhood is called La Défense, "which is kind of the French Manhattan." Though the offices are "not as beautiful as McKinsey's office – not even as good as KPMG (which is also located at La Défense)," the offices are "mostly open space, though some managers have their own offices." An Atlanta source provides a similar assessment of his office: "I'm not there too often, but it is adequate and in a good location in town."

## Promotion commotion

CGEY has a tenure-based system regarding promotion. "The culture is the exact opposite of the traditional "up or out" policy: no promotion before several years, a very small salary increase (if any)," says one source. Once you're in the company, the way to be promoted, one consultant says, is "you must network and be identifiable by many people. An effort both internally and externally must be made." Also, "a good relationship with your internal career counselor may be vital to your promotion and raise."

An insider provides this in-depth look: "There are two kinds of reviews. The first one is called 'project evaluation' and is made by the project manager. He evaluates the performance of the consultant on a specific client engagement when the engagement is completed. The second review is made at the end of the year and has broader perspective: your performance throughout the year, salary increase, promotion. The consultant is supposed to be guided by a mentor."

## Health is happiness

Consultants had varying opinions on life at the firm. Regarding managers, one found that there was a "strong team in health care." Training, meanwhile, is reportedly "getting better as Cap Gemini continues to split from E&Y services."

Charity work "is 'encouraged,' so to speak." What does that mean? Well, there are some "locally driven" efforts, "while others are national. It can range from family fundraisers for a local trauma center to the national United Way campaigns. It's very much encouraged and organized, but not forced."

## Salary report

Salary increases "are pretty rare and the increase is very small (2 to 3 percent)," says one consultant. However, "after two years at CGEY consultants can generally join a competitor for a 50 percent increase." In addition to these salary schemes, there is limited profit-sharing, which one consultant describes as "paltry."

Benefits include accidental death/dismemberment policies, long-term disability, tuition reimbursement, an employee assistance program, laptop computers, cell phones, an employee referral bonus, and, in some offices, free snacks and drinks.

## Fly away

Since the merger, one source reports, "hours are longer and the working life is much more intense and driven by competition." True though that may be, another source reports, "I have had no problem balancing my work and personal life." Consultants at CGEY are rarely on the beach, and have longish work hours of about 50 a week. The workload spikes "quite a bit – you're usually challenged on multiple deadlines with high volume."

CGEY consultants should also expect a fair amount of travel, which is often arranged on a "3-4-5 schedule. Three nights away, four days [away], and you work for the client all five."

# Towers Perrin

One Stamford Plaza
263 Tresser Blvd.
Stamford, CT 06089
Phone: (203) 326-5400
Fax: (203) 326-5499
www.towersperrin.com

## LOCATIONS

**Stamford, CT (HQ)**
78 offices worldwide

## PRACTICE AREAS

**Towers Perrin:**
Benefit Administration Solutions
Change Management
Communication
Executive Compensation
Global Resources Group
Health & Welfare
HR Delivery Service
Mergers, Acquisitions &
   Restructuring
Organization & Employee Research
Rewards & Performance Management
Retirement

**Tillinghast-Towers Perrin:**
Actuarial and Management
Consulting

**Towers Perrin Reinsurance:**
Reinsurance

## THE STATS

**Employer Type:** Private Company
**CEO (or other title):** Mark V. Mactas
**2002 Employees:** 9,009
**2001 Employees:** 9,000
**2002 Revenue:** $1.44 billion
**2001 Revenue:** $1.47 billion

## UPPERS

- Travel minimal
- Flexible hours and work
  arrangements available

## DOWNERS

- Salaries not up to par
- Employees fairly homogenous

## KEY COMPETITORS

Cap Gemini Ernst & Young
Hay Group
Hewitt Associates
IBM BCS
Mercer Human Resource Consulting
Mercer Management Consulting
Watson Wyatt Worldwide

## EMPLOYMENT CONTACT

E-mail: careers@towers.com

## THE BUZZ
WHAT CONSULTANTS AT OTHER FIRMS ARE SAYING

- "Head-hunting gurus"
- "Who cut my wages?"
- "Strong in insurance"
- "Great HR"

# THE SCOOP

## House of HR

Towers Perrin (TP) is an old hand at human resources consulting, with 70 years of experience under its belt – not to mention 9,000 employees and 78 offices in 23 countries. The company handles three-quarters of the Fortune 1000, along with nonprofits, governments, educational concerns and private companies.

Towers is divided into three areas: Towers Perrin deals with human resources matters (like retirement programs, health benefits, administration, communications, or executive compensation); Tillinghast-Towers Perrin focuses on risk management and actuarial work, and most of its clients are finance or insurance firms; and Towers Perrin Reinsurance, predictably, works on reinsurance.

## A long history

In 1934, four Philadelphians started Towers, Perrin, Forster & Crosby, which specialized in reinsurance and employee benefits consulting. By the 1960s, the firm had a national presence, and was expanding internationally by the 1970s. In 1987, the name was changed to Towers Perrin.

## Shopping spree

The company has been on an acquisition binge since the 1990s, swallowing up several niche consulting firms. Two recent purchases include Delphi Consultants (February 2003), a firm that implements SAP software and Denis M. Clayton & Co. (November 2002), a British broker that specializes in insurance and reinsurance. Also in 2002, TP strengthened partnerships with BrassRing, an e-recruitment software company, and Authoria, an HR software firm. In 2001, the company joined with J.P. Morgan/American Century to combine TP's defined-benefit administration and health/welfare services with Morgan's defined-contribution and investing know-how.

## Library dwellers

Towers Perrin publishes surveys, special reports, studies, and *Towers Perrin Monitor* (a monthly benefits issues newsletter for clients) and *Perspectives* (occasional opinionated dispatches on recent events). The publications look at trends in benefits, compensation, HR management, financial services, risk management, pension funds, health care and executive compensation in countries where Towers has offices. The firm conducts surveys and researches compensation and benefits data to help its own clients make informed decisions. TP also publishes an almost-daily news digest, accessible on its web site, that summarizes news and developments affecting HR policy and strategy.

Books that TP has published recently include *Web-Based Human Resources,* a how-to book on implementing and maximizing HR software and hardware; and *Making Mergers Work*, which covers HR's role when a company is undergoing a merger. Other publications include shorter, research-heavy reports, often based on surveys that TP conducts. Titles include "Survival: Can Rebranding Save Your Organization?" and "Perspectives on Retirement Financial Management," a case study on how to handle pension plans.

# GETTING HIRED

## Picky, picky

Towers posts jobs online and recruits at universities (the 75 it visits are listed on its careers site). However, Towers Perrin can be picky. "In San Francisco, we only look at Berkeley and Stanford. It varies by line of business – executive compensation, change management, etc. tend to recruit at better (i.e., Ivy or equivalent) schools," says one source. Another consultant notes, "I went to a small liberal arts school and ended up here through an alumni contact who works here and had to fight very hard to get me an interview. Top performers can come from many places, and TP should be more willing to review nontraditional candidates."

Towers Perrin contacts candidates to set up interviews – on campus if Towers reps are visiting, via phone if not. "Undergraduates and grad students are hired through on-campus recruiting throughout the year, and recruiting is centralized for some lines of business," notes an insider. This is a behavioral interview, discussing interests and qualifications. The second round involves a day-long sojourn to a local office. Depending on the position, three types of interviews might be conducted: experiential interviews (who you are and what you've done), hypothetical-situation interviews (how you would respond in various working situations) and case studies (you'll be asked what factors the client should consider, what facts you'll need, alternative approaches, your evaluation and prescription, and potential obstacles). Fittingly for an HR specialist, Towers Perrin's web site is quite transparent about the interview process and the qualities new hires should have (teamwork, persistence and integrity rank high).

In total, candidates can expect four to six interviews. One candidate who received a job offer from TP describes the interview process: "I was invited to an interview process that started at 3 p.m. on a Thursday. They split the [candidates] into two groups of six. Each group did the same things but in a different order. First, we were given an introductory presentation about the company, benefits, culture, and so on. Then we took a tour of the building. We had to take two tests – one was a visualization test (seeing if numbers were the same) and the other was a graphical data test (analyzing charts). I interviewed with two people. Some of the questions were: How do you prioritize your work? Describe a time when you had to handle a difficult situation with another employee and how did you handle it?" Case questions are also used, insiders say. Junior-level candidates interview with all levels of consultants, while mid- to senior-level consultants will meet only with senior employees.

TP does offer summer internships, which one former intern describes as "a very good experience that enabled me to learn about the benefits industry and improved my technical skills." The intern package for summer 2003 in Dallas, according to one source, is $4,800 per month.

# OUR SURVEY SAYS

## Life in the Tower

Upsides of Towers Perrin, one source says, include "fairly good job security, flexible hours and an autonomous work environment." It's said to be a "fast-paced firm filled with very intelligent people, though sometimes people can forget that work can be fun or should be fun." Insiders like their supervisors: "You learn your job from very intelligent and capable people but sometimes their communication skills may not be the best," says one consultant.

The company is involved in community service, including volunteer projects with "paid leave to conduct volunteer work," "regional community involvement" and "supporting charities and employees who are raising money for charities like cancer, heart association, etc."

TP gets high marks for diversity regarding women. However, regarding minorities, "Towers Perrin is not diverse," assesses one employee.

## Homebodies

Travel is quite minimal at TP, and many consultants don't travel at all, though "travel requirements vary depending on line of business." Agrees another consultant, "Work/life balance is very different for everyone." Hours range from 40 to 50 hours a week, our sources report, and workload "spikes pretty frequently."

## Healthy pets in Chicago

The quality of offices "varies," though "offices in larger markets – New York, San Francisco, Boston, London – tend to be very nice." Likewise, perks vary from office to office. Most employees get laptops, and some get cell phones. San Francisco denizens get gym discounts and sports/theater tickets, while Chicago employees get pet insurance and free snacks.

## Salary spasms

One source of complaint for TP employees is compensation. "TP pays at the 50th percentile. They can try to be cheap," says one consultant. "Pay is on the lower side, but has improved with new compensation strategy rollout," notes another insider. The company should "pay top performers what they are worth (at least in the middle of the pay range)," says a source. The firm "used to provide profit sharing" but does not currently.

## Fast tracks

Since the "firm is not really up-or-out, high performers can advance quickly, even into MBA level positions without a graduate degree." "Your billable hours and knowledge get you through the P1-P4 levels. Your actuarial exam progression or post-graduate degree plus industry knowledge get you to the P5 (bonus eligible) level and above (P6) is consultant," reports another consultant.

"Work/life balance is very different for everyone."

— *Towers Perrin consultant*

# BearingPoint

1676 International Drive
McLean, VA 22102
Phone: (703) 747-3000
Fax: (703) 747-8500
www.bearingpoint.com

## LOCATIONS

**McLean, VA (HQ)**
162 offices worldwide

## PRACTICE AREAS

Broadband Solution Centers
Customer Relationship Management
Emerging Technology – Mobile
  Solutions
Enterprise Solutions
Government, Education and Health
  Care Solutions
Homeland Security
Infrastructure Solutions
Integration Services
Managed Services
Strategy & Business Process
  Services
Supply Chain Management

## THE STATS

**Employer Type:** Public Company
**Stock Symbol:** BE
**Stock Exchange:** NYSE
**CEO:** Rand Blazer
**2002 Employees:** 9,300
**2001 Employees:** 10,000
**2002 Revenue:** $2.37 billion
**2001 Revenue:** $2.86 billion

## UPPERS

- "Young professional interaction"
- "Great pay and fringe benefits"
- Reasonable office hours
- Philanthropic efforts

## DOWNERS

- "Lack of respect, caring, loyalty to employees"
- Training lacking
- Career path unclear
- "The focus on making numbers

## KEY COMPETITORS

Accenture
Cap Gemini Ernst & Young
Deloitte Consulting
IBM Global Services

## EMPLOYMENT CONTACT

Sean Huurman
Director of Recruiting, America
E-mail:
us-consultrecops@bearingpoint.net

## THE BUZZ
WHAT CONSULTANTS AT OTHER FIRMS ARE SAYING

- "Growing, leading edge"
- "Name is a branding disaster"
- "Name in health care, pharma"
- "Old wine in new bottle"

# THE SCOOP

## New name, same skills

BearingPoint may have a newish name (which, if you're wondering, refers to "setting direction to an end point," according to the company) but it retains the skills and services that made KPMG a true Big Five consulting firm. Spun off from Big Five firm KPMG, LLP in January 2000, BearingPoint (which until October 2002 was known as KPMG Consulting) has been making a name for itself ever since, forming new alliances to help grow the business-systems integration area. The firm, rebrand or no, still offers consulting for financial services, consumer and industrial markets, communications and content, high tech and public services. BearingPoint boasts more than 17,000 employees worldwide.

## A bit of history

KPMG Consulting was established as a separate company in August 1999. The unit was also buoyed by Cisco System's $1 billion investment that year. Cisco, which now owns a 10 percent stake in BearingPoint, was one of the many beneficiaries of the February 2001 public offering. In May 2000, KPMG Consulting became the first Big Five (now Big Four) consulting firm to file for an IPO. KPMG LLP no longer holds a stake in BearingPoint; with the IPO, the company sold off its entire investment.

## Taking wing

BearingPoint continues to go international. The IPO included operations in the United States and 15 other countries (Canada, Argentina, Brazil, Mexico, Colombia, Costa Rica, Guatemala, Ireland, Israel, Japan, New Zealand, Nicaragua, Peru, South Korea and Venezuela). The company has since expanded by acquiring international consulting practices from KPMG International in Australia as well as market rights in parts of Greater China. In June 2002, it announced an agreement to acquire KPMG Consulting AG, the German, Swiss and Austrian consulting practices of KPM. The acquisitions were all closed successfully by October 2002.

The firm's boldest, and perhaps most controversial, move came in May 2002, when it signed a letter of intent to acquire most of Andersen's global consulting operations (including those in the United States) in a deal reportedly worth up to $284 million. With the deal, the firm increased its global workforce to more than 16,000 employees. By June, the firm had completed the acquisitions of the independent consulting units of Andersen Worldwide in Australia, Brazil, China, Finland, France, Hong Kong, Japan, Korea, Peru, Singapore, Spain, Sweden and Switzerland, and had hired approximately 1,600 former Andersen Business Consulting employees in the United States.

## Say my (new) name

On October 3, 2002, KPMG Consulting became BearingPoint, a switch that took effect immediately and with impressive deftness – new e-mail addresses, business cards and letterhead were available that same day. The switch follows a trend among consulting firms with Big Five accounting backgrounds: Deloitte Consulting toyed with the idea of becoming Braxton Associates before opting against the change in April 2003, and PwC Consulting briefly renamed itself Monday before being acquired by IBM in August 2002. BearingPoint reports that the name resulted from a worldwide poll of employees, as well as a private branding firm, and was chosen from among 550 possibilities. No word as to the runners-up.

## Shifting bearings

Since (or in spite of) the name change, BearingPoint's business has been strong, despite a few notable bumps along the way. Early in November 2002, CFO Robert Lamb Jr. left the company for an equivalent position at FleetBoston Financial, his prior employer. In December 2002, the firm announced a restructuring of operations in Germany, Austria and Switzerland (formerly KPMG AG) that included a workforce reduction of 700 people; according to the press release, the downsizing and related expenses had been accounted for in the KPMG AG acquisition deal. A separate round of layoffs, sparked by excess capacity, came in January 2003, when between 450 and 500 consultants in North America and the Asia Pacific region got their walking papers.

## New faces

BearingPoint has taken on some new high-level employees in 2003. Met by the BearingPoint welcome wagon in April 2003 was Robert Falcone, who joined the firm as CFO and executive vice president. Falcone was formerly CFO at Nike. Two new board members – Albert Lord, CEO of Sallie Mae, and J. Terry Strange, the former vice chairman of KPMG LLP, joined BearingPoint's board of directors in early 2003, raising the number on that board from six to eight.

## Rebuilding the world

In January 2003, BearingPoint delivered a new financial management system to the government of Afghanistan, helping the country to rebuild in the post-Taliban era. Completion of this $4 million contract provides core processes and trained personnel to enable Afghanistan to track the more than $4 billion in international aid it is expected to receive. In March 2003, the company announced a second contract award with Afghanistan, a three year, $39.9 million contract from the United States Agency for International Development (USAID) to deliver an economic reform program in that country.

Also in January 2003, the firm won an $8.5 million contract with Hyundai Motor Company to implement SAP R/3 software at a new plant in Montgomery, Ala., and got the go-ahead from the U.S. Department of Defense to proceed with the third phase of a security project the firm had begun in 2002.

In February 2003, BearingPoint picked up a $24 million contract from the government of Ireland. The project involves the modernization the country's processes and technologies for handling passport applications. The firm also picked up a new principal: Christopher Formant joined BearingPoint as executive vice president for financial services.

## GETTING HIRED

## Patronage

The firm maintains a searchable job system, which includes a "career network" allowing registered candidates to receive e-mail notification of new positions that match their interests. One BearingPoint insider believes the firm "uses resumes of available candidates to win work, then looks to hire them." Another suggests, "The best way to get in is through a direct recommendation for a specific project by someone who is well respected by the manager of that project."

Hiring is "generally through referrals," according to one source. Another insider notes, "The company does not actively recruit at schools." Although some respondents mention a "hiring freeze," the firm says it continues to recruit for a "number of positions."

# OUR SURVEY SAYS

## Bearing it

There are many good points to working at BearingPoint – one source describes the culture as "very competitive with a large emphasis on teamwork" – but some insiders express dissatisfaction with the firm. Much of it centers on "the move from a partnership model to an American-owned public entity," as one puts it. He continues, "The senior leadership seems to be more interested in pleasing the 'shareholders' rather than its employees or clients." Another source says the firm "has gone from a partnership to a 'corporate.' For example, I don't believe anyone would make any effort to even contact me if I were to put in my papers – though I am one of the top earners [in my specialty]."

Not surprisingly, this has had an effect on the atmosphere. "I don't think that we have a culture, which is why our turnover rate is so high," says one insider. He continues, "There is a lack of loyalty from management to staff and from staff to management." Another says the problems have crept into the compensation and promotion system. He wants BearingPoint to be "truthful with employees – link rewards to the annual performance evaluation process. For example, last year the annual salary reviews and decisions on rewards were completed prior to the completion of the performance evaluation process."

## Moving up the food chain

Regarding promotions, we hear from one source, "Although [the firm is] not strictly up-or-out, one is expected to continue to progress in order to grow as a consultant to improve yourself and the company. The up-or-out philosophy holds truer for management positions." Another says, "the regular promotion time is two years to the next level, with six initial levels until reaching senior management. At that point it is sales-based."

## Online training

One respondent tells us that BearingPoint has "an online Learning Management System where you can enroll for anything that catches your fancy." However, he continues, there are "no real training facilities – I was asked to manage with available online training, rather than attend a one-off session for a new product that I am actually implementing." A colleague notes that training is the "first thing to go when money is tight." One person points out, "Earning consultants don't have much opportunity to attend technology classes at the office during the week."

## Giving back

Insiders mention a number of social concerns that BearingPoint helps. One consultant says, "The firm sponsors many community events around where our clients and offices are located." Another adds, "We participate in and sponsor numerous events for the [local] Air Force base, Boys/Girls Clubs of America, Special Olympics and numerous other charities through our company's own foundation."

## Travel-lite

Travel requirements are generally light. One insider notes, "Some consultants are on long-term projects in other cities requiring them to travel four to five days a week for eight to 18 months. However, in the public services line of business, the majority of consultants work out of their home city and travel only when needed for their specific projects (site visits, focus groups, interviews in other cities, etc.)." Another relates, "I work physically away from my home office, but in close proximity (less than 10 miles)."

In summation, one consultant states, "The firm is great for people who are looking to advance in the consulting world and have the attitude to succeed. It is hard to tell if you like the business or not until you become ingrained in it."

# DiamondCluster International Inc.

Suite 3000
John Hancock Center
875 N. Michigan Avenue
Chicago, IL 60611
Phone: (312) 255-5000
Fax: (312) 255-6000
www.diamondcluster.com

## LOCATIONS

Chicago, IL (HQ)
11 offices worldwide

## PRACTICE AREAS

**Growth:**
Market Penetration • New Business Development • New Growth

**Operations:**
Execution Excellence • Operations Strategy • Turnaround Management

**Technology:**
Architecture Assessment and Strategy • IT Assessment and Strategy • IT Portfolio Assessment and Strategy • Outsourcing Advisory • Security Assessment and Strategy • Technology Program Management

## THE STATS

**Employer Type:** Public Company
**Stock Symbol:** DTPI
**Stock Exchange:** Nasdaq
**Chairman and CEO:** Melvyn E. (Mel) Bergstein
**2002 Employees:** 843
**2001 Employees:** 1,141
**2002 Revenue:** $203 million
**2001 Revenue:** $259.3 million

## UPPERS

• "Greater responsibility on smaller teams"
• International environment
• "It feels like a big family"

## DOWNERS

• Lack of formal training
• Lots of travel required
• "The economy and our susceptibility to it"

## KEY COMPETITORS

Accenture
Booz Allen Hamilton
Boston Consulting Group
McKinsey

## EMPLOYMENT CONTACT

www.diamondcluster.com/careers

## THE BUZZ
WHAT CONSULTANTS AT OTHER FIRMS ARE SAYING

• "Rising star"
• "Cutting edge, mindshare"
• "All travel, all the time"
• "Too techy - no strategic vision"

# THE SCOOP

## A multifaceted gem

DiamondCluster International (as it's known) is a management consulting firm that helps its clients develop and implement growth strategies, improve operations, and capitalize on technology. DiamondCluster is headquartered in Chicago, with offices across Europe, North America and South America.

The firm was established in 2000 through the combination of Diamond Technology Partners, founded in 1994, and Cluster Consulting, founded in 1993. DiamondCluster's 600 consultants currently serve Global 2000 clients in such industries as financial services, consumer and industrial products and services, telecommunications and energy, health care and insurance, as well as public sector organizations. The firm works in both strategy and IT consulting.

## A virtually great idea

Consultants in North America live in locations of their choice (though undergraduate hires must reside in Chicago for two years). DiamondCluster consultants keep in touch in person through regular two-day meetings called "All-Hands." The All-Hands meetings were temporarily suspended but are now held quarterly.

## A really killer app

A key source of exposure for DiamondCluster is the renowned *Unleashing the Killer App*, a bestseller by fellow Chunka Mui and e-commerce expert Larry Downes. The book exhorts its readers to follow seemingly counterintuitive wisdom like "cannibalize your markets" and "give away as much information as you can." In December 2000, Mui was recognized by *CIO* magazine as one of the "Ten Masters of the New Economy."

Other sources of (good) exposure for the firm are the Diamond Fellows, a network of experts who provide clients with a broad range of perspectives on engagements and interactions throughout the year.

## Raising intellectual capital

As a way of boosting its output of intellectual capital even further, DiamondCluster has established a number of study centers and joint ventures devoted to researching various aspects of the high-tech industry. In September 2001, the firm opened the Chicago-based Center for Technology Innovation, a conceptual laboratory where the company develops ways to help clients better integrate high-tech methodologies. The firm also operates the Center for Market Leadership, based in Boston, which examines the drives behind market dominance. And in March 2002, it announced the first round of funding for DevLab One, a joint venture with Motorola and Northwestern University's Information Technology Development Laboratory that will turn University-developed wireless solutions into market-ready products. DiamondCluster also hosts "The Exchange," a forum of C-level executives that explores ways of succeeding in a technology-transformed marketplace.

## Singing an e-business tune

During the dot-com boom, DiamondCluster (and, before November 2000, Diamond Technology Partners) swam with the e-business flow, enjoying significant revenue growth and increased business. Revenues for fiscal year 2001 were up 90 percent over the previous year – to $259.3 million – thanks to a surge of new clients and the Cluster merger. In February 2000, the firm struck an alliance with the Big Three automakers to combine their B2B exchange initiatives into one online marketplace. And in April 2000, the firm teamed with Morgan Stanley Dean Witter and Silgen Holdings to start a new company, Packtion, a B2B marketplace for the global packaging industry.

## Diamond in the rough

By 2001, however, DiamondCluster was beginning to feel the pain of the economic slowdown, exacerbated by the popping of the dot-com bubble – its bread and butter at the time. Despite CEO Mel Bergstein's direction to eschew doing equity work for dot-coms, a tactic that provided real income and protected DiamondCluster against the crash, the company's earnings still plunged. The watchword at the company, as put forth by Bergstein, was "preserve our assets – our people, our client relationships and our intellectual capital."

In early 2001, DiamondCluster announced a staff-wide 10 percent pay cut, with executives giving up an extra 5 percent. But it wasn't enough; in March 2001, the firm laid off 25 non-consultant employees, and in July it furloughed 200 consultants – one-fifth of its total – for six months at 35 percent of their salaries, with benefits. Consultants were also given the opportunity of a severance package, which a number of them took.

## Saving our assets

In October 2001, DiamondCluster extended its furloughs for another six months and reduced compensation for furloughed employees to 25 percent. The company also withdrew most of the outstanding job offers it had made to graduating college students. In January 2002, Bergstein announced that another 50 to 75 consultants might be furloughed later that year. To help save costs, DiamondCluster folded its journal *Context* in December 2002, citing poor ad revenue and a need to refocus operations.

Aside from the drop in the market, a number of internal factors were said to have exacerbated the company's financial situation, including overstaffing, residual difficulties integrating Cluster personnel, poor implementation of DCI's strategy practice and problems with closing a number of important deals. Nonetheless, Diamond Cluster has been lauded for its employee-friendly approach to the economic downturn, putting off staff reductions as long as possible, even at the expense of profits.

## Sparkles of hope

Things have begun to turn around for DiamondCluster. An encouraging sign was the January 2002 return of Michael Palmer, former partner and founding member. By the summer of 2002, all but 25 of the furloughed consultants in North America had returned to active duty. Bergstein predicted that their European and Latin American counterparts would soon come in out of the cold once regional business picked up – as the engagement announced in January 2003 with Colombia Movil, Colombia's third largest wireless telecom company, indicates.

# GETTING HIRED

## MBAs-only club

Insiders at DiamondCluster report "an active campus recruiting program and a pretty active experienced hire program." While the firm "used to recruit at nearly 20 schools and will most likely do so again sometime," consultants claim that campus recruiting in the U.S. has been cut to less than half that. The schools most commonly named by respondents include Kellogg, the University of Chicago, Wharton, Sloan and Michigan. Top schools in Europe and Latin America also receive visits.

DiamondCluster consultants name a few undergraduate institutions where the firm has been known to recruit, but they advise against getting your hopes up if you try that route. DiamondCluster insiders claim that only MBAs are being considered for campus recruitment. However, as of January 2003, the firm has begun to recruit again at some select undergraduate institutions.

## The process

Applicants to DiamondCluster should expect "standard MBA hiring [with] several rounds of case and behavioral interviews." One consultant tersely describes the process (and likely some of his co-workers): "Tough. Efficient. Short." Resumes are "pre-screened" by the firm's consultants, and interviews are "held by [the] consultants themselves." One DiamondCluster consultant gets specific: "Three first round interviews with experienced consultants (Senior Consultants upwards). Two second round interviews with Partners. Offer within a week of the interviews." Other insiders report very little variation from this model, with two or three rounds of meetings consisting of four or five interviews in total.

Case studies are definitely part of DiamondCluster's evaluation process. The types of questions range from brainteasers all the way to full-blown cases based on actual previous firm engagements. An insider from Chicago says, "Most questions are based on the interviewer's personal experience." A colleague from Boston concurs, stating that interview questions are "based on actual practice cases." Some generic examples provided by insiders include: "Sketch a possible infrastructure architecture for an on-line music retailer"; "Calculate the number of planes in the world in three different ways"; and "Estimate the business potential of opening a hamburger POS in the neighborhood where our office is located."

A more specific case would be "You've been selected to become the Project Manager of a project that is overdue and over budget. Your task is to bring it to the finish line as soon as possible. What immediate steps will you take? What long-term steps will you take? What do you envision being your key obstacles to your success?"

A senior consultant on the West Coast shares his story: "It was summer 1999 and I commuted from Los Angeles to Chicago for a very interesting e-commerce project. Our client was the national leader in its industry and we put together a unique physical/virtual shopping experience from idea through actual creation. It was groundbreaking and received some national exposure." A European colleague describes the summer program as "Excellent, it was the reason I joined the firm." A 2001 graduate from Sloan's MBA program calls the summer program "Very fun –

during the heady dot-com days. We had lots of exposure to senior execs and the other interns were just great." The contact adds, "I'd love to be a summer associate again!"

# OUR SURVEY SAYS

## Unbreakable

The people at DiamondCluster had some very insightful comments about their corporate culture. A Chicago-based analyst says, "Desire to learn and self-motivation are valued more than anything else. People work together and hang out together at night – but this is all by choice, as opposed to mandatory socializing done by other firms." However, a colleague feels the company lost something when Diamond and Cluster became DiamondCluster. "We conducted a merger that diluted two very strong cultures into a confusing new outlook."

One source of concern in every office is the world economic crisis, which seems to have hit the consulting industry especially hard. One insider opines, "The firm has a very exciting, diverse culture. However, due to the current climate of the economy, the culture of the firm has declined." Despite this, there is considerable optimism at DiamondCluster, at least as one of the partners sees it. "With the economy as bad as it's been for as long as it has, it is remarkable how close knit the firm still feels," he says. "People genuinely look forward to seeing each other at the quarterly All-Hands Meetings, which resumed in January after a two-year hiatus." He continues, "Whereas I thought the environment might be somewhat somber, spirits were high, and everyone was genuinely happy to be together again." A senior analyst takes a broad view: "As demand has increased throughout 2002, the DiamondCluster culture has devolved from 'work hard, play hard' to just 'work hard.' The firm's headcount has dwindled through furloughs, layoffs and much unforced attrition, so the workers who remain today are a close-knit group of survivors."

A lingering factor in DiamondCluster culture is the aforementioned merger. A three-year firm veteran says, "The firm still has a split identity between North America and the rest of the world (Europe and Latin America) that stems from the merger of Diamond and Cluster in 2000." He adds, "The North American culture today is the heritage of the former Diamond Technology Partners culture." A colleague in Boston agrees that culture is "not consistent across the firm."

## Diamonds are not forever

If you make it onto DiamondCluster's staff, you should expect to work hard to remain there. The order of the day is up-or-out. A partner reports that the system is "value driven and with clear predefined criteria that are evaluated in each project. Consultants without MBAs can progress in their careers, provided that they perform as expected." A newer staff member (in a different office) disagrees somewhat, claiming that "Promotion at the firm is done under the aegis of a meritocracy, but in reality a lot of politicking goes into it." According to one insider in Europe: "Appraisal cycle is six months. After that, consultants usually rise one sub-level. Each sub-level gives you about a 10 percent raise in base salary. Within each level (Analyst, Associate, Senior Associate, Manager, Principal) there are four sub-levels. So the average consultant moves to the next level after two years." Several respondents confirm the two-year promotion timeline.

DiamondCluster laid off a percentage of its staff in 2002, according to insiders. The figures aren't clear, but reports range from 20 to 40 percent. "There have been incentives for people to leave the firm," reports one consultant. The general opinion is that most of those who left the European offices were counseled out after a harsh round of evaluations, with few official layoffs. U.S. consultants were more likely to have been let go outright. A senior consultant reflects, "We used to be growing quickly enough that we were not an up-or-out firm. The economy has forced a more stringent review process. So our promotion model has moved from a standard of performance to a relative performance basis." In short, be prepared to prove your worth to the firm continually and conspicuously.

## The diversity facet

DiamondCluster has no outstanding issues when it comes to maintaining a diverse staff. They're not outstanding because many firms have similar problems — an inability to attract and keep significant numbers of women and minorities. An insider says, "The firm tries to recruit women. However, due to the tech/business combination, it is fairly difficult to get a lot of female interest in the company." One woman in the home office tells us, "I am one of 15 women in my competency. There are about 130 people in my competency." A Boston insider says, "We have very few women in director-level positions in the firm," adding that the firm has "even less minority diversity." One respondent tells us, "With over 45 nationalities in the company it is very multinational," but that's not the same thing. One European puts it succinctly: "Not a single black consultant in Europe." A Chicagoan says, "the firm tries, but minority interest is minimal –not sure why that is."

Still insiders generally have nice things to say. One woman says she's "accepted, no questions asked." A male consultant adds, "We have a health program that respects domestic partners and have a few openly gay partners, so I think that suggests we do fairly well here." One of the higher-ups says, "We are one of the more accommodating firms that I know."

## Hard work

DiamondCluster's travel requirements tend to affect the firm's work/life balance ratings, especially in Europe. European consultants consistently rated the firm lower on this basis, largely due to "continuous travel [which] makes family life almost impossible." A fellow in Europe claims he has "no private life." An American colleague agrees that "work expectations are high and most people find themselves working more than life balancing to meet those expectations." A high-ranking firm member says it is "because we are trying to get and keep everyone we still have staffed."

A manager claims, "I am managing on two different assignments in two different countries other than my office country." We are told "in Europe, our company has the 4-1 rule which means four days at client side and one day in the home office." However, one person points to "lots of overseas traveling" making it "difficult to come back home over the weekend."

## Compensation in every sense

In an effort to avoid layoffs in a miserable business environment, DiamondCluster has taken the approach of company-wide pay cuts. One insider gets specific: "As part of overall efforts to reduce costs, non-partner employees across the board received a 10 percent pay cut in July 2001 that has not restored; partners took a 15 percent pay cut." Another adds, "We've been receiving restricted stock in lieu of bonuses for two years." There's an employee stock purchase program as well as stock options; however, several respondents called the latter "worthless."

It's not all bad, though, and DiamondCluster does try to keep its people sane. A senior analyst says, "travel preferences are considered and new parents are treated well." One insider feels that "Four weeks of vacation for all employees really helps." Another says that typically there is "no work on weekends."

Benefits include what one insider calls "Hands down, absolutely the best medical, dental and vision insurance around." Several colleagues agree that DiamondCluster has an "excellent health plan." Consultants in Germany also receive company cars. In addition, there is a laundry list of other benefits that varies with location. Some of the more common perks include cell phones, laptop computers, free food and drinks (revoked in some offices), tuition reimbursement and gym membership discounts.

## What about the offices?

While consultants won't be working in the Four Seasons (unless they're staffed to a project there), DCIers should expect to enjoy the physical environment. A senior consultant in an unidentified European city boasts his office has "the best view in the city." His colleague agrees, calling the offices "not overly luxurious but always in the best locations with excellent views."

But how often do DiamondCluster employees actually see these great digs? Not very often, it seems; frequent travel and a high percentage of staffed consultants keep the hallways empty. "Our offices are nice," says a Boston worker, "but I'm not in them very often." Another insider says, "We are never there unless we are on the beach." A Chicago local explains, "Since the company is virtual, most employees do not ever need to visit the office."

## What's best

The people at DiamondCluster tell us they get the most satisfaction out of "the challenging projects," working "right at the intersection of strategy and technology" and, as always, "the people." More than one consultant cites the "great opportunities for international work." Some are keen on the "entrepreneurial," "motivated" atmosphere at DCI, while others look forward to interacting with the many "interesting clients."

DiamondCluster sponsors a number of clothing drives, toy boxes for children and blood drives. One insider says, "Projects include free or discounted consulting for the Chicago Symphony and The Chicago Marathon." Worldwide, the firm also donates and supports several non-governmental organizations. "In a recent project in India," relates one consultant, "the team collaborated with a local NGO that supported children's education and feeding. The team contributed to the education and feeding of more than 1,000 children during that year." A senior analyst says, "Efforts are both organized and grass-roots. DCI workers in general have an eye toward charity."

"People genuinely look forward to seeing each other at the quarterly All-Hands meetings."

— *DCI consultant*

# Charles River Associates

John Hancock Tower
200 Clarendon Street, T-33
Boston, MA 02116-5092
Phone: (617) 425-3000
Fax: (617) 425-3132
www.crai.com

## LOCATIONS

**Boston, MA (HQ)**
College Station, TX • Houston, TX •
Jenkintown, PA • Los Angeles, CA
• Oakland, CA • Palo Alto, CA •
Philadelphia, PA • Salt Lake City,
UT • Washington, DC • Brussels •
Dubai • London • Melbourne •
Mexico City • Toronto • Wellington

## PRACTICE AREAS

Aerospace and Defense • Antitrust
Economics • Auctions and E-
Commerce • Business Strategy •
Chemicals and Petroleum •
Damages • Energy and Environment
• European Competition Policy and
Litigation Support • Finance and
Accounting • Intellectual Property •
International Trade • Market
Analysis • Mergers and Acquisitions
• Metals, Materials and Fabricated
Parts • Pharmaceuticals • Product
Liabiltiy • Survey Research •
Technology Management •
Transportation

## THE BUZZ
WHAT CONSULTANTS AT OTHER FIRMS ARE SAYING

- "Pigeonholed analysts"
- "One of top econ consulting firms"
- "Lack real world experience"
- "Small, but heavy hitters"

## THE STATS

**Employer Type:** Public Company
**Stock Symbol:** Nasdaq
**Stock Exchange:** CRAI
**President and CEO:** James C. Burrows
**2002 Employees:** 490
**2001 Employees:** 484
**2002 Revenue:** $131 million
**2001 Revenue:** $110 million

## UPPERS

- Company promotes work/life balance
- Supportive, reasonable management

## DOWNERS

- Graduate degrees needed for advancement
- Work can be repetitive

## KEY COMPETITORS

Boston Consulting Group
Brattle Group
LECG
NERA

## EMPLOYMENT CONTACT

Sara McQuarrie
Fax: (617) 425-3112
E-mail: hr@crai.com

**DC office:**
Erica Scipio
Charles River Associates
1201 F Street N.W., Suite 700
Washington, DC 20004-1204
Fax: (202) 662-3910

# THE SCOOP

## Charles in charge

Charles River Associates (CRA) was founded in 1965 in Cambridge, Mass., near the banks of the Charles River (hence the name.) Though the firm has a reputation as an economic advisor, it also specializes in strategic management, litigation, and regulation. CRA works with law firms, domestic and foreign businesses, accounting companies, and governments. Revenues for fiscal year 2002 increased 19 percent from the year before, while net income increased 13 percent. For 2003, the company is projecting revenue and earnings growth of 20 to 25 percent.

Its three main practice areas are competition, finance and business consulting. Litigation and regulation-related work account for about 65 percent of the firm's revenue. The goal of the practice is to help law firms and other businesses by providing economic analysis and expert advice on highly technical issues, such as antitrust, mergers and acquisitions, damages, finance, international trade, environmental issues, transfer pricing and regulation. In recent years, CRA has provided consulting services for 19 of the top 25 law firms in the United States and 14 of the top 25 industrial companies.

CRA's business consulting practice, which accounts for the other 35 percent of the firm's revenues, specializes in strategy development, operations management and policy planning. The practice's industry focus is varied, with project representation in aerospace and defense, pharmaceuticals, chemicals and petroleum, transportation, media, sports, metals and materials, energy and utilities and telecommunications. The firm boosted its utility and regulatory consulting capabilities in August 2001 when it acquired a portion of PA Consulting's energy economics practice for an undisclosed sum. And in April 2002, CRA acquired the Chemical and Energy Ventures business of bankrupt consultancy Arthur D. Little for just under $7 million. The purchase added 91 staff members to the firm. According to the company, it has integrated Little employees into the chemical practice "ahead of schedule."

## Experts abound

If you want to move up at CRA, it helps to have a few letters after your name. Senior staff members usually hold an advanced degree. Senior associates typically possess an MBA or Ph.D. and often have at least a master's degree. Usual courses of study include economics, public policy or business. Senior staffers are expected to be experts in a field such as competition, energy/environment, telecommunications, trade, transfer pricing, intellectual property, chemicals and petroleum, electric utilities, materials, metals, pharmaceuticals, transportation, aerospace and defense, finance and financial services or auctions. Sometimes, these consultants do double duty as expert witnesses. Two recent examples: CRA vice chairman and MIT economics professor Franklin M. Fisher was an expert witness in the government's antitrust case against Microsoft, and Steven Salop (a senior consultant to CRA) and a team of consultants helped the DOJ with research that enabled Procter & Gamble's $4.95 billion acquisition of Clairol to go forward in 2001.

## Highly engaged

A look at some of CRA's 2002 projects reveals the scope of CRA's work. The company advised the Tennessee Valley Authority on obtaining financing for restarting a unit at the Brown's Ferry Nuclear Plant in Alabama. In the opposite hemisphere, the consulting firm reviewed the New Zealand port sector and recommended that the government not regulate pricing and competition there – a recommendation the Kiwis adopted.

On behalf of the Investment Management Association in the U.K., CRA studied whether past performance on funds are indicative of future success. CRA looked at funds investing in the U.K. over the past 20 years and found that strong past performance seems to be linked to good future returns. The finding sparked an argument between the IMA and the regulatory Financial Services Authority, which had attempted to curtail use of past performance statistics when funds were selling themselves to the public. Thanks in part to these interesting projects, CRA nabbed a place on *Forbes'* 2002 Best Small Companies list, ranking No. 122 out of 200.

## Hello, world

Since its May 1998 IPO, CRA has increased its rate of international expansion. In addition to its Boston headquarters, the firm operates 15 offices around the world. In 2002, the firm expanded its presence in Mexico City, and in 2003, opened its Brussels office, which is led by Dr. Rainer Nitsche, a specialist in European deregulation and competition policy. The firm also opened an office in Dubai in 2003. CRA's overseas offices have been turning in the firm's strongest performances. In fact, for the fourth quarter of 2002, CRA's president and CEO, James C. Burrows, noted that the London and Mexico City offices made "the most significant contributions."

## A Neu co

CRA's NeuCo subsidiary makes and sells software tools and supplementary consulting services that are focused on electricity generation by utilities. NeuCo was not profitable in 2003. However, CEO Burrows said in the 4Q results that NeuCo has a "strong pipeline of prospective contracts" that should push NeuCo into profitability in 2003.

And things are already looking up. In February 2003, a NeuCo proposal was selected as a winner in President Bush's Clean Coal Power Initiative competition; its proposal regards online plant-management software for a Dynegy plant in Baldwin, Ill.

# GETTING HIRED

A background in finance, economics or mathematics, as well as strong research skills, is essential preparation for a career at CRA. Excellent written and oral skills, as well as a firm understanding of computers, are also key.

Junior staff members – analysts and associates – usually don't have advanced degrees. CRA expects junior consultants to stay at the firm for two or three years before going to graduate school, and it is "extremely rare" for associates to get promotions to senior associate without a graduate degree. (However, some associates do stay longer than three years, as CRA "does not have a policy of encouraging junior staff to exit the firm after a specified period of time.") After CRA, 55 percent of junior employees usually go to MBA programs, 13 percent to public policy programs and 19 percent to doctorate programs (usually in economics).

Applications to CRA are accepted through colleges, referrals and direct applications, and include a cover letter, resume, transcript and writing sample. CRA recruits at "top and second-tier schools" including Ivies, sources say. Candidates who make it past the initial screening are asked to interview (usually on-campus, but, depending on circumstances, at an office). Two junior staffers interview the applicant for about half an hour for skills, experience and interest. "We expect all applicants to have rudimentary knowledge of the firm's services and the analyst position at this interview," says the company. Applicants should also note their office preference, if any, during this time.

At the second-round interview, "the best candidates are flown to [a local] office for a day of interviews and a "job talk" presentation," an insider says. The applicant undergoes several 30-minute interviews with both junior and senior employees. The format ranges from case studies to personal interviews. Applicants to the Boston office are notified of their status within three days of this interview, while applicants to other offices usually hear within two weeks. Offers are made for a specific office.

For candidates with masters' degrees the process is similar. Again, the application should include a cover letter, résumé, and sample of written work, along with the preferred area of specialization and preferred locations. HR reps screen the packets, inviting appropriate candidates for an initial interview. These usually take place at an office or by telephone, and one or two members of CRA's recruiting team interview the candidate for about 30 minutes. Those who pass this round are asked to the CRA offices, where they go through four to six interviews with senior staff members. Candidates usually hear back within two to three weeks.

# OUR SURVEY SAYS

## School days

The culture at CRA is "quasi-academic"; perhaps as a result, the "work is sometimes fairly rote." Nonetheless, CRA is said to possess a "good culture and work environment." The people are said to be "friendly, collegial, very smart, and well trained." CRA supports local community initiatives. In addition, CRA insiders cite other efforts "driven by individuals."

## Striking the right balance

Work/life balance is very, well, balanced at CRA. The company is "very understanding and flexible around client engagements," says one respondent. "Although we sometimes work very hard, we are also encouraged to keep reasonable hours and to maintain a life outside of work," assesses another consultant. Employees seem quite happy with their hours, which usually hover upwards of 45 hours a week, but up to 55 "when on a project." Work tends to spike once or twice a month, "depending upon deliverables."

One aspect that helps is CRA's "office-based culture (i.e. not a tremendous amount of travel)." Consultants report spending one day outside of the office during an average week, though one insider says three days traveling is "the general amount of travel for case teams." The firm claims that "less than 5 percent of junior staff members' time is spent outside of their local office."

## Adding to perks

Benefits at CRA include accidental death/dismemberment, long-term disability, an employee assistance program, gym membership discounts, sports/theater tickets, cell phones, pagers, and laptops.

There's a cafeteria and free snacks available in San Francisco, while Boston employees get a lounge area. Salaries get fairly high marks, and include "stock options" and "annual profit sharing based on a percentage of salary that goes into a 401(k) plan; it's dependent on firm performance."

## Back to class

"You grow at your own pace" at CRA, which consultants seem to like. The firm is apparently "not up or out." But though "BA/BS types can move up if they have the smarts," "it is fairly rare for undergraduates to advance to the upper levels." In other words, "graduate degrees count." What to choose for a graduate subject? "Our special focus (economics) helps. We're not primarily an MBA shop, but we have some [MBAs], and they do fine." Graduate diplomas in hand, employees can expect "generally three to four years between stages [of promotion]."

There was a sprinkling of layoffs in 2002. In the largest practice in the company, one source reports, about seven consultants were laid off from a group of 110. Another source says, "Those few who were laid off were offered consulting [freelance] spots." The firm says it continues to hire at all levels, even outside the recruiting season.

# Hewitt Associates

100 Half Day Road
Lincolnshire, IL 60069
Phone: (847) 295-5000
Fax: (847) 295-7634
www.hewitt.com

## LOCATIONS

**Lincolnshire, IL (HQ)**
86 offices worldwide

## PRACTICE AREAS

Health Care
HR and Benefits Outsourcing
Retirement and Financial
Management
Talent and Organizational Change

## THE STATS

**Employer Type:** Public Company
**Stock Symbol:** HEW
**Stock Exchange:** NYSE
**CEO and Chairman:** Dale L. Gifford
**2002 Employees:** 15,000
**2001 Employees:** 13,000
**2002 Revenue:** $1.72 billion
**2001 Revenue:** $1.48 billion

## UPPERS

- Free lunch – really – and other great perks
- Unusually short hours

## DOWNERS

- Wide range in quality of managers
- Tenure, not merit, is key to promotion

## KEY COMPETITORS

Mercer Human Resource Consulting
Towers Perrin
Watson Wyatt Worldwide

## EMPLOYMENT CONTACT

was.hewitt.com/hewitt/careers/
index.htm

## THE BUZZ
WHAT CONSULTANTS AT OTHER FIRMS ARE SAYING

- "Woman friendly"
- "HR and only HR"
- "Smart people"
- "A bit stodgy"

# THE SCOOP

## Seizing an opportunity

In 1940 Ted Hewitt opened an insurance brokerage in Lake Forest, Ill. After working with his first client, Parker Pen, he realized what the company really needed was a well-designed benefits package for employees. Soon after, Hewitt Associates augmented its actuarial work, with HR consulting eventually offering a broad array of human resources consulting and outsourcing services. Over the years the firm expanded its presence, initially by opening offices in Minneapolis, New York City, Milwaukee, Los Angeles and Dayton. Hewitt stretched beyond the borders of the United States with the creation of a Toronto office in 1976, and opened branches in Paris and St. Albans (outside of London) in 1985. Today, Hewitt Associates is headquartered in Lincolnshire, Ill. and has approximately 15,000 associates in 86 offices (including joint venture operations) in 37 countries. The firm boasts a roster of more than 2,000 clients that includes more than half of the Fortune 500.

## Growing strong

One of the 20 largest management consulting firms in the world as well as the largest benefit consulting firm in the United States, Hewitt is growing rapidly despite the shaky global economy. And 2002 was another fine year. In March 2002, Hewitt-then no. 155 on Forbes' 2001 list of America's private largest companies-registered with the SEC for an initial public offering. The firm went public on June 27, 2002, with an offering of 11,150,000 shares, and raised a reported $211.8 million. Revenue increased 16 percent to $1.72 billion, marking the 41st consecutive year of revenue growth and the ninth consecutive year of double-digit revenue growth.

Hewitt is expecting to continue its growth-its estimates for fiscal 2003 include net revenue growth of 13 to 16 percent, and earnings growth in excess of 20 percent.

## Go east

One area where the firm is hoping to increase its presence is the Asia-Pacific region. Hewitt plans to open its Asia Pacific Measurement Centre (note fancy European spelling) in 2003. The firm's third such endeavor (the other two are located in Brussels, Belgium and Lincolnshire, Ill.), the Centre is designed to manage much of the data the firm maintains and studies it conducts annually. And in September 2001

Hewitt struck an outsourcing alliance with India Pension Services Ltd., thereby becoming the largest HR services provider on the subcontinent.

## Two prongs

Hewitt's two practice areas are outsourcing and consulting. In 2002, the outsourcing group was the company's mainstay. Much Hewitt outsourcing involves the adminstration of client human resources systems. Hewitt adminsters, for example, 401(k) plans and pensions, among other benefit programs. Outsourcing accounted for 65 percent of Hewitt's revenue in fiscal 2002, and consulting accounted for 35 percent of Hewitt's revenue.

The consulting group advises companies on how to handle their human resources problems. Business is self-perpetuating, as most clients need actuarial analysis of defined – benefit plans, compensation reviews and health plan selection each year. However, while net revenue in the consulting business increased 15 percent to $600 million in 2002 – driven largely by the acquisition of consultancy Bacon & Woodrow and by growth in the retirement and health benefit plan consulting-net income dropped 4 percent. The weak spot in consulting: "decreased demand for certain discretionary consulting services over the prior year," according to the company.

## Honor roll

Hewitt has been raking in awards, especially for technical prowess. In 2002, for the third consecutive year, Hewitt ranked on *IDG Computerworld*'s list of best places to work in information technology, rising more than 20 places to be number 34 on the list. It also scored 214th on the *InfoWeek* 500 list, which ranks U.S. companies with revenue over $1 billion on their tech and operational innovation. It nabbed a spot on *BtoB Magazine*'s 100 best business web sites, scoring 87 points out of a possible 100 for its corporate site. In 2001, the firm's tech support center received a Best Practices Award from *eWeek* magazine and *Technology Managers Forum*, and the firm took its place among the "Best in IT" by making the InfoWorld 100 a month later. (It failed to make the list in 2002.)

It's not just the firm's technological savvy that's earning recognition. Hewitt garnered a sixth place spot on *Consulting* magazine's list of the "The 10 Best Consulting Firms to Work For" in 2002. The same year, chief Dale Gifford made *Business Insurance*'s list of the top 10 benefit newsmakers in 2002. In 2001, the firm landed second among local employers in *The Orlando Sentinel*'s list of the Top 100

Companies for Working Families. In 2000, Hewitt earned spots on several lists, including *Chicago Magazine*'s Best Places to Work for in Chicago, *Central Florida Family Magazine*'s Top 100 Companies for Working Families and *Connecticut Magazine*'s Top Places to Work in Connecticut. Hewitt's recognition isn't limited to the United States, though – in 2002, Hewitt won the China HR Consultancy of the Year award from *China STAFF* magazine for the fourth consecutive year.

# GETTING HIRED

## Harvesting Hewitt consultants

Hewitt recruits on campus at approximately 25 schools, including "the big local schools" near its Lincolnshire, Illinois office; while the Bridgewater, N.J. office "typically recruits at Penn State and Rutgers, along with other schools in New Jersey and Connecticut. Very few people are from Tier 1 schools, however." Another target: large universities in the Midwest, South and East (examples include Rutgers, Clark Atlanta University, Indiana University, and Penn State). Candidates on campus should have an academic transcript ready for their first interview. Lots of candidates come in through "referrals," as well.

Hewitt hires for both enty-level and experienced candidates. For the majority of entry-level consulting roles, recruiting is held on campus. Promising candidates then have two phone interviews. Candidates deemed qualified are then invited for on-site interviews. Experienced candidates, on the other hand, may begin the interview process with either a phone or an on-site interview. Promising experienced candidates are then invited to a Hewitt office where they have three or four interviews with associates and learn more about the firm's various departments. Don't worry about case-study questions, for "interviews are all behavioral," says a source.

Typically, associates hired out of college join Hewitt's outsourcing area. Hewitt hires a variety of majors but often gives preference to those in business administration, computer science, MIS, accounting, economics and math. College students who have completed their junior year and hold a 3.0 GPA and above are encouraged to apply for an internship – a very promising route to permanent employment at Hewitt.

# OUR SURVEY SAYS

## Chaotic culture

"The company's culture varies first by practice line, then by engagement team," notes one consultant. Since the company went public, some employees say, its culture has changed from "loose and enjoyable." "Now it's more rigid and political," says another insider.

While not all survey respondents concur with that assessment, most agree that a graduate degree is not necessary for success. "Do your job well and play the game; there's no limit, no matter what the education level," says one; another says, "Promotions are based on performance and potential to do well in higher roles. There are several examples of people with only undergraduate degrees moving into MBA-level positions." One posits the following explanation for such a system. "I've understood there to be a unspoken policy of having to 'put in your dues' and be worked extra hard wtih tremendous amounts of overtime (with no additional compensation) before one can be promoted. One can typically expect to move up to a quality assurance manager position after two to three years. There is no need for an MBA and going back to get your MBA is not encouraged because it is viewed as yet another way to try to leave the company."

The firm laid off somewhere between 50 and 200 employees in 2002, according to our sources' estimates. "It was nothing on the scale of other consulting firms," says an insider. "However, many associates were put on improvement programs, which effectively is a way to fire people or get them to quit without having to pay for unemployment or a severance package."

## Power hours

Most survey respondents report workweeks of about 45 hours, relatively low for consulting firms. However, those workdays have been full lately. "We haven't experienced any down time in the time that I've been employed here," notes one insider. Beach time doesn't really exist at Hewitt, say insiders. "Our projects last a minimum of a year, so there is rarely any time where you are 'on the beach.' If anything, Hewitt understaffs all its projects, so once you're off a project, you're automatically put on another one, because everyone's already working at or above capacity."

## Staying close to home

Travel requirements are minimal at Hewitt. Additionally, insiders report that "the firm is considerate about work/life balance" and there are "many programs available to employees to assist in this area." Another source reports that work hours are "very unpredictable." One consultant carps, "We do not receive extra compensation for the extra time worked (i.e., no bonuses or overtime)."

## Prevalent perks

The citations Hewitt has received for being a good employer are reflected in its benefits package. Health-wise, Hewitt offers several varieties of medical plans, along with dental and vision plans. Money-wise, Hewitt makes an annual contribution to retirement accounts based on pay, and matches 401(k) contributions at 100 percent, up to 2 percent of base pay. At the end of each fiscal year, Hewitt provides a profit sharing contribution that vest immediately. It offers paid disability, long-term disability, and life insurance. Relaxation-wise, Hewitt gives 16 days vacation to employees with up to five years of service; after that, employees get an additional day off each year, up to a total of 21 days. There's also a sabbatical-like program called "Splash," where employees get additional time off after five-year increments-that is, after the first five years, you get an extra week off; after the first ten years, two weeks; fifteen, twenty, and thereafter, three weeks off.

Hewitt also provides tuition reimbursement at 85 percent for approved courses, up to a max of $5,000 a year. Tuition expenses beyond that limit are banked and reimbursed in future years at a reimbursement rate of $5,000 annually. The firm also offers less common perks, such as paying for cab fare home "if you are ever unsure about your ability to get home safely after an evening out – or if you believe anyone else in your party is at risk," up to $5,000 in adoption-related reimbursement plus one week of time off, reimbursement of child care costs if you and your spouse are out of town on business or you're working quite late, reimbursement for pet-sitting when you're on a business trip, and meals, snacks and (nonalcoholic) beverages at the office. There is such thing as a free lunch!

Each employee can take two days' paid time off each year to volunteer for human services or educational causes, and the company matches up to $500 in donations to educational institutions. There's also time devoted to "charities, tutoring and food drives," and "Junior Achievement."

## Lax leaders?

Judging from our survey, Hewitt consultants have varying opinions of their managers. Some say they're quite pleased with them, while others say that "managerial skills that these managers have are nonexistent or minimal at best." Another notes that while their project management skills may be up to par, "they lack the subtle people skills that are required of someone in their position." One reason for this, this source posits, is that "managers are often promoted when they are not ready, which causes additional problems."

## Boot camp

The training at Hewitt seems solid. "[Hewitt] provides five weeks (depending on your position) of training for new employees," says one insider. Another consultant opines that "initial training is helpful and there are opportunities to take additional training classes."

## Right by everyone

Consultants seem to like that women are well-represented at Hewitt. "The firm is very diverse with respect to women. I would say that the office is comprised of at least 45 percent women, possibly more. Looking at the project manager level, the ratio drops a little to around 35 to 40 percent, and at the delivery group manager level, it drops to around 20 percent," says one source. Insiders find that minority representation is almost as good. "There are several minority groups represented in my office," says a source, noting that most are of Asian descent. And "above the project manager level, racial diversity is almost nonexistent," reports one consultant. Meanwhile, "Hewitt is accepting of gays and lesbians. I know of a couple people who are out at work and I also know of others who are closeted. There is a gay and lesbian group at Hewitt. Overall, being gay is a non-issue," says a source.

## Salary squabbles

Some insiders find that salary "seems very low compared to other consulting firms – while your total compensation may be somewhat comparable to other firms, your base salary is very low. The only financial growth you have is through annual (not semiannual) raises, which are calculated off of your low base pay." There is "profit sharing and long-term incentives," and it has "provided company stock, but that may have been a one-time occurrence." According to Hewitt's SEC filings, in December 2002 its compensation committee established a framework for how employees would be paid. The firm adopted a "pay-for-results" structure that pays according to the business unit and individual performance; the new structure also makes company stock a large part of the compensation equation, which gets larger as salaries increase.

# 24

# Stern Stewart & Co.

135 East 57th Street
New York, NY 10022
Phone: (212) 261-0600
Fax: (212) 581-6420
www.sternstewart.com

## LOCATIONS

**New York, NY (HQ)**
12 offices worldwide

## PRACTICE AREAS

Business Management and Strategy
  Consulting Communication and
  Training in Value Concepts
EVA Incentive Compensation Design
EVA Value-Based Performance
Fairness Opinions and Valuations
Financial Restructurings and
  Recapitalizations
Financial Strategy and Policy
  Guidance on Mergers, Acquisitions
  and Divestitures
Litigation Support, Expert Witness
  Services
Measuring and Managing Brand
  Value
Software for Financial Modeling and
  Valuation
Worldwide MVA/EVA Databases

## THE STATS

**Employer Type:** Private Company
**Managing Partner:** Joel M. Stern
**2002 Employees:** 200
**2001 Employees:** 250

## UPPERS

- Strong training in finance
- Good salaries

## DOWNERS

- Low morale
- Hands-off management

## KEY COMPETITORS

BearingPoint
Boston Consulting Group
L.E.K. Consulting
Marakon Associates
Monitor Group

## EMPLOYMENT CONTACT

E-mail: careers@sternstewart.com

## THE BUZZ
### WHAT CONSULTANTS AT OTHER FIRMS ARE SAYING

- "EVA, EVA, EVA"
- "The luster is wearing thin"
- "Masters in their niche"
- "Good in Asia"

# THE SCOOP

## The EVA company

Joel Stern, the head of Stern Stewart, is also its marquee name. This Columbia University professor introduced the concept of EVA in the early 1980s. EVA stands for economic value added, and measures economic profit. The equation Stern Stewart uses: EVA equals the net operating profit after taxes, minus a charge for what was invested at first (capital times the cost of capital). That is, EVA only counts earnings once the shareholders have gotten their minimum required return back.

Stern Stewart's consulting projects are usually based on EVA. The consultants look at every aspect of their client – its HR programs, its compensation strategy, which business lines it's investing in – and tries to bring all of those into line with the goal of maximizing EVA. More than 300 companies, such as Coca-Cola, Siemens and Sony, have undergone this shareholder-centric analysis; more recently, Stern Stewart has extended its client base to companies as far flung as Tata Tea, a Calcutta, India, tea company.

EVA has gained popularity outside of Stern Stewart, too. Goldman Sachs and Credit Suisse First Boston use it as a way to value stocks, while CalPERS (California's large and influential pension fund for state employees) uses EVA to evaluate its investments.

## Retaining the lead

Other companies have introduced similar analytical frameworks, including Marakon and the Boston Consulting Group (which poetically dubs its system the "Total Business Return"). But because it was the originator of value measurement tools, New York-based Stern Stewart is, for the moment, the leader of the fiscal measurement pack. It stays on top of the game, in part, with marketing: seminars, publications and articles "evangelizing" EVA. Senior partner and founder G. Bennett Stewart III, the original "EVAngelist" (believe it or not, an officially trademarked term), wrote *The Quest for Value*, a treatment of value management. Other publications include *The EVA Challenge, EVA: The Real Key to Creating Wealth* and the quarterly *Journal of Applied Corporate Finance*, published in conjunction with Accenture.

## Publishing power

Another important tool in Stern Stewart's arsenal is its annual market value added (MVA) ratings. MVA measures the difference between a company's market value (equity and debt) and the capital that investors have poured into it over the years (loans, retained earnings, paid-in capital). "If MVA is positive, it means that the company has increased the value of the capital entrusted to it and thus created shareholder wealth. If MVA is negative, the company has destroyed wealth," the company notes. These rankings are almost always picked up by major news outlets such as *Fortune*, *CFO Magazine*, the U.K.'s *Sunday Times*, Germany's *Capital* and Canada's *Financial Post*. Another influential list ranks top executives according to how efficiently they use available capital.

EVA services are also available through two software programs, FINANSEER®, already in use by over 500 corporations, and EVAntage®, an add-on to Standard & Poor's Research Insight that provides a financial analysis of 1,300 non-finance companies.

## GETTING HIRED

Undergraduates with a background in finance, accounting or economics can apply for the analyst position. Associates should hold an MBA or an equivalent higher degree and have several years of professional experience. Overall, Stern Stewart looks for candidates with strong analytical and computer skills. The company looks for driven, self-motivated individuals with an entrepreneurial bent.

The company does recruit on campus at Rochester, Columbia, Michigan, NYU, University of Chicago and University of Virgina, among other schools. "If someone's interesting enough from another school, we'll take a look," says an insider. Candidates should have "a substantial amount of finance and accounting" on their transcripts, and "finance majors" are preferred.

The hiring process usually starts with a phone or initial screening interview. In that, expect "a lot of finance questions – 'If you had to value a company, what would be the different valuation methods you'd use?' up to complex questions like preferences of debt versus equity, when to use convertible debt, or the cost of financial distress," says one person who interviewed for an analyst position. "For the on-campus recruiting effort, which is 30 minutes to an hour, if it's a case question, it's very simplified," notes another analyst. If the candidate passes the initial interview, the next step is a full day of interviews, usually at one of the offices. Questions are similarly finance-heavy, but the company doesn't lean on traditional case studies, we hear. "The questions weren't so formal that you'd need to get a piece of paper out and make critical decision-making answers. It's more, 'You have two companies, who's doing better and what's your basis?'"

# OUR SURVEY SAYS

## Smart Stern Stewart

In line with Stern Stewart's approach to consulting, within the company there's a "focus on results" as well. It's one of the "best places for finance" consulting, our sources say. The firm is said to foster "intellectual curiosity" and be small enough that there's "opportunity to make a difference." It's not all joy. "There's a strong academic competitiveness," notes one analyst, but adds he has "a lot of good friends among analysts and associates."

## Always the hours

While in the past, "hours for analysts and associates sucked, 70 to 80 hours a week minimum plus weekend work," we hear that hours – especially in the New York office-have decreased greatly. "You can get away with coming in at 9 a.m. or 10 a.m. and leaving at 6 p.m., and you'll get your work done," says a source. Another consultant with a higher tolerance for long hours reports, "Sometimes there are the traditional gruesome hours, but in general it is quite OK, 60 to 70 hour weeks."

## Salary squabbles

While consultants report that the salaries are quite high for consulting, bonuses appear to be a point of contention. Bonuses are set up as "basically profit sharing, but since it's a partnership we don't see the inputs to the level of profit that we generate," says a New York source. "And we just found out our bonuses have been used to pay off losses from other offices. So while we technically made money from last year," the bonuses don't reflect that. "The games being played with the bonuses are one of the most demotivating contributions to the morale problem," this consultant says.

## Through the ranks

Though Stern Stewart does not have an up-or-out system, and "there is no time requirement for each position," there's an understanding that "after a while, below-average performers leave on their own." One thing that will get you ahead at Stern Stewart: "bring business. This is a major issue for advancement. There have been cases of outstanding people who rose to VP without an MBA, just because they brought in business and kept clients happy." Also, "a lot of our VPs have moved up from the associate analyst level, and we hire quantitative analytical people at that associate analyst level."

There are a few complaints that top brass is too hands-off. "Sometimes, people know they're not necessarily good managers so we get no management; or we don't know about what's going on within the company, from a managerial perspective as well as with the client," says one junior consultant. A consultant in one of the satellite offices reports that "we have the ability to run our local office with minimal interference, which is great. But sometimes a little bit more oversight and management from above would be healthy." Another insider carps, "Numbers geeks don't always make the best managers."

## Slimming the pyramid

There have been layoffs "on a worldwide basis" in the past year, but only in some offices. New York seems to have been hit particularly hard, down to about 60 consultants from a high of 100 two years ago. "The cuts were fairly senior," says a New York source. "Also, there have been a substantial amount of people leaving for one reason or another, and those positions – partners and VPs – haven't really been replaced."

## Basic training

Training at Stern Stewart kicks off with "a two- to four-week training session, where we give a general finance overview, then go in and teach them everything they need to know about EVA. Then they apply it in mock case studies." Stern Stewart's academic atmosphere helps make it an "excellent environment for learning." And "a lot of the training gets done on the job," though "we can request any training we deem important – we just lack the time to do it."

## An I-banking makeup

"If you think of a stereotypical workplace environment, especially in finance, where most of the men are professionals and most females are admin, that's basically where the women are at Stern Stewart," says a New York-based source. "It's less than one-third professional females." Ethnic diversity also has room to grow. In New York, a source says there are "two black people in our office – one assistant, one receptionist; there are two Asians – one analyst and one VP; and several Latin Americans."

# 25 NERA Economic Consulting

50 Main Street
White Plains, NY 10606
Phone: (914) 448-4000
Fax: (914) 448-4040
www.nera.com

## LOCATIONS

**White Plains, NY (HQ)**
Cambridge, MA • Chicago, IL •
Ithaca, NY • Los Angeles, CA •
New York, NY • Philadelphia, PA •
San Francisco, CA • Washington,
DC • Brussels • London • Madrid •
Rome • Sao Paulo • Sydney •
Tokyo

## PRACTICE AREAS

Antitrust/Competition Policy •
Commercial Litigation •
Employment/Labor Economics •
Industry Focus • Market
Design/Strategy • Product
Strategy/Pricing • Risk Management
• Securities Litigation • Valuation

## THE BUZZ
WHAT CONSULTANTS AT OTHER FIRMS ARE SAYING

- "Leading economic consulting"
- "Calculator jocks"
- "Solid and thorough"
- "Sleeping on laurels"

## THE STATS

**Employer Type:** Subsidiary of Marsh
& McLennan
**Stock Symbol:** MMC
**Stock Exchange:** NYSE
**CEO and President:** Richard T. Rapp
**2002 Employees:** 500
**2001 Employees:** 430

## UPPERS

- Worldwide reach and influence
- Supported by Marsh & McLennan,
  a major consulting player

## DOWNERS

- Sounds like a government agency
- Low profile

## KEY COMPETITORS

LECG
Lexecon

## EMPLOYMENT CONTACT

**U.S.**
NERA
50 Main Street
White Plains, NY 10606
Fax: (914) 448-4040
E-mail: recruitingteam@nera.com

**London and Brussels**
Recruitment
15 Stratford Place
London W1N 9AF
Fax: +44.20.7659.8501
E-mail: londonrecruitment@nera.com

# THE SCOOP

## The big money

National Economic Research Associates (NERA) is the one of the world's biggest economic consultancies; CBS Marketwatch called it *the* biggest in April 2002. The firm, sibling of the Mercer group of consultancies and a subsidiary of Marsh & McLennan, brings the insight of 500 consulting economists to bear on all matters of competition, valuation, employment and market strategy – over 45 services in nine practice areas. NERA was founded in 1961, and acquired by Marsh & McLennan in 1983.

In its 42 years of service, NERA has had wide-reaching effects on governments and businesses worldwide. Among the firm's claimed triumphs are: the deregulation of the U.S. airline, European energy and U.S./European communications industries, developing the commission structure of the U.S. stock exchanges providing supporting testimony in the Microsoft, British Airways, American Airlines and Visa antitrust suits, determining the value of class-action suits against stock issuers, Dow Corning, American tobacco companies, gun manufacturers and health-related agencies and helping to develop the emerging field of intellectual property law.

## Studies of note

NERA is a full-service consulting firm, but its primary emphasis is on research and reporting of trends in its areas of specialty. Recent examples of completed studies include *Legal Leading Indicators*, a January 2002 survey of corporate legal spending trends; and *Practical Solutions for Intercompany Pricing*, a December 2002 analysis of transfer pricing policies.

## International expansion

Despite its name, NERA is not merely "national." It's international. Seven of the firm's 16 offices are located outside the U.S., including locations in Brussels, London, Madrid, Rome, São Paulo and Sydney. In April 2002, NERA opened its first Asian office (in Tokyo). Previously, the Sydney office handled much of NERA's work in the region. The Tokyo office focuses on international transfer pricing, including valuations for transactional and customs purposes. It also provides advisory services on public policy and structural reform, business strategy, valuation and risk management with a concentration on energy, telecommunications, health care and financial services.

In September 2002, NERA extended its British reach by acquiring LBE (Law & Business Economics Ltd.), an Oxford-based consultancy specializing in competition policy, M&A and business strategy, all with an economic bent. Terms of the acquisition were not disclosed. Mark Williams, who founded LBE in 1995, joined NERA as a Director based in the firm's London office.

# GETTING HIRED

## Stand up and be counted

NERA's employment info says the firm is "always looking for qualified candidates," but neglects to describe those qualifications. However, both recent graduates and experienced economists with a taste for applied microeconomics will find a welcoming environment at the various offices. U.S. candidates are filtered through a central recruiting office in White Plains, while those seeking work in other countries are directed to one of five other contacts in Europe, Asia and Australia.

# "Mars has never had mass layoffs or aggressive reviews."

# — Mars consultant

124 Mason Street
Greenwich, CT 06830
Phone: (203) 629-9292
Fax: (203) 629-9432
www.marsandco.com

## LOCATIONS

**Greenwich, CT (HQ)**
San Francisco, CA
London
Paris
Tokyo

## PRACTICE AREAS

Strategy Consulting

## THE STATS

**Employer Type:** Private Company
**CEO:** Dominique G. Mars
**2002 Employees:** 250
**2001 Employees:** 300

## UPPERS

- Job stability – no layoffs
- Regular job reviews

## DOWNERS

- Haphazard "apprenticeship" training
- Patriarchal feel

## KEY COMPETITORS

Bain & Company
Boston Consulting Group
Marakon Associates
McKinsey & Company
The Parthenon Group

## EMPLOYMENT CONTACT

Francine Even
124 Mason Street
Greenwich, CT 06830
Phone: (203) 629-9292
E-mail:
recruiting@usg.marsandco.com

## THE BUZZ
WHAT CONSULTANTS AT OTHER FIRMS ARE SAYING

- "Quality but less known firm"
- "Bright sparks"
- "Sleek salesmen"
- "Sect"

# THE SCOOP

## Toujours fidèle

Frenchman and Harvard Business School graduate Dominique Mars, then a director of BCG, founded Mars & Company in 1979. The firm's founding principle? Mars would "guarantee the exclusivity of its services to each client, thus limiting itself to a select number of them." Hence, Mars never takes on clients who are competitors of other clients. It bills itself as "the only consulting firm of any consequence to guarantee 'fidelity'." Mars & Co. therefore serves only a limited (and highly exclusive) group of companies. The firm's clients are usually Fortune 100 or similarly powerful international companies and normally the top corporation in an industry. For the sake of discretion, Mars does not publish the names of its clients. In fact, it does not even reveal them to prospective hires until very late in the interview process.

Mars focuses on business strategy – helping clients allocate their resources in order to maximize returns. It also assists clients with international acquisitions, joint ventures and other methods of penetrating foreign markets. Like many strategy consulting firms, Mars defines "critical paths" (strategies) for its clients, but it does not facilitate implementation. Currently at 250 consultants, the Mars master plan is to grow to 400 to 450 consultants, with 30 to 40 clients.

## General knowledge

Though the firm's consultants work in five separate offices, the company is extremely integrated – in many cases, client teams are composed of consultants from two or more offices. Because its clients come from so many different industries, Mars associates gain familiarity with a wide variety of industries and tasks, and all Mars consultants are generalists.

## Taking care of its own

Promotion from within is the norm – indeed, "as a matter of policy, Mars & Co. only promotes from within," the company notes. The structure of the company is that of an "apprenticeship:" junior staff become senior staff, then go on to mentor the incoming employees. The company also has an "unwavering belief in a meritocracy." This means that "there is no pre-determined promotion schedule at any level within the firm. People are promoted as soon as they can successfully handle a more demanding role." However, the firm tops out at the VP level; Monsieur Dominique is the one and only partner and shareholder.

## The HBS connection

Mr. Mars is a Harvard Business School grad, and another major player at the firm has serious HBS ties as well: Malcolm Salter, HBS prof extraordinaire, is the company's U.S. president. Salter has been a major force behind the development of the firm's business concepts. Insiders add he "has a pretty extensive list of contacts on his Rolodex," which he often uses to bring in new clients.

# GETTING HIRED

## Trip to Mars

Mars & Co.'s interviews are usually conducted by senior employees. They take place in office, and the company is looking to see whether candidates "can become catalysts for change in major organizations."

Recent college grads who've majored in engineering, math, economics or the hard sciences and recent MBAs with an undergrad degree in those subjects; ought to contact the recruiter for the relevant office. Along with the usual criteria – analytical background, aptitude for teamwork, sense of humor, fabulous communicative skills and willingness to travel – Mars & Co. wants "catalysts for change who stand by their findings," "a power of persuasion tempered with humility" and "the intellectual power, mind-set and physical stamina to thrive in a deadline-driven environment."

Says one insider, "Lately, Mars has not run a formal recruiting program, which is why they are not as well known on campuses as they should be." The process in the U.S. now: "Resumes are submitted to the Greenwich or San Francisco offices and reviewed internally. If Mars is interested, candidates are contacted for interviews." Applicants can expect "two to three rounds of interviews, with two to three interviews per round."

Some say Mars relies heavily on case studies, while one France-based source reports it's "quite rare to have business cases. It's usually a discussion on motivations and past experience." Undergrads and those who hold degrees in science start as associate consultants, while MBAs start as consultants. The company does not hire more senior positions from outside of its ranks. It is reportedly "not in the firm policy to have interns."

# OUR SURVEY SAYS

## Life on Mars

Mars is described as having a "family-like feel to it." One consultant finds it a "very patriarchal firm. In Greenwich, an insider says, "There are about 100 consultants and everyone knows each other. This is nice when working on new projects, but it also means there is no place to hide." Martians hang out outside of the office, too. Sources report "sports leagues throughout the year," Friday pizza lunches, and happy hours every week. "The attitude is fairly laid back, with the understanding that everyone works hard."

Clients are "major international players." At Mars, you get "excellent clients (excellent exposure), and "good teammates." "The biggest plus I can think of," remarks one consultant, "is stability. Mars has never had mass layoffs or aggressive reviews, counseling people out. This is truly remarkable."

The Greenwich offices are said to be "nice. At least half of the consultants commute in from New York City each day." The San Francisco offices "are in a downtown office tower."

## Hitting the road

Mars is reported to have "a pretty good work/life balance relative to other top-tier consulting firms." The hours range from 40 hours when on the beach, to "60-80 when staffed definitely long," assesses one source. The balance is "depending on who you work with, of course, but they tend to pay attention to your family structure."

One helpful aspect is Mars tends "to send single people on trips more than married people. Everyone is expected to travel when asked, but Mars works to ensure that they don't make your life difficult." Travel engagements "can be as short as a month to as long as six months, but extended travel engagements are the exception, rather than the rule, so it isn't too terrible." On those engagements, however. Consultants often travel out Sundays, and don't have Fridays in the office.

When not on extended assignments, "on average people are out one to two days per week," says a source. "For the most part, travel is limited to meetings and initial research trips at the client site, and most of the work is done in our office." Mars tries not to "send people overseas unless they request some time away from the office."

## Managers are from Mars, consultants are from Mars too

Descriptions of the Mars brass range from "generally considerate" to "very smart" to "management is an unknown word in this firm." Many seem to agree with one assessment: "[Managers] are not at all arrogant, and are, for the most part, very nice. However, some of them can seem detached at times." There's "no transparency and no internal communication; don't ask anything, they would say 'no'," says one vexed employee. Also, "since Mars senior managers are not accustomed to engagements with travel, it means they don't always know how to manage them well when they do arise."

## Salary says

Mars has "good pay and good benefits," assesses one source. "The salary is competitive with other top-tier consulting firms, and bonuses depend on the economic climate," reveals another. There is no profit-sharing – "everything goes to the chairman, who owns 100 percent of the equity!" says a source.

Perks include laptops and gym membership discounts, and "usually two 'leisure/sport' weekends are offered by the firm, like a ski weekend."

## Promotion commotion

An advanced degree seems helpful for a good career at Mars. "Most people at Mars have some sort of technical degree. This is not a requirement, but it is strongly desired at Mars. There are lots of former engineers and science PhDs, and obviously there are also a large number of MBAs from the usual schools," says an insider.

Mars "does not have a strong 'up or out' culture," we hear – "once you're in, there's not much fear to have." However, these days, "promotions are rare given the depressed economy." "Only the really outstanding ones get promoted now," notes one source. Newbies can expect "two years or more" at the assistant position before moving to the consultant position, and "three years minimum from consultant to senior." Here's how advancement works: "Promotions are completely at the discretion of Mr. Mars and don't come at any regular interval. When you are ready, you get promoted, but it is usually after a longer time period than other consulting firms." Performance reviews "take place at the end of each project and on the consultant's anniversary of joining Mars. Raises are given each year on your anniversary."

## Sink or swim training

Training gets low marks from respondents. There's "no training," says one consultant. Another insider says that "training is very limited, and is mostly 'on the job.'" Because training is "apprenticeship based, it depends completely on who you're learning from," notes another. "The people that are hired are already smart and have quantitative skills, so training is not a big issue," concludes one consultant. Another consultant notes that "only foreign language lessons are provided."

# Hay Group

The Wanamaker Building
100 Penn Square East
Philadelphia, PA 19107-3388
Phone: (215) 861-2000
Fax: (215) 861-2111
www.haygroup.com

## LOCATIONS

**Philadelphia, PA (HQ)**
73 offices worldwide

## PRACTICE AREAS

Compensation and Benefits
Corporate Governance
Employee and Customer Attitude
   Research
Executive Assessment, Selection
   and Development
Organizational Effectiveness
Work and Organizational Structure
Work Design

## THE STATS

**Employer Type:** Private Company
**CEO:** Bernd Schneider
**2002 Employees:** 2,200
**2001 Employees:** 2,260

## UPPERS

- High degree of autonomy
- Separate tracks for managers and consultants

## DOWNERS

- Lack of teamwork, coordination between offices
- Mediocre pay

## KEY COMPETITORS

Hewitt Associates
Mercer Human Resource Consulting
Towers Perrin
Watson Wyatt Worldwide

## EMPLOYMENT CONTACT

www.haygroup.com/Careers/
   Overview.asp

 **THE BUZZ**
WHAT CONSULTANTS AT OTHER FIRMS ARE SAYING

- "Innovative approaches to HR"
- "Wallpaper"
- "Strong reputation"
- "Specialized, boring"

# THE SCOOP

## Hay fever

With 73 offices in 38 countries, Hay Group is one of the top five HR-focused management consulting firms worldwide, according to *Consulting* magazine. Clients include almost half of America's 1,000 biggest and Canada's 500 biggest companies, more than a fifth of Europe's 500 biggest companies, and almost a third of the largest companies in Australia and New Zealand. Hay Group is also growing in Asia, and opened offices in Moscow, Istanbul, Shanghai and Costa Rica in 2002.

Founded in 1943 in Philadelphia – where it is still based today – Hay Group began as a side project for Edward N. Hay, the head personnel officer at First Pennsylvania Bank. His first big engagement, a contract with General Foods to evaluate 450 management jobs in 1945, enabled Hay to quit his job and devote himself full time to the "people and jobs" consulting firm. It wasn't until the 1960s that Hay Group began expanding, first to Toronto, then both nationally and internationally. The growth and success led to a buyout by ad giant Saatchi & Saatchi in 1984. However, then-CEO Chris Matthews countered with a management buyback in 1990. Hay Group has remained privately held by its own management ever since.

## Online and on top

Today, Hay Group retains its focus on management consulting in the human resources domain. In 1997 the Hay Group introduced the Hay PayNet, the first interactive, online compensation information system. The Web-based tool allows clients to access compensation statistics, including base pay, bonus and benefits for specific industries or jobs. A revamped model with added capabilities, unveiled in 2000, remains a strong component of the company's services. Hay also performs custom surveys. All told, Hay Group's compensation databases contain more than five million records from thousands of major corporations around the globe.

Hay's management consulting arm is a highly regarded specialist in such areas as job evaluation, salary management, performance measurement and incentive plans. It also provides executive coaching to clients such as Gillette, Reuters, Shell and Sony. In December 2002, Hay allied with Adaptiv Learning Systems to develop a software program meant to teach resilience in the workplace.

## Getting published

Hay Group helps *Fortune* compile its annual list of the 100 World's Most Admired Companies. The rankings are based on nine attributes, including quality management, financial soundness and community responsibility.

In February 2000, Hay Group teamed up with *The Financial Times*, providing content for the newspaper's online Career Advisor Channel, which contains industry profiles and salary data for over 100 jobs in up to four different management levels. Hay also publishes an annual Employee Survey Benchmark Report, which breaks down employee satisfaction by job, region and industry. Companies use the overall satisfaction report to get a sense of how workers feel about their jobs or compare overall satisfaction against their own employee satisfaction surveys.

## Strong and sensitive

"Emotional Intelligence" is a catchphrase Hay likes a lot. The term was popularized by psychologist Daniel Goleman in his book of the same name and its many sequels. His advisory practice based around the concept has led to a partnership with Hay that offers seminars, assessment tools and consulting on emotional intelligence.

# GETTING HIRED

Hay's web site lists open positions broken down by country of origin. The firm tends to recruit at each country's major universities, especially those with "economics, law, business administration, psychology and technical studies" programs.

After an interview, a candidate may be invited to take several tests, including "psychometric testing" or similar personality evaluations. A "presentation and communication test" may also be thrown in. Interviews might be conducted with as many as three employees and usually include a "case analysis and case study." Says one European source, "We do three or four interviews with various senior people after which the chosen candidates are invited to a three-month trial period where they are 'attached' to a senior colleague. Based on the experience, it is decided among senior colleagues whether or not the candidate should stay."

# OUR SURVEY SAYS

## Free and easy

Hay's consultants offer accolades for an "open, ambitious, quality-driven, fun" culture they call "highly flexible" and "completely free." "You have the freedom to be who you want to be and fulfill your obligations according to your own agenda," says one consultant. Inside the firm, you'll find "people with very different personalities, profiles, working styles, etc." – yet outside the firm "work and personal life sometimes mix." Colleagues are called "extraordinary people," "excellent both professionally and socially." One thing consultants especially appreciate is that "senior experienced consultants can get on with client work without having to divert time into management."

## Equilibrium

The work/life balance depends on home office location but, in general, it seems to be pretty decent at Hay Group. "There's complete freedom to manage one's working time provided targets are met, and many people work special and reduced contracts," says one source. Another reports, "Travel varies by office and by job. Some consultants choose to work most with international clients, in which case they travel frequently. Others concentrate on their local market, in which case they travel less. It's also different depending on the country in which you work – small European countries require minimal travel, large ones require more. The U.S. market requires extensive travel." Hay offers four weeks' vacation to start.

Hours in Australia are "long, an average of 14 hours a day," reports one antipodal source. In other locations, our sources report 50- to 70-hour weeks. Beach time is nonexistent – "our way of working doesn't really allow for people to be on the beach," notes one source, and another consultant echoes, "There is more than enough work."

## Gliding up

Hey consultatnts are promoted by performance. "People can stick at a level for many years if they are happy with it," says an insider. Another consultant confirms, "there are many who do not move higher than senior consultant." So what gives a consultant the upper hand at Hay? "Promotion is based on personal growth (measured against clear objectives) and on commercial results, client satisfaction and innovation," says one source. Another consultant adds that promotion is "subject to passing certain accreditation test and showing an ability to lead and win projects." A degree is not decreed. "In our branch of the firm you can go as high as you want regardless of your degree. Your success in Hay depends on your success as a consultant – your ability to solve clients' problems and gain the confidence of clients to help them solve their problems and sell projects."

Hay did undergo layoffs this year, firing 12 workers in the United Kingdom, but according to consultants, "Hay has almost never reduced staff. This was a blip." "Usually it was merely a case of people who should have gone anyway leaving faster," explains another consultant.

## Perk talk

Compensation is rated as middling by the consultants we surveyed. "Profit sharing is available only to partners," notes one source. Another (European) source says "Compensation at Hay is usually very competitive. As it is our business to know what other companies pay, we must be competitive with our own staff."

Perks include a "home phone allowance" and a car allowance in certain locations. Along with standard health and insurance, some sites offer tuition reimbursement, laptops and gym membership discounts.

## Do your thing

Hay seems to be a place where self-starters go far. "Hay is a unique experience in management consulting," says one source. "It allows individual personalities to flourish where many other firms in the branch take a much more militaristic approach. At the same time one must be very self-motivated, for Hay does not over-manage its people. On the contrary, one must carefully manage one's own career." Supervisors get very high marks. Remarks one consultant, "When I consider a different job I worry most about not liking my new boss as much as I like my current one. We have a good mutual understanding – some might say friendship."

## Women bring in Hay

The company gets very high marks for diversity. "About half the consultants are women," estimates one source. "I have never seen an aversion to women in our firm. We have women in positions at all levels," says another insider.

# "We have women in positions at all levels."

## — Hay Group insider

# OC&C Strategy Consultants

330 Seventh Avenue
11th Floor
New York, NY 10011
Phone: (212) 244-3550
Fax: (212) 244-1117
www.occstrategy.com

## LOCATIONS

**London, UK (HQ)**
New York, NY • Amsterdam •
Brussels • Düsseldorf • Hamburg •
Paris • Rotterdam

## PRACTICE AREAS

Consumer Goods
Financial Services
Industrial
Media
Retail
Private Equity
Technology & Communications

## THE BUZZ
WHAT CONSULTANTS AT OTHER FIRMS ARE SAYING

- "Excellent strategists"
- "Disoganized, in decline"
- "Local powerhouses"
- "Too small to be a real player"

## THE STATS

**Employer Type:** Private Company
**Founding Director:** Chris Outram
**2002 Employees:** 350

## UPPERS

- Comprehensive training program
- "Genuinely good atmosphere" maintained by management
- Broad range of projects, no pigeonholing

## DOWNERS

- No strong diversity effort
- Small presence in North America
- MBA internships currently suspended

## KEY COMPETITORS

Bain & Company
Boston Consulting Group
McKinsey & Company

## EMPLOYMENT CONTACT

**U.S.:**
E-mail: recruitment@occstrategy-usa.com

**London:**
Katherine Day
OC&C Strategy Consultants
The OC&C Building
233 Shaftesbury Avenue
London WC2H 8EE
E-mail: Recruitment@occstrategy.com

**France:**
Sophie Sliman
E-mail: contact@occstrategy.fr

# THE SCOOP

## Quiet strategists

Founded in England by current director Chris Outram and a handful of colleagues back in 1987, OC&C Strategy Consultants has grown to eight offices in Europe and the U.S., with more associate offices in Italy and South America. The firm also maintains a close working relationship with Value Partners, an Italy-based consultancy.

OC&C focuses specifically on strategy issues, which it claims separates it from mainstream management consulting firms that increasingly turn to outsourcing and IT-related engagements to boost business. OC&C consultants (there are more than 200 of them) serve clients in all sectors, including heavy industry, media, consumer industries, private equity, technology convergence and financial services. In addition, the firm delves into pro bono engagements; notable beneficiaries include the World Wildlife Fund, the Multiple Sclerosis International Federation and the Rotterdam Philharmonic Orchestra.

## Working at OC&C

The average project has four or five team members working for eight weeks, but varies considerably. Average hours for a consultant are 55 per week; the firm also has an "amber light" system intended to keep people from consistently working more than 60 hours. Typically, OC&C consultants spend half their time working at the office, another 25 percent at nearby clients, and 25 percent traveling.

# GETTING HIRED

## Independence in hiring

Sources tell us that "hiring is done via the local offices; each office looks after itself." OC&C hires associate consultants straight from universities "continuously," with the formal recruiting season occurring from November to January. The firm has a "traditional" internship program, recruiting during February and March for an eight-week period in the summer. One insider informs us, "This year, our internship is for undergraduates only. We usually have an MBA internship as well, but it's on hold due to the economic downturn."

Philosophy majors take heart: At OC&C, your degree "doesn't matter. We are very subject-blind." Education in any field is welcomed because consultants and associate consultants work across all sectors.

# OUR SURVEY SAYS

## Fun and moderation

The people who work at OC&C describe a "fun culture" and a "genuinely good atmosphere." In fact, the firm's structure includes a "Ministry of Fun," essentially a group that organizes small perks, outings and other activities to keep the mood light. A source at the London office notes that consultants there enjoy a "game room" where consultants can take a break with "table football, darts, pool and things like that."

OC&C also offers a "very cooperative and collaborative atmosphere," according to consultants. "We don't think at all of other people here as competitors," says one insider. "It's easy and expected to seek help when you need it. People here are very supportive." The support comes from above as well. "We try and hold to 53-55 hours per week," notes one consultant. "The partners track our hours, and you're flagged when you consistently work 60 hours or more. An 'amber light' goes on and the firm reviews your work load to see how they can make things better."

In addition to the 55-hour week, a respondent tells us OC&C consultants do "a lot of work in their own offices." He confirms the company's stated policy of "about 50 percent of your time is spent in the local office, 25 percent at nearby clients, the rest is 'real' travel." Despite the firm's attempts to moderate the workload, "crunch times are a bear" and consultants do suffer "a loss of personal flexibility in [one's] schedule."

## Learning the ropes

Because of OC&C's generalist approach and the company's average "four to six week" project length, consultants "can be doing any sort of project at any time." This means everybody requires training at some point to be at the top of his or her game. One source simply rated the company's training as a "10" on a scale of one to 10. Another goes into more detail. "Your first week is an international training course, hosted at a different location each year. Everybody goes to this, even the experienced people – it's a yearly international get-together." He continues, "The second week is procedural and general training. Some time later, you get the basic finance course. Six to 12 months later, they follow up with advanced finance." In addition, "every now and again, an employee or principal will host a semiformal internal training session." And since employees need to sell work as they advance in position, "higher-up people get client sales training."

## The road to glory

A source provides details on the promotion track at the firm. "Out of university, you join as an associate consultant. You will most likely be promoted to consultant after two or three years, then to principal after a similar period, then on to partner or director." MBA holders typically start as consultants. He notes, "we've had people make director in eight or nine years," and "people have reached the top without MBAs and done perfectly well." A colleague adds that the promotion process is "not strictly up-or-out, promotions are phased according to ability."

# First Manhattan Consulting Group

90 Park Avenue
19th Floor
New York, NY 10016
Phone: (212) 557-0500
Fax: (212) 338-9296
www.fmcg.com

## LOCATIONS

**New York, NY (HQ)**

## PRACTICE AREAS

A/L and Portfolio Management
Business and Operations Strategy
Customer Relationship Management
Deal Structuring
Distribution Strategy
E-Commerce and Multimedia
    Strategy
Marketing and Segmentation
    Analyses
Organizational Design
Productivity and Cost Structure
    Management
Rapid Cycle Market Research and
    Testing
Risk Management
Technology Alliances/Outsourcing
Technology Strategy and
    Architecture

## THE STATS

**Employer Type:** Private Company
**President:** James McCormick
**2002 Employees:** 90
**2001 Employees:** 100

## UPPERS

- Smart, finance-whiz consultants
- Transferable skills taught

## DOWNERS

- Brutal hours
- Training minimal after first year

## KEY COMPETITORS

Booz Allen Hamilton
McKinsey & Company
Mercer Oliver Wyman

## EMPLOYMENT CONTACT

Recruiting Coordinator
90 Park Avenue
New York, NY 10016
Phone: (212) 455-9224
E-mail: recruit@fmcg.com

## THE BUZZ
WHAT CONSULTANTS AT OTHER FIRMS ARE SAYING

- "Consulting to i-banks, what's
  more prestigious than that?"
- "Slavedrivers"
- "Smart, smart people"

# THE SCOOP

## We'll take Manhattan

First Manhattan Consulting Group (FMCG) is a niche firm, focused almost entirely on working with financial services companies. FMCG offers advice on strategy, risk management and technology for these companies.

The client group is, obviously, heavily weighted toward finance. Since its founding in 1980, the company has worked with 80 percent of the 70 largest U.S. bank-holding companies, insurance companies, international banks from 22 countries, national and regional brokerages, telecom companies, Internet firms, and technology vendors.

## On the job

FMCG maintains a merit-based performance system. It's looking for certain qualities in its fast-trackers, including good project management skills (writing reports, managing analysts, planning, organizing); client skills (running client meetings with panache and skill, and handling clients); expert knowledge (especially in banking or insurance, and the ability to become a "thought leader" in a particular practice); analytical and conceptual skill; and professional demeanor. While analysts are not pushed into business school after two or three years, the firm does reimburse tuition for top business school qualifiers.

Teams usually range from two to six people, and always include at least an executive and an analyst. Analysts can expect workweeks between 60 and 80 hours, and usually balance two or three projects at once. Travel is, of course, standard. While the sole FMCG office is in New York City, clients have been as far-flung as Australia, Dubai and Singapore.

All entering analysts go through two off-site training sessions. Professors and FMCG execs and analysts lead the programs. The first is an introduction to FMCG and the role of the analyst; the second features a role-play of an engagement.

# GETTING HIRED

FMCG usually hires between 10 and 15 people for each analyst class. The firm seeks in its hires "exceptional intelligence, analytical ability, computer capability, and communication skills. Individuals selected also demonstrate a high energy level, a willingness to work very hard, and a belief in their personal responsibility to improve the end product." Occasionally, the company hires MBAs with a financial-services background. However, FMCG does not recruit on business school campuses, so MBAs should contact the recruiting department directly.

There is a 10-week summer internship program for college juniors; those interested should contact the recruiting department for more information.

For more information on top consulting employers and consulting careers, go to the Vault Consulting Career Channel at http://consulting.vault.com

- Detailed 40-page employer profiles on top employers like McKinsey, BCG, Bain, Accenture and more
- Surveys of employees at hundreds of consulting firms
- The only job board on the Web dedicated to consulting jobs – The Vault Consulting Job Board
- Case interview guides and one-on-one case interview prep

# http://consulting.vault.com

"Entrpreneurial, non-hierarchical and flexible, with a focus on creativity rather than a rigid process."

— *Watson Wyatt consultant*

# Watson Wyatt Worldwide

1717 H Street, NW
Washington, DC 20006
Phone: (202) 715-7000
Fax: (202) 715-7700

Watson House, London Road
Reigate, Surrey RH2
9PQ, England
Phone: +44 1737-241144
Fax: +44 1737-241496
www.watsonwyatt.com

## LOCATIONS

**Washington, DC (HQ)**
**Reigate, Surrey, UK (HQ)**
87 offices worldwide

## PRACTICE AREAS

Communications
Compensation
Group Benefits and Health Care
HR Technologies
International Investment
Organization Effectiveness
Retirement/Defined Contribution

## THE STATS

**Employer Type:** Public Company
**Stock Symbol:** WW
**Stock Exchange:** NYSE
**President and CEO:** John J. Haley
**2002 Employees:** 6,200
**2001 Employees:** 6,100
**2002 Revenue:** $710.5 million
**2001 Revenue:** $700.2 million

## UPPERS

• Interesting clients and projects

## DOWNERS

• Management strategy not
  coordinated

## KEY COMPETITORS

Accenture
Hewitt Associates
IBM BCS
Mercer Human Resource Consulting
Towers Perrin

## EMPLOYMENT CONTACT

www.watsonwyatt.com/careers/
opportunities.asp

## THE BUZZ
WHAT CONSULTANTS AT OTHER FIRMS ARE SAYING

• "They own the pension niche"
• "Bit old-fashioned"
• "Worthy"
• "Limited in focus"

# THE SCOOP

## A long, proud history

With more than 6,300 employees in 30 countries, Watson Wyatt boasts an impressive global presence. The firm has a long and complex history as well. R. Watson & Sons was founded in the United Kingdom in 1878, and advised government and companies on pension and insurance matters. Over in the U.S. in 1946, B.E. Wyatt and his co-founders started the Wyatt Company as a consultant for defined-benefit plans. It branched out into different service areas, and, in the 1980s, into different countries, adding offices in Asia, Europe, Canada and Latin America.

In 1995, the two firms merged, and operate as a partnership divided in half. Watson Wyatt & Company is headquartered in Washington, D.C. and has 4,100 associates in 62 offices in the Americas and Asia-Pacific regions. It is also a subsidiary of Watson Wyatt & Company Holdings, a NYSE-traded firm. The privately held Watson Wyatt Partners, on the other hand, is the leading European consulting partnership, with headquarters in Reigate, U.K. The two operate globally as Watson Wyatt Worldwide, specializing in employee benefits, human capital strategies, technology programs, and insurance/financial services. In Europe, Watson Wyatt advises 73 percent of the Fortune Global 500 companies headquartered in Britain and almost half of the U.K.'s 100 largest corporate pension funds.

## HR goes online, ushered by Watson Wyatt

Watson Wyatt has long been a champion of Web-based HR management programs. The centerpiece of its Internet strategy is the eHR package, which offers clients a full-service platform for benefits and staffing administration, as well as 401(k) management and employee training. The company releases research papers and reports concerning Internet-based benefits administration; a section of its web site allows companies to participate in a survey that compares them against 700 other employers. In December 2002, the firm introduced what it calls an eStatement, which permits subscribing employees to access personalized messages, compensation and benefits data in real time. Watson Wyatt also has a number of partnerships with HR software makers and consulting firms, including Siebel Systems, Workscape, Synhrgy and Gabriel, Roeder, Smith & Company.

## Outposts overseas

Watson Wyatt's international offices turned in exceptionally strong performances during 2002, particularly the firm's outposts in Australia, Mexico and Asia. In August 2002, Watson Wyatt Mexico added an important firm to its portfolio: Soluciones Estratégicas de Remuneración, an HR specialist, gave the firm 12 more consultants in Mexico, whose clients include several large auto, pharmaceutical, tech, consumer products and financial services companies. The firm opened a fifth office in China (Shenzhen) at the end of 2002.

## Financial fixings

Fiscal year 2002 (Watson Wyatt's fiscal year-end is in June) was a solid one. Despite an altogether crummy economy the company increased its revenue 1.5 percent from 2001, to $710.5 million. Profits grew 6 percent, to $47.1 million. The company says that for fiscal year 2003, it expects high demand for advice on pension plan governance, stock option strategies and rising health care costs.

Though there were layoffs at the end of 2002, that doesn't mean there's no advancement at the firm. Indeed, in May 2002, Watson Wyatt promoted 24 European associates to partner – the largest number of new partner promotions it had ever made in one year.

As well as being one of the largest HR firms in the world, Watson Wyatt is also part of the still-small coterie of publicly traded consulting firms. The company had its initial public offering in October 2000, announcing 5.6 million shares priced at $12.50 per share – though the actual opening price was $14.88 (a healthy 20 percent jump). On the first day of trading, the shares quickly rose to over $16, making the first-ever IPO by a benefits consulting firm an overwhelming success. (The firm prudently retained 75 percent of the total shares.)

## Oh, you shouldn't have!

Watson Wyatt racked up numerous tributes in 2002. *The London Sunday Times* named the firm 71st of 100 on its "Best Companies to Work For" list; it's made the ranks in each of the three years the list has existed. *China Staff* magazine named it the "Hong Kong HR Consultancy of the Year" for the fifth consecutive year. And *Business Insurance* magazine named Maureen Cotter, Watson Wyatt's global director of group and health care benefits consulting, to its "35 Rising Stars" list covering the commercial insurance and risk/benefits analysis industries. Finally, *Consulting* magazine ranked Watson Wyatt seventh on its list of "The 10 Best Consulting Firms to Work For" in 2002.

## Branching out

People management resources (PMR), a research division of Watson Wyatt Worldwide, identifies and publishes best practices case studies for improving people management. Watson Wyatt Data Services, another subsidiary, is a searchable database containing national and international reports and surveys concerning global compensation, benefits and employment practices information. The HR Scorecard Alliance, launched in November 2002, is a Web-based survey that measures best practices for HR for execs from large companies – IBM, GE and Allstate were initial members. Execs access the survey to gauge the cost effectiveness of programs or priorities for HR.

In January 2003, Watson Wyatt announced a new practice in its North American wing, which it dubbed workforce planning. Part of the benefits consulting group, workforce planning will help organizations plan for staffing – or downsizing. Jane Paradiso was named practice leader of this group.

# GETTING HIRED

Watson Wyatt projects it will hire about 140 recent grads in 2003. If you'd like to be among this number, go online. Hiring is mostly done through the Watson Wyatt web site (www.watsonwyatt.com/careers) or through on-campus recruiting. "The undergrad process is consistent, with interviews and application forms," says a source. In the U.K., Watson Wyatt recruits undergrads from Oxford, Cambridge and other top universities.

Watson Wyatt's web site allows eager job hunters to search a database of currently available jobs and to apply for them online. According to the company, "a degree or background in computer science, communications, mathematics, economics, health care or business will provide a foundation for success with Watson Wyatt," though "many of our associates have degrees in the sciences, humanities or the law."

# OUR SURVEY SAYS

## Culture gap

Our respondents note that culture and work/life balance "varies by practice" and "depends on the office." It's "entrepreneurial, nonhierarchical and flexible, with a focus on creativity rather than a rigid process," notes one respondent. A European consultant isn't quite as pleased, noting that "in my office and practice at the moment, partners are looking out for themselves, and there's lack of teamwork." Also, this consultant notes, "there's no global culture."

The firm gets good marks for its community service – though there's "very little pro bono" work, each office undertakes its own campaign.

## Home of Dilbert?

Some consultants carp that management seems uncoordinated. "The left hand often doesn't know what the right is doing, so there's some frustration with turning ideas into an aligned strategy here," says a source. Another complains about "the politics – Dilbert works here." However, that's not an across-the-board feeling. "I think it's a great place to work – the firm's resources are directed at making its people happy and productive," says an insider.

## Home front

At Watson Wyatt, work/life balance is fairly, well, balanced. "It's hard work, but there's a lot of attention to making sure you have a life," says one source. Just as the hours are "reasonably flexible," so is travel – insiders report traveling about one to four days a month. Fifty-hour weeks are the norm. The company did undergo a handful of layoffs in some practices, including communication and technology, in 2002. The offices are about par for consultant firms, sources say. "It depends on the office," says an insider. Another says, "they're not over-the-[top] luxurious, but I've been in BCG and McKinsey offices and they weren't any nicer."

## The job track

Those without advanced degrees can thrive at Watson Wyatt, where there are "not many MBAs" and no up-or-out policies. "Promotions come from a couple of things: a record of performance, a lot of confidence and self-salesmanship – plus a powerful sponsor," explains a source. However, "promotions take a while" – occurring about "once per year" – and "some who are not partner material still get there because they have been around a long time."

## The salary equation

"Compensation," intones a consultant, "has fallen behind in recent years, and is now uncompetitive." Perks, however, are quite attractive. Eligible associates can expect 25 percent of their year-end bonus is in the form of stock options, vesting over a two-year period at 50 percent per year. In addition, Watson Wyatt matches 401(k) contributions at 50 percent of the first 6 percent contributed. The firm's compensation program includes a base salary, bonus opportunities, stock options, an array of health and welfare benefits, paid time off and pension and savings plans.

175 West Jackson Boulevard
Chicago, IL 60604
Phone: (312) 856-0200
Fax: (312) 861-1340
www.grantthornton.com

## LOCATIONS

**Chicago, IL (HQ)**
51 offices nationwide

## PRACTICE AREAS

Accounting
Business Advisory
Tax

## THE STATS

**Employer Type:** Private Company
**CEO:** Edward Nusbaum
**2002 Employees:** 3,200
**2001 Employees:** 2,700
**2002 Revenue:** $400 million
**2001 Revenue:** $380 million

## UPPERS

- Good compensation
- Teamwork emphasized

## DOWNERS

- Consulting not as respected as accounting
- Confusing promotion process

## KEY COMPETITORS

BearingPoint
Cap Gemini Ernst & Young
Deloitte Consulting
IBM BCS

## EMPLOYMENT CONTACT

See job listings' specific e-mail contacts.

## THE BUZZ
WHAT CONSULTANTS AT OTHER FIRMS ARE SAYING

- "Small but good reputation"
- "Middle market"
- "Excellent"
- "Should stick to accounting"

# THE SCOOP

## Old-timers

Grant Thornton (GT) has been around since 1924, when a 26-year-old Chicagoan named Alexander Grant founded an eponymous accounting firm. Then, as now, the company planned to serve the middle market. The firm grew slowly in its first decades, gaining speed through the 1960s as it expanded internationally. In 1980, Alexander Grant (the firm) helped form, and became a member of, Grant Thornton International, an umbrella organization with member and affiliate offices in 110 countries around the world. Combined, Grant Thornton firms have about 21,500 employees and earn nearly $2 billion in global revenue.

In 1986, Alexander Grant changed its name to Grant Thornton. The firm added the LLP to its name in 1995 when it became a limited liability partnership. As of 2003, Grant Thornton LLP, headquartered in Chicago, has more than 315 partners in 51 offices around the nation. While such numbers render GT one of the world's largest professional services firms, it remains just outside the circle of mega-firms comprising the Big Four. And like those firms, GT has augmented its services with consulting.

## Growing up

The company has expanded upon its accounting roots. Today, its practices include assurance, compensation/benefits, international issues, M&A transactions, general management consulting, tax consulting and valuation. GT typically targets middle-market companies.

In October 2002, the company launched a Business Risk Services practice, which will help clients analyze and deal with technological, operational and financial risks. It also developed a tool called ASAP, launched in December 2002, that pinpoints areas in which clients can cut costs, be more efficient, or manage risk.

The firm seems to have profited from Arthur Andersen's downfall, absorbing a number of that company's employees and offices since June 2002. It's added former AA staffers and offices in Charlotte, Greensboro and Raleigh, N.C., Columbia, SC, Milwaukee, New York, Orlando, Albuquerque, Cleveland, Cincinnati, Tampa, Tulsa, San Francisco and Vienna, Va. All told, those acquisitions added 60 partners and more than 550 employees to Grant Thornton's staff. In January 2003, the company acquired Brueggeman and Johnson PC, a Seattle-based valuation firm.

## Tech tack

In February 2002, Grant Thornton announced a strategic alliance with Minnesota-based Adaytum to resell the financial-software maker's e.Planning program, which helps companies manage their budgeting processes in close to real time. In October 2000 GT sold its 450-person e-business consulting group, now known as Experio Solutions, to Japanese computer giant Hitachi in a $175 million deal.

## Trouble, trouble

But Grant Thornton's past few years haven't been entirely rosy. In October 2001 the FDIC filed a claim against the firm, accusing it of misleading regulators about fraud and negligence at the First National Bank of Keystone. And in May 2000 the Carnegie International Corporation, an Internet support company, filed a $2.1 billion suit against GT, alleging that it had fraudulently failed to provide contracted accounting services. In July 2001, in a twist that eerily foreshadowed the Enron/Andersen scandal a few months later, Carnegie asked for a default judgment after it learned that a GT senior partner had deleted e-mails. The judgment was denied when the e-mails were recovered and produced in court. More tangles ensued in November 2001, when GT admitted it had unknowingly withheld other key documents during the discovery phase of the trial, leading the judge to suspend the proceedings until an investigation could be completed. The trial concluded in 2003.

Grant Thornton replied, somewhat vituperatively, to the suit. "Imagine," said Grant Thornton, "a company that goes from selling gym equiptment to providing 'adult content' phone lines to touting itself as a telecom company, where one of its founders leads a cult that believes aliens are communicating with him through his cats and recently pleads guilty to criminal charges for an alleged murder for hire plot against the firm's chairman, has yet to file its 2002 10K report from March of this year, has liens filed against it by the IRS and State of Maryland for back taxes, and now seeks $2.1 billion in damages from your company, when the most it ever generated in annual revenues was less than 1 percent of this amount."

## Chin up

Despite Grant Thornton's legal struggles, the company continues to keep up with, and even outpace, its larger competitors. Fueled in part by those acquisitions, the firm has been gearing up to make a name for itself. In January 2003, it placed second in *Public Accounting Report*'s quarterly audit ratings – the first time a non-Big Four

(Andersen was by then defunct) firm had placed in the top two. The rankings measure the largest net gain in revenue for the quarter.

# GETTING HIRED

GT recruits at a handful of schools, including "University of Wisconsin campuses and Marquette University," "any school on the A-list," and "most of the top business colleges in the country."

Though "we hire most of our new employees through campus recruiting, experienced hires may come from recruiters, ads or referrals." Grant Thornton's web site has a fairly helpful career page with a link to its job listings. Those not going through on-campus career centers should send resumes and cover letters directly to their GT regional office of choice. "We use an internal headhunter," one source notes.

Cover letters should include career objectives and salary history. While the interview process varies, it is essentially a 20- to 30-minute meeting that includes a review of educational experience and career interests and a discussion of the firm's teamwork environment. Successful applicants then undertake an office visit that consists of interviews with three GT professionals, a panel of recent college grads and lunch with staff members and partners. Case studies are not usually used, though "individuals responsible for hiring are pretty free to set their own criteria." Candidates should expect to hear back from GT within a week.

# OUR SURVEY SAYS

## Accounting rules

Since 84 percent of Grant Thornton's revenue still comes from audit and tax, the culture still seems to be slanted toward that service group, insiders say. "Everything is oriented toward employees who are involved in accounting – the paperwork, the AICPA rules, etc., often do not apply to us but if one has to do it, everyone does, is the rule around here," says a source. "Consulting is not treated as highly as the accounting side," remarks a consultant.

Depite GT's accounting orientation, many consultants enjoy GT culture. It's "friendly and down to earth, yet results oriented," says one. Another finds the firm "very family-oriented and light on politics." The company's team ethic seems strong:

"It's more of a team environment [than the Big Four], with far fewer lone wolves. And I don't think egos are as huge," says one consultant. "This is the happiest place I've ever worked." Consultants hang out after hours, too – one consultant, who recently moved to a new office, describes his experience as "add water, instant social life."

## Stay at home

The company has "very strong work/life balance initiatives," says one source. However, approval of work/life balance is not universal. "I have worked in the same group for my five years here and am in my third location – I moved the first time they moved us, now they moved us back and my commute went from 18 minutes to over an hour inbound and closer to two hours to get home. I have to heat up my supper every night," says one consultant.

On the bright side, travel schedules appear to be relatively light. While a few consultants report traveling from one to three days a week, most say they stay in the office almost all the time, or "travel once per month." Another plus is the ability to work from home: "The work I do can be done remotely, so I work from the office or home. There are occasional trips to local clients, rare trips to clients out of the immediate area, and I have done one extended road trip when the client needed on-site support," says one insider.

Hours can vary. Most people reported working about 50 hours a week, with some reporting up to 60, and another clocking in at 45. "The work load is erratic, with few slumps," says a source. But if you "manage your workload," the amount of work doesn't usually "spike too often."

## Reviewing promotions

While some respondents were satisfied with the promotion process, many described it as unclear. Says one fan, "We have yearly reviews, where you set your goals. You get periodic performance feedback from a counselor or mentor, and there's a year-end roundtable process. Then each person's performance at the end of the year is rated; that rating determines your bonus, pay increase and promotion." Nods another consultant, "Promotions come at a good pace. I have seen people go from senior consultant to senior manager in my five years here and seen that very qualified people are making senior consultant and partner in good time." However, others describe the promotion process as fuzzy, with one calling for a "clear articulation of promotion policies." "Promotions require patience. It's not strictly up-or-out, for there are many people at the firm who linger in their current position," says a source.

## Up the ladder

One point of contention is whether consultants need an advanced degree to move forward. "An MBA is not required to advance," says an insider. But another reports that "you cannot advance without a graduate degree or CPA certification," and "currently our structure is very top heavy so there is not much room for advancement." "Several of our partners have no advanced degree, but advanced degrees are a factor in advancement," muses one insider.

Meanwhile, though promotion is "not totally up-or-out depending on location and need, you're strongly encouraged to move up." Underperformers can expect to be "marked for deletion" (Sounds ominous, no?) That's especially the case in small offices: "The smaller offices have less flexibility to keep people who don't advance."

Another dilemma is how long to expect to stay in each position. "Senior, two years. Manager, five to six years. Partner, 15-plus years," reports one succinct source. Says another, "You can expect to move from supervisor to manager in two years if you're a go-getter." A third places bets on "two years to senior, five years to manager, three years to senior manager, 13 years to partner. "At the upper levels, says one source, time frames are abandoned; promotion at those levels "has more to do with longevity and performance."

There were layoffs (or should we say deletion marks?) in "certain locations" and practices during the last year, though the "firm added over 70 new partners." "In my section, we lost about 30 percent this year," says one consultant. Still, the "firm continues to grow nationally."

## Decent comp, but not much in the way of raises

GT's compensation gets solid marks from our respondents. One insider cites GT as offering a "competitive salary," and another agrees, "The money is good." There is 401(k) matching, "bonuses for new business solutions, profit sharing and rewards for goal achievement." However, one respondent contends that there is "lots of work now, but no meaningful raises."

## Long list o' benefits

Standard benefits at Grant Thornton include medical, vision and dental coverage; a 401(k) with matching; and options for long-term, life, and accidental-death insurance. In the Madison, Wisc. location, we hear many consultants get cell phones, PDAs, event tickets, laptops and a cafeteria. Nashville employees get a cafeteria, laptops, and tuition reimbursement. In New York, it's laptops, an employee-referral bonus, a cafeteria, tuition reimbursement, pagers and day care. Chicago denizens get cell phones, event tickets, tuition reimbursement, laptops, gym discounts, employee-referral bonuses and a dry cleaners. Whew.

## Happily hands-off management

Respondents characterize Grant Thornton management as hands-off yet caring, for the most part. "I have found GT to be a great place to work. It has a caring management style which places the welfare of our employees at the top of their agenda," says a brand new partner. "The primary partner has been hands off in a good sense. He's been interested in promoting my career and getting me to partner ASAP. He positions me to have all the client contact. I'd say he's very supportive," says one consultant. The hands-off style pleases some ("there's little micromanagement") while alienating others ("there's a lack of feedback from superiors").

Others report slightly different views. "I have little respect for those above me," says one manager. A senior consultant says the manager above is "afraid of superiors – with good reason, given all of the layoffs – and of our clients." One respondent bemoans the "new supervisors who don't understand the client base, and the old supervisors with no people skills who resent your good relationships with your clients."

## Range of offices

Not surprisingly, office quality varies by location. D.C. gets low marks, with "a very loud work area, most people in cubicles, and no natural light." Kansas City is also low on the office quality scale. Madison is above average, sources say, while Nashville, New York and Chicago are all reportedly great spaces.

## Remote training

Training is "not great but improving," by some accounts. "Who gets training depends on who makes the most noise and on favoritism," says one senior consultant. But another consultant finds it "wonderful. As an effort to decrease the cost of travel, there's an Internet training program that's live and interactive."

## A welcoming place

"The female/male ratio is still a little out of whack, but the professional practices managing partner is a woman," says a source. One woman notes that there is "no place for nursing mothers to pump." (The firm notes that there is an office in Chicago devoted solely to mothering.)

GT is a fairly diverse place, according to respondents. "Here, there are African-Americans and a lot of Hispanics. It says a lot for the organization," says one source. However, another insider finds that "this place is pretty white/Asian." Overall, diversity with respect to race gets fairly high marks.

With regard to gays, lesbians and bisexuals, there are "openly gay people at the partner level," says one source, and another insider reports that "the few that I know of are treated well."

## Giving back

In some locations, the firm is active in community service. A Madison source says the office there is "very involved with the United Way," Easter Seals, and Big Brothers/Big Sisters." In D.C., there is a "Jeans Day for various causes that are at least respectable at first glance – $5 and you get to wear jeans. Young single individuals are very involved in worthwhile endeavors." In Chicago, there are "many activities, like pro bono consulting, fund raisers, and charitable involvement."

# Kurt Salmon Associates

1355 Peachtree Street, NE
Suite 900
Atlanta, GA 30309
Phone: (404) 892-0321
Fax: (404) 898-9590
www.kurtsalmon.com

## LOCATIONS

**Atlanta, GA (HQ)**
25 offices worldwide

## PRACTICE AREAS

**Consumer Products Division:**
Corporate Finance
Fulfillment (Logistics and Operations)
Information Technology
Merchandising
Strategy

**Health Care Division:**
Facilities Planning
IT
Strategy

## THE STATS

**Employer Type:** Private Company
**CEO:** William B. Pace
**2002 Employees:** 700
**2001 Employees:** 800

## UPPERS

• Management supportive and smart
• Interesting projects and clients
• Telecommuting and flexible hours

## DOWNERS

• Salaries below the norm
• Few learning/training opportunities
• Travel affects team spirit

## KEY COMPETITORS

Accenture
A.T. Kearney
Booz Allen Hamilton
Deloitte Consulting
IBM BCS
McKinsey & Company

## EMPLOYMENT CONTACT

**Americas**
RecrNA@kurtsalmon.com

**Asia-Pacific**
RecrAPAC@kurtsalmon.com

**Europe**
RecrEU@kurtsalmon.com

 ## THE BUZZ
WHAT CONSULTANTS AT OTHER FIRMS ARE SAYING

• "A leader in their field"
• "Fluffy"
• "A champion for retail"
• "Niche player"

# THE SCOOP

## From hosiery to consumer consulting

In the 1920s, a young man named Kurt Salmon was working at a stocking factory in his native Germany but soon became disenchanted with hosiery and took up engineering. His fascination with clothing lasted, though, and when he moved to the United States in 1930, the textile engineer found that apparel manufacturers were always asking his advice. Salmon opened his consulting firm, which specializes in the retail, health care and consumer goods industries, in 1935. Since then, Kurt Salmon Associates has expanded across the globe, and today employs approximately 800 people.

## KSA today

Major groups within the company's retail and consumer products division include corporate finance, strategy, merchandising, information technology and fulfillment. Although Kurt Salmon Associates is smaller than most of its management consulting competitors, it is the largest firm specializing in the consumer goods and retail industries. In its retailing group, KSA focuses on clients' supply chains and technology – from sourcing, manufacturing and distribution to sales and replenishment. Its information technology teams address technology opportunities from developing e-business strategies to selecting and implementing enterprise-wide software solutions. In its health care group, KSA looks at facility planning, strategy and IT for hospitals and private practices.

Kurt Salmon Associates experienced substantial growth in the 1990s (though it has shed about 100 employees since 2000). At least 80 percent of its business comes from previous clients. KSA engagements usually last anywhere from six weeks to a year or more. The firm serves a wide variety of companies whose annual sales range from $100 million to billions of dollars. These include both manufacturers and clients in all channels of retailing, such as mass merchants, direct marketers (Internet and catalog), do-it-yourself shops, and specialty and department stores. The firm's focus has moved up the supply chain over the years from operations to retail, and a current focus is expansion into consumer products. Clients include Tiffany's, Nike, Liz Claiborne, Talbot's, Timberland, Polo/Ralph Lauren, DuPont and Food Lion.

## Acquisition fever

In the past few years, KSA has snapped up several firms as part of its internal growth strategy. What makes these companies attractive, according to KSA, is their ability to add to the firm's services and fit into KSA culture. In May 2000, KSA acquired MMM Consultancy Group, a leading European logistics consulting firm based in the U.K. Five months later, Kurt Salmon Associates' health care consulting practice, Hamilton HMC, acquired Space Diagnostics Inc., a consultancy specializing in hospital and health care planning services. (Hamilton HMC had been formed in 1986 with the acquisition of Hamilton Associates.) The division has since emerged as a leader in its field, advising on such issues as strategy, facilities implementation and technology. With the merger, the combined entity took on the Kurt Salmon Associates name. In November 2000, KSA purchased Chicago-based TransTech, a developer of Internet-based applications and enterprise solutions; it sold the unit in 2002.

In 1998 KSA launched an M&A advisory practice that has acted as exclusive financial adviser in a number of important transactions. The investment banking subsidiary, KSA Capital Advisors, is a licensed broker-dealer and a member of the NASD. The group leverages the industry knowledge of KSA's senior consultants to provide transaction expertise on M&A, capital formation and financial advisory projects. The career track for KSA Capital Advisors differs from KSA proper, though the interviewing process is the same.

KSA currently offers B2B and B2C e-commerce consulting services to retailers and consumer products suppliers, focusing especially on improving supply chain effectiveness. To bolster KSA's IT and e-business practice, the firm has software alliances with, among others, PeopleSoft, JDA, QRS and Manhattan Associates.

## A fast Pace

The firm's biggest recent acquisition came at the tail end of 2000, when it announced it would acquire Swander Pace & Company. Swander Pace, a food, beverage and packaged goods expert, made a neat addition to KSA's retail, consumer products and health care savvy. Swander Pace kept its San Francisco base and most directors, some of whom stayed on to lead KSA's combined strategy practice. Just over a year after KSA and Swander Pace joined forces, KSA named William B. Pace, one of the founding partners of Swander Pace, CEO of Kurt Salmon Associates effective March 1, 2002. Erstwhile Kurt Salmon Associates CEO Peter G. Brown continues in his role as chairman, while longtime KSA executive David A. Cole was named chairman emeritus.

# GETTING HIRED

## Beating the bushes

KSA looks for long-term hires – and man, does it look hard. KSA "had one of the most strenuous hiring processes," says an consultant. "KSA looks for those that eventually will run the firm, not two-year interns," adds another source. The process starts with a resume screening. KSA posts jobs on its site, and also recruits at a mix of top business and engineering programs, including Emory, Columbia, Stern, Georgia Tech, Kellogg and University of Michigan. The first round consists of an interview on campus, in a KSA office, or via phone – and a two-hour analytical test (unless if it's a phone interview). The second stage includes in person interviews (in an office or on campus). Finally, a full-day office visit invitation is extended, where candidates will have several more interviews with various levels of employees, followed by a personality profile. This round includes a case interview.

For retail case interviews, candidates should expect a specific project or problem scenario; they'll have to walk the interviewers through their solution. "The case study primarily focuses on process/performance improvement-type opportunities," says an insider. For the health care group, the questions "will present a current client deliverable and ask the prospect to analyze findings or give feedback on observations and recommendations," says one consultant. The company is looking for a "logical thought process" in interviewees' answers. Some business knowledge is also necessary, and "for experienced hires we would require a higher degree of industry knowledge in the case study."

## A high bar

An advanced degree is required for some groups, such as health care; in others, it may simply give candidates an edge. "We tried an analyst role (undergraduate degree) but haven't had a lot of success with it. There is a very hands-on approach to what we do and an analyst tucked away in an office somewhere doesn't get the sense of what is happening on the client site," explains a health care consultant. College grads can join the firm on the retail side, however. MBA hires usually have two to three years of work experience, come from the top 10 percent of their class and have prior experience in consulting, retail or consumer products. Prospective hires in the health care division should have an MBA or MHA on top of two to five years of related experience. Fluency in a second language and additional degrees are considered pluses for all groups. Occasionally, there are limited summer internship opportunities, and interns often go on to work full time at KSA. The 11-week internships give a taste of life at KSA. Interns are staffed on a single project, and travel, make presentations and talk to clients.

# OUR SURVEY SAYS

## Cuddly culture

KSA is lauded as small and supportive. "You call everyone by their first name and call anyone if you need anything," says an employee. "The culture of the firm is a big selling point for all those who interview at and join the company. The culture is very open and not cutthroat," says another. Management generally keeps an eye out for the worker bees, too. "There is a general concern for your career track within the firm. The principals realize that to continue our success there needs to be growth among the consultants and managers. Thus they are very helpful in advancing your career in the industry and within the firm," explains one consultant. "The managers at KSA offer a lot of flexibility and attempt to provide consultants with a balanced lifestyle," adds another. KSA is also said to be "a very ethical firm, which has refused work on more than one occasion rather than overpromise to a client, or do something that would compromise the principles of the firm."

## Nice-as-pie managers

Still, employees report that the quality of their direct supervisors can be inconsistent. "It's dependent upon project staffing. [They] can be really good or really lousy," says one respondent. Some say management can be "too nice," sugarcoating performance reviews, and many say there's a lack of high-level communication. Insiders also seem to be sensing more competition, particularly as the economy – and the management – dictates that all consultants pull their weight.

Management gets high marks for the integration of Swander Pace employees; most of the original SP employees are still in the San Francisco office, and "it's still quite family-like," says one. Consultants also single out the strategy practice as "small, cohesive, fun, interactive." "I have quite a bit of confidence in our management team. Our current team has charged ahead in difficult times," says an insider. "Also, I have received personal attention and follow-up to both work issues and travel/quality of life issues."

KSA tries to improve quality of life in its office locations, too, supporting Junior Achievement "with a strong firm commitment," March of Dimes, Hands On Atlanta, and United Way ("our campaign is HUGE," brags one insider), along with doing pro bono charity work.

## Fly KSA

KSA requires a lot of traveling. Depending on the service group and type of project, KSA consultants may travel up to four or five days a week. In one group, consultants habitually relocate to each of their projects, living out of a hotel room or apartment until they're finished. A more senior consultant "will fly out no earlier than 7 a.m. Monday morning and will be back home no later than 7 p.m. Friday." Upper-level employees' travel schedules vary depending on project requirements. The upside is, as one consultant says, "I still feel that I maintain a very independent schedule and can adjust my personal time off around the peaks and valleys of project cycles."

And KSA consultants travel in style. "We rarely let clients cap us on expenses, so we fly when and where we want (don't have to route through other cities to conserve on airfare) and stay and eat well on the road," divulges a senior consultant. Moreover, consultants seem happy to spend time on site with interesting clients. "There is no other way [other than working at KSA] to interact with this caliber of institutional clients on a consistent basis," says one KSAer. In keeping with KSA's flexible management policies, "rigid guidelines are available to limit excessive travel, if a consultant wants to call on them. But generally, the firm's penchant for putting 'client interests first' drives one to do whatever it takes to get the job done," says a consultant.

All this travel can translate into a lack of team spirit. "It's difficult to connect with people when you are not on the same project. Everyone travels so a sense of community and long-term team building is hard to achieve," says one employee.

## Softening training

Training, once a forte of KSA's, has "declined a lot over the past two years as the market softened and funds for training were limited." The analytical and technical training have seen the effects. "This is an area where I would like to see more investment," says a source. Another insider adds that KSA is resuming some formal training, and "the training programs are very beneficial when they were occurring regularly." The company notes that it is reinstituting training that had previously been postponed or canceled.

Informal development is also a cause for concern among employees. "The staffing model currently doesn't support professional development. There are not enough new people to whom I can pass on work and skills I have mastered. This is largely due to the turn in economy," says one consultant. Another insider echoes, "Project staffing is often driven more by availability than developmental considerations."

## Cute cubicles

The offices are generally pleasant, according to KSA insiders. The Atlanta headquarters places some consultants in cubes "that are way too small for someone with several years of work experience and a graduate degree." In Minneapolis, by contrast, managers and consultants "have their own offices (with a door) and a window." Chances are, you won't be spending much time there anyway, given the travel requirements.

## On the rebound

After a tough 2001, in which the company laid off employees, KSA's staff seems to be rebounding well. "Yes, we did go through the painful process of adjusting our people capacity, but we have been hitting our targets since then and coming out stronger," says one. They're now looking to their future with the company. There is a slight up-or-out process, though "98 percent move up." The promotion criteria is "clear and fair": three to five years as a consultant – where you "contribute practically from the day one walks in the door," five to seven as a manager, and then a promotion to principal. The key part of promotion to principal/partner is "the ability to sell work and enhance the image of the firm," explains a source. That said, "every consultant is hired with the expectation of making principal or partner," adds another. That's where much of the up-or-out comes in. "If you are not in an ownership role after 12 to 15 years, few individuals stay on past that timeframe."

## Talking about compensation

"We believe our firm to be among the lowest in the sector for salaries," carps one respondent; consultants consistently find salaries to be one of the downsides of working at Kurt Salmon Associates. (The firm counters that salaries are comparable with thoes of competitors' in most service groups.) "We've always relied on our firm to have a culture that is so appealing that people are willing to trade off economically. However, that culture is changing (and not for the better) and compensation has not," explains another. The company states that salaries in the strategy group are not as high as top-tier firms, but believes the group's lifestyle proposition counters that; within the rest of the firm, a company rep says, salaries are comparable. Benefits include 401(k) matching after three years, maxing out at 4 percent matching after six years. "There is also a retirement fund that is contributed to but is very heavily weighted to age, time with the firm and salary – it doesn't accumulate much in the early years," says one insider. The health plan options "suck more than a schoolteacher's," and vision is included only if you select the HMO plan. "We have an attractive health care plan comparable to our competitors," maintains the company. However, perks such as stock options, a company car for upper management, an on-site gym (Atlanta only), life and disability insurance, and laptops and cell phones help counter the sting of the salary/benefit package.

## All in the family

KSA gets high marks for diversity. "It's great overall, but somewhat rocky for new mothers who want to maintain full-time jobs as consultants," one consultant acknowledges. As with many firms, there are "lots of opportunities for females at the consultant/manager level, but no good role models at the principal level." A female consultant sees a bright future for women at KSA: "There's an increasing number of women hired and promoted, and opportunities are increasing as more women achieve success in the firm," she reports.

Regarding minorities, KSA is said to be an accepting place. "What I like best is that minority status is really a nonissue," says one (white) consultant. "We've done very well in the last year or two on hiring minority candidates," agrees another insider.

KSA gets singled out for its attitude toward gays and lesbians. We have plenty of people with different sexual orientation at all levels in the firm," notes one employee. Another consultant observes, "The firm seems extremely progressive in this area for what might be thought of as a conservative firm. Recent policy changes have included benefits for domestic partners. Significant others are welcomed at parties, and there are at least a couple of gay partners that I am aware of."

1800 Sherman Avenue
Suite 700
Evanston, IL 60201
Phone: (847) 492-3600
Fax: (847) 492-3409
www.zsassociates.com

## LOCATIONS

**Evanston, IL (HQ)**
10 offices worldwide

## PRACTICE AREAS

Analytic Data Warehousing
Compensation Systems
Customer Segmentation
Decision Support Systems
Forecasting
Geographic Deployment
Mergers
Micromarketing
Product Marketing Strategy
Resource Allocation
Sales Force Size and Structure
Strategic Market Research

## THE STATS

**Employer Type:** Private Company
**Managing Directors:** Andris A.
Zoltners and Prabha K. Sinha
**2002 Employees:** 500+
**2001 Employees:** 650

## UPPERS

- Relaxed, congenial culture
- In-depth training

## DOWNERS

- Drab offices
- Uneven workloads

## KEY COMPETITORS

Accenture
Booz Allen Hamilton
Navigant Consulting

## EMPLOYMENT CONTACT

www.zsassociates.com/careers/apply
/contactlist.html

## THE BUZZ
WHAT CONSULTANTS AT OTHER FIRMS ARE SAYING

- "Lots of opportunity to travel"
- "Number crunchers"
- "Good at what they do"
- "Very specific"

# THE SCOOP

## Consulting, from Z to S

ZS Associates is an Evanston, Ill.-based marketing and sales strategy consulting firm. It works on marketing and sales strategy, solving problems such as changing customer needs or which business units should do which promotions. Two Northwestern professors, Andris Zoltners and Prabha Sinha (hence ZS), realized they could help real businesses with their academic research in pharmaceuticals and founded the firm in 1983.

The pharmaceutical industry is still the mainstay of ZS business; today, ZS advises companies in 19 industries and 70 countries. The majority of ZS work is for large multinationals, but its expertise spans the field, with experience in everything from over-the-counter markets to biotechnology research. Almost half of the firm's engagements involve strategic marketing and sales analysis; other ZS specialties include forecasting sales and geographic sales territory alignment.

Nevertheless, ZS is branching out beyond pharmaceuticals. It has made efforts to appeal to a wider spectrum of industries (including financial services, consumer products and high tech). In January 2002 it sold its Cozint subsidiary, a specialist online health care research and consulting firm, to British information firm United Business Media for $10.5 million.

## International accents

The company is growing fast while retaining loyal customers. In fact, its first customer in 1983 is still a customer today, and more than 80 percent of its business comes from repeat clients. The firm is also rapidly expanding overseas. Approximately 28 percent of ZS engagements take place outside the borders, and it has offices in such locales as Frankfurt, London and Paris. In 2002, ZS opened offices in Toronto and Milan, and it will open a Tokyo office in fall 2003. All employees have the chance to work or even be based overseas (depending on overseas work eligibility).

## Degrees of professionalism

Employee-wise, the company saw a 43 percent jump in staffing between 2000 and 2001. In 2002, employee turnover was about 20 percent, with the number of employees remaining more or less constant. True to its professorial roots, ZS is looking for well-educated types: more than half of the employees hold MBA or MS degrees, and about one tenth hold PhDs. Employees are, on average, 29 years of age. ZS has employees work in teams of two to six people, which includes some combination of business associates, operations research analysts and business information specialists working with a consultant, a manager and/or a principal. The firm approaches larger projects by assigning a separate team to each facet of the case.

## Training wheels

Training is an important part of ZS's approach. New employees undergo a two-week orientation where they learn about the company and its processes. After that, specialized courses are offered each month, and first-year consultants can expect to spend about 20 days out of the first year in training, including brown-bag presentation series, skill-building courses and expert sessions. Also, each employee is assigned a "professional development manager" who acts as a mentor, a liaison with project managers and schedulers, and an administrative manager, helping with hours, vacation and performance reviews to move the career forward.

## Mapping progress

Since its founding, ZS Associates has produced a number of mapping software programs to assist its sales and marketing initiatives. Its first, the aptly named MAPS, was released in 1983 and since has been updated as MAPS 2000. Mappix, another program, can be fed data, which it then displays geographically. And eMaps, released in 2001, is a Web-based program that enables field managers and central offices to coordinate sales and marketing alignments more easily.

## GETTING HIRED

Entry-level applicants to ZS have several options. Business associates need a BA or BS in accounting, business, economics or marketing; liberal arts majors who have had a lot of math and quantitative coursework are also considered. Associates handle research and presentation duties on the consulting team. Another entry-level position is business information specialist. These specialists structure data for the consulting team; candidates for these positions will need a BA or MS in computer-related fields, communications, physics, engineering, business or math. Operations research analysts address strategic and tactical issues using quantitative and analytic abilities to analyze data. For all positions, GPAs of 3.5 or higher are desired, along with the usual battery of consulting skills: leadership, attention to detail, oral and written communication, analytical ability, and a strong work ethic.

At the more advanced levels, MBAs and PhDs usually come in as consultants. Consultants typically hold MBAs or MA/MS in marketing, economics, applied physics, math, psychology, or engineering- or science-related majors. Those with an advanced degree plus significant work experience can come in as managers.

The process consists of an "initial resume screen, then first round interviews – usually two – either on campus, or at our office or by phone. Then comes a more intensive second round, with cases, problem solving, panel discussions and more interviews. Sometimes there is a third round to probe more details. University transcripts and test scores are required for application, along with a resume," says one source. As that source indicates, case studies are used: "structured and unstructured, quantitative and qualitative cases" can be put forth.

Another source gives this version of the hiring process: "Resumes are screened and the top candidates are interviewed on campus or are given a phone interview (web site write-ins). The first round interview consists of a case and a behavioral segment. Candidates are screened for personality (nice, bright, alert, quick on the draw) and for their ability to problem solve (both quantitatively and qualitatively). Second round interviews consist of one or two cases (one quantitative and one open ended) and numerous behavioral interviews. (The typical second round interview lasts four to five hours.) Candidates are screened for the same qualities as in the first round."

# OUR SURVEY SAYS

## Easygoing culture

ZS's culture, by most accounts, is "very laid back and informal." It's a "relaxed atmosphere where the work is the most important thing and not politics," notes one consultant. Co-workers are described as "friendly – each person is kind and genuine. Daily life is highlighted with many funny moments." Another positive – ZS is a "meritocracy, not based on titles, but on the work and knowledge one has and possesses." One downside is that "the company is growing rapidly, which has been leading to a few growing pains lately."

## Roadies

The consultants we surveyed report traveling from two days a month to two days a week. "ZS locates its offices near clusters of clients to minimize travel, which is why the Princeton office is so large," notes one source.

Hours can vary, but most weeks seem to be about 65 hours at ZS. "Sometimes whole months are spikes – others are all 40-hour weeks," notes one consultant. Another insider reports that "typically, there is one spike per month in which I will work 85+ hours for a week."

## On the beach (but just at Cancun)

ZS tends to staff all of its consultants. "You work when there is work, but there's flextime available," says an insider. Says another, "ZS is very conscious of unstaffed resources and does its best to match office resources with client demand. It is not uncommon for someone to be working in the Princeton office but staffed on a project in Evanston or Chicago." A third summarizes, "there is always plenty to do at ZS – we are never 'on the beach' except when we go to company celebrations." Literally. Luckily for those at the firm in 2003, "ZS did take the entire company to Cancun for a week for its 20th anniversary."

## Iffy offices

Offices get middling reviews. The Evanston and Chicago branches seem to be decent enough, while in Princeton, "ZS applies its operations research approach of optimizing performance for minimum investment to all aspects of its practice. The argument is made that overhead is minimized to maximize bonus and other monetary return. The result is a very cheap-appearing office with abysmal office supplies and minimal support staff."

There is, however, an on-site gym at the Princeton location. Other ZS perks include a cafeteria, free snacks, tuition reimbursement and gym-membership discounts. ZS does have "very competitive health benefits, vacation time and insurance coverage," says one consultant.

Salary components include a 401(k) and a 3 percent match. The firm also offers an "all-expenses-paid trip to Cancun" for training and morale purposes.

# Fair treatment

Supervisors get reasonably good marks from ZS consultants. One remarks that "ZS previously promoted consultants (to managers) based on their ability to get large volumes of work done accurately. Unfortunately, this does not select for the most organized and well-trained managers. Consequently, there is a significant initiative to standardize project management tasks and requirements to ensure that associates and consultants are not exploited as resources (relative to work/life balance and respect for personal time). This initiative has not taken complete hold as of yet." For the most part, people sound enthusiastic about their managers. "ZS is a great place to work. I've been at a few big and a few small companies and this place is by far the best. People are treated fairly and respectfully. It is what you make of it, career-wise."

Training at ZS is widely praised. "ZS maintains its academic roots and is constantly providing training opportunities," observes one consultant.

# Moving up and moving out at ZS

"Promotions are made based on merit," ZS-ers say, which is something they seem to like. That means that degrees aren't necessary – "consultants without master's degrees can move up" – but in truth degrees are helpful. "The average time to becoming partner is six years – less for people who join with a graduate degree," says a source. Here's how advancement works: "Increasing skills lead to increasing responsibilities, which then lead to promotions. High performers advance quickly, and low performers tend to leave. People who have joined at all levels, with all sorts of degrees, have made it to partner. This includes people with bachelor degrees, technical degrees or PhDs, as well as the more typical MBAs. So the degree you have is not the key – the quality of your work is."

Due to the economy, though, the "rapid advancement" ethos seems to be slowing somewhat. "Previously, ZS experienced 20 percent year-on-year growth," says a source. "With recent developments in the economy, pharmaceutical industry, and ZS growth limits, promotions have been slowed significantly. As of 2001, an advanced degree consultant could expect to make manager after two years. The current expectation has changed to three or even three and a half years. The argument being made is not that ZS has become 'top-heavy' but that the requirements to make manager have become more stringent due to increased performance pressures."

ZS "has never laid off people due to lack of work, neither last year nor any other year. Nor has ZS ever reneged on any offers, nor 'deferred' new people's start dates," avows one source. But another counters that, at least in the Princeton office, the bottom 10 percent were asked to leave. "These were not called layoffs, however, but were referred to as people being 'counseled out.' Counseling someone out occurs when the individual is deemed a poor fit for ZS, either culturally or performance-related," says this source.

## Diversity rules!

"Women and minorities abound around here," agree most consultants we surveyed. The racial breakdown, in case you're interested, according to one consultant, is "principal ethnicity: Caucasian. Secondary: Asian/Chinese. Tertiary: Indian." As for women, "the current ratio is about 50/50. As you move up the ladder, there are fewer women. This exists in all firms and industries."

## Helping hands

Community involvement depends on the office, it seems. In the Chicago location, "everyone took one day off last year to build a playground. There's a big commitment to charity by management." In Evanston, though, there's "not too much" community involvement: "Mostly people are left to do what they want, and are supported as needed."

"ZS maintains its academic roots and is constantly providing training opportunities."

— *ZS consultant*

# 34 PRTM

1050 Winter Street
Waltham, MA 02451
Phone: (781) 647-2800
Fax: (781) 647-2804

1503 Grant Road, Suite 200
Mountain View, CA 94040
Phone: (650) 967-2900
Fax: (650) 967-6367
www.prtm.com

## LOCATIONS

**Waltham, MA (Atlantic Region HQ)**
**Mountain View, CA (Pacific Region HQ)**
14 offices worldwide

## PRACTICE AREAS

Acquisition Integration
Capital Asset Management
Customer Service and Support
Marketing and Sales
Operations and Supply Chain
  Management
Product Technology and
  Development
Strategic IT Management Strategy

## THE BUZZ
WHAT CONSULTANTS AT OTHER FIRMS ARE SAYING

- "Great brand"
- "Aggressive environment"
- "Under the radar, high-tech experts"
- "Too products-based"

## THE STATS

**Employer Type:** Private Company
**Managing Directors:** Michael Aghajanian and Michael McGrath
**2002 Employees:** 450
**2001 Employees:** 450

## UPPERS

- "Flexible weekend travel while on client projects"
- "High level of interaction with experienced partners"

## DOWNERS

- "No formal 360-degree review process"
- "Poor top-down communication"

## KEY COMPETITORS

Accenture
Booz Allen Hamilton

## EMPLOYMENT CONTACT

**Western U.S.:**
Attn: Recruiting
Fax: (650) 967-6367
E-mail: uswest@prtm.com

**Eastern U.S.:**
Attn: Recruiting
Fax: (781) 466-9853
E-mail: useast@prtm.com

# THE SCOOP

## Eye on results

With headquarters in both California's Silicon Valley and Boston's Route 128, PRTM is positioned to provide management consulting services to a wide range of industries. The firm is busily expanding its reach into biotech, pharmaceutical, energy, consumer products, government and financial services. The firm is named for its four founders (officially it's Pittiglio Rabin Todd & McGrath), who launched the firm in 1976.

PRTM operates in two decentralized zones, the Atlantic and Pacific, which allows it to focus on regional issues. The Atlantic region is made up of five offices in the eastern United States and four offices in Europe. The Pacific region consists of three California offices and one in Addison, Texas. The firm also has an office in Tokyo.

## Lots of methodologies (and trademarks)

PRTM's practice is rooted in a set of branded methodologies it has developed over the years, so get ready for lots of trademark symbols. Product and Cycle-Time Excellence® (PACE®) was introduced in the mid-1980s as a standard framework for understanding and improving time-to-market in product development for technology-based companies. PRTM has also developed the Supply Chain Operations Reference (SCOR®) model – a toolkit for supply-chain integration and management – in collaboration with the Supply Chain Council and Advanced Manufacturing Research. And the firm offers its Channel Strategies® services, a set of target marketing methodologies, through its marketing and sales practice, and is developing a Total Enterprise Architecture® for its offering in Strategic IT Management.

## Insight and measurement

In addition to its management consulting work, PRTM also publishes *Insight,* billed by the company as a management journal offering "leading thinking for lasting results." *Insight* has a readership of about 50,000 executives worldwide, and is distributed at no charge to subscribers.

PRTM also operates the Performance Measurement Group, LLC (PMG), a wholly owned subsidiary dedicated to benchmarking best practices and core processes.

PMG's customized confidential metrics work hand-in-hand with PACE and SCOR, and are available to subscribers at any time via the Web.

## Adding and allying

PRTM has struck up a number of alliances with software companies to expand its sales channels and service offerings. For example, PRTM enjoys a partnership with Hewlett-Packard to offer a product called PACE-PLC®, for product lifecycle collaboration.

## Continuing education

PRTM touts its rapid career development, fostered in part by its low 4 to 1 ratio of consultants to directors. Internally, PRTM keeps an archive of case studies and surveys accessible through the PMG subsidiary. Industry days and training seminars are also offered for continuing professional development of consulting staff. A professional development plan provides an advisor to every consultant, which means one-on-one mentoring by a director for a period of 18 to 24 months.

They must be doing something right; in November 2002, *Consulting* magazine gave PRTM the top ranking in its annual "Ten Best Consulting Firms to Work For" list. The list is compiled from surveys of the 50 largest management consultancies in the world, published in *Consultants News* as the CN50.

## Changing of the guard

In February 2002, Bob Rabin, managing director of the Pacific region (and the R in PRTM), stepped aside and assumed the role of chairman. In his place, the firm named Michael Aghajanian as managing director of the Pacific region.

At the beginning of 2003, Gordon Stewart was tapped for the role of director of consulting operations in PRTM's Atlantic region. Stewart has over 20 years experience in consulting and led PRTM's European operations for several years before assuming his current assignment.

# GETTING HIRED

## No place for cases

PRTM bucks the trend of testing potential hires with case questions, relying instead on "technical depth, relevant industry experience and a proven track record," according to one insider. Cases aren't unheard of, however. Another PRTMer says, "We use cases intermittently. They are a component of the interview process but certainly less important than other factors." A senior consultant provides some detail: "Our hiring process involves first round and decision rounds. At least five directors are involved in the decision process." Another insider adds, "We hire with the MBA intern and second-year recruiting cycle. BAs are hired once or twice a year based on their school's cycle. External hires are brought in to fill specific business needs as required."

# OUR SURVEY SAYS

## Warm, familial feel

If you're looking for a home away from home, it just might be PRTM. Insiders go out of their way to unanimously emphasize the "family-like" feel of the firm. PRTM has a "small firm feel, although it's a mid-sized firm," says one consultant. "It's remarkable how often Bob (Rabin), Ted (Pittiglio), and Mike (McGrath) are still cited in conversations with the partners," muses another insider. Consultants also consistently praise the partners for fostering a nonpolitical, supportive atmosphere. "We counsel against overt self-promotion," notes one consultant, a surprising thing for any consulting firm. "Colleagues are genuinely interested in helping you, your project team, and the client team succeed. Our culture is close to one exhibited by a high-tech start-up," remarks one veteran consultant. Even though "times have been tough the last two or three years," sums up an insider, "overall, [PRTM's] been a positive place to work given the economic environment, particularly in consulting."

## Maximum chargeability

Hard times call for hard work, and PRTM is no different from any other firm. "Although the firm has excellent values," says one insider, "the tough economy has forced focus away from traditional efforts to maintain and build the culture, in order to drive demand." Another adds, "The extreme focus on utilization creates a high level of tension within the firm." Others confirm the firm seeks "100 percent chargeability" as its goal; most consultants report little beach time, with a "spike" of 16-to18-hour days about once a month.

Despite the pressure, "PRTM is a fun place to work. Project work is very collaborative and mentoring is 'hands on.'" A source says, "Face time in the office is nonexistent; the directors just want you to get the work done and do it well." Several colleagues echo that sentiment. A senior analyst, however, tells us, "Partners manage with an open door policy, making them extremely approachable. The partners' attitude toward all staff, including junior staff, as being valuable members of the consulting teams makes PRTM an ideal place to work throughout, but especially early, in your career."

## A fine balance

"I have worked for three different consulting firms," says an experienced insider, "and of all of them, PRTM cares the most about the personal lives of the individuals that work there." A consultant tells us she "was able to take a four-month maternity leave and come back to a position which enables me to work locally and avoid extensive traveling." In addition, says a principal, "We hold several events during the year to bring everyone's family into the PRTM family."

PRTMers definitely travel and work long hours, though – it's what consultants do. Nobody is surprised by this when they start: "PRTM will stress the realities of consulting during the hiring process," according to one insider. A source says, "Consultants are expected to work long hours and travel four days a week on average, but the firm understands this and works with consultants to minimize the impact on their personal lives." Another confirms, "PRTM utilizes an 'on-site' client service model. Standard travel requirements are leave on Monday morning and return on Thursday evening." Not everybody hates the peripatetic life, though: "Lots of travel comes with the territory and I still enjoy it very much," says a manager.

## The typical mix

The people of PRTM are mostly men, which is common enough in the consulting industry. "Since we have hired a lot of MBAs with engineering degrees, our diversity with respect to women reflects the engineering ratio," says one insider. She adds, "Women rarely advance faster than the 'expected' rates." Another insider feels

PRTM is "quite a diverse organization. About 14 percent of PRTM's worldwide consulting staff are women and 39 percent of the class of 2001/2002 are women."

"Probably like most firms, there is good diversity in the rank and file," says one source about the ethnic mix, "but not enough at the top." Another disagrees: "PRTM is one of the most multicultural firms I have ever seen. The cultural backgrounds and personal/professional experiences is very enriching and a key factor behind PRTM's success, and simply being a fun place to work."

## A learning environment

Our sources characterize PRTM as an excellent place to learn. "PRTM really stepped up training activities over the last two years," says one insider. "There are now more interesting classes available than I can take." Many of these classes are remote learning situations." A manager elaborates, saying, "Our training group continues to identify alternative delivery platforms that fit better with the consulting lifestyle." All this education is as much for the firm's benefit as the consultants'; one person in the DC office says, "Our advancement programs are crafted to encourage consultants to make a career, not just a job, at PRTM." A Massachusetts colleague agrees, "We hire with the mindset that we are hiring future directors."

Insiders lay out the career path in clear terms. According to consultants, "PRTM has four levels: associate, manager, principal and director. It typically requires two to three years to progress through each level, with typical times to director being six to eight years." An experienced team member says, "Consultants are evaluated against an absolute (as opposed to relative) standard at each level. Once a specific standard of performance is demonstrated, consultants get promoted. Consultants who have yet to meet the standard for the next level are mentored so that they grow." While there is "no formal up-or-out policy," respondents say, "there has been a problem of supply exceeding demand. Initially, when the downturn hit, the firm used the opportunity to more aggressively 'counsel out' people who weren't fitting in."

# The Brattle Group

Third Floor
44 Brattle Street
Cambridge, MA 02138
Phone: (617) 864-7900
Fax: (617) 864-1576
www.brattle.com

## LOCATIONS

**Cambridge, MA (HQ)**
San Francisco, CA
Washington, DC
London

## PRACTICE AREAS

Energy
Environment
Finance
General Litigation
Industry

## THE STATS

**Employer Type:** Private Company
**Chairman:** Peter Fox-Penner
**President and CEO:** W. Robson Googins
**2002 Employees:** 128
**2001 Employees:** 124

## UPPERS

• Close-knit colleagues
• Very little travel

## DOWNERS

• Some "grunt work"
• Weak formal training

## KEY COMPETITORS

Abt Associates
Booz Allen Hamilton
Corporate Executive Board
Navigant Consulting

## EMPLOYMENT CONTACT

Megan Dunn
Recruiting Manager
The Brattle Group
Suite 800
1133 20th Street, NW
Washington, DC 20036
Phone: (202) 955-5050
Fax: (202) 955-5059
E-mail: recruiting@brattle.com
www.brattle.com/join/joinHome.html

## THE BUZZ
WHAT CONSULTANTS AT OTHER FIRMS ARE SAYING

• "Strong in regulations"
• "Small, nerdy"
• "Select strategy niches"
• "Stagnating"

# THE SCOOP

## Study skills

Fittingly for a firm whose headquarters are just steps away from Harvard College, Brattle has a slightly academic feel to it. The company consults – both in the boardroom and as expert witnesses – for clients in fields such as energy and economics. The firm was founded in 1990 in Harvard Square; it opened a D.C. office in 1996, a London office in 1997 and a San Francisco office in 2002. The firm also has an affiliate in scenic Wellington, New Zealand, called Simon Terry Associates; which works on deregulation issues in that country.

Brattle's strong academic ties include a panel of "senior advisors," often Harvard, Boston College or MIT professors or researchers. These advisors help guide Brattle as it evaluates market conditions for one client or prepares expert testimony on antitrust matters for another. The firm also publishes reports, presentations and testimony, and many of the consultants publish textbooks and industry titles such as *Power Systems Economics: Designing Markets for Electricity and the Risk Management and Derivatives*.

## Chaos = consulting projects

The world's tumultuous year in 2002 – deregulation, sanctions, and so forth – meant a lot of interesting projects for Brattle. In January, it published a notable report about lifting U.S./E.U. trade and investment sanctions in the aviation industry. The report predicted that such a move would increase transatlantic passengers by 24 percent, intra-E.U. passengers by 14 percent and funnel $5.2 billion annually toward U.S. and European consumers. In July, Brattle performed a study for the Center for International Policy on the potential effect of lifting the U.S.'s travel ban to Cuba. Brattle determined that if the ban were lifted, $415 million would be added to U.S. airlines' coffers (not to mention the joy it would bring to lovers of Cuban cigars). October 2002 saw the company opening a San Francisco office. Heading the office is Daniel McFadden, a Berkeley professor who won the Nobel Prize in economics in 2000. And in December, when El Paso Corp., the U.S.'s biggest natural gas pipeline, was being investigated for manipulating energy prices in California, it was Brattle Group that produced the report saying that El Paso's doings boosted natural gas and electricity prices by $3.1 billion between March 2000 and March 2001. (Brattle's report was commissioned by Southern California Edison Co.)

# GETTING HIRED

Brattle recruits at Brandeis, Brown, Duke, Columbia, Harvard, MIT, Tufts and Yale. Brattle recruiters also "attend the major professional meetings, work with the top schools, seek advice from professors we know" and recruit "largely from economic PhD programs" and "most top graduate schools in the New England area."

Initial screening consists of fit questions, and occurs either via phone or on campus. The second round takes place at a Brattle office, and includes meetings with several consultants. "In the office, you do resume interviews with two or three people at your level, and two or three people above your level." This round usually includes "a lunch" as well. Case studies are posed "infrequently," though "it depends on the person doing the interviewing – MBA associates will tend to go for the case questions." Sometimes, the company asks for a "presentation by the candidate."

Two to six weeks after the office visits, Brattle decides who gets the offers; "the offer is made based on the second round." Applicant backgrounds vary, though almost all have some quantitative heft to them. "At the analyst level, it's based on potential rather than current ability. It's important that you'll fit into the laid-back approach of the office," notes a source.

# OUR SURVEY SAYS

## Cozy and academic

With "a small firm atmosphere" that is "laid-back, friendly, supportive and interesting," Brattle employees find there's "not too much pressure." The firm fosters an "up with people" attitude, where "flexibility and individual relationships matter" and "everyone gets on – there are no politics." "We try to have a lot of fun," and "the employees are genuine people; people enjoy spending time with each other outside of work."

If the play is fun, so is the job. "People are interested in their work," notes one insider; another says that "we also work hard and do great quality work." The work projects vary, it seems. Some lower-level employees find "the smaller size allows analysts and associates a greater project role – if you majored in economics, you truly get to use what you learned in college immediately." However, others say "the day-to-day labor has a large variance between interesting and uninteresting work. There is a fair amount of grunt work mixed in with the more engaging work."

Insiders say it's important to "get" the Brattle culture. "If you're looking for a well-defined role, you're unlikely to find it here," notes one. Another explains, "While having grown significantly during my time here, Brattle's roots remain in a very academic-centered world."

## Reasonable hours

Usually, our respondents say, if you fight for personal time at Brattle, you'll get it. "In general, Brattle does a good job ensuring that people have a balance. However, there are certainly times when that balance is ignored. Ultimately, it's up to individuals to protect their private time," notes one respondent. While "consulting in general is not known for a great work/life balance," notes another, Brattle ranks high relative to other consultancies. It's "better than all the other consultants I know." Agrees another Brattle-ite, "Though [tough work] does hit the fan sometimes, causing late nights, on the whole it's great. Hours are 10 a.m. to 7 p.m. almost every day. And you can take the time quite flexibly."

The consultants we surveyed reported working about 50 hours "in a normal week," and sometimes up to 60, said to be "on the high side of the distribution of effort. During true project spikes, this can go up to 80 hours per week, but this is very rare, and is not typically sustained." Another insider says 80+ hour weeks happen only "once or twice a year." There's a workload spike about once or twice a month, and being on the beach is rare, as there's been "steady work recently." In general, "Brattle has no interest in burning out consultants. One good example of this policy is that employees can bank holidays if they are required to work on a certain day, and use those banked holidays at a later date of their choosing." Notes one source, "If you are proactive in seeking out projects that fit your personal and career goals, it is very easy to manage work hours."

## Travel lite

One nice thing about Brattle, respondents say, is that "there isn't much travel involved for employees below the senior associate level." A London-based source reports "occasional trips of a week to two in foreign countries – perhaps four times a year. Perfect, really." Another source says "travel is quite episodic. I might go several months without a trip then spend two weeks on site. However, modern telecommunications technology has cut the travel level sharply from what it used to be." One consultant sums up: "If you're looking for travel opportunities, Brattle is not for you."

## Degrees of advancement

The general consensus seems to be that promotion policies are "not set" and "not very structured." Undergrads usually start as research analysts – and stay there. "The entry level for undergraduates is research analyst. An analyst will typically stay three years, and subsequently leave or be promoted to research associate. Research associates are also externally hired for some individuals with grad school experience. It is extremely rare for research associates without graduate training to be promoted to associate." Another says, emphatically, "Consultants with only undergraduate degrees cannot move up into associate positions which are typically PhD and MBA level."

For associates, by contrast, it's "easy to get promoted internally if you're good enough. Happy to have you hanging around for quite a while in the same job if you're comfortable and happy with it." However, argues a senior employee, "We hire associates we believe have the potential to be a partner," and while "there is provision for those who don't make partner to stay in a senior scientist role, it does not happen very often."

The usual time frame is "seven years, plus or minus, for a newly minted PhD or MBA to make partner." One consultant suggests that the firm "let associates know when they are expected to become partner and clearly identify barriers that may exist."

If associates don't move up, they might slowly move out; "As usual, some people have been leaving for grad/professional school," and "within the past two years, about six people have been encouraged to leave," though there have been no large-scale layoffs.

## Pouting over pay

Salary is considered decent, though some consultants call for the firm to "revise the compensation and promotion process to better reflect differences in regional offices," for "the pay should be commensurate with the other opportunities candidates of this caliber have." There are "occasional profit sharing bonuses," and the company "offers an annual profit sharing contribution to our 401(k);" one upper-level source notes "bonuses are tied most closely to one's individual utilization." Standard benefits are included, along with cell phones, laptops, gym discounts, event tickets and, in London, "free coffee at the local coffee shop quite often and the odd nice meal." Another consultant counts as a benefit that "Brattle, in many cases, has extended extremely flexible options for people needing nontraditional work schedules."

## Casual, but committed, management

Perhaps owing to the small-firm informality, consultants say the management is "intelligent, committed, engaging, friendly and supportive" but "can sometimes appear disorganized." One consultant helpfully suggests that "employees could learn more and be more effective if project managers provided informal feedback at the end of a project; otherwise, mistakes aren't addressed until the formal review process." One senior employee notes that some associates, "primarily those with PhDs, are initially lacking in real-world experience. But by and large, supervisors are good at giving credit whenever appropriate." One senior analyst says, "the best part of my supervisors is that they go out of their way to help me learn. The worst part of my supervisors is that I don't get much experience in marketing."

## Hot space

Offices get mixed reviews. The London office, in particular, is singled out as stuffy, atmospherically speaking. "We could do with air conditioning," gripes one London employee. Another agrees, "The U.S. offices are much nicer." That opinion seems to be echoed by a D.C. employee, who lauds the "lots of free food and drink, responsive office managers and weekly happy hour."

## Informal training

Training is one low point at Brattle, it seems. "The formal training program is too basic to be very useful," notes one employee; another says there's "not enough formal training." A third agrees that "training is infrequent and largely on-the-job," while another says that there's "good training for incoming analysts, but opportunities become more limited as you get more senior." However, notes one source, "the program is currently being revised, and the initial results are encouraging."

## Debating diversity

As at many consulting firms, Brattle is not incredibly diverse, but not by design. In terms of women, one insider says there's "a very good mix of men and women. 50/50 split with partners, and more women than men at associate level." However, another consultant notes that "I don't think there is any discrimination, but it doesn't appear that they go out of their way to encourage women." A senior employee says, "We've tried to come up with ideas here, too, but unless you're big enough to supply in-firm child care, for example, it's hard for a small firm in this crisis-intensive business to do very much. We continue to work on such issues, but we haven't come up with any magic bullets."

In terms of racial diversity, though the firm doesn't "get many non-Caucasian applicants," "there's a significant amount of ethnicities at Brattle." In terms of lesbians and gays, one source says, "I don't know of any diverse sexual orientations within Brattle. My impression is that people are strictly judged on merit. Ethnicity, gender and sexual orientation don't have a positive or negative impact on an employee's standing."

## Self-service

At Brattle, community service "varies year to year. Generally we encourage employees who want group sponsorship of particular events to let the rest of the firm know. Examples include the Walk for Hunger, food drives, holiday gifts, etc. However, we believe individuals largely should determine their own charitable activities, without being pressured to participate in firm-sponsored ones." Very few consultants request sponsorships, note other insiders, and besides "some office drives around the holidays, there's no formal system for encouraging community service."

# "Training is infrequent and largely on-the-job."

## — Brattle insider

# Strategic Decisions Group

2440 Sand Hill Road
Menlo Park, CA 94025
Phone: (650) 854-9000
Fax: (650) 854-6718
www.sdg.com

## LOCATIONS

**Menlo Park, CA (HQ)**
Boston, MA
Houston, TX
New York, NY
London
Mumbai (joint venture)
Tokyo (joint venture)

## PRACTICE AREAS

Business Strategy
Corporate Strategy
Enterprise Risk Management
Portfolio Strategy
Post-Merger Integration
Risk Diagnostics
Strategic Game Theory
Technology Strategy
Valuation

## THE STATS

**Employer Type:** Private Company
**CEO:** Robin Arnold
**2002 Employees:** 160
**2001 Employees:** 140
**2002 Revenue:** $42 million
**2001 Revenue:** $31 million

## UPPERS

- Teamwork, supportive management

## DOWNERS

- Niche work can be dull

## KEY COMPETITORS

Bain & Company
Boston Consulting Group
McKinsey & Company

## EMPLOYMENT CONTACT

Sydney Higa
Recruiting Coordinator
2440 Sand Hill Road
Menlo Park, CA 94025
Fax: (650) 854-6718
E-mail: recruiter@sdg.com

## THE BUZZ
WHAT CONSULTANTS AT OTHER FIRMS ARE SAYING

- "Risk and decision analysis experts"
- "Very academic"
- "Innovative"
- "Eggheads"

# THE SCOOP

## Back to school, kind of

In 1981, a group of professors with ties to Stanford opened a strategy consulting firm in Silicon Valley, with the intention of running the firm with the collegiality, learning curve and rigorous processes typical of an academic institution. The company was acquired by Navigant Consulting in the late 1990s. In 2000, the current top three executives at Strategic Decisions Group (SDG) – CEO Robin Arnold, COO James Lang, and chairman Carl Spetzler – led a $22 million management buyout. Once again independent, SDG now has 160 employees and affiliates among its seven offices.

## Informed decisions

SDG likes to call its approach to consulting "decision analysis," a term coined in 1963 by Ronald A. Howard, a Stanford professor and SDG founder. SDG's approach uses risk valuation, game theory and portfolio analysis, among other tools, to assess a company's state and the competitive market. It might suggest selling or prioritizing various business lines, maximizing research or asset investments, or bringing in new technologies to help the business grow. SDG says it takes a disciplined, practical approach to consulting – an approach that "has never been among the management fads that periodically capture the attention of the business community."

Repeat clients have made up more than 80 percent of SDG's business since its founding, and the average client signs on for three years. Today, its clients include major biotech, device/diagnostics, pharmaceutical, chemical, tech and energy companies, along with dozens of small or start-up biotech, private equity, media, consumer products, and transportation firms.

## Flat structure

SDG maintains a flat organizational structure and supports merit-based promotions. The merit bar is high, though: all consultants have MBAs or advanced technical degrees, and many have PhDs. Unsurprisingly, these highly educated consultants produce a lot of books. Notable recent books include *The Smart Organization*, a 1999 tome on creating value through strategic R&D by father and son consultants David and Jim Matheson; *Solving the Corporate Value Enigma*, a 2003 guide to creating shareholder value; and *Business Portfolio Management: Valuation, Risk*

*Assessment, and EVA™ Strategies*, a 2000 book whose title essentially explains its content.

## GETTING HIRED

Candidates with a BA or BS should apply for business analyst positions; those with MBAs or other graduate degrees should apply for consultant positions. While business analysts usually leave for graduate school after two to three years, consultants are generally promoted to senior consultant, senior engagement manager and principal.

SDG recruits at Stanford and Dartmouth, in particular, "two schools where we have longstanding affiliations and recruiting activity." It also recruits at Harvard, along with "schools that are local to our offices in Boston, Houston, London, etc."

The hiring process consists of "several rounds of interviews performed by senior consulting staff and partners, with separate interpersonal, business and analytical interviews." Case studies are used: "We try to create a situation where we can see the candidate think and work through a business case and also an analytical case."

## OUR SURVEY SAYS

### Small-firm spirit

The culture at SDG is "extremely open, team-focused, flexible. There's an incredible amount of shared commitment to building and improving the firm." "I respect and learn a lot from my supervisors," says a source. Diversity is reported to be fine with respect to women ("we get a much higher proportion of male applicants, though we have a number of highly respected senior women consulting staff") minorities (there are few minority applicants and hence relatively few minority staff) and gays, lesbians and bisexuals ("it's a relatively diverse staff in this respect").

### Home away from home

Work/life balance is "a high priority," though "in the current difficult market there is a natural shift to being more focused on getting the job done and making some personal sacrifices." Travel seems to be common. "We work at the client site three to four days per week, though it is possible to be away only two to three nights per week," a source says. Hours hover at around 10 a day, with some "very rare" weekend work.

The company does some pro bono consulting, and "we support the Decision Education Foundation, a program to help teens make better life decisions."

## The whole package

SDG does not have an up-or-out policy. "One can learn and grow at one's own pace if you're making valued contributions." However, "it's very rare for someone with only an undergrad degree to move into MBA/grad degree level positions."

The company is doing "everything we can to avoid layoffs, including taking pay cuts instead." (The firm did lay off a number of staffers in May 2003.) Salary is reported to be average for the consulting industry, though "profit sharing and professional development expenses" are part of the compensation package.

Benefits include an employee assistance program, gym discounts and free snacks. The offices are reported to be "very nice, beautiful," particularly in Boston.

## Train early, train (not so) often

According to the company, all new consultants attend a three-week orientation in Menlo Park, including a two-week mock case study, while business analysts spend one week doing a mock case study. Employees also get formal training throughout the year that's targeted to their level; each also receives a stipend to spend on publications, conferences or courses. One respondent assesses the training as "decent," though notes there is little ongoing training. "Most of the really important learning happens on client projects." The firm holds frequent informal "staff development forums" at lunchtime, where consultants can eat and attend presentations on recent SDG engagements.

# PA Consulting Group

123 Buckingham Palace Road
London, UK SW1W 9SR
Phone: +44 20 7730 9000
Fax: +44 20 7333 5050
www.paconsulting.com

## LOCATIONS

**London (HQ)** • Boulder, CO •
Cambridge, MA • Chicago, IL •
Houston, TX • Los Angeles, CA •
Madison, WI • New York, NY •
Princeton, NJ • Arhus, Denmark •
Auckland • Cambridge • Beijing •
Belfast • Birmingham • Buenos
Aires • Copenhagen • Dublin •
Frankfurt • Glasgow • Helsinki •
Hong Kong • Jakarta • Kuala
Lumpur • Lysaker, Norway •
Manchester • Melbourne • Moscow
• Munich • Paris • Prague •
Stockholm • Sydney • Tokyo •
Utrecht, the Netherlands •
Wellington, New Zealand

## PRACTICE AREAS

Business and Corporate Strategy •
Economic and Environmental
Analysis • Human Resources
Consulting • Operations Consulting
• Program and Project Management
• Systems Integration and IT
Consulting • Technology and
Innovation

## THE BUZZ
WHAT CONSULTANTS AT OTHER FIRMS ARE SAYING

- "Strong in public sector"
- "Kid's paradise"
- "Better than Big Five"
- "Students' consulting group"

## THE STATS

**Employer Type:** Private Company
**CEO and Chairman:** Jon Moynihan
**2002 Employees:** 4,000
**2001 Employees:** 4,000
**2002 Revenue:** $500 million
**2001 Revenue:** $529 million

## UPPERS

- Fast-paced, challenging
  assignments
- Limited layoffs
- Intelligent, fun-loving co-workers

## DOWNERS

- Constant travel
- Consultants expected to sell work
- Lack of projects due to the
  economy

## KEY COMPETITORS

Accenture
Cap Gemini Ernst & Young
IBM BCS
McKinsey & Company

## EMPLOYMENT CONTACT

**Americas**
Julie Davern
PA Consulting Group
315A Enterprise Drive
Plainsboro, NJ 08536
Fax: (609) 936 8811
E-mail:
julie.davern@paconsulting.com

# THE SCOOP

## London calling

PA Consulting Group is one of the biggest names in the British management consulting world. Based in London, it's just starting to make its presence known in the U.S. It manages projects from e-business systems to consumer-products designs, and focuses on implementing – not just proposing – solutions. "We do fascinating work that is both appreciated and used by clients (tactical work rather than pure strategy work)" avers one source.

## Growing in the United States

With almost 4,000 employees in 40 offices worldwide, PA Consulting is the world's largest employee-owned practice. Founded in 1943, the firm stepped up its U.S. presence with the October 2000 purchase of Hagler Bailly, Inc. for approximately $96 million, giving it about 600 employees in nine offices across America. (Still, one PA source reports that the "lack of a brand in the U.S. is making it extremely difficult to sell work.") In June 2001 PA opened its Strategic Information Management capability, a suite of information processing services, in New York. While a planned merger with fellow consultancy Arthur D. Little fell through in January 2001, PA says it's still aiming to build its presence in the United States.

Twenty-seven percent of PA Consulting's revenue comes from its IT work; the firm focuses the rest of its energies primarily on management, systems and technology consulting, with an emphasis on the life sciences, government, transportation, energy, manufacturing, telecommunications, interactive media, infrastructure and development and financial services industries. Through its venture capital arm, the firm is also involved in a range of activities including wireless communications, drug-delivery technologies and online HR solutions, some of which it has spun off into successful businesses over the last few years.

## Awards podium

PA Consulting's work has received a number of accolades. At the sixth annual Management Consultancies Association (MCA) Management Practice Awards, it won five awards – more than any other consultancy – in human resources, production and services management, strategy and business transformation, organizational development, and production and services management. Since the MCA awards started, PA has won more awards than any other firm, claiming 30 percent of all awards given. In March 2002, it was named to the *Sunday Times'* (London) "100 Best UK Companies to Work For," ranking third for fairest promotion processes and 10th for fairest pay. One of its clients, the Female Health Company, won the Queen's Award for a product PA had helped market, a female condom called Femidom; another client, Evian, won a WorldStar Packaging Award for the bottle design that PA had come up with.

# GETTING HIRED

## Hiring phase

"Recruitment has phased down in the last few years," according to insiders; at the Los Angeles office, one source reports "we are currently in a hiring freeze." Hiring processes differ greatly depending on the practice and the location, but in general, "the firm has a very thorough and well thought through recruitment process," says an employee. (Others disagree, calling it "long-winded" or "inconsistent and lackluster"). In the U.S., "we hire about one out of every 250 people that make it to the interview stage," says a New York-based source." PA recruits at top business schools such as Sloan and Harvard, along with schools close to each office – UCLA and Claremont for the L.A. office, for example; recent hires also came from University of Chicago, Princeton, Duke, UNC and others.

## Targets sighted

In Europe, PA Consulting recruits at a handful of top tier schools, such as Oxford, Cambridge, Imperial, University College London, Manchester, Edinburgh, Trinity College and University College Dublin for the U.K. practice, and the Norwegian School of Management (BI), Norges Handelshøyskole and NTNU for the Norway practice. Experienced staff is generally preferred to freshly-minted grads. "The graduate selection process is tough enough as they generally select people from just a handful of universities to which they have ties, or they take people with relevant experience in consulting or in the field (e.g. government)," says a European consultant. And for recent grads, the bar is set high. "In order to get an interview you have to be among the top 10 percent of students (grades) and additionally have shown social skills and commitment," says another European source.

## Structured interviews

Though our respondents report different hiring processes, one general structure seems to exist. Usually, a candidate will submit a resume, which is followed by a telephone screening with an HR rep. The next step is another call "with a high level member of the appropriate practice." If that goes well, the candidate is invited to an interview day, where they take a critical reasoning exam, followed by two to seven interviews and a lunch with current employees. Afterwards, there's "a group session where prospective employees tackle a problem as a team." Sometimes the day ends with a writing test. After passing this stage, they advance to the final round, "a videoconference with one of our worldwide senior partners."

The three on-site interviews will usually include case studies. "These vary considerably depending on the level at which the candidate is interviewing. Often these are developed by the interviewers based on projects on which they've worked," reveals a source. Another consultant notes these cases are "relevant to recent assignments and topical issues, e.g. cost reduction within retail banks." A third source gives a case-study example: "A (named) electrical utilities company considers to acquire a competitor in an other country. How would you value the different units of the acquisition target, and which external factors have to be considered and/or addressed?" Think about clear reasoning rather "than getting to a 'correct' answer," advises one consultant.

For senior hires, the process can differ. One such hire reveals his experience: he had worked with a VP at PA before, and heard through him that "a 'tailor made' position for my background" existed in PA Consulting. "I submitted my resume, which was vetted both internally and by the client. After being told I was the preferred candidate and accepting, I underwent all of the formal background and reference checking required of any candidate."

The firm rarely hires interns. "This decision is made by each practice. Last summer, my group took on two summer interns, but this was because one member of the team took it upon himself to bring them in from his alma mater," says a consultant.

# OUR SURVEY SAYS

## Cultural blend

Consultants report the London office holds the most influence and power, which is both good and bad. "Although the British still run the operations, they're quite entertaining, and don't subscribe to the same office politics that we see in the U.S. As a result, people tend to be more open and willing to make jokes," says an American insider. The downside, as a New York-based consultant relates, is that the "focus is on taking care of those who work in the London office at the expense of everyone else." A D.C. consultant suggests the company "recognize that one culture does not fit all countries and allow for variation that aligns with the culture of each country."

Outside of any international issues, consultants describe a professional, friendly, hardworking firm "with a very positive and 'can-do' culture" – thanks in large part, they say, to the employee ownership. PA is "professional and ethical, with a strong focus on providing quality services for clients based on team work and harnessing the best from individuals," says one source.

However, consultants also report the company is quite frugal – "picky and cheap," says one; "penny-pinching," according to another. The stringent expense report policies are criticized by consultants. "All we seem to worry about are expense policies that make no sense," says one. For example, "PA employees are unable to expense lunch when traveling, which gets annoying very quickly," says a consultant.

## All about the bonus

PA's frugality, in many employees' views, extends to its salaries. "In the U.K. you get paid 40 percent less than in the U.S., though London is one of the most expensive cities in the world," says a British consultant; another European employee says that "despite having good performance reviews I earn less than one of my peers who has less experience. I find this demotivating." Salaries in the U.S. "have been frozen, except with promotion," says a source, while "raises have occurred in parts of Europe." (The firm says that salaries are no longer frozen.) "In real terms we have all taken pay cuts over the past 18 months," says a consultant. "I think we are underpaid considerably considering the hours and extra work we are expected to do," says another source. "Comparative base salary when times are off is low compared to other companies," reports another insider.

Bonuses are a different matter. "In general, PA compensation policy is to pay median salary and then to offer the potential for incredible bonuses," says one consultant. According to one source, a few years ago top employees received between 100 and 400 percent of salary for their bonuses. "A portion of each year's bonus is in the form of company stock which vests over three years," explains another – according to one source, that portion is at least 10 percent, are at most 30 percent. "PA's share price has seen a dramatic increase from the late 1980s until now, and many of the old school partners will be rich when they retire," says an employee.

However, since bonuses are tied to both the individual's performance and his group's performance, "star performers in practices that make less money overall get screwed because of poor performance on the part of others," says a respondent. Candidates should note that bonuses are paid in April for the previous calendar year – "therefore, whenever you quit, you lose at least four months' bonus or up to 16 months' bonus should you quit before your bonus is in your bank account," says a source. And when the market is bad, bonuses are lower. "It's a great scheme on paper – a low-median base salary and high bonus philosophy – but it's sometimes felt that the base is too low, especially in tough market conditions where bonuses (no matter how committed or hard you work) just don't bring total remuneration in line," says one consultant.

## Perfectly fine perks

Benefits include what one U.S. employee calls a "great 401(k) contribution on the part of PA – they contribute 6 percent of salary for every consulant that vests 20 percent in two years, and 100 percent in three." Perks vary depending on location, but many sites include a company car (including gas), on-site gyms, cell phones, health care (though a much higher amount of the premium has been passed onto the consultants," says a U.S. consultant), laptops, long-term disability and accidental death/dismemberment.

## Clear careers

Respondents applaud PA's promotion process, describing it as meritocratic with an "excellent annual review process." "Promotion is based on demonstrating, for at least one year, attributes expected in the higher rank – e.g. meeting sales and utilization targets," says one source. The general path is eight to 10 years from junior consultant to partner, with promotions taking place every two to three years. Several employees note that "MBAs are not necessarily required to advance."

PA has no up-or-out process. However, weak performers do get fired occasionally; the firm has seen dozens of layoffs in the last couple of years. Consultants note, however, that the cuts were "all on the basis of individual performance" and "mostly at the analyst/admin levels, nothing like what has happened at the other firms." One employee, in fact, says that "the firm has been too soft on non-productive individuals thus far."

## Logging hours

One way of avoiding the layoff axe is to studiously avoid being unstaffed. "If you are off the clock, then this is very much viewed as an issue that you individually have to resolve, either through getting back on or through completing insightful, thought-leading work," says a consultant. Advises another, "Just make sure you're not too often on the beach." Beach time varies widely. Some consultants were almost never on the beach in 2002, while others report being there more than 20 times. "This is a tough time for the industry, so most of us are spending more time on the beach than we would like," explains a source.

Consultants can expect normal consulting hours: 35 to 45 hours a week when not working on a project, 60 to 70 hours when working for a client ("If you don't work these hours you will not be promoted as quickly or be successful in this line of work," notes one consultant), up to 90 hours "on fast-paced assignments, sometimes months in length." When working out of a client's office, especially, consultants "are expected to 'work until the job is done' or at minimum work client hours," says a source. And it seems to work out in the end: "PA does consider hardship (i.e., nights per week spent away from home) when determining bonus," says a respondent.

## Roadies

Though work hours seem long, the vacation policy is "very generous," many consultants say. The minimum vacation time is four weeks. Travel varies greatly, but consultants are generally expected to travel close to home, and most report traveling at least once a week. "This is dependent on the nature of the work sold. Some colleagues are on assignments of three months or more and only return to base once every six weeks," says an insider. Meanwhile, "you can get clients close to office if you need to for family reasons." While some employees report working weekends "without fail," others "are positively encouraged not to work the weekends."

## Training time

The company gets high marks for its focus on training, but respondents disagree about whether that training is effective. With five to eight days of in-house training each year, it's "excellent," says one. Others disagree. "It's basically training in techniques and company policy rather than knowledge. No training assistance is given for people to progress in their technical areas." Many consultants note external training "is difficult to get approved," and training is not especially available to those at lower levels. "We are improving," says a source, "but very few, if any, of our training courses are of a comparable standard to what is available externally."

## Mentor structure

Just as employees are divided on the formal development opportunities, they're equally divided on the informal mentoring system at PA. Many say there's little supervision and a lot of independence, which they like. However, "it was two weeks after I joined before [my supervisor] even spoke to me," reports a recent senior hire. The mentoring structure at PA includes a line manager who directly supervises the employee, a mentor who guides the employee throughout their career, and a buddy to help with insider knowledge of the company. "Together, these three people can easily and effectively help guide a staff member," reports one employee. Another disagrees, saying, "at PA, there is very little feedback, coaching or management outside the formal twice-yearly process. The general perception is that senior managers and partners are judged almost entirely on numbers, and so place little importance on managing or developing people." Another insider echoes this sentiment, saying, "being so profit-focused, [managers] do not have the time to put into developing or mentoring subordinates."

## Sharing space

The offices get middling responses. D.C. locals describe their outpost as "frugal" with "no privacy and low ceilings." In several European offices, too, consultants say the layout could use some work. "The open space can get noisy," and other spaces are "badly arranged and organized." The problem with this, says one, is that "open plan offices are not conducive to a high degree of concentration when required, consequently one has to 'hide' in order to obtain the right conditions to enable good work to be completed. If the desks were divided by screens such that you were not forever visible, as is the case in other firms, it might improve the situation." On the bright side, one source says PA Consulting offices are almost always in terrific locations.

# Corporate Executive Board

Suite 6000
Washington, DC 20006
Phone: (202) 777-5000
Fax: (202) 777-5100
www.executiveboard.com

## LOCATIONS

**Washington, DC (HQ)**
London

## PRACTICE AREAS

Corporate IT
Corporate Sales
Corporate Strategy
Finance
Financial Services
General Counsel
Human Resources
Marketing
Operations Management

## THE STATS

**Employer Type:** Public Company
**Stock Symbol:** EXBD
**Stock Exchange:** Nasdaq
**Chairman and CEO:** James J. McGonigle
**2002 Employees:** 997
**2001 Employees:** 725
**2002 Revenue:** $162.4 million
**2001 Revenue:** $128.1 million

## UPPERS

- Intelligent staff – advanced degrees abound
- Spikes in work typically predictable

## DOWNERS

- Supervisors often research whizzes, not manager types
- Not ideal for high-powered consulting types

## KEY COMPETITORS

First Manhattan Consulting Group
Gartner

## EMPLOYMENT CONTACT

Recruiting Department
2000 Pennsylvania Avenue, NW
Washington, DC 20006
Fax: (202) 777-5100
E-mail: jobs@executiveboard.com

## THE BUZZ
### WHAT CONSULTANTS AT OTHER FIRMS ARE SAYING

- "Uppity, sharp"
- "Report writers"
- "Pretty smart"
- "Rising star"

# THE SCOOP

## Burnishing best practices

Corporate Executive Board (CEB), which once had a reputation as a think tank, has now positioned itself as a research and advisory firm. The firm tends to shy away from the "consulting" label, pointing out that it does not help "members" (what other firms might call clients) implement solutions, nor does it charge on an hourly or daily basis. Instead, CEB offers "membership," meaning access to its proprietary research and to fast answers to their toughest questions. CEB research focuses on issues related to corporate strategy, operations and general management. The firm focuses specifically on identifying management initiatives, processes and frameworks of use to its members. At best, boasts CEB, "our work is able to shape strategic debate and to accelerate tactical implementation in even the most prestigious organizations."

## In the past

CEB began as an outgrowth of The Advisory Board's health care group, eventually becoming a separate corporate practice in 1997. Two years later CEB went public, raising $155 million. Although the chip and the old block would seem like natural competitors, The Advisory Board focuses only on the health care industry, while CEB researches all other industries.

CEB had a strong 2002, with revenues rising more than 25 percent to $162.4 million, profits rising more than a third to $29.6 million, and 79-cent earnings-per-share, a 33 percent rise from 2001. Client renewal rate and subscription renewal rate were the same as in 2001, at 90 percent and 82 percent, respectively. Since its 1999 IPO, CEB's stock price has more than tripled. For 2003, the firm is predicting 25 percent minimum revenue growth.

Today, CEB's more than 1,800 blue chip clients include American Express, Coca-Cola, Sony and AOL Time Warner; members include more than 70 percent of the Fortune 500 and more than half of the world's top 300 financial institutions. More than 30 percent are non-U.S. companies, coming from 30 countries on six continents. CEB's services are typically provided on an annual subscription basis.

## Bigger backyard

CEB's on the road to expansion. The number of staff based in Washington, D.C. increased 22 percent in 2002 to 179. The firm is also beefing up its presence in

London, introducing expatriate and foreign national benefits as it increases staff in that city by 50 percent.

## The breakdown

CEB organizes its research into various members-only web sites, called 'councils,' customized for specific types of content and clients. Some examples include the General Counsel Roundtable (corporate lawyers), Financial Services Operations Roundtable (back-office finance professionals) and the Corporate Leadership Council (human resources). The Board also offers in-person briefings and presentations and executive education. The quantity of business information it has produced is remarkable: 80 massive studies and 13,000 research briefs each year.

## Nice job!

With its impressive growth in 2002, CEB shot to the top of several industry lists. The firm ranked No. 54 on *Fortune's* annual ranking of the "100 Fastest Growing Companies" for 2002, No. 13 in *Business Week's* annual ranking of "Top 100 Growth Companies" and No. 11 in *Forbes'* annual ranking of "200 Best Small Companies."

# GETTING HIRED

## Bookworms wanted

Research is the mainstay of CEB. As the company says, "If you're just out of school and loved doing term papers, the Corporate Executive Board may be a good fit." The research angle is usually strategic, management or best practices, such as looking at deregulation policies facing a gas company or figuring out how corporations have successfully improved their sales force productivity.

For recent grads, the short answer research associate position is the usual entry point. Research associates research and write five- to 50-page strategy briefs for members. CEB is looking for a great academic track record (especially in the liberal arts), intellectual curiosity, leadership, maturity, strong written and verbal communication skills, and good time management skills.

For MBAs interested in research, there are three options. The first is called "strategic analyst." These analysts interview, conduct research with experts, and make presentations on tight deadlines. Helpful qualities include the ability to find hidden or sensitive data, distilling information well, articulating findings well, analytical ability, independence, and working well under pressure.

Other senior positions include "consultants" and "practice managers," who boil down clients' problems, make recommendations to the clients, work on new product development and launch and manage P&L for the content side. Travel is required about 10 to 20 percent of the time. Requirements include three years at a consulting or law firm, an MBA or master's in economics, and a track record of problem solving, love of business content, writing, and leadership.

## Interview hurdles

Though the company is "growing like mad and hiring like mad," it can still afford to be "very selective on new entrants, especially on the research side." It recruits at Ivy League schools, Northwestern, the University of North Carolina, the University of Michigan, Stanford and University of Chicago, as well as prestigious schools in D.C., Virginia and Maryland.

The first interview takes place over the phone, and, sources say, usually includes questions like "Why did you choose your major? Why are you interested in working at CEB? Walk me through your resume. Where do you see yourself in five or 10 years?" It's necessary to prove not only that you have the right qualifications, but also that you understand what CEB does – and what you hope to gain from a career at CEB.

The second interview is a two-parter. "You interview with managers from different research programs. They ask baby cases and help you with the answer. They don't really care if you figure out the right answer, since that's not what this business provides anyway. They want to know how you would think about the question, what kinds of questions you would ask to get at the information and that you can think of the different areas to attack to find the information." Says another source, "CEB does use case questions, but not the typical brain teasers found among consultants like 'How many pennies are in the Washington Monument?' CEB case study questions generally stem from questions we receive from our members/clients, such as what factors should be considered when divesting a business unit."

The second interview might begin with, say, someone from the Corporate Strategy Board and the Corporate Leadership Council. While candidates should familiarize themselves with each of the councils and the work they do, our sources say, there's no need to become an insta-expert. "I do remember that I had a hard time because I had no idea how the insurance industry worked, but [my interviewer] helped me through it. I got an offer a few weeks later." That time frame seems to be standard for successful applicants – "A final response should be known within a couple of weeks of the final interview."

# OUR SURVEY SAYS

## Young and healthy

Insiders say the Corporate Executive Board is a happy place for the young and eager. "The company is really best suited for young professionals. For many CEBers, it's their first job out of college and the friendships formed (and frequent company-sponsored happy hours) attest to the youthful nature of the company," says one insider. Indeed, research associates are almost always "fresh out of college," while managers "are just out of grad school with their master's or two years work experience or something comparable." "CEB employs hundreds of smart, motivated, hardworking 20- and 30- somethings who can log plenty of hours, but also reap great rewards," says an insider.

CEB has recognized in the last few years that it has mommies and daddies on staff as well. To support its parent-employees, CEB offers generous flex time and telecommuting options. Approximately 7 percent of CEB staffers take advantage of the telecommuting option, working from home at least eight hours a week. CEB also offers emergency backup day care. In addition, CEB consultants have formed a club called the CEB Parents Affinity Group; members take to the company intranet to exchange info on babysitters, health care and other quotidian details.

## School smarts

Don't put those schoolbooks in storage just yet. "The culture at CEB is one of its strongest selling points," notes a consultant, and that culture seems to be reminiscent of an honors program at college. One insider reports that CEB-ers are "the ultimate snobs about schools and credentials, but if you are smart and completely dedicated to gaining experience and developing in your field, the company will definitely offer benefits." Another finds that the youthful atmosphere can be problematic: "Under a veneer of youthful pleasantness, the firm is rampant with intellectual orthodoxy, and poorly adjusted people who don't seem to understand how the real world works." However, others note employees' "top schools," "interest in a variety of area" and "incredible intelligence." CEB is, says one source, "a dynamic environment where thinkers thrive."

## Baby bosses

One wrinkle in the company's youthfulness is that "managers are young and often not very experienced in providing good leadership," several respondents note. Says one, "It can be hard to take direction from an incompetent manager since they are only a year or two ahead of you." Managerial skills also seem to vary greatly: "Getting a good manager is very important to feeling like you can survive the job," and "if you have a good manager they will try to get you the projects that interest you." The long hours, combined with the lack of guidance, can be frustrating for some. "You work long hours on tons of projects and it's questionable if anyone even reads the final project because you hardly ever get feedback from the client on your work; that also means that it is essentially your manager who you aim to keep happy, not the client."

CEB consultants do have the chance to weigh in on their supervisors – the firm has a biannual review process, where employees review themselves, their superiors and any direct reports. Because consultants are reviewed twice a year, they have twice as many opportunities to move up. It's common for entry level CEBers to be promoted within a year.

## Load balancing

Hours at CEB, our sources say, generally hover around 55 to 60 hours a week. "Relative to investment banking and full-scale consulting companies, CEB has more normalized hours," says an insider. "There will be times when you will be working long days – 12 or more hours – but for the most part, you can expect to be home at a reasonable hour to go to the gym, watch television, socialize, etc." However, "you will not work 40 hours a week any week you work there," says a consultant. "Having worked in consulting before where I put in regular 15-hour days," muses another source, "I am grateful to CEB for the ability to get out of work by 6 or 6:30 p.m. on most nights. There are exceptions, of course, but normally the workday is 9-10 hours."

On the other hand, deadlines breed long hours. "Obviously, the closer to the due date of deliverables, the longer the work week becomes," says one consultant. The unpredictability factor is especially high in research positions. "Within custom research, work loads spike every other week. It is not very predictable in that regard! You need to have great flexibility and excellent time management skills," notes one source. Another consultant quips, "Spike is my middle name."

All the work does have a payoff, though. "If you work long hours in the office it pays off really fast; you can work from home pretty easily and your manager can make it easy on you," we hear; also, "they are understanding about personal issues and you can even work from home every one in a while if your projects permit."

## No frequent flyer miles here

Travel demands are minimal at CEB, especially for researchers. "For most people, there's little or no travel, and for most researchers, there is very little. But enough to be fun once in a while," says a consultant. The requirements are "contingent upon the position. Within research, you might expect to travel a few times a year (depending on your level). However, if you work in Content Delivery or Marketing, you can expect to be on the road more than 50 percent." Though "some of us travel massively," most consultants can reasonably expect not to get too many seat upgrades from their employment at CEB.

## Extra perks

The company also provides, in D.C. at least, pre-tax "Metro fare, 24 paid days off and sick time you can use without giving an explanation" and the option to work from home. "Each business unit gets $500 a quarter which is used at quarterly team outings – like at restaurants or bars etc. for the team to 'bond.'" There's an employee lounge, some reimbursement for tuition, movie passes, and gyms, day care assistance, and general medical/dental/life/disability insurance. Some find that "given the lower-than-industry-standard salary, the CEB benefits package is quite impressive!" Others disagree, saying, "The lack of reimbursement for very fundamental things is shockingly poor." Indifferent reimbursement for cell phone bills irks many insiders, for example.

## Rapid development

Thanks in part to the company's growth, new consultants can advance quickly at CEB. "As long as you get your projects done on time, you can move up pretty fast because the company is in a steady growth phase," says a source. Echoes another consultant, "Speaking from the research perspective, upon acceptance one can expect to advance as quickly as he or she promotes his/her abilities. With talent comes promotion. Although it may seem slow-moving initially, once you have demonstrated solid aptitude, you are recognized and will be promoted. If you start as a research associate, you can expect advancement within six to twelve months, and from there, another six to 12 months for the next promotion." Indeed, according to the company's web site, when staff members get their twice-yearly reviews, about a quarter of them are promoted.

Consultants say that promotion is by both talent and tenure. One insider says that "you are either really good at what you do as an RA and get to move up; or you work at CEB so long that you are the best by default. This means you are an RA in your second year and have established yourself and are going to be better than the younger members on your team – at that point, if you want to advance, you pretty much can." A degree isn't necessary, either: "It's definitely possible for undergrads to go to MBA-level positions." A few others find CEB to be more of an up-or-out sort of place, though. "With fairly constant growth, there are always opportunities for 'stretch roles' into new functional programs. High performers should expect to be rewarded with both promotions and raises, while low performers should not expect to last very long in a given position (although internal mobility across programs and job functions is fairly common)," says one employee.

The flipside to the period of extended growth is an oversupply of RAs. They may be the "backbone of the company – but there is lots of competition for the few positions to advance." Insiders aren't complaining about the growth, though. "CEB has yet to lay off any employees," several consultants note happily.

## Unsupervised

Again, CEB's fast pace of expansion proves both a blessing and a curse regarding management. "It's a fast growing company, and [supervisors] are probably one of the company's weaker points. Oftentimes, individuals are promoted based on merit – which is great – however, this does not make them a good manager! There are always exceptions to the rule and the company is improving, but you certainly do want to know who your manager will be and how best to manage him or her."

## Educational vacuum

"Curiously, for an executive education company," says a source, "there really isn't any training. There's a one-time course for new syndicated consultants, but ongoing education is not reimbursed or provided." That seems to be a big minus, according to CEB consultants. "The conventional wisdom in the firm is that participating in an internal training program qualifies one for their position. There are no opportunities whatsoever to receive any training outside of the firm," says a consultant. As for the minimal training provided, one employee "would grade it above average, though [it is] not remarkable. Most of what you need to learn is process and that is discovered on the job." The firm says that it provides extensive in-house training on topics like management skills, graphics creation, writing and presentation skills and other job topics. On average, CEBers attend 45 hours of training per year.

## Minimalists and cubists

Offices are not the high point of a CEB career, employees say. "Fast growing, entrepreneurial companies do not put much into office space! You can expect the basics and you'll most likely share an office – if you have an office," says a source, adding "Cube life is the norm, but quite congenial." However, another employee gripes that "offices are exceptionally bad," and remarks that "senior management (who occupy rather massive corner offices) are untroubled at putting (no kidding) MBAs, lawyers, former investment bankers and Harvard PhDs in cubicles."

## Diversity across the Board

Women are well-represented at CEB. "At least half of the employees at CEB are women." "There certainly is disparity in senior level management, but it is improving – slowly." Agrees another, "It's getting better – there are some women who have reached the consultant level, more who have advanced in member services and marketing." As of 2003, women made up 31 percent of the senior ranks at CEB.

There are "a few examples of diversity at high levels, but the senior strategic research community tends to be white and male." That might be changing, though. "Diversity seems important to the company but I saw a majority of white RAs with some Asians and Indians and one or two black people – so I'd say it's partially interested in diversity." "I love the company, but it *needs* more ethnic minorities!" says a third. Meanwhile, being gay or lesbian seems to be a non-issue: "Having several friends at the company who fall into this category, it is something with which CEB has no problems."

## Community connections

CEB is active in the D.C. community. "It's significantly involved with various community activities and employees are encouraged to participate. Monthly letters are sent to all employees to alert them to coming events in which they can participate," notes one employee. There's an Advisory Board Foundation where "all sorts of community/charitable events are encouraged and often sponsored," which reportedly "does a good job." According to the company, almost half the staff walks in the Fannie Mae Help the Homeless Walkathon. Other popular programs include the Greater D.C. Cares Day and Christmas in April (fixing homes in D.C.). CEB's ServiceCorps awards grants to nonprofit organizations based on volunteer hours of CEB staffers ($70,000 has been donated since 1998 through this program) and critical needs. Consultants can earn up to three days of paid time off through volunteering.

# Dean & Company

8065 Leesburg Pike, Ste. 500
Vienna, VA 22182-2733
Phone: (703) 506-3900
Fax: (703) 506-3905
www.deanco.com

## LOCATIONS

**Vienna, VA (HQ)**

## PRACTICE AREAS

Strategy Consulting

## THE STATS

**Employer Type:** Private Company
**Chairman & CEO:** Dean Wilde
**2002 Employees:** 70
**2001 Employees:** 70

## UPPERS

• Lots of responsibility at lower
  levels
• Lack of hierarchy

## DOWNERS

• Lack of office choice – had better
  like suburban DC
• Work lacks variety – had better
  like tech!

## KEY COMPETITORS

Bain & Company
Boston Consulting Group
McKinsey & Company

## EMPLOYMENT CONTACT

E-mail: recruiting@dean.com

## THE BUZZ
WHAT CONSULTANTS AT OTHER FIRMS ARE SAYING

• "Small but nice"
• "Mercer Management boutique"
• "Egotistical"
• "Quantitative"

# THE SCOOP

## Techifying strategy firm

Based in Northern Virginia's tech corridor, Dean's practice reflects its surroundings. Dean works with large corporations such as telecom titan AT&T as well as small firms, private equity funds and tech startups. A mix of capital markets know-how and strategic problem solving is the hook that seems to keep clients returning to Dean. Indeed, Dean measures its success against whether its clients' profitability has improved.

Dean itself fits into the "small firm" category. The firm is also highly selective – a quarter of its consultants have PhDs, and the company recruits primarily from top Ivy League schools.

## Wilde roots

Dean was founded in 1993 by Dean Wilde and two senior consulting colleagues. Wilde, the firm's chairman, was previously an executive vice president at Strategic Planning Associates (SPA) and subsequently at Mercer Management Consulting (Mercer was formed by the merger of SPA and TBS in 1990), where he ran the worldwide telecom and technology practice and was a member of the board of directors. He is also a visiting lecturer at the MIT Sloan School of Management.

## The Delta model

One of Dean's keys is what it calls "The Delta Model," based on a 2001 book Wilde co-wrote with Arnoldo Hax, a professor at MIT Sloan. This model suggests old managerial frameworks are somewhat outdated, especially since the Internet and other new technologies have changed the face of business. The model asks companies to position themselves based on a concept called "customer bonding," the degree to which customers are emotionally invested in the products they buy and use.

How can companies achieve some degree of this so-called bonding? Through one of three strategic positions, according to Dean. The first, and most traditional, approach is called "best product:" companies either make their product cheaper or better than the competition's. Wilde and Hax aren't thrilled about this approach, arguing that it makes the competitor, rather than the customer, the central focus. "The obsessive concern with the competitors often leads to imitation and price war, resulting in rivalry and convergence – the worst of all deals." Companies following "best product" strategies create limited bonding; customers won through this method are easily lost when competitors introduce new and improved products. The authors seem to see this focus on the product itself as an outmoded approach. A better tack, they say, is what they've termed the "total customer solution," where product design, price and positioning are centered around an understanding of what the customer wants, regardless of what's already out there.

Finally, the "system lock-in" option looks at the company, the customers, the suppliers and especially the "complementors." A complementor company offers products or services that round out the client's portfolio. With this approach, the client company would court the complementor (usually external, but occasionally an internal division) to work in tandem – thus making the whole package more enticing to a customer. From there, companies can create a self-perpetuating cycle where more complementors help attract more customers, and vice versa. The challenges with this approach, the authors say, are to create such a lock-in without seeming monopolistic and then to sustain it. That's where Dean comes in.

## Joining forces

What the Delta Model preaches, Dean practices. It's allied with several highly specialized consulting firms to round out its expertise – usually, they're experts in an industry or a function. Some of these include American Management Systems, PowerSim, C-Change, Riversoft and LCC.

In terms of investing, Dean works primarily with Lindsay Goldberg & Bessemer, a multi-billion dollar private equity fund, on a variety of deals. Dean handles the due diligence and advisory functions, while LGB handles the financial side. Occasionally, Dean works in exchange for equity plus cash. Historically, the LGB funds have averaged returns of 30 percent a year. Each investment is about $75 to $200 million.

## Speeding up

Dean says it has a "speedometer," rather than an "odometer," approach to the professional development of its employees. That is, performance, not time at the firm, dictates promotion. The company uses a comprehensive career review process centered around detailed feedback that will accelerate a worker's career. Each consultant is paired with a career adviser, an informal mentor who plays an important role in supporting the individual's development. There's also an upward feedback process, in which analysts and associates review managers and VPs on their managerial skills. (Not coincidentally, sharp Dean consultants can use this process to learn more about developing their own managerial skills.)

This "simple, flexible and nonhierarchical structure" applies to running the firm, too. A management committee composed of the firm's senior professionals addresses major policy and strategy questions, while the managers lead the day-to-day casework. The remaining management and administrative functions are spread among the consultants and other professionals.

# GETTING HIRED

First, a brief discussion of Dean & Company's promotion structure. The typical progression is analyst (entry level) to associate (MBA or PhD level) to managers (normally promoted from within; they have day-to-day case responsibility). Each of these roles usually draws on areas such as research (collecting data), analysis, problem solving, communication (meetings, feedback), talking to clients, and planning and structuring the analytic approach.

Analysts perform entry level tasks on case teams, researching and crunching numbers, but are also responsible for what Dean chooses to call the "business 'so whats'" of their analysis. They should possess keen analytical skills, be handy with computers, strong researchers, good communicators and possess sparkling interpersonal skills. The best analysts can be promoted to the associate level without an MBA. Dean helps pay for business school for top analysts who agree to rejoin the firm after graduating from an MBA program.

Associates start out as generalists and begin to specialize as they move toward becoming managers. They'll handle broad research, analysis, problem solving and some management. Associates should expect to travel two or three days a week, and work on one case at a time at first, handling multiple cases as they move up. Applicants should be good at analytics and business problem solving, skilled at communication, deft with clients, quick learners, good at structuring problems, and act and think like a CEO.

Dean offers internships to first year business school students and undergraduate juniors. Interns are staffed on project teams, and are reviewed in the same manner as full-time employees. "It was great," enthuses one former intern who's now a senior consultant.

Dean recruits on campus at a handful of undergrad schools: Dartmouth, Harvard, Princeton, University of Virginia, Wellesley and Yale. It also recruits through the business schools at MIT (Sloan) and Harvard, as well as at numerous PhD programs. At these schools, interviews take place during fall and winter. There's an on-campus "company presentation," says an insider, then "three rounds of interviews." There's a "first round case interview on campus, and the second round is two case interviews on campus," says an employee; at least one partner will be interviewing each candidate.

Associate candidates also have a third round of interviews at Dean's office. "Successful candidates demonstrate the ability to think in a logical and well-structured manner about the case issues and communicate insights and options clearly," reveals the company; its web site has an aptly titled presentation, "How to Crack a Case," available at www.deanco.com/docs/HowToCrackACase.pdf. An insider elaborates, "Cases are based on actual firm case experience and are designed to test one's ability to reason through a case-like problem." Those who receive offers are invited to visit the Vienna offices – a "sell day," says a source, where they'll conduct one-on-one discussions, get exposure to the firm's mission and principles, and go to social functions. The interview process is "pretty efficient – we're good at making decisions very quickly," reveals a source.

# OUR SURVEY SAYS

## Culture club

Insiders report that Dean's culture is "open and collegial – people are really willing to help." Because it's a "small firm" with "hardworking people," everyone gets "a lot of responsibility." Supervisors are also praised for their "open-door policies." The workers are "bright and friendly," and Dean is praised for its "firm-sponsored social events."

## Balancing lifestyles

"Work/life balance is very dependent upon the project you are working on and the manager/partner you are working with," says one consultant. Echoes another, "There can be very large differences to the averages for travel and work hours." A third consultant says that in terms of travel, there's a "wide variation among consultants, not all of it driven by personal choice or desire." However, "if you're lucky, there's very little travel." Dean has a centralized staffing process that provides employees input on staffing decisions.

## Moving on up

Organizational structure seems to be relatively fluid at Dean, since there's "no up-or-out policy" and a "lack of hierarchy." "People with undergraduate degrees can and do move up to MBA-level positions," says a consultant. However, that takes work: "Management is fairly conservative in promotions. They want to see proven work at the next level before they promote," reveals a source. That means there's no usual timeframe for promotion, either. "Time to advance depends very much on the individual," says a consultant. "[Promotion is] based upon performance," says another, "but promotion seems to have slowed from prior years." Though the company has not undergone layoffs "within the last year," "offers were delayed by six months" for the class that graduated in 2001.

## Clocking in

Consultants report 60-hour workweeks are not uncommon, though again, it's "highly variable and based on the project." Unstaffed time is reportedly rare.

## Home sweet office

Dean has but one office, and consultants love to talk about it. Some consultants love that there are "no cubes" at Dean – "All analysts and associates share an office with one other person – no professionals in cubes." Another insider cherishes the possession of "a door to close if necessary." But some insiders don't love the decor. "It needs a refresh," says one employee. The location – "out in suburbia, next to a mall" – isn't peachy for everyone either. "Not a pleasant office location," carps a consultant.

## In search of women

The makeup of the office is "homogenous", says one consultant. "We try, but don't do so well" in terms of minority hiring, says another. "Minorities are underrepresented in the firm,," one source says. "We have been increasing our hiring of women of late," reveals another consultant.

## Putt-putt perks

Consultants give high marks to Dean's salary, rating it at the high end of the scale. There's no profit sharing "until you reach the manager level." Bonuses and perks include an on-site gym (at the D.C. office), laptops, concert tickets, Monday firm-sponsored social events (including the highly regarded in-office Putt Putt Golf Tournament. No, really) and the daily joy of business casual dress in the office.

# "Simple, flexible, nonhierarchical structure."

## — Dean source

# Giuliani Partners

5 Times Square
New York, NY 10036
Phone: (212) 931-7300
Fax: (212) 931-7310
www.giulianipartners.com

## LOCATIONS

**New York, NY (HQ)**

## PRACTICE AREAS

Corporate Security
Crisis Management
Emergency Preparedness
Financial Management
Public Safety
Private Equity
Risk Assessment

## THE STATS

**Employer Type:** Private Company
**Chairman and CEO:** Rudolph Giuliani

## UPPERS

- Prestigious, high-powered leadership
- Backing from Ernst & Young
- Practice areas are hot buttons

## DOWNERS

- No established track record
- High level of scrutiny
- Limited range of focus

## KEY COMPETITORS

Bain & Company
Boston Consulting Group
Booz Allen Hamilton
Mayor Mike Bloomberg

## EMPLOYMENT CONTACT

Phone: (212) 931-7300

## THE BUZZ
WHAT CONSULTANTS AT OTHER FIRMS ARE SAYING

- "More political consulting than business?"
- "Small firm, big name"
- "Coattails"

# THE SCOOP

## The next challenge

He was an attorney for New York and the U.S. Government. Then he was New York City's iron-fisted mayor. Now, Rudolph Giuliani is working for himself, as chairman and CEO of Giuliani Partners (GP), a private equity and management consultancy specializing in security and risk assessment. The firm came into being in January 2002 as a joint venture between Giuliani and the accounting and professional services firm Ernst & Young.

## Experts on the coattails

Many of the top executives at Giuliani Partners are former City Hall advisors who followed Hizzoner into private practice. Among the notables are VP Tom Von Essen, former fire commissioner and head of subsidiary Giuliani Von Essen; partner Dennison Young, from Giuliani's days as a U.S. Attorney; partner Tony Carbonetti, former City Hall chief of staff; VP Rich Scheirer, former head of the Office of Emergency Management; partner Michael Hess, formerly the city's corporation counsel; partner Bruce Teitelbaum, a former advisor; VP Bernard Kerik, the former police commissioner; and communications director Sunny Mindel, formerly Giuliani's press secretary.

## Rudy, year one

The firm's first engagement was announced in May 2002, a strategic alliance with Nextel Communications to improve public safety message systems in the U.S. by reducing interference and maximizing the useful exchange between authorities in multiple jurisdictions.

Also in May 2002, pharmaceutical company Purdue Pharma engaged Giuliani Partners to develop a number of prescription drug-related projects, including an early warning network to spot and stop prescription drug abuse trends, a national standard for monitoring prescriptions and programs to help prevent smuggling.

GP and Aon Corporation, a holding company of insurance brokerages and underwriters, allied themselves in October 2002 to provide a broad array of crisis management services to major corporations worldwide. GP's responsibilities in the partnership include providing short- and long-term crisis management solutions, developing processes for handling emergencies and advising on emergency communications procedures. Aon's experience in this field includes the Special Risks Counter-Terrorism Team, formed in 1997.

## What's next?

In March 2003, Giuliani Partners announced two more strategic alliances. The first, with commercial real estate services firm CB Richard Ellis, is essentially a knowledge-exchange program; Ellis clients will have access to GP's risk assessment and management expertise, while Giuliani clients will gain the real estate insight of the 10,000-employee CB Richard Ellis. The second alliance, with business intelligence technology group Cognos, combines the two companies' skills to provide corporate performance management solutions to public and private sector firms. GP will utilize Cognos Metrics Manager, Cognos Series 7 and Cognos Enterprise Planning software to create corporate accountability and performance measurement programs.

Speaking of corporate accountability, there's some chance that GP's CEO may find himself repairing the shattered images of some of the more notorious names in the recent economic downturn. Giuliani has been linked, at least since November 2002, to David Matlin, the head of an investment group that has been trying to take over WorldCom. The proposed reorganization plan would place Giuliani as chairman of the bankrupt telecom. Giuliani and Tom Von Essen also entered into negotiations with Tyco in December 2002 to bring new life to the troubled company's fire and security unit, which includes alarm company ADT.

## GETTING HIRED

## It's not what you know

Early reports state that all of the original five managing partners and 15 associates at Giuliani Partners are friends and/or former colleagues of the ex-Mayor. This suggests that the usual means of getting hired by a consulting firm don't apply here, though *BusinessWeek* stated in October 2002 that the staff had more than doubled in size since the firm opened for business. Contacts at venture partner Ernst & Young may be helpful – the two firms are in the same office building – but there is no public information on how to get one's foot in the door at Giuliani Partners. The company's web site is no more than a placeholder as of June 2003.

"It is by no means a requirement for applicants to have German language skills."

— *Droege consultant*

# Droege & Comp.

Poststrasse 5-6
40213 Dusseldorf
Germany
Phone: 49-211-86731-0
Fax: 49-211-86731-111
www.droege.de

## LOCATIONS

**Duesseldorf, Germany (HQ)**
New York, NY
Beijing
Hamburg
London
Moscow
Munich
Singapore
Sydney
Vienna

## PRACTICE AREAS

M&A
Operations
Restructuring/Turnaround
Strategy/Marketing

## THE STATS

**Employer Type:** Private Company
**CEO:** Walter Droege
**2002 Employees:** 345
**2001 Employees:** 315
**2002 Revenue:** $128.2 million
**2001 Revenue:** $111 million

## UPPERS

• Hands-on, interesting projects
• Entrepreneurial spirit at company

## DOWNERS

• Competition between employees
• Long hours, short deadlines

## KEY COMPETITORS

A.T. Kearney
McKinsey & Company
Roland Berger Strategy Consultants

## EMPLOYMENT CONTACT

Droege & Comp., Inc.
Attn: Recruiting
405 Lexington Ave.
35th Floor
New York, NY 10174
Phone: (212) 557-7616
Fax: (212) 577-6788
E-mail: recruiting@droegeusa.com

## THE BUZZ
WHAT CONSULTANTS AT OTHER FIRMS ARE SAYING

• "Successful in Germany
" "Dubious second tier"
• "Local hero"
• "Lack know-how on top issues"

# THE SCOOP

Founded in 1998, Germany's Droege & Comp. (pronounced DROY-guh, and yes, they say "and comp") counts both large publicly traded companies and mid-size firms among its clients. The firm splits its energy among three practice areas: strategy and marketing, operations and efficiency, and restructuring and turnaround. Clients are mostly European, and tend to have an interest in global expansion. Droege is working on its own global expansion, too, beefing up its presence in the English-speaking world. Industry-wise, Droege focuses on manufacturing (which makes up 44 percent of its business), financial services (32 percent), and retail/service (24 percent).

## The ups and downs of company structure

Droege is a smallish firm and relatively unbureaucratic. Consultants work in teams that include clients, and are given a lot of responsibility and autonomy. Consultants' salaries are tied to the client's performance, so "only measurable results count," says one consultant. On the flipside, this organizational structure leads to long hours and short deadlines.

The performance-based commitment holds at upper levels, for Droege's motto, "know-how plus equity," isn't just talk. Droege actually invests in some of the companies it is advising. The venture wing is called Deutsche Investors' Capital (DIC). DIC invests in companies undergoing restructuring, which Droege sees as a further commitment to its clients.

## Weathering the storm

Despite persistent worldwide economic doldrums, Droege performed better in 2002 than in 2001, increasing revenues by 15 percent and adding 30 more employees to its payroll. Droege also welcomed some major new clients, such as ITT, Namasco, and German heavyweights Kloeckner, Madaus and Eurobike. "In general terms, Droege is targeting, among other customers, the German Fortune 100 firms as well as the U.S. Fortune 500," says an insider.

## Research intensity

Droege is known for its thorough research reports and benchmarking studies. One particularly popular study is "Benchmarking USA," Droege's annual look at the state of German companies with American subsidiaries. Droege conducts its research in collaboration with universities, government entities and corporations. It's also published several books; currently on the market, some about restructuring management, doing business in the United States, a Six Sigma handbook, and reevaluating e-business.

# GETTING HIRED

## No German required

The hiring process at Droege is said to be both "elaborate"and "very quick – quite a feat! " It took three weeks from my application to finish interviews and receive my offer letter," says one Droege consultant. The company recruits at NYU's Stern, Columbia Business School, Harvard, Thunderbird and major German universities, and posts jobs in newspapers and on job web sites.

The process consists of several interview sessions with case studies and tests; they're looking for how well a candidate structures and analyzes a problem. Each candidate is also asked to give a brief presentation at the beginning of his or her interview in front of the local office's staff; all of these staff members will later rate the candidate.

The key to working at Droege is a master's degree, preferably an MBA or master's in engineering, science or IT. "There's a lot of emphasis placed on education," confides one consultant. Beyond education, Droege says it is looking for "individuals with superiority and leadership competence, winning manners, a sense of humor, originality and individuality, and the necessary people skills." Time spent abroad, particularly internships or work abroad, is also a must. While German language ability is helpful, it's not necessary. "With regards to language skills, some of our employees in the U.S. have German language skills, but the majority do not. It is by no means a requirement for applicants to have German language skills," says a source. Another consultant points out that knowledge of German "opens the door for potential assignments in Germany, if desired."

Internships (here called "trainee programs") are a solid way to get a foot in the door at Droege. Trainees often function as a consultant's aide, helping out with benchmarking studies or aiding clients on site.

# OUR SURVEY SAYS

## Performance pressure

Droege maintains an up-or-out system. "As an above average performer, you can expect a promotion every 18 to 24 months," says one consultant. Adds another insider, "All start as consultants, and promotions are performance-based. Educational requirements are very high." One insider says the normal time frame is "two to four years at the consultant level, then another three to four years at principal before becoming a partner." The firm says that fast track promotions are common at Droege, with consultants promoted every year.

## Life at the office

Droege gets average to good marks on diversity with respect to women, minorities, and gays and lesbians. Offices are considered pleasant. However, consultants don't get to spend a lot of time there, as "local projects are not generally the norm," says one consultant. "[You] can expect to be on the road for four days per week." Notably, the New York office is located in the Chrysler Building.

## Up with comp

The consultants report they're quite happy with their salaries – "compensation is above average," says one consultant. Employee referral bonuses, laptops and good ol' life insurance are part of the package. For higher-ups, "starting with the principal level, company stocks are issued in parallel to other forms of compensation," says a consultant.

## Boot camp

A career at Droege typically starts with an orientation period, where the Droege mission is driven home, and quantitative skills are honed. After that, consultants are thrown right into their maiden assignments, and get on-the-job training with occasional evaluations from supervisors. There is a Droege & Comp. Academy for special skills, but as one consultant says, "The problem is to find time to schedule the classes."

# Aon Consulting

200 E. Randolph Street
Chicago, IL 60601
Phone: (800) 438-6487
Fax: (312) 381-6032
www.aon.com

## LOCATIONS

**Chicago, IL (HQ)**
140 offices worldwide

## PRACTICE AREAS

Compensation
Employee Benefits
Human Resources Outsourcing
Management Consulting

## THE STATS

**Employer Type:** Subsidiary of Aon
Corporation
**Stock Symbol:** AOC
**Stock Exchange:** NYSE
**Chairman and CEO, Aon Consulting:**
Donald C. Ingram
**2002 Employees:** 7,800
**2001 Employees:** 7,400
**2002 Revenue, Aon Consulting:**
$1.05 billion
**2001 Revenue, Aon Consulting:**
$938 million

## UPPERS

• Flexible hours
• Strong work/life programs

## DOWNERS

• Slightly bureaucratic feel
• Lack of cohesion between the
many offices

## KEY COMPETITORS

Deloitte Consulting
Hewitt Associates
Mercer Human Resource Consulting
Towers Perrin
Watson Wyatt Worldwide

## EMPLOYMENT CONTACT

jobsearch.aon.newjobs.com

## THE BUZZ
### WHAT CONSULTANTS AT OTHER FIRMS ARE SAYING

• "Intrigued"
• "Fingers in too many pies"
• "Neat presentations"
• "Risk, risk and more risk"

# THE SCOOP

Aon Consulting is a subsidiary of the world's second-largest insurance brokerage, Aon Corporation. Aon's offerings began with pure human resources consulting, which grew out of Aon's benefits practice, founded in 1982. Today, offerings have grown to expand beyond benefits consulting, HR outsourcing and compensation consulting. Current offerings include more traditional management consulting on mergers and acquisitions, customer and employee loyalty, process improvement and Six Sigma, and advising on internal communications.

## Targeted expansion

Still, Aon remains true to its roots as an HR consultancy. One of its strong suits is analyzing workforce productivity, especially for companies that have undergone changes. A number of purchases have rounded out Aon's HR offerings. In 1997 Aon acquired Pecos River, a change management firm, and the following year it bought Rath & Strong, a management consultancy. 2001 saw Aon add three firms to its fold – ASI Solutions, an HR consultancy located outside Philadelphia; Groupe Prevention Progesst (which is really spelled that way), a Canadian management consulting firm; and Actuarial Sciences Associates, a New Jersey-based provider of administration and compensation solutions.

In December 2001, Aon restructured its consulting operation by bringing its management-related endeavors under one group, Aon Management Consulting. The new practice, which functions as a subdivision of Aon Consulting, is primarily a merger of the Pecos River and Rath & Strong offerings, capitalizing on Rath & Strong's Six Sigma suite of HR management solutions.

## Dial up

Aon Consulting landed a huge outsourcing contract in the summer of 2002 with AT&T. The agreement, which spans seven years, dictates that Aon will provide administrative and account-management services for the telecom giant. In addition, Aon will build tech software and hardware for AT&T's HR and payroll groups.

## Study hard

Aon Consulting publishes a number of studies each year. Most notably, the massive "United States @Work" study, which has been conducted annually since 1996, surveys employees to measure their loyalty and attitude toward their companies and supervisors.

## Solid results

Aon Consulting's revenue grew steadily throughout 2002, ending the year at $1.054 billion, a good 12 percent above the previous year's results. The company said the AT&T outsourcing contract was a large part of that jump, as well as healthy growth in continental Europe and the Pacific region. In the U.S., the company, unsurprisingly, endured the deferral of some projects by clients. And despite the economic tumult, 2001 was also a solid year – that year, the firm's revenue spiked 22 percent to $938 million, a jump also attributable in part to the ASI acquisition.

## Striking a work/life balance

As a firm that advises clients on HR offerings and strategy, it's fitting that Aon has a rich HR program. It supports flexible work arrangements, including telecommuting, job sharing, unusual hours or compressed workdays. It also has several career-development programs in place, including Aon University, which tutors employees on various subjects, such as risk management and sales. There's also a mentoring program that pairs new employees with more seasoned ones they can turn to for advice. Should employees get a case of wanderlust, Aon is willing to transfer them to an overseas office for a short-term assignment.

## GETTING HIRED

Aon takes resumes through its web site. (Access the database at: jobsearch.aon.newjobs.com). The firm also does limited on-campus recruiting. "The process was initiated by a recruiter and would involve one interview with the hiring manager and a HR rep on the same day. The questions were related to my past experience as it related to [consulting]," reveals one source.

## OUR SURVEY SAYS

## Megacompany

Dress at Aon is "business casual," reflecting the "informal environment." One consultant agrees, "The culture is somewhat relaxed. Dress code is business casual with jeans permissible on Friday."

The company as a whole has a rather "impersonal larger company" feel, sources say, that can be "high stress and fast paced." "The corporate parent has somewhat antiquated HR policies and practices, tuition reimbursement is micromanaged, there's no PTO time, and there is a very labor intensive attendance tracking system, for example," says one source. Also because of its size, some can feel left out: "Because we are not located with the corporate office, some feelings of isolation and segregation exist," says a source.

Being in a big company also has pluses, such as "a vast array of resources that can be utilized" and "a large infrastructure of specialized services."

## Working on promotion

Though one consultant reports that "advancement [is] limited" at Aon Consulting, another source qualifies this by saying "the opportunities for advancement are there, but few and far between. Management sets very high expectations on its employees and occasionally at review time compensates for hard work." Another insider finds that "the firm takes into consideration experience, performance of one's current role and anticipated performance in a promotional role. A degree is considered where it is deemed applicable for the position." Training at Aon Consulting includes "work-specific classes to increase knowledge."

## A good balance

Consultants praise Aon for its "flexible" hours and work arrangements. "Several employees have telecommute privileges and work from home one or more days per week, though they are primarily IT-related types," says a source. Another consultant opines,"Aon is a good firm to work for in that they are flexible enough (if you are considered a valued employee) to accommodate for the individual's personal demands, like children."

Hours "range depending on the time of year." For one consultant, typical hours are 8 a.m. to 4:30 p.m., while another works "in excess of 40 hours per week" during the end of the financial year.

 **LECG**

2000 Powell St., Ste. 600
Emeryville, CA 94608
Phone: (510) 653-9800
Fax: (510) 653-9898
www.lecg.com

## LOCATIONS

**Emeryville, CA (HQ)**
26 offices worldwide

## PRACTICE AREAS

Antitrust
Claims Services
Energy
Entertainment, Media and Sports
Environment and Insurance Claims
Finance and Damages
Health Care
Intellectual Property
Mergers and Acquisitions
Public Policy
Strategy
Telecommunications
Transfer Pricing
Transportation

## THE STATS

**Employer Type:** Private Company
**Chairman:** David J. Teece
**2002 Employees:** 575

## UPPERS

• Intellectually rewarding work

## DOWNERS

• Some layoffs

## KEY COMPETITORS

Charles River Associates
FTI Consulting
Lexecon

## EMPLOYMENT CONTACT

Recruiting Coordinator
Fax: (510) 653-9898

## THE BUZZ
WHAT CONSULTANTS AT OTHER FIRMS ARE SAYING

• "Great West Coast presence"
• "Good reputation, sometimes not
  matched in execution"
• "Great for economic consulting"

# THE SCOOP

## The wild green yonder

LECG (short for Law and Economic Consulting Group) provides a variety of services to the leaders of various industries and governments. In recent years, the firm's highest visibility has come from its work in transportation, specifically the airline industry. The crisis that industry finds itself in has been LECG's bread and butter since 2001; as carriers flirt with bankruptcy, LECG consultants are quoted in an endless stream of news articles regarding the state of air travel.

The firm, founded in 1988 by a group of Berkeley economists and business school professors, grew quickly on the strength of its staff and the relative uniqueness of its focus – not many consultancies base their business on economic and legal issues. LECG made a brief run as a public company when it had an IPO in December 1997. By August 1998, though, Navigant had swallowed LECG in a merger, citing LECG's expertise and "more PhDs than any other company in our market." That relationship was short-lived; LECG management bought their company away from Navigant in October 2000. Since that time, LECG has operated as a private concern.

## Do you want wings with that?

The airline industry has been in trouble for a long time, even before the attacks of September 11 weakened confidence in the safety of air travel. Price wars, route reductions and labor disputes have plagued major and minor carriers alike, and LECG has been there through it all. In particular, Dan Kasper, a managing director for the firm, has been quoted again and again as each new development comes to light. Kasper has provided insight on the troubles (and, in some cases, bankruptcies) of United, US Airways, Continental, JetBlue, American and Southwest.

## Bioconsulting

While LECG gets its name in the papers through providing expert opinions and advice on the airline industry crisis, the firm has been busy in other fields as well. Economist John Urbanchuk completed a study for the Illinois Soybean Association in December 2002 on potential benefits of a soybean-based "biodiesel" fuel industry. The study found that Illinois could increase its gross economic output by more than $6 billion over 10 years by providing a tax incentive for biodiesel. Also that month, LECG released a report on establishing a "single payer agency" universal health care system in Massachusetts; such a system "would cost an extra $3 billion to $6 billion annually but would provide rich benefits to every person."

# GETTING HIRED

## Where will you start?

Typically, undergraduate hires at LECG have access to three positions in the company's research staff: research analyst, associate and senior associate. Most undergrads hired into the company begin as research analysts and are promoted into the other positions, but direct hires are not unheard of. Senior staffers bear titles that are variants of economist or consultant, and most have MBAs, PhDs in economics or finance, or other advanced degrees.

An insider notes, "Research associates are recruited from select colleges and universities. Entry level PhDs are recruited directly and via annual meetings (e.g., American Economic Association). Most MBAs are hired laterally." Another confirms LECG recruits "at universities, through professional associations and referrals." Entry level candidates are drawn from "Ivy League and top 20 colleges."

# OUR SURVEY SAYS

## A little information

LECG insiders are fairly positive about aspects of the firm. One insider calls the culture "extremely positive, especially for individuals that value intellectual curiosity and independence." Another describes LECG as "collegial and entrepreneurial." Philanthropic ventures such as "volunteer charities" are undertaken "to a limited extent."

## Moving up, moving out

If you're planning on staying, consider this tip from a well-placed insider: "Promotions are strictly performance based but are not strictly 'up-or-out.' They typically occur after one to three years. Promotion to partner level requires significant business generation." Another points out, "Occasionally, consultants have been promoted without an MBA, but that requires unusual talents." Even in the rocky economy, LECG has managed to spare its staff the massive cuts other firms have suffered. "Staff was reduced by fewer than 20 worldwide," according to one source.

For more information on top consulting employers and consulting careers, go to the Vault Consulting Career Channel at http://consulting.vault.com

- Detailed 40-page employer profiles on top employers like McKinsey, BCG, Bain, Accenture and more
- Surveys of employees at hundreds of consulting firms
- The only job board on the Web dedicated to consulting jobs – The Vault Consulting Job Board
- Case interview guides and one-on-one case interview prep

# http://consulting.vault.com

# Value Partners

32 Via Leopardi
Milan 20123
Italy
Phone: +39 02-4854-81
Fax: +39 02-4800-9010
www.valuepartners.com

## LOCATIONS

**Milan (HQ)**
Rome
São Paulo

## PRACTICE AREAS

Automotive
Consumer Goods
Corporate Social Responsibility
Energy and Utilities
Financial Institutions
Health Care
Real Estate
Technology
Telecommunications and Media
Transportation

## THE STATS

**Employer Type:** Private Company
**Managing Director:** Giorgio Rossi
Cairo
**2002 Employees:** 275
**2001 Employees:** 197

## UPPERS

- "No perceived hierarchy"
- "Continuous growth"

## DOWNERS

- "Lack of internal organization"
- "Communication issues inside the firm"

## KEY COMPETITORS

Bain & Company
McKinsey & Company

## EMPLOYMENT CONTACT

**Europe**
E-mail:
recruitment@valuepartners.com
**South America**
E-mail:
talita.onghero@valuepartners.com

## THE BUZZ
WHAT CONSULTANTS AT OTHER FIRMS ARE SAYING

- "Just Italy and Brazil"
- "European-focused"

# THE SCOOP

## First Italy, then the world

Value Partners is one of the largest consultancies in Italy. Founded in 1993 by Giorgio Rossi Cairo, Vittorio Giaroli and 13 other ex-McKinsey partners, the company has grown rapidly, doubling in size between 2000 and 2002 (the firm now has over 300 consultants), taking on such major clients as Telecom Italia, Merloni, Pirelli and Fiat. And though the firm bases most of its consultants in Milan and has only two other offices (in Rome and São Paulo) its affinity for the international consulting scene is more than idle talk – the firm has completed more than 150 projects in 20 countries on six continents.

## Bringing Italy up to date

In January 2000, Value Partners launched VP Web, a sister company dedicated to IT strategy, which has since expanded into Brazil. In December 2000, Value Partners opened the Golden Mouse Fund, a partnership with Arner Bank, to provide seed money for Italian telecom and media start-ups. Value Partners repeated its success with VP Web twice more: VP Tech, an 80-person practice focused on IT security solutions, was set up in 2001 and VP Finance was launched in 2002.

## The Bain of Value Partners' existence

Value Partners learned a difficult lesson in the cutthroat world of global consulting when, in October 1997, virtually its entire São Paulo office quit to join Bain & Company, which then opened an office in the city. Value Partners took the case to court in Boston, Bain's hometown, where it won a $10 million jury verdict against Bain in December 2002. The jury found that Bain had engaged in unfair competition with Value Partners and had interfered with Value Partners' existing and prospective contracts and business relationships. The jury awarded Value Partners the entire compensatory damages the firm had requested at trial. Bain is appealing the verdict.

# GETTING HIRED

### La dolce intervista

Predictably, Value Partners looks for employees with international flair. But even more than an interest in global business, prospective employees should have the knowledge to back it up – a degree in international relations, engineering or economics, along with fluency in at least one European language other than English. While Italian is not required, anyone with a working knowledge of the language will have a big advantage. In the United States, the company recruits MBAs exclusively and visits Harvard, Columbia, MIT, Wharton and Stern every year. In Europe, Value Partners recruits MBAs at INSEAD, LBS, SDA Bocconi, MIP and IESE.

The interview process at Value Partners is elaborate. After receiving resumes, the company invites a select number of candidates to a preliminary interview. If that goes well, the candidates return for a second and third round, and finally a recruiting day, where they meet with two or three principals. If they pass through all the interviews, they receive an offer. The preliminary interviews center upon an applicant's CV (or, more familiarly, resume), but the second and third involve case questions.

# OUR SURVEY SAYS

### Entrepreneurial culture

Insiders at Value Partners, when describing the culture there, are prone to call it entrepreneurial – it's the single most common observation by far. One source, by way of emphasis, reiterates part of the company's credo: "Honesty – Entrepreneurship – Collaboration." An American transplant agrees, noting the firm is "relatively entrepreneurial, with little bureaucracy and office politics." His colleagues concur; one describes the atmosphere as "collaborative, challenging and respectful of personal needs and growth path." Another consultant appreciates the "sound, fact-based, 'ex-McKinsey' approach" taken on projects, as inspired by the founders. One mentions the "nonconformist culture and limited bureaucracy." A high-level source notes the "strong focus on ethics, both in professional and personal relations." The offices are "comfortable, but low profile (by choice)," according to one person. Another raves about his location: "in the center of the city near a park!"

Sources remark on the "good trade-off of job satisfaction and living standard" found at Value Partners. One consultant notes there is a "careful balance between personal and professional commitment, but we are always very busy." Another insider agrees, "Work is always a lot, but the atmosphere is very friendly and there's attention to personal and family issues."

## Good news on growth

Unlike so many other consulting firms, Value Partners is enjoying a growth spurt. The firm's site crows about a 29 percent growth rate over its 10 years of existence, and comments from insiders reflect this: "We are in a constant growing trend;" "Only a few people laid off because of the strong company growth;" "Firm growth is stable." People rarely leave (the firm claims a startlingly low 11 percent turnover rate), and can expect to be promoted every two to three years if they perform well. For those who don't perform brilliantly, a source says the policy is "not strictly up-or-out, but it follows this principle." Another says it's "selective but 'open.' I would describe it as 'slow up-or-out.'"

## MBA not required, but welcome

Value Partners has two entry level positions, business analyst for those right out of school and associate for those with an MBA or at least two years of consulting experience. From there, employees will advance to engagement manager, senior engagement manager and, if all goes well, principal. An insider tells us, "consultants with only undergraduate degrees can move up to MBA level positions/partnership," though another says it is "hard for non-MBAs to get MBA positions. The firm sponsors employees for MBAs." Estimates on reaching partner level vary; one source says, "seven to eight years from analyst to partner," while another claims, "The best path allows one to be elected partner in eight to 10 years starting from the entry-level position (business analyst)." One optimistic soul sees "approximately six to seven years [from analyst to partner]."

Another point of departure from other consultancies is the level of training that employees receive. While most of it is "on the job," one source feels it is carried out "with excellent directors." A high-level source says there is both "on-the-job and structured training." Another says, "a lot of effort is dedicated to training, but there is large room for improvement. It's a training issue, rather than my firm's issue, however."

# Braun Consulting

20 W. Kinzie
Suite 1600
Chicago, IL 60610
Phone: (312) 984-7000
Fax: (312) 984-7033
www.braunconsult.com

## LOCATIONS

**Chicago, IL (HQ)**
Boston, MA
Dallas, TX
Indianapolis, IN
New York, NY

## PRACTICE AREAS

Business Intelligence
Business Strategy
CRM
Customer & Marketing Analysis
eBusiness
Enterprise Applications

## THE STATS

**Employer Type:** Public Company
**Stock Symbol:** BRNC
**Stock Exchange:** Nasdaq
**Chairman and CEO:** Steven J. Braun
**2002 Employees:** 285
**2001 Employees:** 435
**2002 Revenue:** $45.9 million
**2001 Revenue:** $76.7 million

## UPPERS

- Solid background in technology
- New leadership is driving positive changes
- Short, focused engagements keep the job interesting

## DOWNERS

- Layoffs fueled by plummeting demand
- Internship program on hold
- Uncertain reputation in strategy consulting

## KEY COMPETITORS

Accenture
Deloitte Consulting
Digitas

## EMPLOYMENT CONTACT

**Experienced consultants:**
Phone:(888) 284-5621
**Campus recruiting:**
Phone: (888) 284-5628
www.braunconsult.com/careers

## THE BUZZ
WHAT CONSULTANTS AT OTHER FIRMS ARE SAYING

- "Mix of strategy and IT"
- "D.O.A."
- "Tech-focused"
- "Losing steam"

# THE SCOOP

## Brains and Braun

Braun Consulting is a hands-on professional services firm with roots in IT consulting. Founded as Braun Technology Group in 1993 by Steven Braun, the firm focused on business intelligence and data warehousing. Today, the firm combines technical know-how with strategic and organizational capabilities to serve its clients. Offerings include customer relationship management, business intelligence and custom application development.

Steven Braun's company continues to beef up its business strategy practice while retaining its technology implementation capabilities. Early successes in business intelligence left Braun with a tech-savvy reputation – not a bad thing to have in any consultancy. Braun Consulting approaches many of its projects from the customer's perspective, using its understanding of customer behavior to shape the client's business. Broad-reaching strategy isn't Braun's forte. The firm focuses instead on specific challenges and the ever-important ROI (return on investment) for clients.

## Slimming down, adding lean muscle

Recent years have not been kind to Braun. The firm faced a large drop in demand in fiscal 2002, with sales falling 40 percent to $46 million. Measures undertaken to stabilize the business have included a headcount reduction of 25 percent (including 63 employees cut loose in December 2002), various cost-cutting actions and consolidation of space. The firm completed a yearlong stock repurchase plan in November 2002. That same month, the firm appointed Craig Lashmet to take over the presidency from Steven Braun. Braun will remain as chairman and CEO.

## C-level project work

Braun wants more business at the C-level – from chief marketing officers, that is. In August 2002, Braun Consulting made a direct bid to become the consultancy chief marketing and sales officers turn to when they seek to fine tune their customer relationship management strategies. One of the first efforts in this vein was a survey Braun co-authored with the American Marketing Association and Deep Customer Connections Inc. According to the study, "Marketers are being held back not by budgets or poor planning or bad campaigns, but by a lack of alignment of the various functions within their companies."

Braun's health care practice earned recognition in late 2002, with two of its disease management Internet portals winning awards. The Web Marketing Association gave www.psoriasissupport.com the nod in October 2002 for Outstanding Achievement in Website Design and Development. That site, along with www.msactivesource.com (dedicated to providing information to sufferers of multiple sclerosis), won the top spot in separate categories in *eHealthcare Strategies & Trends Magazine*'s annual eHealthcare Leadership Awards, published in December 2002.

## Muscle shirts

In other growth-related news, Paul Bascobert, an executive VP at Braun, e-mailed the firm's New York employees in November 2002, saying a dress code would be imposed until the publicly traded firm's stock doubled from 75 cents to $1.50. "We are already teeing up the best dressed, worst tie contests and philanthropic fundraisers that let people dress casual as rewards," the message continued. "In summary, we intend to have a little fun with it." While acknowledging "logically, not much" rationale for linking business attire to stock performance, he stated it was a reminder that "what we do each day is incredibly important." Bascobert claims the New York office instituted the policy on its own. Regardless of the source of the change, the stock price has risen 40 percent since November and held steady around $1.05 through May 2003 – short of the goal, but still noteworthy. There's no word on whether the New York office is still wearing full business dress.

## GETTING HIRED

## Powering in

Braun maintains a comprehensive careers page on its web site. There are separate sections for all aspects of employment at the firm, from support and infrastructure all the way to senior execs. Undergrads, MBA/graduate degree holders and experienced consultants may search available positions, read employee profiles, learn about the available benefits and view upcoming campus events. Job applicants should use the site to submit a resume.

A word of warning about seeking an internship at Braun: the 2003 summer programs were cancelled, and hopefuls are encouraged "to revisit Summer 2004 internship opportunities during our Fall 2003 recruiting initiatives." These programs are standard 10-week summer associate and consultant programs for students about to enter their senior year or who have completed their first year of business school, respectively.

615 N. Wabash Avenue
Chicago, IL 60611
Phone: (312) 573-5600
Fax: (312) 573-5678
www.navigantconsulting.com

## LOCATIONS

**Chicago, IL (HQ)**
38 offices worldwide

## PRACTICE AREAS

Claims Management and Analysis
Corporate Restructuring
Data Discovery Services
Financial and Transaction Advising
Government Contracting
Litigation and Investigation
Operations Advising and
    Management

## THE STATS

**Employer Type:** Public Company
**Stock Symbol:** NCI
**Stock Exchange:** NYSE
**Chairman and CEO:** William M.
Goodyear
**2002 Employees:** 1,368
**2001 Employees:** 1,320
**2002 Revenue:** $258.0 million
**2001 Revenue:** $224.6 million

## UPPERS

• Employees enthusiastic about
  company, work
• Posh offices

## DOWNERS

• Just emerged from lawsuit tangle
• Racial diversity needs work

## KEY COMPETITORS

Accenture
Booz Allen Hamilton
Hewitt Associates

## EMPLOYMENT CONTACT

Christine Bedalow
Director of Recruiting
175 W. Jackson Blvd., Suite 500
Chicago, IL 60604
Phone: (312) 583-5700

## THE BUZZ
WHAT CONSULTANTS AT OTHER FIRMS ARE SAYING

• "Doers"
• "Rollup of some mediocre firms"
• "Solid consulting"
• "Recovering after implosion"

# THE SCOOP

## Risky business

When companies are in trouble, Navigant Consulting, Inc. (NCI) steps in. That means its litany of services includes litigation, finance, restructuring, operations, strategic advice and data discovery. It remains a primarily domestic firm; all but three of its 38 offices are in the U.S. (the others are Calgary, Toronto and London). There are more than 1,000 professionals on staff and more than 1,300 employees total. In 2002, revenue rose 15 percent year-over-year to $258 million. The company said that in 2002, demands for its health care, asbestos and data discovery work were strong, but the energy and water practice declined.

## Navigating history

NCI has worn many hats over the years. One recent incarnation was the Metzler Group, which went public in 1996; that was a coalition of several consulting firms, including Bookman-Edmonston (which retained its name and is now a division of NCI, where it works on water resources issues). During the next three years, Metzler snapped up several more firms, including Peterson Consulting (confidential fact-finding for businesses under investigation), Barrington Consulting Group (construction and government contracting), and PENTA Advisory Services (financial advice). These firms then became business units of Navigant. In 1999, the name was changed to Navigant Consulting, Inc. 2001 saw the company acquire two more firms, Chambers Associates (a specialist in public policy consulting) and Barba-Arkhon International (a specialist in claims analysis for construction and government disputes).

It didn't stop there. In June 2002, NCI bought the Government Contracts Consulting wing of Arthur Andersen LLP; in September 2002, the firm bought The Hunter Group, a St. Petersburg, Fla., health care consulting firm. Barrington Energy Partners added strength to Navigant's energy and water practice when it was acquired in July 2002, as did the addition of Arthur D. Little's Advanced Energy Systems and Technology & Innovation Management consulting practices in April 2002. Finally, in August 2002, NCI launched a corporate restructuring practice, led by Dan Williams, a former managing partner for Arthur Andersen in the same area. This practice has 75 professionals drawn from several Navigant business units, including Peterson, PENTA and Barrington.

# GETTING HIRED

Job applicants should have degrees in finance, accounting, engineering, computer science or economics. NCI does recruit on campus, for the D.C. office at William & Mary, University of Virginia, Lehigh, Villanova, Georgetown, Virginia Tech and others depending on the year and recruiting season," says a source. Navigant also offers a summer associate internship.

After an initial on-campus interview, some applicants are invited to a second round in the NCI office, where they'll meet each other and the consultants while undergoing intensive interviews.

The firm's professional structure is fairly standard: associate consultant (undergraduate degree), consultant (one to two years' experience with either undergrad or graduate degree), senior consultant (three to five years' experience or two years plus a graduate degree), senior engagement manager (five years' experience or three years plus a graduate degree), principal (responsible for new business development and bringing in $1 million a year, with either eight years' experience or a graduate degree and five years' experience), director ($2 million in annual revenue, 10+ years' consulting experience), managing director (practice area management, 12+ years' experience, and bringing in $5 to $20 million in revenue each year), and senior managing director (practice group management, $20 to $60 million in annual revenue, and 15+ years experience).

# OUR SURVEY SAYS

## Navigating office life

The culture gets high marks from respondents, who characterize it as "fun and enthusiastic." Consultatnts are said to be "very well rounded." The company engages in nonprofit work, with an "annual group charity event." While the offices are rumored to be very nice, at least one employee takes issue with that: "I believe the firm uses its funds inefficiently. We purchase artwork, yet cut employee compensation," this consultant snits.

Work/life balance seems to be reasonable enough for a consulting firm. Hours range from 45 to 60 hours a week, which consultants find "long," and work tends to spike several times a month, "usually two out of four weeks," says one source.

## Steering employees upward

Promotion at Navigant is centered on "merit-based advancement," and there can be "fast advancement for those who are interested and capable." There is "no up-or-out policy," though there were layoffs in 2002 – estimates are that about five consultants were dismissed.

Salary is rated in the middle of the range, and includes a "reduced price stock-purchase plan." At least one consultant suggests the company "increase bonuses when the firm performance merits it and increase the frequency of bonus distribution."

Benefits include an employee referral bonus, long-term disability insurance, laptops and sports/theater tickets. The D.C. office has an employee lounge and an on-site gym, while the Baltimore location offers a cafeteria.

# Analysis Group

111 Huntington Avenue
Tenth Floor
Boston, MA 02199
Phone: (617) 425-8000
www.analysisgroup.com

## LOCATIONS

**Boston, MA (HQ)**
Denver, CO
Los Angeles, CA
Menlo Park, CA
New York, NY
San Francisco, CA
Washington, DC
London
Montreal

## PRACTICE AREAS

Antitrust • Commercial Litigation •
Energy • Entertainment and Sports •
Environmental Economics • Financial
Institutions • Health Care Economics
• Intellectual Property • Labor and
Employment Economics • Mergers
and Acquisitions • Real Estate •
Securities • Telecommunications •
Transfer Pricing • Valuation

## THE STATS

**Employer Type:** Private Company
**President:** Martha S. Samuelson
**2002 Employees:** 300
**2001 Employees:** 250

## UPPERS

• Informal and accommodating work
  atmosphere
• No cubicles – consultants have
  doors!

## DOWNERS

• "Litigation consulting has a
  strange set of rules that bother
  some people"
• "Not much" community
  involvement

## KEY COMPETITORS

Cap Gemini Ernst & Young
Charles River Associates
Lexecon Inc.
LECG
NERA

## EMPLOYMENT CONTACT

www.analysisgroup.com/c_apply.htm
E-mail: recruiter@analysisgroup.com

## THE BUZZ
WHAT CONSULTANTS AT OTHER FIRMS ARE SAYING

"Strong technical skills"
"Quite focused on telecoms"
"Niche"
"Often a lot of hot air"

# THE SCOOP

## Just analysis, thanks!

In April 2003, Analyis Group/Economics combined operations with its sister company, Integral. Analysis Group/Economics had concentrated primarily on providing financial and economic consulting to law firms and corporations, while Integral's forte was strategy consulting to Fortune 100 companies. The combined company is now called Analysis Group, and features financial, economic and strategy consulting services.

## No secrets here

Analysis Group provides support to clients in a broad range of industries and situations. Whether the firm's research is used in tax planning, litigation, strategy or regulatory matters, the focus is always on the expert interpretation of economic data. Despite the focus inherent in the firm's name, a large percentage of work comes from the firm's litigation practice, which, according to *BusinessWeek*, accounted for half the firm's revenue in 2002. Integral's traditional emphasis, however, has been on helping clients fashion strategies in "disruptive market conditions." (That, for the record, can mean coping with new technologies like the Internet.)

Unlike many consultancies, which refer to their clients anonymously, if at all, Analysis Group provides detailed lists of many clients, cases and activities on their web site, along with the names and biographies of nearly the entire consulting staff. The client list ranges from the Boston Symphony Orchestra to the NFL, from AAMCO to Dell Computer. Analysis Group has represented clients in just about every major American industry, as well as government agencies. (Integral, on the other hand, historically did not provide the names of clients.)

## Who's making the rain?

The consulting field as a whole has been struggling in recent years, with scandals and economic failures reducing confidence in consulting firms and the collapse of the tech bubble reducing the pool of potential clients. Yet Analysis Group claims it has maintained 35 percent revenue growth for the past six years. Company president Martha Samuelson and founder Bruce Stangle state that the litigation consulting boom has replaced (at least for Analysis Group) the merger and acquisition work of the late 1990s. "There were business practices that didn't cause concern when the economy was booming," says Samuelson, "but when it stops booming, it reveals the skeletons in the closet. Those things lead to litigation."

## Well-spoken economists

Analysis Group frequently publishes newsletters and reports based on its research. The firm publishes *Forum*, a quarterly newsletter highlighting a particular practice's current research and other activities. Consultants and their studies have appeared recently in such publications as *Fortune*, *BusinessWeek* and *The Wall Street Journal*. The firm has also published, or assisted in the creation of, numerous research reports on topics ranging from energy to health care to the stock market. Recent publications include Valuing Employee Stock Options: A Comparison of Alternative Models (February 2003); a report for the Federal Energy Regulatory Commission on the 2000-2001 California energy crisis (March 2003); and an article on the viability of online doctor-patient consulting (October 2002). In addition, individual team members and affiliates publish on their own, adding to Analysis Group's academic gloss.

## Movin' on up

The firm announced a number of promotions and new hires in February and March 2003. In February, John Hobster, former Global CEO of Transfer Pricing Services for Ernst & Young and advisor to the British government on that subject, joined the firm's London office as a principal. Prolific Harvard Business School writer and professor Peter Tufano was named an academic affiliate of the firm that month as well. In March 2003, seven senior associates (including four in the Boston office) were promoted to vice president, and another HBS professor, Brian Hall, became an academic affiliate.

# GETTING HIRED

## Outplacement

Much of Analysis Group's practice involves collaboration with leading professors and researchers in prestigious schools. If you're fortunate enough to study under one of them, they could provide a valuable inroad to the firm – make sure your references are in order (and as long as you don't fail their class!) Harvard Business School seems to be a prime source of academic affiliates, and presumably of consultants as well, but the firm reportedly hires from other "leading undergraduate colleges and universities as well as top business schools and PhD programs."

Candidates should possess an attractive mix of "entrepreneurial spirit" and "comfort in a teamwork environment." Applicants for the strategy area of Analysis Group may receive case studies; bank on such cases relating to "disruptive" business conditions.

## OUR SURVEY SAYS

### A firm of friends

Our sources at Analysis Group report good things about the firm's atmosphere. One engagement manager calls the culture "fun and easy going." A peer agrees that Analysis Group is "hardworking but cooperative. Extremely friendly." One consultant describes it as "a firm of friends," but cautions that it's "fun if you 'belong,' not so fun otherwise." A longtime senior consultant terms his colleagues "intellectually very interesting;" albeit "slightly nerdy."

### Home economics

The physical environment isn't the best, according to some consultants. One claims, "The office space and furnishings are old and run-down." On the positive side, one person notes, "Everyone has an office with a door – no cubicles for consultants at any level." The firm notes that it is in the process of updating and remodeling all of its offices; the Washington D.C. office, for example, will move to brand new quarters in 2004, while Boston and New York moved to new offices in 2002.

### Consistent hours, little travel

Analysis Group is said to have a relatively laid-back approach to hours (for a consulting firm). One source says, "Late nights are rare, and the firm is very flexible about family leave." Another notes that there are "some major crunches, but not much travel, and the median workweek is not too bad." However, a dissenter says sudden increases in work hours occur "frequently; based on the timing of cases I'm working on."

Travel isn't a factor for all specialists at the firm, though it is for some consultants. One insider explains, "The management consulting group travels often. The economic and financial consultants do not travel extensively." Another consultant adds, "Principals probably travel eight to10 days per month."

## The promotion treadmill

Accompanying the lack of movement around the country, though, is a lack of mobility within the firm. A long-term employee says there is "no opportunity for advancement without MBA or PhD." "Advancement from analyst to associate is extremely rare without an MBA," says one new addition to the firm. His senior colleague calls such a promotion "almost impossible," attributing this to "a change in policy." He adds, though, that Analysis Group is "growing quickly, adding several staff at all levels of the firm." The firm says it is "extremely supportive" of staff who elect to pursue an advanced degree.

One veteran of the firm suggests the company could improve by "aligning the criteria used for review to more closely match the skills needed by the firm." To this end, Analysis Group has instituted twice-yearly 360 reviews.

# "Advancement from analyst to associate is extremely rare without an MBA."

## — Analysis Group insider

# Corporate Value Associates

12 avenue Kléber
75116 Paris
France
Phone: +33 1 53 65 71 71
www.corporate-value.com

## LOCATIONS

**Paris (HQ)** • Boston, MA •
Amsterdam • Berlin • London •
Melbourne • Seoul • Shanghai •
Singapore • Sydney • Tokyo •

## PRACTICE AREAS

Acquisition Screening & Synergy •
Acquisition Strategy • Business
Definition & Segmentation •
Business Program Alignment •
Business Unit Strategy • Core
Competencies Management •
Corporate Risk Management •
Corporate Value Modeling •
Corporate Portfolio Design •
Customer Centric Value
Enhancement • Customer
Relationship Strategy • Distribution
Strategy (Channels) • E-Business
Strategy • IT Strategic Alignment •
Long-Term Dynamics • Mission
Design • Organizational Alignment •
Post-Acquisition Restructuring • 14
others

## THE STATS

**Employer Type:** Private Company
**Founder and Managing Partner:** Paul-André Rabate

## UPPERS

• Quick-moving, adaptable company
• Fast, merit-based promotions

## DOWNERS

• Very extended travel time
• Squishy, structure-lite firm
  organization

## KEY COMPETITORS

Bain & Company
L.E.K. Consulting
McKinsey & Company
Roland Berger

## EMPLOYMENT CONTACT

**Paris:**
E-mail: recruitfrance@corporate-value.com
Phone: +33 1 53 65 71 87

**Boston:**
E-mail: cvarecruitus@corporate-value.com
Phone: (617) 267-5959

## THE BUZZ
WHAT CONSULTANTS AT OTHER FIRMS ARE SAYING

• "Boutique, international
• "Minor player, occasionally
  surprises"
• "Small and intense, good work"
• "One trick pony"

# THE SCOOP

## All around the world

Corporate Value Associates (CVA) wasted no time in making an international splash when the firm was founded in Paris in 1987. The firm established offices in three other cities straightaway – in Boston, London and Amsterdam. The founders were three consultants who wanted to offer companies consulting based on problem solving frameworks and methodologies. Today, CVA has added offices in Berlin, Seoul, Tokyo, Shanghai, Singapore, Sydney and Melbourne. Industries served include automotive, financial services, retail, telecom, transportation, mining/resources and utilities.

## The CVA approach

When CVA engages a client, it creates a team with client staff and its own consultants. Its argument: this helps train the client employees, and helps project implementation, since client employees buy into the project. CVA partners lead each of these teams.

## Game on!

CVA seems to be quite the convivial workplace. Sports are a big part of life at CVA; the company organizes outings like skiing in the Alps and go-karting. It also sponsors the CVA Dream Team, a competitive sailing team made up of CVA consultants and select university students.

Movement between the international CVA offices is encouraged. That said, each office is run autonomously – as an "independent business," the company says. Breakfasts are a regular part of office life, as are Friday happy hours.

## Training daze

Upon joining CVA, new consultants are taught skills (data collection, Web research, interviewing, slide presentations and financial analysis), and methodology (CVA's problem solving frameworks). After those training sessions, there's a program called the "CVA Challenge." The challenge brings together new employees from around the world for a spirited week of team-building and mock cases. The company also offers ongoing training for upper level consultants and managers.

## The year in review

In late 2002, CVA acquired Lochridge and Company, a small Boston-based consulting firm, thus beefing up its presence in the U.S. Some of CVA's recent engagements have included an economic study for Australia's Cancer Council that explored the best way to organize cancer screening and a strategic review for the Bank of Queensland.

# GETTING HIRED

Applicants' majors are not considered particularly important at CVA. What is important is a demonstration of quantitative skills, people skills (especially "the ability to communicate effectively with people of all ages, backgrounds and nationalities"), teamwork and a solid transcript. Specific skills are not key, though dexterity with computers and language are helpful.

CVA does some limited recruiting, mostly in Paris and Australia and "top undergrad and business schools in the markets in which we operate." Targeted schools include HEC, Ecole Centrale, Forum Trium, Ecole Polytechnique, ESCP, Essec and Supaero, all in France; and the University of New South Wales, University of Sydney, Monash University and the University of Melbourne, all in Australia. Applicants outside of these schools ought to contact the CVA office that interests them directly.

The hiring process includes "three interview rounds." It starts with an interview with a consultant and an associate, followed by two more rounds with a manager and/or partner. All of the interviews involve case questions. A sample question, from an insider: "A manager of a hotel feels profits should be higher. Advise him."

# OUR SURVEY SAYS

## Fleet-footed

The company seems to be a nimble one; it's called "entrepreneurial, fast moving, and with a short line of communication" by one senior employee. A more junior employee reports that CVA "encourages independent thought and action while being very collegial." Personal relationships between staff around the world serve to bind the firm together." The "entrepreneurial aspect" of the firm encourages "thinking and initiative," respondents note. The company does engage in some community service, though "pro bono consulting is done ad hoc, and is driven by partners' local community involvement."

Partners, and other supervisors, are reportedly doing a good job. "Supervision is not completely consistent, but the good supervisors are very good and more than 50 percent," says one source. Respondents also rate the company as highly racially diverse, and having a good male/female ratio. Few people in the Australian offices were born there. Most speak multiple languages," says one source.

## Plane tired

Typically traveling two to four days a week, the consultants we surveyed aren't too thrilled with CVA's stringent travel requirements. "Two days a week is OK, but travel involving more than two months away is much more demanding and fairly common at CVA," says one source. "Significant amounts of travel are required," states another. And "six-months-plus" travel is not unheard of.

Hours, likewise, are fairly long. A partner reports working 60-hour weeks, while a senior consultant reports 60 to 70 hours in the office. Work tends to spike a couple of times a month. "Work plans are based on 10-hour days, which rapidly become a minimum, and 15-hour days are common," says a consultant. Beach time is rare; "our operation in Australasia has been fully booked most of the year," a source based there tells us.

## Speedometer

Promotion is based on a "six-monthly review," and "on merit alone regardless of qualifications. Promotion can be very rapid, with double promotions commonplace." Nor is an advanced degree necessary – "Non-MBAs can and are making it to partner." There's "no [set] time in each grade," says an insider. "People can move as fast as their capabilities allow."

# Putnam Associates

25 Burlington Mall Road
Burlington, MA 01803
Phone: (781) 273-5480
Fax: (781) 273-5484
www.putassoc.com

## LOCATIONS

**Burlington, MA (HQ)**
London

## PRACTICE AREAS

Biotechnology
Medical Devices
Medical Diagnostics
Pharmaceuticals

## THE STATS

**Employer Type:** Private Company
**Managing Partner:** Kevin Gorman
**2002 Employees:** 30
**2001 Employees:** 25

## UPPERS

• Highly focused practice

## DOWNERS

• Better like health care, due to highly focused practice

## KEY COMPETITORS

Boston Consulting Group
Health Advances
IMS Health
L.E.K.
McKinsey& Company
ZS Associates

## EMPLOYMENT CONTACT

Erica J. Wines
HR/Recruiting Coordinator
E-mail: careers@putassoc.com

 **THE BUZZ**
WHAT CONSULTANTS AT OTHER FIRMS ARE SAYING

• "Clever"
• "High turnover"

# THE SCOOP

## Healthy attitude

Putnam Associates is a Burlington, Mass.-based consultancy specializing in the strategy concerns of health care industry players. From both its home office and its European branch in London, Putnam serves companies in pharmaceuticals, biotechnology, medical devices and diagnostics.

Putnam's approach to clients is simply to give good advice; the company line is that nobody knows a client's business better than the client, so a consultant's job is to provide a fresh perspective based on knowledge, experience and research. The firm tries to combine short-term fixes with long-term performance goals – a wise strategy, considering the changing nature of the pharma/tech community and the long time-to-market of some products.

## Good medicine

Medical products travel a long road to market that begins with product development and market assessment. In some cases a need develops for which a medical solution must be found, while in other situations a new drug or procedure is developed and its maker must find a use (or another use for a preexisting drug). Sometimes, a firm has to gain a foothold for its new product against an entrenched competitor.

Putnam has had success at helping companies through these early stages; its case studies indicate that many of its clients are second entrants into particular markets who must compete with established rivals. In one such case, the firm enabled a client's successful drug launch against an established and well-financed competitor in an $800 million market through market segmentation and a series of "war game" simulations of the competitive environment. After two and a half years, the result was a 32 percent overall market share for the Putnam client, with 68 percent of those sales in targeted segments. That's a lot of pills.

In another situation, an established client was concerned its successful but unstructured sales strategy would begin to fail as the market matured. Putnam helped to define and prioritize future sources of growth as well as potential competitive threats. Physician and hospital data were compiled to provide the sales force with zip code-level sales direction to better target the client's areas of strength. By successfully identifying the changes occurring in the market, Putnam's advice to expand the client's field sales force and shift the direction of 30 percent of their sales calls, among other things, caused the client's national market share to increase 3.5 points in one year.

# GETTING HIRED

## Students and specialists

Putnam Associates typically recruits recent college grads for analyst positions, but "experienced undergraduates with one to two years work experience in consulting, banking or health care are also encouraged to apply." Analysts here, as at most consultancies, handle primary research and create forecasts, with travel as necessary; "on average," the firm claims, "analysts work 55- to 60-hour workweeks." Graduate degree holders, as well as exceptional analysts, will be asked to fill consultant positions, reporting directly to a partner or manager. Consultants lead multiple three- to five-person case teams. Senior consultants (and above) sell work.

"Experienced
undergraduates with one
or two years work
experience in consulting,
banking or health care are
encouraged to apply."

— *Putnam insider*

# Buck Consultants

**PRESTIGE RANKING 50**

1 Pennsylvania Plaza
New York, NY 10119-4798
Phone: (212) 330-1000
Fax: (212) 695-4184
www.buckconsultants.com

## LOCATIONS

**New York, NY (HQ)**
59 offices worldwide

## PRACTICE AREAS

Compensation & Benefits Consulting
HR Technologies & Software
Organization & HR Effectiveness
Outsourcing

## THE STATS

**Employer Type:** Subsidiary of Mellon Financial
**Stock Symbol:** MEL
**Stock Exchange:** NYSE
**Chairman and CEO:** Joseph A. LoCicero

## UPPERS

- Well-established firm with a history
- Steady influx of highly experienced people

## DOWNERS

- Competition with better-known firms
- Odd times for human resources

## KEY COMPETITORS

Hewitt Associates
Mercer Human Resource Consulting
Towers Perrin

## EMPLOYMENT CONTACT

Cathy Gushue
Director of Human Resources
500 Plaza Drive
Secaucus, NJ 07096-1533

Phone: (201) 902-2465
www.buckconsultants.com/careers
E-mail: careers@buckconsultants.com

## THE BUZZ

**WHAT CONSULTANTS AT OTHER FIRMS ARE SAYING**

- "Good people, savvy consultants"
- "Merger with Mellon didn't help its prestige"
- "Value long-time employees"

# THE SCOOP

## The Buck starts here

George B. Buck was an achiever in his day. He published the first actuarial report on the New York City Police Pension Fund in 1913. As an inventor, he created and patented the Hollerith keypunch verifier in 1915, selling it to the company that would one day become IBM. And in 1916, Buck went into private practice as George B. Buck, Consulting Actuary. Buck Consultants, the firm that still bears his name, is now a subsidiary of Mellon Financial, with nearly 60 U.S. and international offices.

Buck Consultants provides a full range of HR services and products to its more than 3,000 clients worldwide. The firm's associates develop compensation and benefits packages and analyze clients' HR functions and strategies, outsourcing or implementing the results as required. In addition, Buck hooks clients up with the latest HR technology and software.

## Shopping and growing

Snapped up by Mellon in 1997, Buck has continued to grow through acquisition and partnership. Its banner year for shopping was 2001, when Buck teamed up with several companies. The firm acquired a "substantial" interest in LiveWire Media, a specialist in online communications; it now aids with development of intranet and employee-driven applications. Buck acquired iQuantic (now iQuantic Buck), a San Francisco-based company with expertise in organization performance, compensation and rewards program design, communication and implementation strategies and equity-based pay programs. And Buck also acquired Harbor Technology Group in 2001, turning it into Buck Harbor Technologies. Buck Harbor provides information systems strategy, integration and technology consulting, and Internet-based systems.

Early in 2002, Mellon Financial acquired Unifi Network from PricewaterhouseCoopers. Unifi's human resources outsourcing business, comprising about 2,100 employees, became part of the newly formed Mellon HR Solutions, and its approximately 400-member human resources consulting business was merged into Buck. David Hofrichter, formerly of Unifi, was tapped to head Buck's compensation practice (of which Unifi is a part) in July 2002.

In June of that year, Buck formed an alliance with KnowledgePlanet, an HR solutions provider known for its suite of "human capital management" products. Together, the two firms provide joint services to Global 2000 companies.

## Bucks keep rollin' in

The firm announced several high level appointments during late 2002 and the first half of 2003. December 2002 saw two promotions in Buck's Canadian arm, Buck Consultants Ltd.: Michael McKay became president and CEO, with Peter Hirst moving up to executive vice president. In March 2003, Graham Jarvis joined the company from consulting firm Black Mountain to head Buck's London office. A few months previous, the firm also hired Mark Littlewood to run the office in Manchester.

The firm's newest principal is Jill E. Neilson, who joined the San Francisco office in April 2003 after leaving Aon Consulting. Associate principals added during 2003 include J. Bradford Barlow Jr., also from Aon; Karen S. Gorman, from Gorman and Associates; Margery F. Paul, from the law firm Reish Luftman McDaniel & Reicher; Daniel W. Sherman, from PricewaterhouseCoopers; Gregg Levinson, formerly of Vanguard Group; and Thomas J. Hricik, coming over from Highmark Blue Cross Blue Shield.

# GETTING HIRED

## The other side of Buck's HR practice

Since Buck is a human resources consultancy with strong technological influences, it's no surprise that most of their recruiting is handled online. The form provides access to lists of current job openings, online job application forms, a list of campus events and some pay and benefits details (more info is available at Mellon's careers site). A section called "Reel Buck People" offers brief interviews with employees. (Don't be misled, though – these aren't video interviews.)

# THE BEST OF
# THE REST

# Abt Associates

55 Wheeler Street
Cambridge, MA 02138-1168
Phone: (617) 492-7100
Fax: (617) 492-5219
www.abtassoc.com

## LOCATIONS

**Cambridge, MA (HQ)**
Bethesda, MD
Chicago, IL
Hadley, MA
Lexington, MA
Washington, DC
Cairo
Pretoria, South Africa

## PRACTICE AREAS

Business Research • Clinical Trials
and Medical Affairs • Cost-Benefit
Analysis • Economic Analysis •
Epidemiology Studies • Information
Technology • Market Research •
Performance Measurement •
Program and Policy Evaluation •
Program Monitoring • Registries and
Post-Marketing Evaluations •
Statistical Analysis • Survey
Research • Technical Assistance

## THE STATS

**Employer Type:** Private Company
**President and CEO:** Wendell J. Knox
**2002 Employees:** 1,100
**2002 Revenue:** $184 million

## UPPERS

- Intellectual environment
- Government contracting means
  lots of work

## DOWNERS

- Management heavy
- Recent layoffs

## KEY COMPETITORS

Booz Allen Hamilton
Brattle Group
Kurt Salmon Associates
ZS Associates

## EMPLOYMENT CONTACT

See careers section on Abtassoc.com

## THE BUZZ
WHAT CONSULTANTS AT OTHER FIRMS ARE SAYING

- "USAID studies"
- "Good quality"
- "Good in select niches"
- "Beltway bandits"

# THE SCOOP

## Defensive line

Abt Associates started out as a liaison between the civilian and defense world. Founder Clark Abt figured the advanced technological models used to evaluate for defense systems could just as easily be applied to criminal justice or education programs.

Today, Abt Associates focuses on government, public policy, and health research and consulting. Notably, Abt is one of the largest employee-owned companies in the world, with a staff of more than 1,100.

## German imports

Clark Abt emigrated from Germany to the U.S. at age 11. He founded Abt Associates in 1965 after working as an engineer at Raytheon and serving in the U.S. Air Force for five years. Though Abt relinquished the CEO reins of his eponymous firm he's still chair of the board; Abt has also been active in in helping U.S. port cities firm up their post-September 11 anti-terrorism defenses.

## Environment and government

The company's work ranges from studying pollutants for the Environmental Protection Agency to developing a health care infrastructure in former Soviet republic Kyrgyzstan. Its survey work includes the Centers for Disease Control and Prevention's annual immunization survey, which measures the rate of child immunizations. A sample of other past clients includes BMW, Genzyme, Campbell Soups, Charles Schwab, Kaiser Permanente, Shell, Hewlett-Packard and Merck. The firm has also recently instituted a homeland security program, headed up by Rocco Casagrande, a biologist who had been a United Nations weapons inspector in Iraq before the military action in that country. Another notable engagement: advising down-at-the-heels East St. Louis on the $475 million redevelopment of its riverfront.

Abt has been in the news for several environmental studies. A report it prepared in the fall of 2002 noted that Bush's changes to the pollution rules meant that air pollution would increase, while an April 2002 study determined that pollution from utility-owned power plants causes almost 6,000 premature deaths each year in the U.S. Massachusetts natives may be interested to note that the current Republican lieutenant governor, Kerry Healey, spent almost a decade as an Abt Associates consultant.

# GETTING HIRED

Employment opportunities are listed under the 'careers' section of the company's web site. The firm typically does not recruit MBAs but will hire them for appropriate positions.

# OUR SURVEY SAYS

Abt Associates is said to be a "congenial, laid back, easygoing" work environment with a "left leaning work force" that is "smart and intellectually stimulating." The company does "high quality work," says a source, and strikes a "good balance between family life and work." There were layoffs of about 30 people in 2002; despite this, one source still considers the company to be "very top (management)-heavy." Benefits are said to include accidental death/dismemberment, long-term disability, tuition reimbursement and a cafeteria.

# "Cubes for most, no offices for anyone under VP."

## — Bogart Delafield Ferrier associate

# Bogart Delafield Ferrier

9 Campus Drive
Parsippany, NJ 07054
Phone: (973) 898-9800
Fax: (973) 267-3681
www.bdf.com

## LOCATIONS

**Parsippany, NJ (HQ)**

## PRACTICE AREAS

Alternative Medicines
Biotechnology
Devices/Diagnostics
Pharmaceuticals

## THE STATS

**Employer Type:** Private Company
**CEO:** Robert Lieberman

## UPPERS

- Good location, convenient to NYC and clients
- Company accommodates those who want to travel
- Raises tend to be generous

## DOWNERS

- "Extremely unstructured" culture
- Inequities in compensation structure
- Minimal training

## KEY COMPETITORS

Health Advances
IMS Health
NDCHealth

## EMPLOYMENT CONTACT

E-mail: employment@bdf.com

## THE BUZZ
WHAT CONSULTANTS AT OTHER FIRMS ARE SAYING

- "Bio guys"
- "Unknown"

# THE SCOOP

## Better living through chemistry

Founded in 1985, Bogart Delafield Ferrier (BDF) is a small company (just a single office in New Jersey) focused on both the science of medicine and the art of managing and marketing it. Since its inception, BDF has worked with some of the biggest names in pharmaceuticals, biotechnology and medical devices and alternatives; AstraZeneca, Bayer, DuPont, Glaxo SmithKline and Johnson & Johnson are just some of the noteworthy clients the firm has advised. BDF consultants often comment on pharma and biotech deals to the press.

BDF's location in Parsippany, N.J., might seem odd to the uninitiated. But it's actually a strategic position; the offices and labs of several clients (including Pfizer and Schering-Plough) are located in that part of the Garden State, and it's a short trip from there to New York City.

## Science jumps out of the box

While most consulting firms say their successes are built on innovative, "out of the box" thinking, BDF actually uses this phrase in its motto, calling itself "the place where the business of science steps out of the box." Some of BDF's more notable case studies support this claim. For example, a company with a medical device designed for highly accurate delivery of genes, proteins and small molecules sought advice on its still-developing business plan. BDF recommended the company change its business model to one where the product was packaged with the therapy compounds as a drug/device unit. According to BDF's case study, "Clinical trials confirmed that an older 'generic' compound delivered with the company's new device technology created a 'new drug' with efficacy heretofore unavailable. The combination further yielded substantially greater patent and regulatory exclusivity than would have been possible with the device alone." Since then, the manufacturer has repeated its success with other projects and has considered offering to combine its devices with the drugs of other companies.

In another case, BDF used good old math to solve a client's dilemma. A fertility treatment manufacturer wanted to increase usage of its therapy, in which patients paid $8,000 for a 50-percent effective solution that was not reimbursed by insurance. Combining these factors, BDF recommended the client use performance pricing: successful treatments (resulting in conception) would cost $16,000 but failures would be free of charge; the company would get the same revenue, and patients could attempt the procedure without fear of throwing money away.

## Industry pundit

When Pfizer agreed to acquire Pharmacia Corp. for $53 billion in February 2003, the company became the only drug maker with more than 10 percent of the world prescription market. As reported in *The Bergen County Record*, BDF founder Ian Ferrier commented, "This, of course, is a seminal acquisition." A later article, discussing the effects of this and previous Pfizer mergers on the pharmaceutical industry noted that the drug maker would be eliminating overlapping job functions as it integrated Pharmacia into its structure. Ferrier inferred, "The significant majority will come from the Pharmacia ranks. That's culturally normal of Pfizer, who knows how to run their business their way."

# GETTING HIRED

## Simple medicine

Bogart Delafield Ferrier recruits at top schools nationwide, "particularly Penn, Princeton and Brown," according to one source. The best way to get a foot in the door at BDF, the company says, is to send a resume and cover letter to the main address, care of Human Resources; e-mail is an equally viable alternative. The firm's web site includes brief narratives by a managing principal, a consultant and an analyst to give you an idea of what sort of people you'll be working with.

As one insider at BDF tells us, "candidates interview with senior management only" in what he calls a "relatively quick process." The firm "sometimes" uses case questions, wherein "a project scenario is laid out and the candidate is asked how to approach and manage issues."

# OUR SURVEY SAYS

## Do-it-yourself career building

A source at the firm notes that BDF possesses "no regular performance or salary reviews, and must be prompted by the employee," though when raises come, "the average compensation increase is 10 percent." He continues, "Promotions typically can happen in two to three years, but compensation increases and promotions are contingent on new business development, not excellence in project-related analysis and management." We hear that "consultants without an MBA can advance; however, all staff hold advanced degrees of one kind or another." Additionally, an insider points out, "in general, [there is] little or no training except by managers who go to great lengths to train new analysts." That contact adds there are "no formal training programs sponsored by the firm."

Sources feel this is due to a culture that is "extremely unstructured, with a high level of responsibility and accountability on individuals." They note the "limited leadership from senior management," as well as "high expectations and high intensity work." In terms of office space, though, all BDF consultants are equal: "Cubes for most; no offices for anyone under VP."

## Lots of New Jersey love

The hours aren't brutal, according to our sources; the average week is 50 hours. One person notes, "Spikes often occur due to [the] small staff; say, five or six times a month." The New Jersey location saves a lot of wear and tear on the BDF workforce; one member says, "Limited travel and the ability to manage my own time allows for great flexibility with other commitments." For the more outgoing, the firm "tends to create travel opportunities for those who prefer to travel." Reasonable proximity to three major airports in the area also helps in this regard.

## Sans bonus

Lack of travel is good, but lack of salary equity isn't. A source reveals there have been "no bonuses since 2000." Furthermore, "compensation levels are out of balance." According to the same source, individuals with the same title or level of responsibility "can have salaries that differ by 100 percent." Benefits are "good, but not the best. For example, [there is] no 401(k) match."

# CFI Group

625 Avis Drive
Ann Arbor, MI 48108
Phone: (734) 930-9090
Fax: (734) 930-0911
www.cfigroup.com

## LOCATIONS

**Ann Arbor, MI (HQ)**
Atlanta, GA • Buenos Aires • Kuala
Lumpur • London • Madrid • Milan •
Melbourne • Paris • Porto Alegre •
Seoul • Shanghai • Stockholm •
Zurich

## PRACTICE AREAS

Customer Satisfaction
Employee Satisfaction
Employee-Customer Satisfaction
   Linkage

## THE STATS

**Employer Type:** Private Company
**Chairman:** Claes Fornell
**2002 Employees:** 100
**2001 Employees:** 100
**2002 Revenue:** $15 million
**2001 Revenue:** $10 million

## UPPERS

- Stimulating academic feel
- Short days, little travel

## DOWNERS

- Lack of training
- Little name recognition

## KEY COMPETITORS

Hewitt Associates
Mercer Human Resource Consulting
Towers Perrin

## EMPLOYMENT CONTACT

Jenni Pozar
HR Manager
Phone: (734) 930-9090
Fax: (734) 930-0911
E-mail: hr@mail.cfigroup.com
See HR contacts for specific offices
at
www.cfigroup.com/annarbor_HR.htm

# THE SCOOP

## The customer is always right

CFI Group isn't your typical management consulting company. It's distinctive both in its focus and approach. All CFI Group activities are focused on enhancing the economic value of clients' customer base and human capital, thus (in theory) ensuring financial growth. This approach is grounded in rigorous statistical analysis. In fact, CFI holds a patent (No. 6192319 B1, if you're interested) on its overall "Customer Asset Management" system. As companies continue to supplement traditional accounting data with other, nonfinancial measurements, such as customer and employee satisfaction, the demand for CFI Group's services continues to grow.

CFI is an international consulting firm with 13 company offices in the United States, Europe and Asia, plus local representation in South America and Australia. It has a broad client base of Fortune 1000 companies in a variety of industries, including shipping, retail, banking, telecom, business services, household services and manufacturing. CFI Group's "Customer Asset Management" is based on a basic premise – customer relationships are valuable assets that should be measured and managed in order to optimize customer satisfaction and maximize company profits. CFI Group prides itself on recommending client-specific actions that best leverage those customer and employee assets to enhance shareholder value.

## Fully satisfied

CFI is best known for its connection to the American Customer Satisfaction Index, an economic indicator that runs quarterly in *The Wall Street Journal*. University of Michigan Business School professor Claes Fornell – the CF in CFI Group – created the ACSI, which benchmarks customer satisfaction at more than 200 companies and government agencies. In 1994 CFI developed the measurement software, which it licenses to the University of Michigan's National Quality Research Center. Econometricians use the ACSI as a gauge of consumer spending and corporate earnings growth. CFI Group also provides a customized, more exhaustive adaption of the ASCI methodology to its Fortune 1000 clients.

# GETTING HIRED

CFI says the company is looking for candidates with good communication skills, a strong academic background, "high tolerance for change," the "ability to generate excitement and enthusiasm" and "dependability and productivity." One insider tells us that "there are no MBA-level positions as such; those with graduate degrees in things other than business [i.e. economics or statistics] do well. Research backgrounds are valued." However, most consultants at the senior consultant level have MBAs from top universities, and an MBA is increasingly a requirement for those at the consultant level.

The interview process consists of an "initial phone screening," followed by two rounds of on-site interviews "on multiple days with multiple team members" that hail from all "levels and functions." Candidates are "also expected to put together and give a PowerPoint presentation." The company recruits heavily "at [University of Michigan Business School] because of proximity, and because Claes Fornell is a professor" for that graduate program. While there are no case studies posed "yet, that may change as we alter our hiring strategy." The company has "interns only on an ad hoc basis." And, cautions one source, "As a small company in a buyers' market, we are pretty selective."

# OUR SURVEY SAYS

## Intellectual and academic

The CFI environment is described as "professional, diverse, somewhat competitive," and "cliquish." The company is said to "value innovation and autonomy," and be "a prime place for intellectual curiosity, statistical rigor and customer-focused analysis that often has the ear of top executives." One consultant lauds the "trusting, cooperative environment," liking that there is "plenty of room to contribute in ways that you feel appropriate and great access to top execs at the client." The people "are a great mix of social science academics and strategy consultant MBAs," and they are frequently described as "great people." While CFI is a "small company that isn't well known yet," the silver lining is that there's "none of the nonsense you find at the 'big' firms."

## Likeable hours

Hours aren't too bad at CFI, sources say. "People are expected to work hard, but the firm's especially good with letting people take time off when they need to (family illness, maternity leave, deaths, etc.)," says a source. Another insider describes it as "a very good work/life balance company. I seldom come into the office on weekends, and I am often the last person out of the building when I leave at 6:30 or 7 p.m." Those we surveyed reported workweeks of 45 to 50 hours, on average; one source reports working 50-55 hours a week, "although many others probably work less than that, depending on your career aspirations." The workload can spike about twice a month – "client requests, changes in timelines, presentation or report deadlines all contribute to spikes in our work." Meanwhile, beach time is rare, for CFI "had a good year last year and everyone was well utilized."

## Home is where CFI is

CFI consultants typically stay close to home, averaging "two to four days a month [traveling] for the most part; more for those with P&L responsibility." While travel "varies a lot – I may be gone for one week and then not travel for three" – it is "project specific and is generally done at the beginning and end of a project, to kickoff the project and share results in a formal presentation." One consultant notes the lack of travel is "a strength for those who want top-level client interaction without the normal associated travel. Much of the analysis and program implementation is completed off site from the client."

## Slow promotions

At CFI, "there is ample opportunity for moving up. We are definitely not an up-or-out company." The company has not had layoffs in recent memory – CFI "puts employee retention before profitability," says one insider. "Advancement opportunities may take longer than a McKinsey & Co. or a BCG," says one source, while another source elaborates that "advancement is fairly fast for those with subject matter/technical expertise, but it's very hard for those with a BA only to move up." One source finds that "different opportunities exist depending on your tenure and sometimes your boss. This is an area that is currently being addressed and improving."

## Living the CFI life

Salaries get middling marks. "The base pay is on the low side, but good profit sharing can compensate," says one consultant. CFI offers "profit sharing to partners, and incentives to consultants based on how well individuals and teams perform." The company provides accidental death/dismemberment coverage, along with laptops, an on-site gym, a cafeteria, massages, a lounge area and tuition reimbursement.

Offices are rated as average to good. "I share an office with a co-worker, rather than sit in a 'hoteling cube' as I did at my last employer. Perhaps this is because we're here more often than with typical consulting companies," notes one employee.

The company "supports Planned Parenthood, University Musical Society and Christmas gift giving to local families," does pro bono projects, and matches some donations.

## No time to train

Training, it seems, could use some work at CFI, where there's "not enough time available for proper training" and thus a "lack of training/development opportunities." One enthusiastic source does say that "a variety of training programs are offered, and we are encouraged to stay fresh on latest developments in management."

## Roy G. Biv

CFI is said to be a diverse place. The firm fosters "a very respectful environment for women; we seem to have about 50-50 men and women here, which makes it a more enjoyable environment," notes one source. And "a number of minority groups are represented at CFI Group, including African-American, Hispanic, Middle Eastern and Asian." Meanwhile, "there is no active effort to encourage diversity with respect to [gays, lesbians and bisexuals], but there have been 'out' employees here and it's just not an issue."

"Help is there if you need it but you have to be prepared to learn quickly at the first instance."

— *Edgar, Dunn and Company consultant*

# Edgar, Dunn & Company

2 Bryant Street
Suite 240
San Francisco, CA 94105
Phone: (415) 977-1870
Fax: (415) 977-1879
www.edgardunn.com

## LOCATIONS

**San Francisco, CA (HQ)**
Atlanta, GA
London
Sydney

## PRACTICE AREAS

**Financial Services:**
Differentiation
e-Commerce
Expansion
Profitability
Technology

**Energy Services &
Telecommunications:**
Business Unit Planning
Merger Strategy
Organizational Effectiveness
Strategic Focus
Technology Strategy

## THE STATS

**Employer Type:** Private Company
**CEO:** David Poe

## UPPERS

- Supportive management, culture
- Lots of autonomy and responsibility

## DOWNERS

- Slow promotions – but pressure to rise
- Lack of formal training

## KEY COMPETITORS

Booz Allen Hamilton
Greenwich Associates

## EMPLOYMENT CONTACT

E-mail: recruiting@edgardunn.com
www.edgardunn.com/workingatedc/p
_whoweseek.cfm

## THE BUZZ
### WHAT CONSULTANTS AT OTHER FIRMS ARE SAYING

- "Boutique"
- "Not well known"

# THE SCOOP

## Energy and money

Strategy consultant Edgar, Dunn & Company (EDC) began in 1978. Since its founding, it has focused on two areas: financial services and energy services/telecom. The financial services practice, considered tops in the payments industry, also offers advice on financial technologies and markets, retail financial services, and e-business. The energy services and telecommunications group, meanwhile, focuses on mid-size companies such as utilities or regional telecom carriers.

## Creditable client base

Clients have included more than two-thirds of the U.S.'s top 25 credit card companies, more than 40 European banks and credit card issuers, the world's largest third-party processors and technology providers for the credit card industry, six of the largest investor-owned gas and electric utilities, regional Bell carriers, cell phone service providers, mining companies and two influential public utility commissions. (Whew.)

## Independence days

In 2000, Edgar, Dunn was bought by Commerce One as part of its effort to build out its consulting wing. However, just over a year later, in October 2001, EDC underwent a management buyout, and is an independent company once again.

# GETTING HIRED

To get a job at EDC, candidates should have work experience in consulting or in one of the industries Edgar Dunn targets. Of course, a good academic record, good problem solving and communication skills, and a good ol' "self-starter mentality" are also helpful.

"The higher the position," notes one source, "the longer and more complex the [hiring] process. Up to engagement manager, it takes four to eight interviews and may involve flying to another office." The company is not concerned with just "qualifications, but also the right kind of experience, attitude, fit and reputation. If you fake it or are unsuitable, it is likely that you will be spotted during the selection process."

The company does use case studies, though the "kind and complexity depend on the seniority of the candidate." These cases usually concern market sizing, strategy and operations.

EDC is said to recruit at "top business schools, and also looks at very talented candidates who are from less known (but not less good) business schools and universities."

# OUR SURVEY SAYS

## Support network

The company is reported to be "very collaborative and collegial, with a lot of support," and to offer a "very positive and friendly environment." Consultants get "lots of responsibility from day one, and lots of learning opportunities on specific business areas," and there is "quick exposure to the board level with clients." However, there is said to be "not a lot of industry variety or diversity in assignments." Nor is there a huge amount of diversity in the makeup of the firm: Regarding women and minorities, there are "not many of them around. But this is not intentional, it just happens," ponders one source.

## Pressure and promotion

With long hours – 80 to 90 is the norm – "unpredictable spikes in workload" and a disheartening "amount of travel," work/life balance isn't exactly ducky at EDC. The promotion process can be arduous as well. Though the firm does not hew to an up-or-out policy, "without meeting goals you can forget about a salary rise and bonus." "The firm is very supportive of people's growth and not too keen about letting people go, but promotion is very slow and mainly based on business development/client ownership and quality of delivery." With regard to managers, "help is there if you need it but you have to be prepared to learn quickly at the first instance." Sometimes "you are on projects on your own, and you should be prepared to take responsibility from day one with minimal supervision."

## The whole package

EDC offers a "pension contribution on salary and bonus base, life and long term sickness insurance, and medical insurance." One insider remarks, somewhat dubiously, "There seems to be a degree of profit sharing." Laptop computers are also provided. Offices are "not overly luxurious but very comfortable. There is plenty of space and storage."

# ENVIRON International

4350 N. Fairfax Drive
Suite 300
Arlington, VA 22203
Phone: (703) 516-2300
Fax: (703) 516-2345
www.environcorp.com

## LOCATIONS

**Arlington, VA (HQ)**
34 other locations

## PRACTICE AREAS

Air Quality Management •
Compliance Assistance •
Engineering Design and
Construction Management • EHS
Management • Environmental Due
Diligence • Environmental Impact
Assessment and Planning •
Environmental Sciences &
Engineering • Environmental
Technology Assessment •
Integrated Pollution Prevention and
Control • Litigation Support • Risk
Assessment and Risk Management •
Site Characterization and
Remediation • Solid and Hazardous
Waste Management • Water and
Wastewater Quality Management

## THE STATS

**Employer Type:** Private Company
**Chairman and CEO:** Joseph H.
Highland
**2002 Employees:** 490+
**2001 Employees:** 450
**2002 Revenues:** $70 million
**2001 Revenues:** $63 million

## UPPERS

- Flexible company, supportive of
  families
- Autonomy in highly specialized
  subjects

## DOWNERS

- Clashes between offices
- Training spotty

## KEY COMPETITORS

Geomatrix
GeoSyntec
ICF

## EMPLOYMENT CONTACT

See individual office contacts at:
www.environcorp.com/CAREERS/
    CAREERSset.html

## THE BUZZ
WHAT CONSULTANTS AT OTHER FIRMS ARE SAYING

- "Too small"
- "Green"

# THE SCOOP

## Chemical structure

As its name indicates, ENVIRON (yes, it's all caps) specializes in engineering, science and risk management for firms. That can mean anything from assessing the level of chemicals in water to providing expert testimony during a lawsuit. ENVIRON clients are usually facing some sort of health or environmental challenge, along with other pressing business concerns. Clients include law firms, industrial companies, trade associations, insurers, banks and public sector agencies.

## Toxic engagements

ENVIRON had a whirlwind 2002, opening offices in Beijing and Aix-en-Provence, France. At the end of 2002, the firm established CarbonVentures International, which helps clients measure greenhouse gas emissions and strategize how to deal with them. Some of its engagements during the year were quite high profile. ENVIRON worked on a report for DuPont on whether there was a dangerous level of dioxin in a surface component DuPont had used to pave some California roads. An ENVIRON consultant and environmental engineering PhD testified in a federal court in May that defendants in a class-action lawsuit had allowed toxic chemicals to seep into groundwater in Illinois. An ENVIRON toxicologist testified in a Paterson, N.J., trial that there was no basis for linking chemicals excreted at a former DuPont munitions plant in Pompton Lakes, N.J., to residents' cancer. And in April 2003, ENVIRON began a $350,000 study for Long Beach, Calif.'s Harbor Commission on the feasibility of running ships docked at the Long Beach port with electricity instead of internal combustion engines.

## Library lovers

ENVIRON publishes a number of reports each year, mostly focused on environmental topics. Topics can be as specific as the "Use of Sediment Quality Guidelines and Related Tools for the Assessment of Contaminated Sediment" or as general as "Risk Communication."

# GETTING HIRED

## Green hires

Recent college grads start as environmental sciences/engineering associates. They evaluate air or soil samples for chemical composition and develop plans for chemical cleanup. Environmental associates must have a bachelor's or master's in a related field (like environmental engineering or chemical engineering), good writing and communication skills, computer experience and strong analytical skills.

Another career option is that of "Life Sciences Associate." These associates gather data and analyze in the areas of new product approval, product liability/toxic tort litigation and "quantitative human health and environmental risk assessment." Requirements are similar to the environmental/engineering associate position, except life sciences associates should have a master's or PhD in a related field like toxicology, pharmacology or biology.

Benefits include health insurance, life/accidental death and dismemberment insurance, long-term disability coverage, tuition reimbursement, either a 401(k) or a pension plan and interest-free loans to purchase a PC for home use.

To apply, select one of the office locations and e-mail or mail a resume (visit www.environcorp.com/CAREERS/CAREERSset.html to see openings).

A European source reveals that ENVIRON solicits candidates through "advertising in local (country) newspapers and head hunting." A St. Louis source says there, "referrals are a big one, though we use resumes from outside. In many cases, if you hear someone is looking, you interview them and see if they will fit."

# OUR SURVEY SAYS

## ENVIRON's environment

ENVIRON's "culture is very independent but [people are] very willing to help whenever asked! We operate like a law firm. We are very specialized and have a great group of people and experience." The company is said to be "incredibly supportive of working at home when needed, flexible and incredibly understanding. You don't see the 24-hour a day consulting requirement like other firms." Indeed, reported workweeks range from 40 to 55 hours, and travel is limited to a couple of days a week. "Depending on your work load, you don't travel too much," says a source, "and you can get a lot of work done via the Internet and conference calls."

## Can't we all just get along?

There is some talk of conflict between offices. "I don't like some of the 'turf' wars created in other offices where senior management or partners are more concerned they are getting credit for work than providing the best product for the customer," notes one source. Another consultant reports a lack of "support for this country's operation. " There needs to be "more communication on what type of work is being done in other offices," says one respondent.

## Reaping rewards

ENVIRON is reportedly "wonderful about rewarding for performance – financially and promotion-wise. You can move fairly quickly, and the MBA is not as important as a graduate degree or professional engineer's license. Undergraduates have just the same opportunity to move up – it depends on your performance and credibility." Not only does ENVIRON reward consultants for performance, it also gives back in the form of "client equity that's now available for senior managers. It has a great 401(k) as well."

# First Consulting Group

111 West Ocean Boulevard
Suite 1000
Long Beach, CA 90802
Phone: (562) 624-5200
Fax: (562) 432-5774
www.fcg.com

## LOCATIONS

**Long Beach, CA (HQ)**
20 locations worldwide

## PRACTICE AREAS

**Consulting:**
e-Consulting • IT Strategy •
Performance Improvement

**Integration Services:**
e-Business and Technology Services
Systems Development
Implementation

**Management and IT Outsourcing
Services:**
Discrete/Full Outsourcing
IT Executive Staffing
IT Outsourcing Assessment
Program Management

## UPPERS

- Team spirit among consultants
- Good technical resources and support

## DOWNERS

- Layoffs and a tough time getting contracts
- Management focus on billable hours

## KEY COMPETITORS

Accenture
Cap Gemini Ernst & Young
Deloitte Consulting

## EMPLOYMENT CONTACT

E-mail: recruiter@fcg.com
www.fcg.com/career/buildingcareer.asp

## THE BUZZ
WHAT CONSULTANTS AT OTHER FIRMS ARE SAYING

- "Health care experts"
- "Small 'me-too' consulting firm"
- "Quiet low key firm"
- "Going down the drain"

# THE SCOOP

## In sickness and in health

For 23 years, First Consulting Group (FCG) has been providing consulting, research and outsourcing services for health care, pharmaceutical and other life science organizations. In recent years, the company's expanded to include consulting services. Based out of Long Beach, Calif., FCG has served leading hospitals, 17 of the top 20 managed care firms and every single one of the Fortune Global 500's pharmaceutical and life sciences companies, among other big clients. More than 70 percent of FCG's projects are with repeat customers.

FCG's expertise falls into three categories. The company's operations effectiveness and IT group includes outsourcing, integration, and consulting. The information management group handles subjects like call centers, data warehousing, and application development. Finally, FCG's operations and process improvement group looks at customer relationship management, pharmaceutical research and drug discovery and regulatory approval, among other topics.

## Taking e-nitiative

FCG prides itself on its prowess in both strategy and planning and technology, permitting the firm to plan widespread improvements for its health care and life sciences clients. The company's FirstDocs suite of document management software, which allows providers to move paperwork onto an electronic network, is a popular example of this expertise. In February 2002 FCG debuted the FirstDocs M&S software, which applies the FirstDocs technology to the pharmaceutical marketing and sales realm.

## Shopping around

FCG has made a practice of snapping up small companies that round out its expertise. In February 2003, it acquired Paragon Solutions for $4.2 million. Paragon, which helps companies develop and manage their business software, was folded into FCG's Life Sciences group. In June 2002, it acquired a majority stake in Codigent Solutions Group, a Tennessee health IT company. In November 1998 the company bought the Integrated Systems Consulting Group, a Pennsylvania firm strong in the biotech industry, for $124 million. The following year, FCG bought two British companies: Activa, a document management firm, and SDC Consulting. Hoping to expand its e-commerce practice, the company purchased Doghouse Productions in May 2000 (Doghouse was folded into FCG's health care group in early 2002).

## Year in review

In 2002, FCG turned in financial results that were a bit better than 2001's; revenues rose to $268 million from $266.9 million. The company attributed the increase to two large IT outsourcing contracts that began in mid-2002, including a $96 million contract with Cleveland's University Hospitals Health System Corporation. However, the consulting and systems-integration practices saw their revenues decline.

# GETTING HIRED

FCG sources candidates through "mostly internal recruiting from referrals, blind ads and 'picks' off the Monster board." The interview process, one source says, consists of "a recruiter interview followed by interviews with multiple levels of management and a peer."

FCG posts jobs online at www.fcg.com/career/career_finder.asp, and has an online application form there. Undergraduates are typically hired as associate consultants or consultants, while those with master's degrees are brought on as master consultants.

# OUR SURVEY SAYS

## In fighting shape

Consultants describe a culture that's been affected by layoffs and a tough sales environment but is still thriving. FCG is "collaborative, supportive, professional, and sincere," says one source; another consultant finds the company "hard working, supportive of work/life balance, valuing experience and individual contributions." The "team spirit among members of project teams" is cited by a few respondents as a high point.

However, there's "no job security," says one consultant, and a "management emphasis on billable utilization and cutting costs." Indeed, one respondent finds that "what you did for the [firm] yesterday is of no value – it's [a question of], 'are you billable today?'" "Trying to get clients to buy our services at this time" is a downside, says another respondent.

## Clocking long hours

Work/life balance is not terrific at FCG, respondents say. "Many folks are scared into working [long hours] to keep a job," reports one insider. Another notes that while "peak times are tough, there is a real understanding of the importance of family life." While travel isn't too excessive, averaging one to three days a week, "they are moving to a delivery model that will increase the amount of travel," reports a manager. Hours per week average 54 or so, according to those we surveyed, and that "usually spikes two times a month to support business development or speaking at conferences."

## Shedding the fat

The company seems to have been scaling back training. "They have really cut back on training in the past 18 months," reports one source. Meanwhile, there have been layoffs of "about 100 persons," though one source notes that "I think my company does a good job of notifying people ahead of time if their job is at risk." Promotion-wise, "several positions are plateau positions, promotions can occur every two to four years, and there are no restrictions based on education." The company is still flush in some areas, including "the caliber of technical resources," according to one source.

The company continues to be involved in "multiple community events," sponsoring "blood drives, clothing drives, support for the military, and cell phone drives for battered women."

## Underwater options

Salaries include a 401(k) contribution, and the "company occasionally provides stock options." One source says "the stock options I have received in the past four years are far above current share price (so basically worthless)." Another source opines that the "company could do a better job of rewarding key associates with bonuses when times are tough and they are not making budgets," while a different source agrees FCG could "improve the bonus program."

Perks include accidental death/dismemberment and long-term disability coverage, an employee assistance program, tuition reimbursement, PDAs, laptops, cell phones, free snacks and a cafeteria (in some locations).

# Fletcher Spaght, Inc.

222 Berkeley Street
20th Floor
Boston, MA 02116-3761
Phone: (617) 247-6700
Fax: (617) 247-7757
www.fletcherspaght.com

## LOCATIONS

**Boston, MA (HQ)**
Los Altos, CA

## PRACTICE AREAS

**Strategy Consulting**
Corporate Growth
Health Care
High Technology

**Venture Capital**

## THE STATS

**Employer Type:** Private Company
**CEO:** John Fletcher
**Partners:** John Fletcher, Peary Spaght, Linda Tufts
**2002 Employees:** 40

## UPPERS

- Junior staff can be promoted without graduate degree
- Ample office space, very fine views

## DOWNERS

- Assignments tend towards the short and intense
- Modest training program

## KEY COMPETITORS

Bain & Company
L.E.K.
Parthenon Group

## EMPLOYMENT CONTACT

E-mail: recruiting@fletcherspaght.com
fletcherspaght.com/careers/apply.html

## THE BUZZ
### WHAT CONSULTANTS AT OTHER FIRMS ARE SAYING

- "Boutique, former BCGers"
- "Niche, family-friendly, uppity"

© 2003 Vault Inc.

# THE SCOOP

## Business nursery

Fletcher Spaght, Inc. focuses its consulting practice on what it considers to be its "sweet spot" – technology-based clients looking to grow their companies at a fast pace. Clients are typically funded by venture capitalists or management buyout firms, though some are laboratories within large corporations, universities or government organizations. Approximately one third of FSI's clients are at the initial commercialization stage, another third are established companies enjoying a period of high growth, and the balance are mature businesses seeking new areas of growth.

CEO John Fletcher launched the firm in 1983, intending to apply the strategy analysis methods he picked up at the Boston Consulting Group to emerging companies. In 1986, Pearson Spaght, now President and leader of the Corporate Growth practice, joined former BCG colleague Fletcher. Several years later, the firm changed its name to Fletcher Spaght, Inc. The third partner, Linda Tufts, joined FSI in 1998.

## A-team ops

FSI is composed of three practice groups: High Technology, Healthcare and Corporate Growth. Each offers a number of services, but all include teams headed by practice leaders and principals, who are expected to do hands-on work – in essence, every team is an "A-team." The typical engagement lasts two to four months.

As it's focused on private equity-backed clients, FSI tracks the IPO, M&A and financing of all its clients. Whatever the results of its projects, FSI does not fear feedback – each client is asked to register their perspective on recent work done.

In addition, the company operates Fletcher Spaght Ventures, a venture capital fund specializing in emerging high technology and healthcare companies.

## Generosity of spirit

For a small firm, Fletcher Spaght has made a considerable effort in giving back to the community; the firm names nearly 60 separate charitable organizations in the Boston area that it supports. Time off is provided for philanthropic work.

# GETTING HIRED

## Careers at FSI

Junior staff are recruited primarily on campus. Late fall through early spring is the traditional time for campus visits. Brown, Carnegie Mellon, Cornell, Dartmouth, Harvard, MIT and the University of Pennsylvania are the schools of choice. The firm also solicits candidates from other schools, though it may not interview on campus.

An insider says the process on the inside typically involves the "screening of hundreds of resumes, yielding 30-60 interview invitations for about 20 candidates." The firm makes about 10 offers to research associate candidates a year, and three to five offers to consultant candidates a year.

# OUR SURVEY SAYS

## Counterculture

One insider describes the culture as a "family atmosphere" with a "pretty much open-door policy. You never need to make an appointment with anybody, you just chat. It's friendly." She adds, "Every firm is political – but this is a small firm." Another source claims, "There is a complete absence of politicking" at the consultant level.

One source at Fletcher Spaght avers, "General work life is acceptable." Apparently, "junior staff work considerably fewer hours," though junior consultants are given strict deadlines and must redo work of insufficient quality. "Projects are scoped to allow each team member to bill a 40-hour week," says one respondent. He notes that he stayed at the office "past 9 p.m. no more than 10 times in a year and a half, and worked [on] Saturday no more than three times." Another insider notes that travel is "pretty minimal – almost none, for a consulting firm. Probably less than 10 percent." She says this helps to contribute to a "very good work/life balance."

## Decent diversity

Sources at Fletcher Spaght realize that since it's a "small firm, it's hard to get a broad range" of people working there. Despite this, most feel that the firm has done well in building a diverse talent pool. One person notes there are "a few more women in health care vs. IT, for instance," and this is reflected in the gender balance. In addition, the source feels FSI has "decent diversity" of ethnic backgrounds, especially "Asian and Indian." Another source concurs. "FSI is quite ethnically diverse, and has slightly more female than male employees. The cost of entry is brainpower, manners and cooperativeness – not ethnicity."

# Greenwich Associates

8 Greenwich Office Park
Greenwich, CT 06831
Phone: (203) 629-1200
Fax: (203) 629-1229
www.greenwich.com
E-mail: contactus@greenwich.com

## LOCATIONS

**Greenwich, CT (HQ)**
London • Sydney • Tokyo • Toronto

## PRACTICES

Corporate Finance • Equities • Fixed
Income • Investment Management •
Small Business and Middle-Market
Banking • Treasury

## THE BUZZ
WHAT CONSULTANTS AT OTHER FIRMS ARE SAYING

- "Elite group"
- "Secretive"
- "Very useful research reports"

# THE SCOOP

## A guiding light in rocky economic times

When leading commercial banks, investment banks, brokerage firms, bond dealers, investment managers and other major financial institutions are in need of independent, customized financial information, they very often turn to Greenwich Associates. Founded by Charles (Charley) Ellis in (aptly) Greenwich, Connecticut in 1972, Greenwich Associates today interviews senior corporate and institutional executives in more than 70 countries around the globe to gather its financial market research.

In 2002, Greenwich Associates conducted more than 23,000 interviews with key decision makers in financial institutions to compile its consulting reports. Most of these market studies are conducted and released annually. Other services offered by Greenwich Associates include custom research, white papers, benchmarking studies, online tools and other specialized analytical services.

## All about quality

According to the firm, one of its key missions is to independently measure quality of service. The firm has thus developed a metric called the Greenwich Quality Index (GQI), which is used by clients to compare service quality both within and across financial markets. It's also sometimes used in connection with performance reviews of senior executives. Greenwich applies its index across all its annual research to ensure a consistent baseline for comparing financial service providers (FSPs).

## In for the long haul

Over 95 percent of Greenwich's work is with continuing clients. Greenwich has maintained some relationships for over 20 years – perhaps that's why the consultancy likes to say that "the clients are the firm." Indeed, Greenwich emphasizes that the clients come before the firm. Moreover, the firm is proud that many of its directors have stuck with Greenwich for up to 30 years. Indeed, the firm's founder, Charley Ellis, remained on board until June 2001. (John H. "Woody" Canaday is the current head, appointed in 2000 to succeed Ellis.) Among its clients, Greenwich counts big names like Bank of America, Merrill Lynch, Deutsche Bank, Goldman Sachs, Morgan Stanley and Fidelity Investments.

# GETTING HIRED

Research associates at Greenwich must have a bachelor's degree or equivalent experience, strong organizational skills and analytical abilities and top-notch communication skills. One insider says there are "clear career tracks for talented undergraduates to have professionally meaningful mid- to long-term positions."

Greenwich hires about two MBA associates per year; most associates are hired with a good chance of becoming partners in the pint-sized firm. Greenwich prefers its hires to have two to four years of experience in financial services or financial services consulting organizations. For these positions, Greenwich recruits on campus, though it also accepts referrals from existing staff, and even accepts resumes directly. (Positions are listed on the www.greenwich.com web site.) Interviews may occur either on or off-campus.

The firm also hires "executive interviewers" to help it glean information from financial contacts; these interviewers are independent contractors and typically possess a deep financial and/or marketing background. Profiles of select individuals (the firm employs about 150 interviewers in total) are available on Greenwich's careers page; executive interviewers are recruited separately from associates.

"They work hard at finding engagements."

— *Haverstick Consulting associate*

# Haverstick Consulting

11405 N. Pennsylvania Street
Suite 210
Carmel, IN 46032
Phone: (317) 218-1700
Fax: (317) 218-1701
www.haverstickconsulting.com

## LOCATIONS

**Indianapolis, IN (HQ)**
Chicago, IL
Cincinnati, OH
Cleveland, OH
Dayton, OH

## PRACTICE AREAS

Business Consulting
e-Learning Solutions
Enterprise Application Integration
IT Consulting
Lean Manufacturing
Network Infrastructure
Security
Strategic Design
Web Development

## THE STATS

**Employer Type:** Private Company
**Chairman and CEO:** Stephen C. Hilbert
**2002 Employees:** 234
**2001 Employees:** 250
**2002 Revenue:** $26 million
**2001 Revenue:** $10 million

## UPPERS

- Lots of autonomy
- Flexible schedules
- Energetic, growing company

## DOWNERS

- Lackluster benefits and vacation
- Money-focused management
- Low employee morale

## KEY COMPETITORS

Accenture
DiamondCluster International
Lante

## EMPLOYMENT CONTACT

E-mail:
recruiting@haverstickconsulting.com

## THE BUZZ
WHAT CONSULTANTS AT OTHER FIRMS ARE SAYING

- "Expanding, solid work"
- "Never heard of them"

# THE SCOOP

Established in 1994, Haverstick is a fast growing regional consultancy. In 2000, Haverstick hit the headlines after hiring the former CEO and CFO of Conseco, both of whom had left the insurance giant under pressure as the stock plummeted. Once CEO Stephen C. Hibert joined Haverstick, he tripled its profits, doubled the number of clients and got large contracts from several tech companies. In 2001, he and CFO Rollin Dick declared Haverstick would grow into a $250 million venture within 24 months.

### Enveloping other companies

Since Hilbert took the reins at the consultancy, Haverstick has absorbed three companies, sometimes to the dismay of employees. Late in 2001, Haverstick stepped in to manage the clients of Eviciti, a financially troubled IT consultancy, and took in many of its employees. Then, in July 2002, Haverstick acquired A.F. Kelly, Inc., a consulting firm that had a strong relationship with the Federal government as well as a notable distance learning practice. Hilbert's first acquisition was Innovis, a software consulting firm, in 2000.

### Breaking down the business

Haverstick Consulting, started in 1994 as C/Soft, is the backbone of the business, providing IT consulting. Business Solutions, started in 2001, handles the management and strategy consulting piece of the pie. Strategic Design handles branding and marketing and was also formalized in 2002 Learning Solutions deals with employee training programs, and was established in 2002. All of these practices work in the commercial sector, while the federal sector falls under Haverstick's government solutions subsidiary.

### Bye

In 2002, Haverstick made the undoubtedly difficult decision to shutter unprofitable offices in New Jersey and Minneapolis laying off an unspecified number of employees. But thanks in large part to the well timed government-centric Kelly acquisition, Haverstick is holding on in a rough economy. After all, it's a good time to have the Department of Defense as a client. Other clients include Indianapolis Motor Speedway and the State of Indiana.

## Friends in high places

Haverstick has helped establish its reputation by creating partnerships with Cisco, Microsoft, IBM and other tech giants. The deals give Haverstick partners access to unreleased software, so consultants are familiar with the software before it hits the market. Haverstick has also been expanding its services in health care, manufacturing, security and, with the Kelly acquisition, the delightfully stable area of government consulting.

# GETTING HIRED

Haverstick recruits experienced consultants almost exclusively, and accepts resumes through its web site. For "team level" (entry-level) consultant positions, expect a phone interview first and then an in-person interview with managers. "If that interview goes well, an interview with a technical person will be set up to evaluate technical skills. If that interview goes well, an offer is tendered," says a source.

When Haverstick searches for experienced candidates for a specific job, the process is "pretty rigorous." Candidates are interviewed by the hiring manager or project manager and sometimes the other folks on the project. The customer may also opt to review the candidate's resume. "That doesn't mean they control the hiring process," says an insider, "but if they had a strong objection, the relationship is close enough between my firm and their customers that the firm would listen to any strong objections the customer may have."

For developer positions, applicants may be asked to write code in a number of languages (at least Java and SQL). Candidates should be comfortable working with people (not just machines) and have a strong commitment to teamwork and customers. Most openings target experienced consultants with a minimum of three years of work experience under their belts.

# OUR SURVEY SAYS

## Up with people?

Haverstick consultants say one of the best things about working at Haverstick is its "intelligent," "friendly" workforce. "We have an excellent staff of extremely talented people," says one. "It's very welcoming to new consultants," says another. Generally, they report high satisfaction with their direct supervisors – "my immediate supervisor and the one above him, are great people, and seem to really care about what is going on." However, "as it goes up the line it gets progressively worse," says an employee. Echoes another insider: "My managing director is superb! But his bosses are money [focused]." Many employees report concern with the profit focus of the executives. "Management is driven by margins, and not at all concerned about keeping the people that built the foundation for the company," says one. "We probably spend too much playing the 'numbers' game – weekly revenue estimates – rather than dealing with the reality of the situation," says a source. That may have something to do with size; as another Haversticker says, "Money has changed a successful family-driven company into a company that only cares about the bottom line."

## Long-distance relationship

Many Haverstick employees work off site, and thus find they have somewhat attenuated ties to the company. One consultant reports he only sees a manager one-on-one if something bad has happened; another says he gets about one hour per month with his boss. "My client has more of an impact on my career," says one consultant who works on a government project. Haverstick does make an effort to keep in touch through quarterly meetings, work-sponsored outings and an infomative weekly e-newsletter.

Haverstick gives employees two weeks a year to attend any training they like, and encourages them to obtain certifications; however, because of the red tape involved, very few employees report taking advantage of the benefit. "I've never really been able to obtain training because the company gives me such a run-around in paying for it," says one. Haverstick hopes its new "Performance Objective Plan," which aims to plan training up to one year in advance, will remedy any budget-related training delays.

## Sluggish salaries

Employees report concerns their pay is not quite competitive. Salaries "are lower than the standard in the city and nation," says an Indianapolis-based consultant. Bonuses are "based upon hitting an individual revenue goal and average bill rate per resource," says one employee. "Raises, even for promotions, are small," a consultant adds. The company does award cash for each certification test an employee passes and for each unsolicited letter of praise from a customer. The firm also says it performs an internal benchmarking analysis to produce competitive salaries.

Stock options are "almost a gimmick," says one employee, offered at signing and rarely thereafter. Benefits, meanwhile, are basic; the company contributes to medical and dental insurance, offers a 401k match, and provides a long-term disability insurance package.

## Bending over backwards

Haverstick gets high marks for its flexibility regarding work schedules. Many employees can work from home and adjust schedules to fit in with children's soccer games or plays, provided they work after-hours or on weekends to accumulate the target number of billable hours. "Managers are very flexible on schedules and needs of the family," says a consultant. Adds another, the company has a "clear understanding of the importance of both work and family, and provides the ability to work from home when family issues require it."

Traveling is also adjusted to the consultants' desires. "Managers work with individuals to keep them from traveling when they have family obligations," says a Haversticker. The travel can be minimal – many employees don't travel at all, and those that do usually stick close to home. Some consultants work entirely off site at the client's office, usually located within commuting distance of home, and hardly ever go in to the Haverstick offices. "A 45-minute drive is the farthest away I have had to travel," says a consultant who's been with the company for two years.

Hours seem reasonable compared to other consulting firms. Off-site consultants can be contractually limited to 40-hour workweeks, while those who go to the Haverstick offices report about 40- to 50-hour workweeks. Employees report being "on the bench" (that's what it's called there) a few times a year.

## Offices not posh enough for some

The Haverstick offices are functional, but could use improvement, insiders say. "It gets the job done, but we wish we would move to a better space," one tells us. The color scheme is drab, and the offices are "not upscale enough to entertain high-brow clientele," says another. The firm plans to move from the Dayton office, which attracted most of the negative comments, in 2003.

## Keeping Dayton beautiful

The company has traditionally been involved in community service, engaging employees in projects such as building homes, having a food drive, or building web sites for charities. For example, the Dayton office participates in the exciting Adopt-A-Highway program; Indianapolis supports Habitat for Humanity.

## Men on top?

The top executives at Haverstick are mostly men, and many consultants say that needs to change. As one employee says, it's "mostly white American males" at Haverstick. The female employees we surveyed seem split on whether that's an issue or not. "I have not encountered any problems here," says one female Haversticker. Some point to the lack of an official maternity leave policy as a potential reason for the lack of women. "There is currently no maternity leave over and above what is required by FMLA," says one. The firm says that 13.5 percent of its managers are women, and that 5.4 percent are members of minority groups.

## A bright future

Despite the layoffs and the malaise among many employees, other consultants maintain the firm offers great opportunities. "The future is very bright," says one consultant. The firm is "dynamic," adds another. Many praise its "entrepreneurial" spirit. And despite 2002's layoffs, employees believe the business fundamentals are strong. "The company is solid, no debt, profits, and growing in a down economy. They work hard at finding engagements," says a consultant. Federal work is especially stable. "Because of our DoD client base, there is a good work/life balance. Also, in the current economic climate, the federal sector is going strong," says one consultant.

# Health Advances

9 Riverside Road
Weston, MA 02493
Phone: (781) 647-3435
Fax: (781) 392-1484
www.healthadvances.com

## LOCATIONS

**Weston, MA (HQ)**

## PRACTICE AREAS

Business Plans and Fund Raising
Competitive Analysis
Health Economics and
   Reimbursement Assistance
Market Research
Mergers and Acquisitions
Partnerships and Alliances
Technology Evaluations

## THE STATS

**Employer Type:** Private Company
**Managing Directors:** Mark Speers,
Paula Ness Speers, and Mason (Skip)
Irving III

## UPPERS

• Small, familial feel

## DOWNERS

• Narrow scope of consulting
  activities

## KEY COMPETITORS

First Consulting Group
Putnam Associates
Triage Consulting Group

## EMPLOYMENT CONTACT

Recruiting Coordinator
Health Advances LLC
9 Riverside Road
Weston, MA 02493
Fax: (781) 392-1484
E-mail: rec@healthadvances.com

## THE BUZZ
WHAT CONSULTANTS AT OTHER FIRMS ARE SAYING

• "Qualitative health care group"
• "Knowledgeable, good firm"
• "Smaller clients"
• "Dominated by founders"

# THE SCOOP

## Teaming up for health care consulting

Husband-and-wife team Mark Speers and Paula Ness Speers founded Health Advances in 1992. As the name suggests, the company focuses on the health care industry, with clients ranging from pharmaceuticals to services to medical devices and diagnostics. That focus helps them clarify market strategy and market dynamics, price and promote new products, execute clinical trials, increase sales, figure out expansion or merger strategies – and get paid.

## On the inside

Market research is one of Health Advances' strengths. The consulting firm maintains a panel of 2,000 "thought leaders" in the medical world – experts, health care providers, and doctors – who provide feedback on surveys and ideas. It also has what it calls "unique access" to a few insurers' longitudinal claims data; this allows it to figure out how much a certain treatment of a specific condition might cost.

## Thoughtful and flexible work schedules

The company aims for an informal and flexible atmosphere. A week of 50 hours is the target, and weekends or late nights are said to be rare. Health Advances says it aims to accommodate those who wish to work untraditional work schedules. The company is also involved in community service, which includes four days a year of officewide volunteering, pro bono projects, and donations to one charity each year.

# GETTTING HIRED

Health Advances recruits for its analyst, senior analyst and associate positions at schools including Harvard, MIT/Sloan, and Dartmouth. Analysts must be good at collecting and organizing data, interviewing clients, and preparing presentations; those with coursework in life sciences are particularly suited to working at Health Advances. Associates ought to have life sciences or health care training or consulting experience, strong communication and quantitative skills, and good organizational skills.

# Huron Consulting Group

550 W. Van Buren
Chicago, IL 60607
Phone: (312) 583-8700
Fax: (312) 583-8701
www.huronconsultinggroup.com

## LOCATIONS

**Chicago, IL (HQ)**
Boston, MA
Charlotte, NC
Houston, TX
Miami, FL
New York, NY
San Francisco, CA
Washington, DC

## PRACTICE AREAS

Business Dispute Analysis
Business Strategy
Corporate Finance
Economic Consulting
Financial Advisory
Health Care
Higher Education
Interim Management
Intellectual Property
Legal Business Consulting
Organizational Design
Shared Service Formation
Strategic Sourcing
Valuation Services

## THE STATS

**Employer Type:** Private Company
**President:** Gary E. Holdren
**2002 Employees:** 400

## UPPERS

- Economic consulting a hot specialty
- Experienced leadership making a fresh start

## DOWNERS

- Andersen legacy
- Controversy over United Airlines fees

## KEY COMPETITORS

LECG
Lexecon

## EMPLOYMENT CONTACT

E-mail:
careers@huronconsultinggroup.com

## THE BUZZ
WHAT CONSULTANTS AT OTHER FIRMS ARE SAYING

- " Not well known but kept good Andersen people"
- "Rising but still green"

# THE SCOOP

## Phoenix

Huron Consulting Group is a newcomer to the consulting scene, but one with deep roots. In May 2002, 25 consulting partners rose from the ashes of Arthur Andersen in the aftermath of that firm's accounting scandal-fuled demise. Joined by senior executives from other firms, the new consulting company attracted funding from Lake Capital. In just one year, the firm has grown to 400 personnel, expanded into new business areas and shows real promise.

The firm's president, Gary Holdren, has over 30 years' experience in accounting and business consulting fields. Huron's initial service offerings were in financial disputes, investigations and valuations; strategic and operational consulting and corporate advisory services. The firm intends to grow to 600 employees by the end of 2003.

## Taking advantage

Huron made news with its influential January 2003 report on the leading causes of corporate financial restatements during the previous five years. The widely quoted report revealed that the number of restatements rose 22 percent during 2002 to a total of 330. Joseph J. Floyd, managing director of Huron's financial and economic consulting practice, claimed, "Problems applying accounting rules, human and system errors and fraudulent behavior are the three primary causes for accounting errors." The report also noted that the cessation of Andersen's audit practice forced more than 1,300 corporations to engage new auditors.

In December 2002, Huron scored a major coup when it landed a consulting engagement for bankrupt UAL Corp., the parent company of United Airlines. Huron beat out several other established firms for the engagement; Gary Holdren claimed one key reason was the strong business relationships the Huron team had developed while still employed by Andersen. Huron has already received $500,000 as a retainer. United's creditors started a challenge to this payment and others (including a $1 million-a-month flat fee for McKinsey) in January 2003, feeling such expenses are unwarranted for a company that can't pay its current debts.

## New business for a new business

Huron announced in February 2003 that it would form a new practice specializing in economic consulting. The practice will "conduct economic analyses for corporate clients dealing with strategy, litigation, regulation, valuation and bankruptcy matter," according to the company. Michael J. Moore, a professor at the Darden School of Business and a research associate at the National Bureau of Economic Research, will head the practice. Dr. Moore will operate from both the Chicago and Charlottesville offices, but the staff of undergraduate and PhD economic experts will have nationwide presence.

# GETTING HIRED

## Get in on the ground floor

Huron is still a very new firm, and is continuing to gear up to full capacity, as indicated by numerous announcements throughout 2002 and early 2003 of additional managing director-level hires. Though exact figures were not available, those managing directors need staff to direct, and approximately 150 employees came aboard in the first year of business. The firm's employment page has direct links to open positions; interested candidates are directed to inquire via e-mail. The firm says it is currently seeking "A players" at the analyst and associate levels.

"If you've got the talent, there is no limit to the level attained."

— *IMS Health associate*

# IMS Health Inc.

1499 Post Road
Fairfield, CT 06430
Phone: (203) 319-4700
www.imshealth.com

## LOCATIONS

**Fairfield, CT (HQ)**
101 offices worldwide

## PRACTICE AREAS

Information Management
Managed Care
Marketing
Pricing & Reimbursement
Research & Development
Sales Force Effectiveness

## THE BUZZ
WHAT CONSULTANTS AT OTHER FIRMS ARE SAYING

- "Specialist pharma"
- "Disorganized; dinosaur"

## THE STATS

**Employer Type:** Public Company
**Stock Symbol:** RX
**Stock Exchange:** NYSE
**CEO:** David M. Thomas
**2002 Employees:** 5,700
**2001 Employees:** 5,425
**2002 Revenue:** $1.43 billion
**2001 Revenue:** $1.33 billion

## UPPERS

- "Excellent promotion policy"
- Workload "rarely" spikes

## DOWNERS

- "The long hours"
- Limited scope of work

## KEY COMPETITORS

Aon
First Consulting Group
Superior Consultant Company

## EMPLOYMENT CONTACT

Contact the local office for
opportunities at specific locations.

**Careers page:**
www.imshealth.com/careers/

**Job search:**
www.imshealth.com/ims/portal/front/
BrassRing/

# THE SCOOP

## Go see a specialist

IMS Health is, not surprisingly, built around providing advice, information and support to pharmaceutical and health care industries worldwide. IMS Health's chief services are strategy consulting and market research for drug makers and insurance groups. The company operates from 100 offices in as many countries.

## Healthy history

IMS has been through a number of changes on its way to becoming a 5,700-employee firm that generated $1.3 billion in revenue during 2002. It bears little resemblance to the original Intercontinental Marketing Services launched in 1954. When Wilhelm Frohlich and David Dubow founded the company, IMS was initially focused on pharmaceutical market research, a field then just taking off. The firm remained focused for a quarter of a century, acquiring six other companies and expanding to more than 50 countries.

Two of those firms, Pharmatech and Cambridge Computer (both acquired in 1974), gave IMS a foothold in the just-blossoming world of computer-enabled business. The expertise of these two firms enabled IMS to create MIDAS, a worldwide data analysis service that enabled companies to access IMS databases from terminals in their own offices, in 1979.

In 1980, IMS attempted to diversify into consumer market research, establishing a practice to serve the fashion, apparel and household appliance industries. The 57-office, $170-million revenue company decided to spin off its consumer research interests in 1981, returning its focus to pharmaceutical and health matters. To accomplish this, IMS began another period of acquisition and expansion, absorbing four more firms between 1984 and 1986.

In 1988, IMS was itself acquired by Dun & Bradstreet in a $1.8 billion deal. D&B invested heavily in its new property. In 1996, the drug consultancy was spun off as part of Cognizant Corp., along with sister division Nielsen Media Research. Two years later, IMS and Nielsen became independent public companies. IMS (whose NYSE ticker is RX, naturally) spun off Gartner Group in 1999, and its strategic technologies unit (which became Synavant) in 2000. The firm also sold Erisco Managed Care Technologies that year. These units were replaced in December 2001 with the acquisition of Cambridge Pharma Consultancy, a private consulting firm serving the strategic needs of pharmaceutical management.

## Three awards and one repeat

IMS Health earned a trio of awards during 2001. The firm was one of three finalists selected by the Eastern Technology Council in November 2001 for the 2001 Enterprise Award. IMS Health Canada was named one of Canada's Top 100 Employers, and 48th of the "Best 50 Companies to Work For," by *Globe & Mail's Business Report* magazine, in December 2001. Management consultancy Compass America named IMS winner of the 2001 Compass Data Center of the Year award (bestowed in May 2002), in recognition of the company's efficient data centers. In 2002, the Canadian wing moved up from No. 48 to No. 30 in the "Best 50" rankings.

## On the right side

The year 2002 was marked by two notable legal victories for the company. In September, a German appeals court upheld a favorable judgment in Pharma Intranet Information AG v. IMS Health GmbH, an intellectual property suit centered on IMS' proprietary pharmaceutical tracking service. PI was directed to cease copying and reselling IMS' RPM 1860 product and to pay court costs. In October 2002, IMS was cleared of allegations by competitor NDC Health that the firm's commercial practices in Europe violated European Commission rules regarding competition.

## Meet the new boss - he reports to the old boss

Also in October 2002, IMS Health hired David Carlucci as its first president and chief operating officer. The newly created position reports directly to the chairman and CEO, David Thomas. Prior to joining IMS, Carlucci was general manager of IBM Americas, a $40 billion division of the computer giant. Young consultants and executives in training should take note – Carlucci holds only a BA in political science from the University of Rochester.

## Building a healthy business

The firm has been busy throughout early 2003, forging new alliances to expand offerings and influence. In February 2003, IMS announced a strategic alliance with Harris Interactive, a Web-powered market research firm, to create new business intelligence solutions for health care and pharmaceutical providers. In March, the U.S. business unit of IMS acquired Data Niche Associates Inc., an Illinois-based firm specializing in Medicaid and managed care services.

Also in March 2003, IMS announced a three-year engagement with Pfizer to provide the pharmaceutical giant with data, analytics and advice in Canada and 22 European countries. Under terms of the agreement, IMS will supply business intelligence and associated services to help Pfizer optimize the effectiveness of its field-based teams.

# GETTING HIRED

## Seasoned professionals, please

Sources at IMS Health tell us new hires are "usually via industry press, recruitment agencies and referrals from employees." When asked which schools the firm targets for recruitment, an insider said, "None." Potential IMSers will have to do their own networking.

This is not to say the company has no use for recent grads. One employee says, "The company's promotion policy is excellent. If you've got the talent, there is no limit to the level attained, regardless of qualifications." The firm's employment page includes an anecdote of an administrative assistant earning a BA through the tuition reimbursement program and jumping onto the consulting career track.

# OUR SURVEY SAYS

## Still healthy

One source notes that there were some layoffs throughout the firm during 2002. He says, "This was due to new management assessing the level of resources for each department throughout the organization," and is not indicative of problems in the company. Employees are still happy with the "health care, company car, share options and discounted share purchase" they receive, and think the "remuneration" is a positive point to working at IMS.

The benefits package at IMS Health is solid; in addition to the above, insiders mention "cell phones, PDAs and laptop computers," "employee assistance program," "an employee lounge area" with "free food and drinks," "gym membership discounts," "long-term disability insurance," and "sports and theater tickets" as some of the perks they enjoy. For social and philanthropic efforts, sources say the firm has "regular contributions and fund-raisers for local charities."

# Katzenbach Partners LLC

381 Park Avenue South
Sixth Floor
New York, NY 10016
Phone: (212) 213-5505
Fax: (212) 213-5024
www.katzenbach.com

## LOCATIONS

**New York, NY (HQ)**
Houston, TX

## PRACTICE AREAS

Strategy and Organizational
Consulting

- "Very strong boutique, hip culture"
- "No chance for advancement"
- "Building its reputation"

## THE STATS

**Employer Type:** Private Company
**Founders:** Niko Canner, Marc
Feigen, Jon Katzenbach
**2002 Employees:** 47 (consultants)
**2001 Employees:** 40 (consultants)
**2002 Revenue:** $19 million
**2001 Revenue:** $17 million

## UPPERS

- Growing fast – and hiring
- Management flexible and
  committed

## DOWNERS

- Lack of structure
- Little personal time when traveling

## KEY COMPETITORS

Bain & Company
Boston Consulting Group
McKinsey & Company
Mercer Management Consulting

## EMPLOYMENT CONTACT

Kristen Clemmer
E-mail:
kristen.clemmer@katzenbach.com

**Undergrads:**
E-mail: undergrad@katzenbach.com
**Graduate students:**
E-mail: graduate@katzenbach.com
**Summer associates:**
E-mail: summer@katzenbach.com
**Experienced hires:**
E-mail: experienced@katzenbach.com

# THE SCOOP

The three founding partners of Katzenbach Partners LLC came from deep consulting backgrounds. Jon Katzenbach had been a director at McKinsey, while Marc Fiegen and Niko Canner had co-founded McKinsey's Change Center before leaving in 1996 for Mitchell Madison Group, where they founded the Organization Practice. The firm was founded in 1998 in a New York City townhouse. By 1999, the firm had moved to its current offices in New York's Flatiron district; by 2000, clients included Microsoft and Pfizer. The firm, currently at 47 consultants, is still owned by the partners.

## A select clientele

The company advises on strategy, and, to date, its clients have been in the health care, finance, telecom/tech, energy, and industrial products sectors. Katzenbach does take a slightly different approach to consulting than most strategy firms in that it looks very closely at human performance and how that can be exploited to help the business. The company's approach very much relies on tools that break down 'soft' issues, such as, performance and employee commitment. All the consultants are generalists, and the revenue per professional ranks Katzenbach among the top five consulting firms.

# GETTING HIRED

KPL recruits on campus, but only at top schools. According to consultants, schools that make the cut include "Harvard, Yale, Brown, Princeton, Columbia, Barnard, Wellesley, Wharton, Harvard Business School, Columbia Business School, Stanford, Tuck and Kellogg."

The acceptance rate lingers around 1 percent for undergrad applicants. Candidates don't necessarily need to be business majors; the company says it's looking for people with originality in their work and an ability to inspire who can get things done – in short, leader types. The career path is "pretty flexible," and entry level consultants have led projects such as hiring and managing a PR firm, developing the web site, and organizing the recruiting effort.

The interview process includes the whole arsenal of consulting tricks. Cases might include brainteasers (which test creativity and ability to cope with stress), market-sizing challenges (which measure the ability to do off-the-cuff calculations and make solid assumptions) or business-based case studies (which test how well you attack a real-life situation). The company is looking for structure, logic, synthesis of information and creativity in answers. Additionally, candidates should have a poised, engaging presence, show leadership ability, prove intellectually curious and have relevant work experience. A typical question might be, "How many barbershops are there in New York?" or "How many people fly out of La Guardia on an average Saturday?" "There are also more involved cases based on business situations, e.g. 'How would you improve sales force profitability at X company?'" a source says.

The "rigorous and selective" process usually includes two to four rounds of interviews – "candidates generally interview with at least five people" – some on campus and some at the office. At least one interview is with a founding partner. "We do not use quotas such as 'We will hire five MBAs'; rather, we hire as many people as we meet that really inspire us," says a source.

# SURVEY SAYS

## Small and smart

Now in its fifth year, the company is staying true to its "young, energetic, non-competitive, hip, ambitious, New York" roots. It's "very culture conscious," and that seems to be working, for the firm is reported to be "very open, friendly, transparent and nonhierarchical." People are "smart" and "collegial" with "incredibly diverse interests," while the management has a "commitment to work/life balance." Another Katzenbach plus: "regular outings to cultural events sponsored by the firm."

Consultants find the top brass accessible. "I've gotten to know the founding partners," reports one junior-level employee; another likes that it's "small enough to have personal contact with everyone – resulting in a clear sense of where we are headed and an ability to influence this." Yet if senior staff are around in the office, they may not be as visible on cases: "I'd like more time with senior staff on projects," says one junior consultant.

## Service sector

Katzenbach is roundly praised for its community involvement, though consultants note that they – not the company – usually take the initiative in such events. "We do pro bono consulting work, and research in areas that affect public policy (such as homeland security)," says one. Another consultant adds that "our firm allows people to work 80 percent if they want to pursue personal pro bono interests." There is "a community service project one day a year, as well as a holiday toy drive." Though "the firm will sponsor pro bono projects" with "use of time and in some cases with financial support," they are "primarily driven by individuals with interest."

## Work/life equilibrium

Respondents find the firm is "extremely sensitive to work/life balance issues, and the flexible policies reflect genuine concern and care." That especially seems to play out in the staffing arena: "Our management has worked hard to help me balance my personal and work life – especially through extremely thoughtful staffing decisions," notes one consultant, while another reports that "given personal needs, I have been staffed on local projects." Still, while "many of our projects are New York-based," there are quite a few projects that require travel. On those, people "work especially hard – long hours and not much personal time. The firm recently began having traveling projects and is still learning how to manage them." "Those on traveling projects return to the home office on Fridays. Traveling projects involve long hours. Consultants on traveling projects try not to travel on Sundays, but do sometimes," says a source.

Still, there's "no face time" at the firm, and a "very generous vacation policy, even for new hires." Work usually takes between 45 and 60 hours a week, which most insiders find reasonable; "however, when work needs to get done, we stay late."

## Fast forward

The firm is "growing in a down economy," note our respondents, and "has never laid anyone off" – in fact, "we're hiring constantly." "Consultants with only undergraduate degrees can move into MBA-level positions," says a source; another agrees, "Our promotion policy isn't based on prior experience or education – it is based on your individual performance at the firm." Moreover, it's "not up-or-out – you can stay in a position until the partners feel you are ready to be promoted. But if you are excellent you can be promoted quickly." While the promotion model "is a little unclear," management seems to "encourage promotion from within." Consultants "can advance to the senior associate level after two years."

## Bank notes

Katzenbachians seem fairly pleased with their salaries, rating them on the high end of the scale. They're "very generous," says one source. The firm offers "profit sharing," "full payment of healthcare and insurance benefits" and a "401(k) contribution based off of a percentage of salary." In fact, many say the firm in general is "extremely generous – the health care plan especially, but also small things like theater tickets." Cell phones, snacks, PDAs, tuition reimbursement, gym discounts, laptops, relocation bonuses and sports/theater tickets are all part of the package.

## Training the management

Training consists of a two-week orientation for undergrads, but beyond that, consultants seem divided on how effective – and available – training is. "There should be more formal training, especially for junior people like me," says one analyst. Another remarks that while "some of it is good, it's an all new curriculum and is sometimes scattered." "Training gets a lot of attention, and we can provide input as to how we want to be trained, sometimes I wish there were a more established regimen," comments a consultant. Training enthusiasts, meanwhile, report that "a huge amount of attention is given to training, with engaged, knowlegeable leaders," making it "regular and broad" and "given priority."

Several insiders suggest that the firm "provide training for new managers." "The firm needs to work on improving the quality of its junior and middle managers," says one entry level analyst. Another echoes, "The firm could provide more training in how to manage;" however, the same respondent notes, "[The company] cares about my development and we've had development conversations." Agrees another source, "There are excellent supervisors here, and they are generally extremely interested in employee development." One inside tip: "it seems that people have to really request raises, rather than just get the raise they deserve." The same tipster suggests that the firm "unify the partner relationships – it seems like the four of them sometimes have different agendas."

## Soaring space

The office space gets high marks from consultants. "It's gorgeous, very tasteful, a great location," notes one. Another consultant says that the offices are "well designed and sleek, with rooms for privacy and nice conference rooms. The building we are in is sub-optimal, though." Employees also seem to like the office layout, which is "totally open plan, from Jon Katzenbach down to the newest associate." "The open office keeps things casual," remarks another consultant, "but can be more distracting." Another source muses that "the very carefully thought-out design represents a particular philosophy of the firm." Desk potatoes be warned: "The chairs are extremely uncomfortable."

## Tolerance in the workplace

Katzenbach seems to be a fine place for women. "The commitment is clear, and many women at the lower levels, but no partners and not many principals are women," says one consultant. Another Katzenbacher echoes, "We have lots of talented women in junior positions (i.e., engagement managers), but few at the principal level and none at the partnership level." However, says one woman, "in my opinion our firm is amazing at addressing the needs of women." The company also seems to be pushing for more women: "The most senior group is still heavily male, reflecting trends in the industry and that our senior group has all been hired laterally. Promotion from within has been more than half women. In five years, this will lead to much greater diversity at the top."

Respondents agree that the firm is "happy to hire minorities" and seems "highly supportive of cultural differences." With regard to gay people, there's "extreme tolerance" – almost all the respondents rate the firm as highly diverse in this area. "Many consultants and support staff are gay and out. Benefits are extended to domestic partners, and significant others of the same sex are routinely included in firm events," says one consultant.

# Leigh Fisher Associates

160 Bovet Road, Suite 300
San Mateo, CA 94402-3107
Phone: (650) 571-7722
Fax: (650) 571-5220
www.leighfisher.com

## LOCATIONS

**San Mateo, CA (HQ)**
Washington, DC

## PRACTICE AREAS

Air Cargo • Airfield and Airspace
Planning • Airline Negotiations and
Relations • Airport Privatization •
Airport Security Planning and
Implementation • Commercial
Development and Concessions •
Environmental Planning • Financial
Feasibility and Reporting • Financial
Planning and Business Advisory
Services • Forecasting and
Economics • Ground Transportation
and Parking • Information
Technology • Management,
Organization and Compensation •
Master and System Planning •
Rental Car Facilities Planning •
Simulations and Support • Facilities
Planning

## THE STATS

**Employer Type:** Private Company
**Principal-in-Charge and CEO:** Nick
Davidson
**2002 Employees:** 85

## UPPERS

- Opportunities to see the world
- Profit sharing

## DOWNERS

- Consulting and air travel both not-
so-robust industries
- Training-lite

## KEY COMPETITORS

HNTB
Landrum & Brown
John F. Brown Company

## EMPLOYMENT CONTACT

Employment
Leigh Fisher Associates
P.O. Box 8007
San Francisco International Airport
San Francisco, CA 94128-8007
Fax: (650) 571-5220
www.leighfisher.com/company/
f_career.html

## THE BUZZ
### WHAT CONSULTANTS AT OTHER FIRMS ARE SAYING

- "Low-value engagements"
- "Not bad"

# THE SCOOP

## Consulting takes wing

If you've ever been in an airport, dealt with security and customs, rented a car at the airport or had a drink at the SkyBar, you've probably experienced some of Leigh Fisher Associates' handiwork. If you've ridden an airport tramway between the terminal and the passenger gates, you can thank Leigh Fisher Associates (otherwise known as LFA) for that little piece of convenience as well – they developed it in 1971 as an alternative to moving walkways.

LFA founded in 1946 in South Bend, Ind., to serve all aspects of the burgeoning air travel industry, has grown into a firm with worldwide reach – though it still only has two offices. Helping international airlines and high-volume terminals deal with their business concerns has a way of doing that to a company.

Today, LFA has moved out of South Bend and into San Mateo, Calif., serving the San Francisco International Airport. The firm opened its Chantilly, Va., office in August 2000 to serve Dulles International. From these two locations, LFA provides advice to air carriers and ground facilities on cargo handling, ground transportation, facilities planning, information technology and just about everything else that can be found at an airport – right down to the concessions and duty-free shops.

## Spiffing up airports

The firm conducted a study into a possible merger of the Port Columbus and Rickenbacker airports in Columbus, Ohio; LFA determined that taxpayers would save up to $7.6 million through 2007, as reported by *The Columbus Dispatch* in March 2002, if the two facilities were combined. The municipal committee overseeing the project authorized the firm to plan the workings of the potential new unified port authority.

Also in March 2002, LFA advice moved Harrisburg International Airport to embark on constructing new facilities, including a $91 million terminal and $55 million transportation center, instead of renovating existing structures. The project, estimated to cost $221.6 million in total, would employ as many as 2,000 workers during construction. The new airport would enable more efficient handling of the predicted 10 percent air passenger increase through Harrisburg in 2002, followed by 15 percent in 2003 – which, Leigh Fisher CEO Nick Davidson noted in *The Harrisburg Patriot*, would mark a return to the airport's 1998 level.

# Riding out turbulence

Air travel is an industry in crisis, and Leigh Fisher Associates personnel have been busy helping clients weather the bad times. For example, in August 2002, *The Rocky Mountain News* reported LFA's analysis of the effects of United Airlines' planned Chapter 11 reorganization on the operations of Denver International Airport. The firm predicted that, despite a 27 percent decline in net revenue in 2003, the facility would have sufficient funds to cover its debts until the airline recovered.

Despite the turmoil, some cities are trying to revitalize their local economy by becoming major participants in the air business, and Leigh Fisher is working with them. In February 2003, Mayor Martin Chavez of Albuquerque, N.M., announced that he had engaged the firm to conduct a feasibility study on building an air freight hub. The city, conveniently located near Mexico and the junction of Interstates 40 and 25, has usable land south of its passenger airport for a freight hub; the city has been in discussions with three freight carriers, a handlers union and the state economic development office about the possibilities of such a project.

# GETTING HIRED

## Taking off

Leigh Fisher Associates may be focused on a single industry, but it seeks consultants with a variety of skills. The firm's careers page says students of "architecture, business, computer science, economics, engineering, environmental sciences, finance, urban planning" and other disciplines are all welcome. Candidate background is likewise variable; the principals, managers and consultants have come straight from college, from other consultancies, from government agencies and from airport/airline careers.

Job seekers are directed to apply by mail through LFA's post office box at San Francisco International, or by fax or e-mail for best results. For an idea of what sort of people work at Leigh Fisher, consult the web site's news page for introductions to new hires and biographies of the principals.

"At times, work is your life, but most managers are sensitive to making sure you get enough time off."

*— Lexecon consultant*

# Lexecon Inc.

332 South Michigan Avenue
Chicago, IL 60604
Phone: (312) 322-0200
Fax: (312) 322-0218
www.lexecon.com

## LOCATIONS

**Chicago, IL (HQ)**
Cambridge, MA (2 offices)

## PRACTICE AREAS

Antitrust
Bank Support
Board Advisory
Damages
Employment Discrimination
Intellectual Property
Public Policy
Regulated Industries
Securities
Transaction Support
Valuation

## THE STATS

**Employer Type:** Subsidiary of Nextera Enterprises Inc.
**Stock Symbol:** NXRA
**Stock Exchange:** Nasdaq
**Chairman:** Daniel R. Fischel
**2002 Employees:** 200
**2001 Employees:** 150
**2002 Revenue:** $75.9 million
**2001 Revenue:** $122.3 million

## UPPERS

- "Lots of freedom "
- "Flexibility" of work schedule
- "Collaborative and supportive culture"

## DOWNERS

- "Intense pressure associated with litigation support projects"
- "Lumpy nature of the work"
- "Need to be better at building the brand"

## KEY COMPETITORS

Charles River Associates
FTI Consulting
LECG

## EMPLOYMENT CONTACT

Darlene Serrano
Human Resource Manager
Phone: (312) 322-0200
Fax: (312) 322-0218
E-mail: chgo_recruiting@lexecon.com

## THE BUZZ
WHAT CONSULTANTS AT OTHER FIRMS ARE SAYING

- "Ideological"
- "Good reputation, but ALWAYS on one side of the issue"
- "Good econ consulting firm"

# THE SCOOP

## Unit of a unit

Lexecon is a consultancy dedicated to all things economic and financial. (The very name Lexecon reflects the firm's focus on the intersection of law and economics.). Since 1977, the group has advised industry leaders and law firms on such topics as antitrust, mergers and acquisitions, intellectual property, regulatory support and valuation. Lexecon is the operating unit of Nextera Enterprises, which is itself the independent consulting arm of Knowledge Universe, the Michael and Lowell Milken/Larry Ellison venture.

In recent years, Nextera has sold off its other consulting businesses, which included Strategic Services, Technology Solutions and the human resources consultancy Sibson Consulting. Now Lexecon, its core consulting business, stands alone.

## A helping hand for litigators

One of Lexecon's biggest activities is litigation support. That's a catchall term for providing expert witnesses, performing research and doing whatever else a client needs to get through arbitration, court proceedings and regulatory hearings. Understanding the economic, public policy and financial consequences of actions and decisions in those forums enables clients to form effective strategies. The firm's business consulting practice provides strategic advice on pricing matters such as new business entry and production capacity. Consultants use economic principles to predict those reactions and determine their likely effects on future competition.

Its public policy work has earned the company a reputation as an economic think tank; Lexecon has performed studies on behalf of governmental institutions and trade associations, such as the U.S. Departments of Commerce and Transportation, the SEC, the FCC and the National Association of Securities Dealers.

## Branching out

In addition to its three established practice areas, the firm broadened its business consulting services in February 2003. Board advisory services will provide expertise tailored to the needs of a board of directors, with such focuses as board education and decision making support. Transaction support services will offer private equity investment advice in the energy and utilities industries. Bank support services, not surprisingly, will assist banks in controlling their economic exposure to fluctuations in the energy and utilities sectors.

## Tops in their fields

The firm's name turns up again and again in news reports of legal actions, but in this case it's a good thing. Lexecon is often engaged to support noteworthy lawsuits and regulatory inquiries, such the approval of eBay's merger with PayPal in August 2002.

Lexecon is at the forefront of the regulatory changes occuring within the energy sector. Dennis Carlton, a leading economist for the firm, helped Sun Microsystems gain a preliminary injunction against Microsoft in December 2002 in an antitrust case revolving around Sun's Java Runtime Environment and Microsoft Internet Explorer. In January 2003, Lexecon client Boca Investerings Partnership won a $605 million federal appeal against the IRS for disallowed capital losses.

Lexecon's consultants include recognized leaders in government and advisory organizations. In December 2002, the firm announced that several of its people had been appointed to influential commissions. Two senior Lexecon officers, Susan Tierney and Philip Sharp, are members of the National Commission on Energy Policy, a long-range policy forum for the U.S. government. Jonathan Taylor was named to the Commission to Study the Potential Expansion of Legalized Gaming in the Commonwealth of Massachusetts by acting governor Jane Swift. Joseph Cavicchi was appointed to the Northeast Energy and Commerce Association's board of directors.

# GETTING HIRED

## Lexecon entries

Economic-minded consultants should take a look at Lexecon. A source says, "Analyst positions are recruited every year in the fall on-campus cycle. Consultant positions are recruited on a more as-needed basis." A senior analyst provides these details: "For analysts, there is a short first-round interview at the applicant's school, and then a day of on-site interviews for those that advance to the second round. Second round includes four interviews with various levels of consulting staff, with one or two case questions." Hopefuls should expect questions to be "based on applied microeconomics, public policy or data analysis." An insider provides this example: "The FTC is investigating the merger of two airlines both serving the same route. What might you consider in thinking about whether this merger violates antitrust laws."

The hiring process is termed "selective." Lexecon insiders tell us that the recruitment schools include "the Ivies, Williams, Swarthmore, Amherst and Carleton." You should expect to see a number of people during your interviews; one senior consultant says "the entire firm" participates in hiring.

A consultant says, "Lexecon offers an excellent three-week training program for new analysts. The firm also offers in-house and external training and professional development opportunities on an ongoing basis, including tuition reimbursement for [supplementary] undergraduate and graduate classes in related fields." He adds, "Unfortunately, there is no formal training program for consultants." Another source says the training program was "useful to get our feet wet and to get to know the other new analysts." At lower levels of experience, promotion is "generally rapid and merit-based."

## OUR SURVEY SAYS

### Respectful and academic

Insiders at Lexecon describe the culture as "relaxed in tone, serious in substance," with a "quasi-academic and informal culture." One source notes the "high level of respect for the individual. Everybody, top to bottom, is on a first name basis." A longterm employee says life at Lexecon is "rather like a PhD seminar – know your stuff, but have a good time arguing." Another agrees, calling the firm's atmosphere "nearly academic, except without anything but enjoyable conflict during debate."

### Cycling around (or not)

Most of our sources say the work at Lexecon is "cyclical" – understandable for a firm that concentrates on economic cases. A young analyst says, "At times, work is your life, but most managers are sensitive to making sure you get enough time off." However, another analyst claims, "I am constantly finding myself sacrificing my personal life for work. At this point in my life, I don't mind as much and it isn't a great concern." It doesn't have to be that way, though; a more experienced employee adds, "Recognizing the nature of the work, colleagues at Lexecon have great respect for each others' personal plans and commitments and are always willing to help one another during deadline time."

The workload isn't affected by travel, though. A source explains, "Since our work does not require on-site analysis, business trips are usually for a one-day client meeting. Most analysts only travel once or twice a year. Consultants, on the other hand, are more likely to travel (e.g. once a month)." Another concurs, "For non-partners, travel is generally one or two days a month."

## Bonus?

Some Lexecon insiders mention a problem with the firm's bonus system, but it's not the usual one (i.e., their nonexistence) – Lexecon is more than happy to pay bonuses. It's the metric used to determine the size and timing of bonuses that elicits gripes. A source mentions the "hours-based bonus system" non-partners use. That consultant calls it "useless when business is slow, because you still have deadlines where you work 80 hours a week, but not enough work the rest of the time to meet the minimum number of hours." Another source confirms the "volatile" work pace, with a range from "when slow, 20-25 hours" all the way to "extreme." Another Lexeconian says, "The range is probably between 30 and 90 hours." Others agree the firm could benefit from "improved bonus calculation."

## Relax (do it)

One of the nice upshots of not having a travel-based business model is the ability to have personal space. "Lexecon has an excellent office space," says one respondent. "Unlike many other consulting firms, each member of the consulting staff at Lexecon (including analysts) has his or her own office." An insider rejoices, "No cubicles!" A source in Boston describes the location: "Spacious, private, needs updating." Another insider tells us, "We are about to move, as we've outgrown this office. That said, the style is nice and functional but not ultra-luxurious."

"No cubicles!"

— *Lexecon consultant*

# Mercator Partners LLC

89-93 Thoreau Street
Concord, MA 01742 USA
Tel: (617) 896-8000
www.mercatorpartners.com

## LOCATIONS

**Concord, MA (HQ)**
Reston, VA
San Francisco, CA
London

## PRACTICE AREAS

Strategy

## THE STATS

**Employer Type:** Private Company
**Chairman:** Michael Davies
**2002 Employees:** 20 (consultants)
**2001 Employees:** 15 (consultants)

## UPPERS

• Ability to contribute to small,
  growing company

## DOWNERS

• Tech sector not exactly robust

## KEY COMPETITORS

Bain
Boston Consulting Group
McKinsey & Company

## EMPLOYMENT CONTACT

Recruiting Coordinator
Mercator Partners LLC
89-93 Thoreau Street
Concord, MA 01742 USA
E-mail:
careers@mercatorpartners.com

## THE BUZZ
WHAT CONSULTANTS AT OTHER FIRMS ARE SAYING

• "Solid"
• "Too big for boots"
• "Elitist"
• "PhDs and electronics"

# THE SCOOP

## A strategic helping hand for tech

Name an industry that desperately needs good, sound advice and consulting. If you picked technology, you'd be absolutely correct. That's how Mercator Partners came to be. Founded in 1998, Mercator Partners has the tough task of consulting to technology business and private investment firms. The firm focuses specifically on helping clients craft business strategies to help them cope with the everchanging domains of mobile and broadband tech.

## Optimism

The firm, in addition to working with information, communications and technology companies worldwide, also provides counsel to private equity firms still interested in investing in technology businesses. Some of these investors include Berkshire Partners and Carlisle & Company.

## Team Mercator

Michael Davies and Charles Gildehaus founded Mercator Partners in 1998. Davies, currently the Mercator Partners chairman, has a background in consulting and mobile communications; he worked with Nokia and Apple in the early 1990s to develop the first PDA with digital cellular connectivity. Gildehaus worked in corporate finance at investment bank Merrill Lynch and top law firm Cahill Gordon. He subsequently helped create several successful start-up ventures as a founder, advisor and board member before founding Mercator Partners.

# GETTING HIRED

Mercator Partners is a small and growing company, so candidates had better be interested in helping the company grow. The firm says successful candidates must have demonstrated aptitude for numbers and analysis. Preferred candidates will also have experience in technology industries (Internet, telecom, wireless, etc.) and strong computer skills.

# Milliman USA

1301 Fifth Avenue
Suite 3800
Seattle, WA 98101
Phone: (206) 624-7940
Fax: (206) 340-1380
www.milliman.com

## LOCATIONS

**Seattle, WA (HQ)**
Albany, NY • Atlanta, GA • Boise,
ID • Boston, MA • Chicago, IL •
Columbus, OH • Dallas, TX •
Denver, CO • Hartford, CT •
Houston, TX • Indianapolis, CA •
Irvine, CA • Los Angeles, CA •
Milwaukee, WI • Minneapolis, MN •
New York, NY • Omaha, NE •
Philadelphia, PA • Phoenix, AZ •
Portland, ME • Portland, OR • Salt
Lake City, UT • San Diego, CA •
San Francisco, CA • Seattle, WA •
Shawnee Mission, KS • St. Louis,
MO • Tampa, FL • Washington, DC
• Hamilton, Bermuda • Hong Kong •
London • São Paulo • Seoul • Tokyo

## PRACTICE AREAS

Health Consulting Services
Life and Financial Consulting
Services
Pension, Employee Benefits,
Investment and Compensation
Consulting Services
Property/Casualty Consulting
Services

## THE BUZZ
### WHAT CONSULTANTS AT OTHER FIRMS ARE SAYING

- "Excellent client products"
- "Good in health care"

## THE STATS

**Employer Type:** Private Company
**President and CEO:** Patrick J.
Grannan
**2002 Employees:** 1,700
**2001 Employees:** 1,700
**2002 Revenue:** $324 million
**2001 Revenue:** $301 million

## UPPERS

- Generous profit sharing setup

## DOWNERS

- Lack of formal training

## KEY COMPETITORS

Hay Group
Hewitt Associates
Mercer Human Resources Consulting
Segal
Towers Perrin
Watson Wyatt Worldwide

## EMPLOYMENT CONTACT

Job postings list job-specific
contacts; see:
www.milliman.com/careers/
    job_postings_by_title.asp
Send resumes at
www.milliman.com/careers/
    apply_for_a_position.asp

# THE SCOOP

## Rainy day people

Milliman got its start on a (presumably rainy) day in Seattle in 1947. Today, the firm has more than 1,700 employees in 35 U.S. cities.

Milliman USA employs a wide assortment of experts: actuaries, accountants, medical-savvy professionals, legal diehards, marketing whizzes and IT superstars. Those experts handle the core four practices: life insurance (mergers, demutualizations, product design), property and casualty insurance, employee benefits (defined benefit pensions, multi-employer/public plan practices, 401(k) administration and investment) and health care. About half of Milliman's $324 million in 2002 revenue came from the employee benefits group, 30 percent from the insurance and finance practice, and 20 percent from the health care practice. Milliman has worked on more than 75 percent of all life insurance industry mergers and has worked for more than 80 percent of the largest property and casualty insurers.

In May 2003, Milliman USA acquired IBM Business Consulting Services' Insurance Actuarial Software group, which makes valuation software for insurers. In November 2002, it acquired the institutional investment firm Dorn, Helliesen & Cottle.

## Going global

In May 2001, what was then Milliman & Robertson joined with 22 similar firms – all actuarial and consulting – to form a worldwide partnership called Milliman Global. The Yankee branch dropped the "& Robertson" and rebranded as Milliman USA. With more than 100 offices in more than 30 countries, the global operation had revenues of $432 million in 2002 and 2,800 employees. Given its global partnerships, Milliman has been involved in a number of cross-border deals: restructuring Lloyd's of London, consulting for Japanese life insurance companies and, the firm claims, "the first insurance actuarial assignment in China."

# GETTING HIRED

Milliman posts jobs on its web site; candidates can submit their resumes at http://www.milliman.com/careers/apply_for_a_position.asp. "Referrals are a major source of new employees," reveals one source. And since the company hires "as needed," recruiting "varies by office, but not much goes on."

# OUR SURVEY SAYS

## Celebrating culture

Milliman consultants rate its culture as tops, especially lauding its "flexibility" and the "challenge" of working there. The company is "active in community projects." Once at Milliman, consultants are promoted "based on performance;" degrees like an MBA are "irrelevant, since we are actuaries." The company "fosters promotion from within," says one source. However, there is reported to be a "lack of structured training." Work hours range from 45 to 60 hours a week, spiking about four times a month. Travel is fairly minimal, hovering around zero to two days per week for those we surveyed.

## Rounding it out

Perks include a "quite generous" "profit sharing plan" that comes out to "10 percent of compensation plus an employer match." Other cushy plusses include accidental death/dismemberment, long-term disability coverage, an employee assistance program and an employee referral bonus. Offices are reported to be just fine, and that's OK with insiders; you "wouldn't want [them] too luxurious," says one penny-conscious source.

"You know what people do, there are no politics, you perform and you get rewarded for it."

— *Novantas associate*

# Novantas

100 Park Avenue
New York, NY 10017
Phone: (212) 953-4444
Fax: (212) 972-4602
www.novantas.com

## LOCATIONS

**New York, NY (HQ)**
Singapore
Toronto

## PRACTICE AREAS

Banking
Brokerage
Information Services
Insurance
Telecom
Utility Services

## THE STATS

**Employer Type:** Private Company
**Firm leadership:** Run by partnership
of 15

## UPPERS

- Lots of contact with partners
- Structured, meritocratic promotion
  process

## DOWNERS

- Lack of brand recognition
- Weekend work is expected

## KEY COMPETITORS

Bain & Company
Booz Allen Hamilton
First Manhattan Consulting Group
Greenwich Associates

## EMPLOYMENT CONTACT

E-Mail: resumes@novantas.com

## THE BUZZ
### WHAT CONSULTANTS AT OTHER FIRMS ARE SAYING

- "Good boutique, young crowd"
- "Too small"

# THE SCOOP

## Holding itself accountable

In October 1999, senior partners from Bain, Booz Allen Hamilton, and First Manhattan Consulting ditched their old gigs and banded together to launch Novantas in New York City. The partners all had backgrounds in financial services and wanted to start a consultancy with higher accountability and more quantitative results than traditional consultancies offered. "We develop agreed metrics in advance, and we gauge success based on these measures. We try to tie the measures to those that the market judges [clients] by," the firm says. What's more, Novantas' billing structure is based on the results it gets for the client – so the firm has a big incentive to get things right the first time.

Initially, Novantas' offerings focused on Internet strategy for financial firms. Today, Novantas' clients also include insurers, utilities, and telecom companies. The firm, which has expanded from five to 60 professionals, counts 50 international clients.

## Working in tandem

Novantas takes an "insider" tack to consulting, operating in teams with the client. The company treats each engagement like a full-time job. This starts with the "job interview" (the pitch meeting) and carries through outlining the project (the job description), starting the work (introducing Novantas as the client would introduce a new employee) and evaluating the work (regular performance reviews). There's also a focus on mentoring. Novantas has a 6:1 ratio of management to staff, allowing younger employees to have personal relationships with directors and partners. Teams are led by managing directors, and range from two to eight consultants in size.

## Venture services

Novantas Ventures focuses on turnarounds for financial firms. It offers advice in areas including screening and due diligence, management, credit evaluation, finance, operations, technology and legal/regulatory, along with connecting banks to financing (Novantas has a group of investors committed to venture investment).

## Company chat

The company has a password-protected idea exchange center on its site. Here, clients can read articles and opinion pieces from consultants, look at strategies Novantas has used with past clients, or get information on industries. There's also a message board where clients can critique in-process articles or discuss current events and issues affecting their work.

## Technology in focus

Novantas has developed several software products. Call center products include those focused on retention (e.g., customizing phone reps' scripts to be effective with various demographics), leads (a browser program for reps that screens and profiles potential leads and selects the most appropriate pitch), productivity and service-linked selling (converting customer service calls into sales calls, again, by selection of the best script). In September 2002, it allied with StarTek, further rounding out its call center outsourcing products and services.

One product of interest to potential bankers is Market$im, a popular tool that simulates life in the banking world, having players (usually students studying banking) work in teams to develop marketing, management, pricing and other strategies for their faux retail banks.

## GETTING HIRED

What is Novantas looking for in new hires? In its own words: "high 'get-it' quotient (i.e., are you smart?)," "obsession with problem solving," "comfort in the absence of structure," "intense self-discipline and intellectual productivity," objectivity, determination, "social grace, confidence and interests (are you fun to be with?)," demonstrated achievement and "decisiveness (can you draw conclusions without waiting for all of the data?)." According to one insider, Novantas recruits on campus at "almost exclusively Ivy League schools; in 2002, it was Yale, Harvard, Penn, Cornell and Columbia." However, "we have not been doing graduate recruiting" for MBAs.

Advanced degrees are not necessary, though many staff members have an MBA or master's. For more senior positions, consulting experience is quite helpful. Hiring is competitive. "We shoot for classes of 10 to 15 people, so we basically took two or three from each top school last year," notes one source.

## The process

A phone call from a junior employee – outlining the recruiting process – comes first. Then, midlevel employees conduct interviews on campus, looking for problem solving skills. Case questions make up the bulk of these interviews. The interviewer is looking for a specific approach (not to be confused with a specific answer – there is usually more than one correct solution). Applicants need to show they understand the problem, outline a framework for analysis, come up with a hypothesis, use analytical techniques and basic business concepts to tackle the problem and come up with a creative, convincing answer. Novantas says its cases are not riddles – there won't be hidden information the interviewer hasn't revealed. More guidelines, along with examples of cases, are available on Novantas' web site (see www.novantas.com/joinus/case.htm).

Candidates who pass the case round are invited to the New York office for final interviews. They meet members of the company and interview with one or more partners. This is the chance for candidates to ask questions about the firm and for the company "to assess the candidate's quantitative and qualitative skills." "On Super Saturday, [candidates] have four case study interviews back to back. The goal is to be very intense and make sure that a lot of people have seen them, and we make sure we have some time to talk to them," says an insider.

Summer interns are selected in a similar manner, except that associates handle everything but the final rounds. Would be interns apply through Jobtrak or similar sites, and the associates choose "30 or so that we're interested in, then call them and interview them." Interns go through a "two-part interview process that takes between 30 and 45 minutes; the first is a qualitative/behavioral interview with brainteaser questions, and the second is a case study." The associates select a handful of candidates for review by a manager or principal, who makes the final decision.

## What Novantas wants

While interviewers are "not necessarily looking for technical skills," "analytics and creativity" count for a lot. "In strategy consulting for the financial services industry, it's necessary to have a strong quantitative background and do analytical thinking. The real key is when you get into case study questions. We're looking to see how you think, analyze, lay out and dissect. If you get it wrong, that's okay, but we have to understand why you got it wrong," says a source. This insider suggests candidates "be very structured" in approaching case studies. Some brainteaser questions are also thrown in, such as "How fast does the earth travel around the sun?" or "What is the angle between the hour and minute hand of the clock at 9:45?"

A personable approach is also important. "Our goal is to get [new associates] on the client site with us, so they need to be client-facing, and being able to interact is a bare minimum. One of the requirements is, 'Can I picture myself in six months leaving this person on a client site for a couple of days to collect data?'" says one source. Or, as another consultant puts it, candidates must pass the Pittsburgh airport test: "Would I want to spend six hours in the Pittsburgh airport with this person?"

No single major rules. "We've ended up getting a handful of liberal arts folks that really impress people with their get-it factor," says an insider, "and we have brought in everything from applied math to operational research majors."

# OUR SURVEY SAYS

## Size doesn't matter, really

Tiny Novantas flies under the radar, which is "both a benefit and a drawback," says one source. "You probably have a lesser known brand than the next place." However, adds another consultant, "we're growing, so there's no intent to stay small forever and there are great benefits. We all know each other, and it's a meritocracy – because it's small, there's no bull. You know what people do, there are no politics, you perform and you get rewarded for it." One associate notes Novantas is "an hourglass-shaped organization (as opposed to the dreaded pyramid, or worse, inverted pyramid), with a lot of partners and associates but not a huge middle management layer. This means we have a great associate class: very young, very intellectual and very close. We all go out at least once a week. At the same time we get a lot of direct exposure to senior partners."

## Seeing it through

The culture is "collegial and very ambitious" and "definitely intense," sources say. The people are "very smart and fun." "Our mission is around what we call applied customer science, which is marketing strategy and application. We're not a strategy company that sits in New York and hands off a document," summarizes one source. "Instead we have projects from three months up to a year where we really help the client apply it. It doesn't mean we're implementation experts, but we stick around while the implementation goes through."

## Road rules

Novantas consultants travel, and travel a lot. "You're definitely expected to be willing to travel up to 100 percent. But because we are about 70 percent financial services, a good portion of clients are in New York City," says a source. "You generally travel Tuesday through Thursday, with Monday and Friday in the office," reports one consultant. "There are some projects where you're out four or five days a week for a month, and some where you're at the site just three or four times over six months," reports another source.

That can mean a lot of time away from the office, which in New York is "right up by Grand Central," and is set up "in offices, not cubes, with two people per office."

## Everybody's working for the weekend

Hours usually range from 60 to 70 a week, going as low as the high 40s or up to "80-plus or 90 on crazy weeks." Consultants can expect to be on the beach for "four weeks out of 52," but even then hours "vary depending on pitches" you're working on.

Meanwhile, "weekend work is a part of life. It's not expected every single weekend, but when you're on a project, it is expected." And it's not just lower-level employees: "If we have to work weekends, it's rare that we don't have one day off. And the partners, who all have families, don't say on Friday 'this is what I need' and disappear until Monday morning; they'll take time out of their family lives on Sundays" to come in.

Partners are still, by all reports, fun-loving folks. "One partner is a heavy sailing guy, so we pull the 70-hour weeks, and on Sunday we go sailing on Long Island Sound." Another consultant echoes this, saying "We try to balance work with social activities. There's a soccer league with a Novantas team, so every Tuesday 10 people go and play at Chelsea Piers." In sum, as one source says, "I don't know if the work/life balance is healthy, but it's fun."

## Staffing decisions

Analysts are quite involved with clients from the start. "We're very on-the-ground with our analysts. You pull them into the client site, they learn and are part of the team, and we often leave the analysts" to deal with clients on site, says a source. Teams are generally three to four people, and "analysts are staffed on one project at a time, managers staffed on one and a half or two, and principles are staffed on two to four."

## Advancing associates

Each associate is assigned a managing director to whom he or she reports. "They make sure we're busy, and when we're on the beach we'll go to them and help them with a proposal." The assigned MD is in the room during the reviews. Reviews are "given by someone who you've never worked for, who does a 360-degree interview process. They'll interview other associates you've worked with" along with superiors.

Sources describe the promotion process as fair. "It's the purest meritocracy that I've ever been a part of," says one source. "Reviews are really well structured because they're really comprehensive; they rate you precisely on your skill sets, like spreadsheets or databases or communication or presentation, along with overall feedback on strengths and what you need to improve on," reports one insider. Consultants can expect "one and a half to two years to become a senior associate, at which point it's another year or two to become a manager." There's not an "up-or-out point, but there's definitely a drive – we're willing to promote everybody in a class if they're all doing well. While we don't tell people they have to go, after two years they weed themselves out pretty well."

## On-point managers

In addition to the assigned MD, each associate gets a mentor at the manager or principal level. "You're probably already friends with your mentor, so it's very easy to go up and say, 'I'm having a problem with this,' or 'I'm running into a partner on this issue.'"

Managers in general receive good comments. "Throughout a project, some managers will manage you differently. Some will be very specific about, 'This is the right way to do this thing,' while others will gently guide you more by example."

## Bonus time

Salaries at Novantas "fall on the high end," and are described as "pretty good, but not the best." Thus, "in the first couple of years [compensation equals] salary with a healthy bonus proportion." Afterward, "as you hit manager, principal and especially higher levels, the bonus becomes much more substantial." One source reports the "first-year bonus is up to a third of your salary, and it jumps up pretty significantly from there." Benefits include standard health, cell phones, Internet access at home, laptops, payment for dinner and cabs home after 8:00 p.m. and some compensation for relevant books or materials.

## Learning fast

Training at Novantas has been "in development over the last three years, and we've brought in flavors of what folks have experienced at other places." This year, training included a "three-day workshop off site with the whole new analyst class" with "a focus on technical skills – getting people up to speed on hardcore math and business/financial" material. Also, "there's a managerial training plan in place, which is for once people get to senior associate." "We'll basically have some type of training every six weeks" after that, notes one source, which can be "a self-study course or a core class we'll be teaching, taught by more senior associates with subjects like finance accounting, financial services or banking industry overviews."

## A slight imbalance

We hear the racial diversity at Novantas is about average. "There are several ethnicities, but the majority of people are Caucasian, though not by a huge amount," says a source. As for women, diversity is temporarily out of whack in 2003. "Several females left to work elsewhere. It's happenstance right now – it's never been like this before," says a source. "I don't think it was that we pushed them out. I don't think it's an intimidating place to work." While Novantas doesn't have an old-boys feel, this source says, "it has a sports team feel. Women working here tend to be pretty athletic with strong personalities."

# R.B. Webber & Company

2637 Marine Way, Suite 100
Mountain View, CA 94043
Phone: (650) 903-7500
Fax: (650) 903-7575
www.rbwebber.com

## LOCATIONS

**Mountain View, CA (HQ)**

## PRACTICE AREAS

Strategy
Technology

## THE BUZZ
#### WHAT CONSULTANTS AT OTHER FIRMS ARE SAYING

• "Small, nice, high-level"
• "Pure strategy"

# THE SCOOP

## The fountain of consulting youth

R.B. Webber is young – the firm is less than a decade old, and half of the consultants are under 27. The firm advises its Silicon Valley neighbors on management and tech strategy. Its client base ranges from start-ups to large public companies, and its expertise is in the technology field. Internet/e-commerce, software, wireless data and services, computer hardware and electronics, telecom and networking equipment are all part of R.B. Webber's repertoire, along with financial services, medical devices and biotechnology.

While R.B. Webber focuses on technology, it's the business end of technology on which the company's foundation lies; they wouldn't implement a software system, for example. Cases are relatively short (eight to 12 weeks) and usually concern a "big picture" issue: i.e., market strategies, figuring out price points or advising on mergers and acquisitions.

## Spinoff city

Two affiliates of Webber include The Entrepreneurs' Funds and BCG ValueScience Center LLC. The Entrepreneurs' Funds is a venture capital investing practice that has put more than $150 million into high-tech (and mostly client) companies. Some of the companies it's invested in include AvantGo, CommerceOne, Intraware, Persistence and Sagent. ValueScience took shape when Webber found itself providing custom valuations to dozens of clients; it standardized those valuations to help link market dynamics and company performance to valuation. These analyses help execs and investors get a sense of how a company is doing and guide management and investment decisions.

# GETTING HIRED

Looking to work at Webber? You'll probably have to start with a college transfer application. Webber recruits exclusively at Harvard, Stanford, Yale and MIT. "We only hire out of four schools; I think that's pretty darn selective," says one analyst. Applicants can expect three rounds of interviews, the final one performed by the firm's managing director. "There's one recruiting cycle each year to bring in a new class of analysts in the fall," says a respondent. And "at least some of the interviews will be a case, usually about a technology company" or "based on recent client work," say sources.

"We're looking for very smart, entrepreneurial people with backgrounds in finance and technology. Independent thinkers and leaders are especially appreciated," says an analyst. Business or engineering majors are preferred, but not required. If you didn't concentrate in one of those subjects, your extracurricular activities and/or previous work experience should show a fascination with the business of technology. "Culture is really important to Webber, so when candidates are assessed for hire 'firm fit' is very important," says a source.

# SURVEY SAYS

## A tight-knit group

R.B. Webber seems to promote a chummy atmosphere among its analysts. "The junior staff is tightknit, and hosts many extracurricular activities," says one young analyst. It's not just lip service; another agrees, "we have a pretty strong analyst culture – we all tend to hang out together during lunches and weekends." Analyst activities such as hiking or skiing trips are commonplace.

That bond helps fortify what one employee calls the company's "strong work/life balance." Also helping: the fact that "almost all the clients are in Silicon Valley, which means less travel" – virtually none outside the Bay Area. One analyst reports having to travel only twice since starting at Webber a year ago. And, adds another analyst, "our model is not one that places consultants on-site at the client." Even at the higher levels, sources say local travel is the norm. "As a principal, my challenge is to find local clients; to the degree I am successful in this, the less I travel," says one higher-up.

## No face time

Employees are generally very happy with their hours. "As with all types of consulting, we have ups and downs – I have been here until two in the morning (but only once in my six months of work here), and most of the time am able to fit everything into a 60-hour week, which is amazing in the consulting world," says a source. Most report working between 50 and 55 hours a week. "The firm culture is very flexible in terms of hours and vacation. As long as you do your work well, no one expects you to put in 'face time,'" says an analyst. There's a "good attitude overall that this is not a 24/7 job. Work hard, do your work well, and have a life."

Consultants may have a life, but they don't have downtime. "Since we are staffed on two projects at a time, it is very rare that we will ever be 'on the beach.' This can be tough because we don't get breathing room between projects, but nice because we don't get stuck working on the same thing every day," says a respondent.

## Making contact

Webber gets praise for letting junior employees work directly with partners and clients. "Often it will only be an analyst, manager and partner on a case and I will be working with a partner every day. I feel lucky that I can walk into almost any partner's office any time I want – I know that my friends at other consulting firms can't do this," says one junior analyst. Another says there's "a lot of exposure" to both clients and partners, even for entry-level analysts.

## Managing up

Junior employees say they hold management in high regard, calling their supervisors "intelligent," "competent," and "nicer than any of the partners I used to work with at my former firm (a traditional global strategy consulting firm)." Since many of Webber's senior employees started out as analysts, they have empathy for the junior employees, say respondents. "Partners really care about developing their employees," says one insider. "They know how to work with analysts well," agrees another consultant. "Oftentimes they were analysts themselves so they can talk 'at our level' and know what to expect from us." "Managers come from the ranks of the junior staff and are in touch with the reality of the work," says one source. One consultant goes so far as to say there's "lots of love here." Most of the senior staff were partners or consultants at top consulting firms like Bain, McKinsey and BCG or executives at Fortune 500 companies before joining R.B. Webber.

## No degree necessary

The fact that so many partners and managers were junior employees also speaks to Webber's "meritocratic, not rigid at all" promotion policy. "The meritocratic system ensures supervisors that one respects," assesses one respondent. MBAs are not necessary for MBA-level positions. "Analysts have been promoted to manager after proven competency and a certain number of years with the firm," says a respondent. Another source says analysts should expect three to four years of hard work before moving to an engagement manager position. Of course, the MBA won't hurt consultants any; the firm is home to many MBA graduates, mainly from Harvard and Stanford.

## The salary tradeoff

One area where employees aren't quite as happy with Webber is in its salaries. "Our salary is on the low side for consulting firms, but we argue that we make up for that with the experience and type of work analysts get to do. And we have good hours," says a source. Another reports that compensation usually runs 25 percent below larger consulting firms, but "it is made up with quality of life factors and the learning opportunities that the firm provides." The firm counters that its salaries run roughly five to 10 percent below the industry standard.

Managers, principals and partners can participate in the firm's affiliated venture fund. Moreover, "principal/partner compensation is directly tied to revenue production and billing. I wholeheartedly support this. It reinforces the belief that results matter," says a principal/partner.

Benefits include an on-site gym, dry cleaners, disability and accidental-death coverage, an employee lounge area and free snacks. One unusual perk: Consultants are invited to wine tastings at the founder's Napa vineyard!

## Frugal feel

Webber's Mountain View digs draw middling responses from employees, who bemoan the suburban location and long commute from San Francisco, where many of them live. "The location of our office is tough," groans one consultant. Inside, employees say the office is bare bones, though "we all have our own cubes and enough space." Another describes the philosophy behind the spartan decor, saying, "We're not into fancy furniture and amenities like that. We share the frugal start-up mentality of many of our clients who are tech start-ups."

## Hit the ground running

Training at Webber is mostly on the job, which works decently, most analysts say. "We had training in the summer when we started and will have occasional updates throughout the year," says one analyst. Continues another, "On-the-case training is huge – managers are constantly making sure that we are really learning from the work that we are doing." The lack of training is a problem for some, though. "Part of being a small firm means you lack the scale and infrastructure to develop really robust training programs," says a respondent. First-year associates' main responsibility: presentations. That means researching, interviewing, doing financial modeling, attending conferences and working with a case team to figure out a solution. Associates work directly on client teams – and never just one.

## More women needed

"The firm is definitely male-heavy. We are trying to change that with future recruiting efforts but it is something we need to work on. There is no preference for men, but the people we end up hiring tend to be men," says a source, adding that out of eight analysts, three are women. Moreover, there's "not much female representation at the top, but women are afforded the same opportunities as men in the firm," says another. And while there are a number of Asian and Indian employees, "we have had limited success attracting African Americans," says a respondent.

# Right Management Consultants

1818 Market Street
33rd Floor
Philadelphia, PA 19103-3614
Phone: (215) 988-1588
www.right.com

## LOCATIONS

**Philadelphia, PA (HQ)**
More than 300 U.S.-based and
international offices

## PRACTICE AREAS

Career Transition
Executive Coaching and Assessment
Leadership Development
Organizational Consulting:
Organizational Performance
Talent Management

## THE STATS

**Employer Type:** Public Company
**Stock Symbol:** RHT
**Stock Exchange:** NYSE
**Chairman and CEO:** Richard J. Pinola
**2002 Employees:** 3,000
**2002 Revenue:** $472.1 million

## UPPERS

- Pleasant work environment
- Emphasis on employee
  development

## DOWNERS

- Emphasis on making financial
  numbers
- Pressure to work long hours

## KEY COMPETITORS

Hewitt Associates
Mercer Management Consulting
Towers Perrin

## EMPLOYMENT CONTACT

E-mail: careers@right.com

## THE BUZZ
### WHAT CONSULTANTS AT OTHER FIRMS ARE SAYING

- "Great 'people' guys"
- "Worked with them – useless"

# THE SCOOP

## When you're right, you're Right

For over two decades, Philadelphia-based Right Management Consultants has been an aide to clients in times of trouble, stepping in when companies lay off people (they're the ones hovering about the conference room, severance information in hand) and offering career consulting. Services include talent management, transition leadership development and organizational performance.

Right's career transition services begin before layoffs or firings. It designs a program for terminating employees, coordinates how employees will be notified, coaches managers on how to proceed, helps prepare PR statements explaining why the layoffs occurred, and connects ex-employees with Right's services. Employers can then track how (and what) the laid off employees are doing via Right.

Its organizational consulting services also center around people and their careers. Along with organizational performance, Right specializes in leadership development (assessing and coaching leaders) and talent management (selecting talent, managing performance, developing careers, retaining high performers and managing succession).

## The art of layoffs

Right also publishes a number of research studies. The best known is the quarterly "Career Confidence Index" report. This report measures how employees feel about their career prospects and the job market at large, through a survey of 500 to 1,000 full-time workers in 17 countries. Other reports include "Global Severances Practice Survey," "Lessons Learned from Mergers & Acquisitions: Best Practices in Workforce Integration," "PeopleBrand" and "Retaining Employees During Critical Organizational Transitions."

## Turning tides

The firm can speak with personal authority on some of these topics, having recently undertaken several acquisitions which led to organizational transitions. In March 2002, Right acquired Coutts Consulting Group from 3i (a European venture capital company) for $105 million. The acquisition of Coutts, Europe's biggest career consulting firm, gave Right increased presence in Europe and Canada, and bumped the firm up to a second place position in the Japanese market. Also in 2002, Right acquired ADC in the Netherlands and Aston Promentor in Denmark.

Right has also recently launched two new practices. In September 2002, it added a global practice for aviation, aerospace, defense and related technologies; in April 2003, it created an "agility practice" that helps companies in flux (broadly defined to cover everything from responding to competitive pressures to implementing new software to managing a merger) define goals and manage their way through the change.

## A good report card

All this change seems to be benefiting the company. Right snagged the No. 5 spot on *Forbes*' 2002 list of the 200 Best Small Companies, based (most likely) on its 126 percent EPS year-over-year and its five-year average EPS growth rate of 44 percent. The firm was also reported to have sales growth over the previous twelve months of 71 percent and a five-year average sales increase of 22 percent.

Indeed, recent financial results back up its placement on *Forbes*' list. While many consulting firms struggled in the soggy economy, Right thrived. Revenues for the year climbed 48 percent, from $315.4 million in 2001 to $466.3 million in 2002. Profits doubled, going from $19.2 million to $38.3 million. Career transition services accounted for over 80 percent of the company's revenues, with the remainder coming from its consulting offerings. The career transition group delighted in record revenue growth, with revenues increasing 52 percent during 2002, while organizational consulting revenues grew 38 percent.

## GETTING HIRED

Insiders note that the way to get a foot in the door is "mostly by references and recommendations." The interview process includes "use of assessment instruments" including, one source says, "psychometric profiling." Candidates "must have the relevant experience, qualifications and maturity as prerequisites. The ability to bring in business is another plus." One insider advises that "consultants must have an MS degree, and most organizational consultants have doctoral degrees (in counseling, psychology, etc.)"

# OUR SURVEY SAYS

## The Right approach

Employees rate themselves as quite satisfied with life at Right: "It is an extremely pleasant place to work with openminded people; it's progressive and understanding." "The environment is superb." "There are quality people and interesting clients."

However, an unwanted focus on the bottom line was reported. "The consultants and staff are bright, caring people," says one source, "in an uptight, accounting-dominated organization." A different source reports there is a "stress of selling and making numbers as a publicly traded company."

While "quality varies widely" among supervisors, they get moderately high marks. There are "highly professional [supervisors] who are constantly transferring their knowledge and experience to their employees," notes one consultant. Another source finds that "superiors are very competent and are willing to share their knowledge." And a third insider notes, "My boss/supervisor travels excessively and therefore I have a free hand to manage the business."

## Production line

While "the company leaves employees free to use their time," there is said to be "a lot of pressure to produce and lots of weekend and night work. It's tough on relationships." Hours are reportedly "an average of 40 hours a week," though "it depends on the week's demand." Meanwhile, travel is not too demanding: "full-time organizational consultants travel approximately two days per week."

Training is said to be quite good. "In three years with the firm, I received more relevant training than I did in the previous 17 years," says one source. Offices are also said to be good, "very nice" in Houston especially.

The firm is involved in community service, offering "pro bono outplacement services to companies that go under, when hundreds of employees are 'thrown out' without any support. It's also very supportive of community work."

## Bonusless

Salaries are rated fairly high, though there is reportedly "no other compensation" besides the salary check. Benefits include accidental death/dismemberment coverage, long-term disability insurance, free cell phones and laptops, sports/theater tickets and some profit sharing.

# The Segal Company

One Park Avenue
New York, NY 10016
Phone: (212) 251-5000
www.segalco.com

## LOCATIONS

**New York, NY (HQ)**
Atlanta, GA • Boston, MA •
Chicago, IL • Cleveland, OH •
Denver, CO • Hartford, CT •
Houston, TX • Los Angeles, CA •
Minneapolis, MN • New Orleans, LA
• Philadelphia, PA • Phoenix, AZ •
Pittsburgh, PA • Princeton, NJ •
Raleigh, NC • San Francisco, CA •
Seattle, WA • Washington, DC •
London • Toronto

## PRACTICE AREAS

Administration and Technology
  Consulting
Corporate Consulting/Public Sector
  Consulting/Taft-Hartley Plan
  Consulting
Communications Consulting
Human Resources Consulting
(Sibson
  Consulting)
Investment Consulting (Segal
  Advisors)

## THE STATS

**Employer Type:** Private Company
**CEO:** Howard Fluhr
**2002 Employees:** 1,000
**2001 Employees:** 750

## UPPERS

• Don't have to advance to stay at
  firm
• Good benefits and work/life
  balance

## DOWNERS

• Promotion criteria unclear
• Firm policies somewhat
  intransigent

## KEY COMPETITORS

Hay Group
Hewitt Associates
Mercer Human Resources Consulting
Milliman Global
Towers Perrin
Watson Wyatt Worldwide

## EMPLOYMENT CONTACT

www.segalco.com/careers/opportunit
ies.html

## THE BUZZ
WHAT CONSULTANTS AT OTHER FIRMS ARE SAYING

• "Great benefits"
• "Getting smaller, backwards"

# THE SCOOP

## A long history

Back in 1939, when employee benefit plans were just becoming part of the American corporate landscape, the Segal Company established itself as an actuarial and consulting firm. Today, many benefit plans have roots in Segal's early work. Segal's clients employ more than eight million employees worldwide, primarily in the United States and Canada but also in Puerto Rico, the Virgin Islands, the Bahamas and Europe.

## All about the employee

Segal has practices in three areas: corporate and nonprofit, public sector (local, state and federal governments, state retirement systems and health plans, and other governmental agencies) and multiemployer (that is, benefit plans jointly administered by labor and management trustees; Segal's clients in this area include national, regional, state and local funds in a wide variety of industries). Segal consulting focuses on employee benefit, compensation and human resources matters.

## You must comply

Segal does not have a law practice, though it works with clients through its compliance practice to make certain all applicable laws and regulations affecting benefit plans are carefully followed. Compliance consultants also provide a separate service called CrosscheckSM, which checks a client's administrative procedures and plan operations to make sure the plan is in compliance.

Segal stays on top of the information game with publications, seminars and workshops. Its publications include newsletters produced for each market it serves covering benefits, compensation and HR issues, bulletins (news about major regulatory or compliance changes), and other electronic publications, including periodic surveys on benefits and HR issues. Seminars and workshops are held regularly to address news or legislation in the benefits arena, and clients are welcome to attend.

## A plethora of affiliations

Two affiliations in particular give Segal a global reach. The first is membership in the Multinational Group of Actuaries and Consultants (MGAC), a group of independent consultancies that share advice, resources and best practices to help with the international benefits planning needs of their clients. The second is with Polak International Consultants, Inc., an HR consultancy with an international focus.

The company is also an active member of many, many other groups including the American Benefits Council, the College and University Professionals Association, the Employee Benefit Research Institute, the Employers Council on Flexible Compensation, the Government Finance Officers Association, the International Foundation of Employee Benefit Plans, the National Association of State Retirement Administrators, the National Coordinating Committee for Multiemployer Plans, the Profit Sharing Council of America, the Society of Human Resource Managers, SPARK (the Society of Professional Administrators and Recordkeepers), the State and Local Government Benefit Association and WEB, a Working in Employee Benefits network.

## Subsidiaries and divisions

Segal has a subsidiary run separately from the parent company: Segal Advisors, an investment consultancy that offers advice to Taft-Hartley, public and corporate retirement plans. Segal Advisors' 170 clients control more than $45 billion in assets in 250 benefits plans. In January 2002, Segal acquired Sibson Consulting, a leading human capital consultancy, now run as a division of Segal.

# GETTING HIRED

## The road to Segal careers

Segal's a place where long careers are the norm – CEO Howard Fluhr started in the actuarial department in 1969. Unlike typical consulting firms, Segal's positions and prerequisites are quite diverse. College grads often start as associate analysts in areas such as health care where, for example, trainees would help managers prepare budgets and financial reports, price benefit plans and prepare bid specifications. For this position, Microsoft Office and Excel proficiency are key, as is a background in math and analytics and good communication skills. For most health care practice positions, previous health care analysis experience is also helpful. Experienced positions range from actuarial (analysts for health and retirement benefits), to consulting (on benefits programs for corporate, multiemployer or public sector clients), managering (corporate and technical staff) and compliance specialists (researching and writing about regulatory issues).

Segal does hire interns. Those interested should send a resume to intresumes@segalco.com, and should specify the location(s) they are interested in and the type of work (the kind of knowledge or skills they want to use or hone).

# OUR SURVEY SAYS

## A good balance

The atmosphere at Segal is described as "pleasant," with "the work of each individual valued." One conservative consultant says, "We are sometimes a little slow to react to change, which is also good in many respects." The firm is "involved with all kinds of community [activities] from charity runs to home development projects." A source finds that "as a privately owned consulting firm that does not answer to Wall Street, work/life balance is significantly better than at the other consulting firms. The reality of remaining competitive in terms of work product and compensation has resulted in some deterioration of the work/life balance over the past few years." Still, hours are said to hover around 45 to 50 hours a week – not bad for consulting – and travel isn't too demanding. (One source says, "I probably only need to travel away from our home area a couple times per month and generally on day trips.")

## Room for everyone

At Segal, "the promotion policy is developed to fit the individual – there is no one policy that all employees must adhere to," says an insider. "There is certainly opportunity for those consultants who want to advance, but there is a good place for those consultants who would like to find a niche and perform in that niche very well." However, one consultant calls for "more clearly defined promotion policies."

Segal has, so far, "never undergone blanket layoffs. There have been times when people were laid off for behavior or performance, but we have never, say, cut 10 percent of our workforce."

## The benefits of a benefits consultant

Fittingly for a benefits consulting company, Segal offers comprehensive benefits to its own staff. These include medical and dental coverage, life and disability insurance, tuition reimbursement, sabbaticals (eight weeks after 15 and 25 years), profit sharing (vesting at 10 percent per year, fully vested after five years), a pension plan, a retiree health plan, a reimbursement program for certain expenses (employees get a $10,000 lifetime allowance that can be used to obtain reimbursement for expenses such as health clubs, closing costs, financial planning, child care and burial), employee referral bonuses and domestic-partner coverage. A source says there are also "spot bonus awards."

# Sibson Consulting

One Park Avenue
New York, NY 10016-5895
Phone: (212) 251-5901
www.sibson.com

## LOCATIONS

**New York, NY (HQ)**
Atlanta, GA • Chicago, IL • Los
Angeles, CA • Princeton, NJ •
Raleigh, NC • San Francisco, CA •
London • Toronto

## PRACTICE AREAS

Employee Effectiveness
Leadership Performance and Rewards
Sales and Marketing

## THE STATS

**Employer Type:** Subsidiary of The
Segal Company
**Segal President & CEO:** Howard
Fluhr
**Sibson COO:** Vincent C. Perro
**2002 Employees:** 133
**2001 Employees:** 152
**2002 Revenue:** $34.4 million
**2001 Revenue:** $38.0 million

## UPPERS

• Segal alliance strengthens brand
  name, offerings

## DOWNERS

• Some culture questions post-
  integration

## KEY COMPETITORS

Hewitt Associates
Mercer Human Resources Consulting
Towers Perrin

## EMPLOYMENT CONTACT

Patty MacRae
E-mail: pmacrae@sibson.com

## THE BUZZ
WHAT CONSULTANTS AT OTHER FIRMS ARE SAYING

• "Highly professional"
• "Limited scope of practice"
• "A blue chip specialist firm"
• "Very 'niche'"

# THE SCOOP

## Sibson, Segal's baby

Sibson Consulting, a division of the Segal Company, was acquired in January 2002 from Nextera Enterprises for $16 million plus an amount based on future operating results. Sibson specializes in human capital consulting – improving performance, efficiency and motivation among employees. Segal folded its human resources innovation practice into Sibson upon purchase and brought in Nextera COO Vincent C. Perro to continue running the new division.

## All about Sibson

Sibson began more than 40 years ago as Sibson and Company, a compensation consulting firm based in collegiate Princeton, N.J. It was acquired by Nextera, another consultancy, in 1998 and sold to Segal four years later.

The company advises when a client is in a risky situation, such as acquiring or being acquired, strategically redefining itself or under performance pressure. "Sibson prides itself on delivering maximum impact in engagements with high degrees of uncertainty and risk, complex economic or employee dynamics and large scale change," the company states. The people-focused consulting leads to revenue growth, profit improvement and better customer and employee retention, according to the firm.

Financial services, professional services and health care are Sibson's specialties, though the firm consults across a wide variety of industries – more than half the Fortune 500 companies are current or former clients.

## The triumvirate

Three practices make up Sibson's human capital offerings. The first, employee effectiveness, examines what benefits (both monetary and not) can make an employee a better, more loyal, worker. Services in this area include talent management, compensation and incentives, performance management and HR department strategies.

Where employee effectiveness focuses on rank-and-file workers, the leadership performance and rewards practice looks at the top managers. How can they be retained? What are the appropriate pay vehicles for top management? Is performamce linked to strategy in ways that will help the firm succeed? Sibson offers analysis of executive compensation and benefits, assessments of what competing firms are doing and leadership coaching to answer these questions.

The third practice is sales and marketing. This group looks at the sales organization, asking how companies can achieve their financial and growth objectives. The practice looks at the company's sales organization structure and rewards strategy to ensure they match the company's business objectives. The practice also fashions customized solutions to help clients become more effective at sales.

# GETTING HIRED

## Analysis, please

Sibson is looking for candidates with strong analytical and problem solving skills, a solid business background and understanding, with good listening and communicating skills. There are four levels of positions.

Associate consultants support client teams by researching, interviewing, leading focus groups, analyzing data and presenting findings. Associates should have a strong academic background with a degree in quantitative or research curriculum, and the transcript or work history should show success in problem solving, leadership, self-management, and good oral and written communication skills.

Consultants help manage the team and the work plan to meet deadlines. They are the liaison to the client, as well as coaches to the junior employees, and perform complex analyses to find answers to client issues. Later in a consultant's career, he or she will go on business calls with principals. Consultants should be good at problem solving, analytical project management, business knowledge, organizational behavior and process facilitation. Ideally, they'll also have knowledge of strategy, human capital issues, sales and marketing consulting and/or an understanding of topics like strategic planning and pay and performance programs.

Senior consultants do the same work at a more advanced level, leading the project team, handling the client and promoting Sibson. They do high-level analysis, establish themselves as experts in their field and develop and close new business. They most often come from a consulting background, whether with Sibson, another consulting firm or internally from within a corporation.

Finally, principals are expected to do the lion's share of business development, along with making the firm visible by giving speeches and writing articles. They'll manage multiple projects at the same time, help recruit staff and conduct training. Principals will need a strong reputation in the industry, usually as a partner, with a track record of analytical, business development and consulting success, and an of-the-moment knowledge of where the industry stands today. They should be experts in one or more of the following: business strategy and implementation, human capital, sales, marketing and service strategy, channel strategy and customer segmentation, and sales force effectiveness.

# Superior Consultant Company

17570 West Twelve Mile Rd.
Southfield, MI 48076
Phone: (248) 386-8300
Fax: (248) 386-8301
www.superiorconsultant.com

## LOCATIONS

**Southfield, MI (HQ)**
Alpharetta, GA • Ann Arbor, MI •
Cheshire, CT • Pittsburgh, PA • San
Diego, CA • Woodland Hills, CA

## SERVICES

**Consulting**
Applications Delivery
Financial Systems
Strategy Formulation
Systems Integration

**Outsourcing**
Application Management
Business Process Outsourcing
Facilities Management
Full-service IT Outsourcing
Interim Management
Remote Networking and Help Desk
Services 24/7

## THE STATS

**Employer Type:** Public Company
**Stock Symbol:** SUPC
**Stock Exchange:** NASDAQ
**CEO & Director:** Richard D. Helppie Jr.
**2002 Employees:** 586
**2001 Employees:** 658
**2002 Revenue:** $84.1 million
**2001 Revenue:** $86.7 million

## UPPERS

- "Casual work environment"
- Recent big contracts

## DOWNERS

- Limited international opportunities
- Health care concentration not ideal
  for consultants craving cross-
  industry assignments

## KEY COMPETITORS

Cap Gemini Ernst & Young
Computer Sciences Corporation
Electronic Data Systems
First Consulting Group

## EMPLOYMENT CONTACT

E-mail:
recruiting@superiorconsultant.com
www.superiorconsultant.com/
    Company/careers.asp

**THE BUZZ**
WHAT CONSULTANTS AT OTHER FIRMS ARE SAYING

- "Boutique health care IT"
- "Healthy"

# THE SCOOP

## What a name!

Some firms are named for their founders or their primary practice areas. Others are named to evoke certain concepts, or just because the name sounds good. Superior Consultant Company appears to be named for direct marketing: "Our consultants are the best – just look at our name." The company may not be the biggest (586 employees, $84.1 million in revenue for 2002), and best is a nebulous concept, but Superior has a winning attitude. Superior's credo is "Superior Knowledge, Solutions, Value and Results," which it abbreviates as KSVR.

Superior is the primary operating subsidiary of Superior Consultant Holdings Corporation, incorporated in October 1996, of which CEO Richard Helppie owns 30 percent. Helppie founded Superior as a solo practicioner in 1984. Today, Superior works with health care industry clients, connecting online technology to traditionally offline business processes. Services include business process and IT outsourcing as well as management and IT consulting services to health care organizations with a strategic focus on hospital systems and integrated delivery networks. The firm claims to have served over 3,000 clients as of May 2003.

## Health care for health care

Increasingly, health care organizations have faced increasing scrutiny over issues of patient safety, privacy, security, financial performance and clinical excellence. Superior's services are designed to give clients in every sector of the industry the sorts of tools and strategies they need to serve customers effectively, improve the quality and safety of clinical care, secure and authenticate online health care transactions, reduce costs, and ensure compliance with evolving government and industry regulations, including Health Insurance Portability and Accountability Act of 1996 (HIPAA) regulations.

HIPAA calls for administrative simplification in order to allow patients better control over their own records, as well as better access for the physicians they choose. The act also includes numerous provisions to protect patients' privacy rights.

## Internal medicine

Superior enjoyed growth for 15 consecutive years following its founding in 1984. In 1999, however, the health care industry was shaken by new government regulations. The Balanced Budget Act and HIPAA put significant pressure on health care providers' financial performance and operational expectations. Players in the industry fought to remain viable and competitive in the changed environment.

The shakeup affected Superior as well. The health care industry slid into recession. Health care consulting firms, computer services organizations, general consulting firms – all faced a tough, competitive market. Health care organizations suffered – and Superior suffered along with them. From a high of $149.4 million in fiscal 1999, Superior has seen its net revenues slide to $84.1 million in fiscal 2002. The firm also shed more than 80 consultants during 2002, bringing the headcount down to 586.

## On the mend

Superior started a reorganization in 2001 to meet the challenges of the extant environment in the health care industry. CEO Helppie added a new chairman, president and CFO to his team. Superior has also flattened the organization, eliminating layers so as to more nimbly deploy the talents of Superior consultants. The firm has also embarked on research and development designed to better align Superior services and solutions with the challenges facing the health care industry. The 2002 layoffs were part of this strategy as well; laid off consultants were offered outplacement, retraining, extended benefits and severance.

In early 2003, Superior completed a rotation of its board chairman position, appointing director John L. Silverman as chairman. Silverman, an independent health care consultant and a member of the board since 1997, serves on four other corporate boards and is the former CEO of health investment firm AsiaCare Inc.

A few months later, in June 2003, the firm appointed a new national health care information technology adviser. Walter C. Zerrenner, recently senior vice president and CIO of New York Presbyterian Hospitals, rejoined Superior after a two-year absence to take the post. Zerrenner will advise clients and perform selected strategic consultations interim management (read outsourcing) engagements. He will also serve as mentor to CIOs of hospitals working with Superior.

## Partnerships and deals

In 2001, Superior began a strategy of pursuing outsourcing engagements, constructing a processing center in Dearborn, Michigan for that purpose. A subsequent major development for the firm was a 10-year outsourcing engagement for Central Connecticut Health Alliance, undertaken in May 2002. The deal, valued at more than $100 million, requires Superior to supply outsourcing services for applications, data centers, desktops, networks and telecom. The CCHA project is the largest such contract in Superior's history.

Superior won another major bid in 2003, this time with Agnesian HealthCare. The Wisconsin-based nonprofit health care system selected Superior in May 2003 to fill a seven-year, $35 million total outsourcing project after a competitive bid process. According to the terms of the contract, the consultancy will provide a full network infrastructure upgrade, applications, data center, help desk and desktop services, as well as telecommunications support. Superior will also give HIPAA-related support and advice. The firm says it has $700 million in the outsourcing pipeline for 2003.

## GETTING HIRED

Superior Consultant maintains a complete list of available positions on its careers page. Applications, including a cover letter and resume, should be e-mailed to recruiting@superiorconsultant.com, referencing the listed job code for prompt consideration. Many of the company's consultants have held C-level former positions at hospitals, health plans, HMOs and universities. Superior also welcomes returning employees, which it calls "boomerangs."

# Triage Consulting Group

221 Main Street, Suite 1450
San Francisco, CA 94105
Phone: (415) 512-9400
Fax: (415) 512-9404
www.triageconsulting.com

## LOCATIONS

**San Francisco, CA (HQ)**

## PRACTICE AREAS

Contract Negotiations
Litigation Support
Managed Care Education
Managed Care Payment Reviews
and Collection
Reinsurance Audits
Risk Pool Settlement
Silent PPO Review

## THE STATS

**Employer Type:** Private Company
**Founding Principals:** Rich Griffith,
Jim Hebert, Patti Lee-Hoffman
**2002 Employees:** 130

## UPPERS

- Generous vacation policy
- Young, social employees
- 45-hour weeks the norm

## DOWNERS

- Four days' travel per week
  expected
- Offices cramped

## KEY COMPETITORS

Abt Associates
Accenture
Hewitt Associates
Kurt Salmon Associates
Mercer Human Resources Consulting

## EMPLOYMENT CONTACT

Kim Comstock
Fax: (415) 512-9404
E-mail: info@triageconsulting.com

## THE BUZZ
### WHAT CONSULTANTS AT OTHER FIRMS ARE SAYING

- "If you want to do health care, this
  is the place"
- "They get top tier kids to do 3rd
  tier work"

# THE SCOOP

## Chasing bills

Triage draws its name from the health care industry and, indeed, that's what it specializes in. Think of it as a bill collector and advice giver. In 1994, three co-founders – Rich Griffith, Jim Hebert and Patti Lee-Hoffmann – started Triage in order to offer financial advice to hospitals. In the Bay Area, virtually all hospitals are Triage clients.

Triage specializes in making people pay their bills. Hospitals hire Triage to collect on bad debts. Triage consultants review contracts and agreements to find underpayments, then tries to make those debtors pay. The consulting firm also looks at ways in which hospitals can minimize underpayments in the future. So far, Triage's managed care payment reviews have retrieved over $100 million for over 60 clients. Of that, 40 projects have brought in $500,000; 20 projects have brought in $1 million; and 12 have brought in more than $2 million. Since Triage's fee is based on how much it collects, hospitals need not pay up front.

## How it works

Triage begins by comparing managed care account data to contracts in order to find underpayments. Then the company calls and follows up until the debtor hands over the cash due. After the money is paid, Triage makes further recommendations to the client and teaches them account review and negotiating tactics. Triage also offers a number of other services, including advising on risk pool settlement, contract negotiations, silent PPO reviews, litigation support, reinsurance audits and managed care education.

## Making work fun

Triage places its consultants on-site Monday through Friday, though occasionally consultants return to Triage's California headquarters at the end of the week. In addition, instead of returning home, an employee can remain on site on Fridays and fly a friend out, or use the flight amount toward airfare for a different destination. Four weeks' vacation is standard for first-year consultants, and company outings to Giants games or the California Culinary Academy are frequent.

Triage places a heavy focus on training. Associates attend 14 training "modules" a year, which are sandwiched in between projects. New senior associates get management training, and senior associates, managers and principals often get together to listen to expert lectures and discuss the direction of the company.

# GETTING HIRED

## California recruiting

College grads at Triage start as associates. Next up on the hierarchy chain is senior associate, manager and principal. The company says candidates should have taken courses in business administration, economics, health services and/or math.

The company recruits at "mostly California schools," including, insiders say, on-campus visits to Berkeley, Stanford, UC Davis, UC Santa Barbara, UC Irvine, UC San Diego, UCLA, Santa Clara, University of San Francisco and Cal Poly. "If your school isn't approached by Triage, you have to contact the HR person with your resume. If your experiences and academic credentials match what we're looking for, you'll be contacted for on-campus interviews (or in-office interviews if you're not on the list of schools)," notes an insider.

The interview process includes a "first round for 'fit,' usually on campus," "followed by an all day on-site interview." The "second and final round" includes meeting with "principals and doing case studies, and meeting with associates as well." "It gives you a chance to meet seven to 10 people, including a couple of partners. Besides them learning about you, you get a chance to really understand what we do. After that, you're either contacted with an offer or just contacted," says a source.

Case studies are used in the second round. "The cases ask candidates to work through a typical managed care underpayment by absorbing claim information and understanding contract provisions," says one source. However, another source calls the case studies "more just a common sense math quiz." A third source summarizes, "our case question involves the bread and butter of our firm, which is conducting a review of a specific health care financial analysis on a few fake medical claims. You get walked through it, so don't worry, it's not like a tough business case."

# OUR SURVEY SAYS

## Young and healthy

Respondents commonly describe Triage as a "young, energetic firm." "The firm is a great transition from college to the working world. 95 percent of the company is in their mid- to early twenties, so that makes for a youthful, fun atmosphere," notes one consultant. The "extremely collegial" feel spills into personal life, too: "We socialize after work at happy hours, at team events when staffed out of town, and build strong friendships with co-workers. Several Triage employees even live together and travel together. Last year, a group of associates and senior associates went on safari in Africa," says another source. Triage has "a Culture Squad, as well as a Social Responsibility Squad, which plans several company events each year." The firm is described as "lively, exciting, friendly, challenging, the perfect mix of social and corporate experience!"

Despite the enthusiasm, a few respondents have complaints about the actual work at Triage. "The job can be at times tedious or repetitive," notes one insider, while another source says a downside is that "the type of work we do is very specific." Moreover, spending your day chasing delinquent health care accounts can leave you with "few transferable skills," warns another Triage pro.

## Having a life

Triage pays a great deal of attention to its employees' work/life balance, sources say. "As far as consulting goes, I think you'd be hard pressed to find a firm that has more respect for work/life balance," asserts one source. While "work/life balance varies by project," "45 to 50 hour weeks are the norm for associates and senior associates," and you "rarely work more than 50 hours per week." "Work/life balance is paramount, and whenever employees have specific needs (i.e. weddings, babies, etc), the firm always accommodates effectively," avows another employee.

Those we surveyed reported working 40 hours at the low end to 50 hours at the high end. Work is said to spike "very rarely," for although "it gets tough sometimes, everybody always helps each other get things done in time, I never feel overwhelmed." Work pace is "hard during the week, but Fridays are relaxed and everybody can make their happy hour." There is "not a lot of beach time," for there is "lots of new work," "and if there isn't, there is recruiting, etc. to be done."

## On the road again, and again...

According to our sources, travel is excessive at Triage. Almost everyone we surveyed reported being out of town four days a week, on average. "In almost three years with Triage, I have been staffed in San Francisco only once," says a source, though another consultant counters that consultants are "sometimes staffed in town for months at a time." In general, though, "we typically work Monday through Thursday on our clients' sites, many of which are in Southern California." In conclusion, "you cannot work here unless you are willing to leave town for Monday through Thursday 70 percent of the year (30 percent of clients are local)." Not surprisingly, "the travel can sometimes become tiring, especially when flying to client sites more than 1,000 miles from San Francisco." However, "you earn sabbatical time for every day you travel to use towards a LONG (i.e., months) vacation after a couple of years."

## Earned rest

The vacation policy is roundly hailed as generous. "The amount of paid time off is excellent (four weeks at the associate level), and we are allowed to 'roll over' 80 hours to the next calendar year, so it's possible to have six weeks of vacation in a given year. Also, there is a sabbatical program that allows employees to take time off between their fourth and fifth years at the company, based on how many out-of-town hours they accrued in the first four years with the company," says an insider.

## Sharing the wealth

Salary rates fairly high on the scale, sources say. "The bonus is the profit sharing," and this year, at least one associate expects his/her portion to be $10,000. A senior associate reports that "Triage provides profit sharing beginning with the first full calendar year completed. Last year, my profit sharing was 17.5 percent of my base salary. The profit sharing in 2003 may exceed the amount given in 2002. There is "no client equity or 401(k) matching" addition to almost 10 training modules tailored specifically to our managed care payment review work, the firm offered a 'mini-MBA' program to experienced senior associates last year. The courses were taught by UC Irvine professors," says a source. Another source says, "If you like training, here is the place for you. Day-long trainings every few weeks as an associate give you a chance to learn more and reunite with your new hire group."

## Fitting in

The office space seems to be a low point of life at Triage. (Get someone on that, stat!) "Our office is terrible," opines one consultant, "with low quality desks, phones, services, etc." It "can get crowded at times, but we're moving in a couple months to a much larger office," says an insider. "Since we have a Monday to Thursday travel policy and Fridays in the home office, Fridays tend to be the day where the office is most crowded," reports another source. Adds yet another consultant, "The location near the waterfront in [San Francisco's] financial district cannot be beat."

## A helping hand

Triage is said to be involved in "lots of charities," along with "many opportunities for community service, fun-runs, etc." There is "a committee dedicated to community service opportunities," which translates into "almost too many to list, but off the top of my head: We do a canned food drive every holiday season, we participate in a pen pal program with a local elementary school, we run a marathon that benefits cancer research (I think), we do work for an ecological group once a year, we do soap and shampoo drives for the homeless, we go Christmas caroling at a senior citizens home." Adds another consultant, "we do business clothing drives, adopt families at Christmas and Thanksgiving, participate in food distribution at a local shelter around Thanksgiving, field several teams of runners at the Organs 'R' Us Relay (Calistoga to Santa Cruz) every year, donate blood and register with the National Marrow Donor Program and have an active Social Responsibility Squad to look for new ways to be involved with our community." Whew.

## Development

"Responsibility comes quick" at Triage, where "associates get promoted to seniors in two years." (One and a half years "if they excel.") One source says promotion "to the manager level comes three to four years after that," though a different source puts it at four to five years. "The principal level is estimated to be five years away from that," notes an insider.

"An MBA is not necessary to be promoted – in fact, it will not help at all," one consultant notes, and another consultant adds that "there are no MBA level positions. Triage does not reward or value graduate degrees. They prefer to promote from within." However, "we've yet to promote a principal that started as an associate." The company does not currently have an up-or-out structure, but one source reveals that, "there have been associates who were 'counseled out' of the company." Another source says, "I hear that we are leaning toward instituting an unspoken up-or-out policy." The firm has managed to avoid layoffs so far. "We hired 40+ associates last year and expect to hire 35 to 40 this year."

## What women want

Triage is said to be quite women-friendly. One consultant estimates the percentage of women at two-thirds, one "the majority," one 55 to 60 percent, and one 65 to 70 percent. "Two of the five principals are women," and "of the partners, half are female, half male. Guys, where are you?"

With regard to race, the firm seems to be fairly diverse. "The firm is ethnically diverse. If we are lacking in some minority group, it is because our pool of applicants may lack that group," says one consultant. Another says "there are white, black, Latino, Asian and South Asian employees at Triage." With regard to diversity regarding gay people, though, insiders shrug. "There are no openly gay Triage employees," says a source.

# Trinity Partners, Inc.

Prospect Place
230 Third Avenue
Waltham, MA 02451-7528
Phone: (781) 487-7300
www.trinitypartners.com

## LOCATIONS

**Waltham, MA (HQ)**

## PRACTICE AREAS

Data Management
Strategy Consulting

## THE BUZZ
### WHAT CONSULTANTS AT OTHER FIRMS ARE SAYING

- "Need critical mass"
- "Emerging"

# THE SCOOP

## Focus on pharma and biotech

Founded in 1996, Trinity Partners works exclusively with health care companies – biotech, pharmaceutical and medical device firms. Clients are largely based in the Northeast, though a few are in Europe or located across the U.S.

Trinity takes a two-pronged approach to consulting, working on both strategic and data management issues for clients. Whatever the problem, data is at the heart of Trinity's solution, and consultants should be comfortable working with IT-based market analysis.

## Loyalists

As a small, rapidly growing and relatively new firm, Trinity has eschewed bureaucracy in favor of a casual environment. There's no dress code and no clock-punching, and several employees described the culture as "laid back." There is, however, hard work: Trinity demands long hours and lots of initiative from its employees. Also, don't expect a dotcom-like atmosphere – just because there's no dress code doesn't mean there are foosball tables. The combination of challenging work and a laid back atmosphere seems to be working well for Trinity, which has seen only two people leave since the company was founded.

# GETTING HIRED

Trinity recruits on campus at Harvard, Dartmouth, MIT and a few other northeastern schools. At these schools, the first round takes place on campus, followed by two to three rounds at Trinity's offices. "The later rounds consist of half-day interview sessions that test not only a candidate's intelligence and problem-solving skills, but also their potential fit into the Trinity family and lifestyle," says a staffer. Trinity also accepts e-mailed resumes, in which case the initial interview is handled over the phone.

Trinity is looking for graduates from top schools who have demonstrated quantitative ability, analytic skills and leadership experience both at school and in the workplace. Programming skills and computer proficiency are both helpful, and majors in economics or hard sciences are preferred.

Study up on the health care industry before a Trinity interview. Case questions are almost always specific to this field, focusing on market sizing, strategic problems or brain teasers. Typical questions: "Estimate for me the annual U.S. revenue produced by X drug that treats the nausea caused by chemotherapy in cancer patients," or "Why has Company X made less money than predicted on their prescription drug for osteoporosis?" One employee cautions, "We are not impressed by people who either know nothing about the industry (but you don't have to be an expert!) or who really falter on case questions. Even if you don't get the right answer, have a framework and follow it. At least you will appear more polished than a candidate who stumbles blindly around the case."

# OUR SURVEY SAYS

## Office space

Trinity moved to new offices in 2003, and the digs get high marks from employees. Each consultant gets an office (occasionally shared), there are good views and it's spacious. The office is "a great place to work," says an employee. "Tremendous," agrees another. The only drawback seems to be the Waltham address. "We don't hang out as friends enough because of our suburban location," says one employee.

## Fair pay

Trinity consultants are very happy with their salaries, and upper-level employees participate in profit sharing. "The managing partner is a very generous man and is extremely fair with compensation. I feel valued as an employee and as a person," says one consultant. The tradeoff is that "benefits are light," as one respondent says. The company matches 3 percent of 401(k) contributions, offers dental insurance and pays for half of health insurance. Material perks include free food and drinks, event tickets and laptops.

## No beach, no fun in the sun

Trinity consultants consistently harp on the two weeks' allotted vacation, especially since they are never "on the beach." Trinity is also not forthcoming enough with holiday time, report insiders. "Work hours for most staff are quite reasonable for consulting, with only a few exceptions," says one consultant, "but the subpar vacation policy and fair to average holiday schedule, coupled with typically demanding consulting work schedule, can lead to accelerated burnout for some staff."

Short vacations aside, management is reported to be sensitive to work/life balance, though the lines often blur. "Because we are a small firm, when there is work to be done, it has to be done, almost regardless of the impact that this has on life outside of work," says one employee. However, another consultnat counters, "A lot of [work] is self-imposed. Most managers recognize when someone is overworked and encourage them to take time off or go home early. Commitments (weekends or nights) are almost always honored if they are scheduled ahead of time." Trinity consultants report workweeks of 50 to 60 hours during normal times. One upside in the travel-heavy consultant world: travel at Trinity is infrequent for lower-level consultants, usually limited to day trips once or twice a month. Senior employees travel up to once a week.

## Unstructured management

Supervisors are lauded for their intelligence and honesty, but their hands-off management approach translates into a lack of structure. Consultants say it's unclear what happens at the meetings of the high-ups, and there's little feedback about performance. As one consultant says, "They've given me a lot of freedom and entrusted me with responsibility. However, there is not a lot of mentoring or development from the company leadership."

That's echoed in concerns about the company as a whole. The firm could use "a clearer organizational structure, better communication, and more formal training" for its employees, say insiders. "The small company atmosphere sometimes leads to less clear corporate structure than some employees desire," says one respondent.

The sink-or-swim philosophy transfers to employee training, too. "The job is definitely for people who are inclined to independent learning," says one analyst. That's good and bad news. "Rather than spending the first week learning how to format Excel spreadsheets, associates are brought in on a very high level," says one consultant.

## A meritocracy

Trinity bases its promotions almost purely on merit, a policy lauded by insiders. "Thus far, I have found Trinity's promotion process to be ideal. One is not judged on number of years in the firm or whether or not he/she has an MBA. Promotions are based on merit, performance and potential – the way it should be," says one consultant. Another echoes, "Trinity is a true meritocracy: If you do great work, there is no limit to your position or your success."

In hiring, too, Trinity appears to look only at merit. The firm has approximately four minority consultants out of 30 employees, average for the industry. "It seems as though we don't actively go out and recruit [minorities]. We hire the best person for the job, regardless of minority status," says a consultant. Women haven't made it to the upper levels of the company – yet. "Women are much more prevalent at the lower levels in the company today, but that is a direct result of their recent entry to the company. The women that have been with the company for years have matured through the company in the same way as men," says one consultant. "As Trinity Partners grows, the number of senior women should grow as well."

---

For more information on top consulting employers and consulting careers, go to the Vault Consulting Career Channel at http://consulting.vault.com

- Detailed 40-page employer profiles on top employers like McKinsey, BCG, Bain, Accenture and more
- Surveys of employees at hundreds of consulting firms
- The only job board on the Web dedicated to consulting jobs – The Vault Consulting Job Board
- Case interview guides and one-on-one case interview prep

# http://consulting.vault.com

---

"Promotions are based on merit, performance and potential - the way it should be."

— *Trinity Partners consultant*

# Vantage Partners

Brighton Landing West
10 Guest Street
Boston, MA 02135
Phone: (617) 354-6090
Fax: (617) 354-4685
www.vantagepartners.com

## LOCATIONS

**Boston, MA (HQ)**

## PRACTICE AREAS

Improving Management of Key
Relationships
Increasing Return on Negotiation
Enabling Cross-Matrix Collaboration

## THE STATS

**Employer Type:** Private Company
**CEO (or other title):** Run by
partnership of six
**2002 Employees:** 36
**2001 Employees:** 30

## UPPERS

- "Casual, fun atmosphere"
- Academic writing opportunities
- "Intellectual challenge – my brain
  gets a workout every day"

## DOWNERS

- "Nowhere to be promoted"
- "Performance expectations can be
  unclear"
- New firm, many processes still not
  in place

## KEY COMPETITORS

Accenture
A.T. Kearney

## EMPLOYMENT CONTACT

Associate Recruiting Coordinator
Vantage Partners
Brighton Landing West
10 Guest Street
Boston, MA 02135
Phone: (617) 354-6090
Fax: (617) 354-4685
E-mail:
recruiting@vantagepartners.com

 **THE BUZZ**
WHAT CONSULTANTS AT OTHER FIRMS ARE SAYING

- "Niche"
- "Allows a lot of responsibility"

# THE SCOOP

## We can work it out

Vantage Partners is a small firm focused on the field of relationship management. Everything from building and implementing new business alliances to negotiating deals to helping companies deal with internal conflicts falls under the rubric of Vantage's brand of expertise. Members of the firm are responsible for such helpful books on the subject as *Getting to YES, Difficult Conversations* and *Making Partnerships Work: A Relationship Management Handbook*.

## It's academic

Vantage Partners exists as proof that networking in school pays off. The five founding directors of this management consultancy were members of the Harvard Negotiation Project at Harvard Law School, created in 1979 to investigate all aspects of negotiation and conflict resolution. Furthermore, they all served as director at the firm that grew out of that project, Conflict Management Inc.

## Teaching companies to fish

Vantage seeks to make effective negotiation and relationship management part of a client's normal business structure, by building the necessary processes, skills and attitudes into a company. In a sense, Vantage loses every client it gains because when the project ends, the client has learned to be self-sufficient.

There are three Vantage divisions, each focusing on different pieces of the relationship puzzle. Vantage Partners is the consulting arm. The other divisions are Vantage Training and Vantage Technologies.

Vantage Training offers workshops based on techniques elucidated in publications by Vantage partners and consultants. Some notable courses are Effective Negotiation Skills (based on *Getting to YES*); Managing the Difficult Conversation in Business (based on *Difficult Conversations*); and Strategic Relationship Management.

Vantage Technologies is a software solution provider, giving clients the online tools to effectively cope with diverse relationships. Its chief offering is Partnersmith, a comprehensive system for strategic relationship management (SRM).

# GETTING HIRED

## Need-based hiring

If larger firms are a hiring factory, Vantage is more like an artisanal boutique when it comes to choosing new consultants. As a small firm focused on a single aspect of consulting, Vantage can afford to pick only those applicants it needs, when it needs them. "We do not have routine hiring cycles," confirms one insider. Another adds, "We recruit undergraduates and experienced graduates as needed." These hires typically have one to three years of post-grad experience. Vantage also offers a summer internship program.

When asked where Vantage recruits new consultants, the common response was "Harvard and Wellesley." One respondent notes, "We also look at resumes that are sent to us directly from visitors to our web site." The interview process itself involves a wide cross-section of Vantage consultants. An insider relates: "After a telephone screen, a group of candidates attends a full day of interviewing at our offices, which allows us to get to know the candidate better and allows the candidate to learn more about what it is like to work here. The recruiting team then debriefs the day and the partner in charge of hiring decides whether or not to extend any offers." A colleague adds, "Associates manage the hiring process and are integral to the final decision on who to accept."

Applicants are asked to solve a case study – typically "a slightly fictionalized account of an actual client project." "We use an example that's very specific to our context," says one respondent. The firm says the case is based on a real engagement with the names of all parties changed.

# OUR SURVEY SAYS

## An East Coast think-tank-y consultancy, with dog

Vantage associates describe the company atmosphere as "collaborative." One insider says, "associates work closely with partners, and the exchange of feedback is highly encouraged." Another calls it "very friendly, laid back, and open." "Vantage likes to describe itself as a cross between an academic think tank, a San Francisco start-up and an East Coast consulting firm," relates an associate. "We are completely casual all week long, break regularly every Thursday to enjoy 'snack time' provided by an employee on a rotating basis, and get visits from one of the partner's new puppies regularly."

## The well-balanced consultant

Life must be good for Vantage employees – they don't even complain about travel requirements or work hours, two common gripes among consultants. Travel, according to one associate, "is highly variable, but generally low. We don't 'set up shop' at a client for weeks at a time. Usually, if you visit a client, it is once a month for a few days." Another adds, "People's travel preferences are taken into account when we make staffing recommendations – if people really don't like to travel, their needs are generally accommodated." A third provides this explanation: "Since our consulting deliverables are based on our own methodology and tools, we do most of our work out of our own office."

As to office hours, Vantage consultants expect to work 45 to 50 hours a week, with "dramatic swings," at least in the eyes of one insider. Most report that work spikes bring the hours up to 70 or 80 a week, occurring "about a quarter of the time." Another consultant points out "there is no expectation of 'face time.'" "As long as the work gets done, it does not matter where or when," one respondent informs us. (Vantage clarifies that while there is no expectation of face time in the office, there is a certain amount of face time with clients expected.) That insider adds that "associates are allowed to manage their own time" and, for example, may "work from home when necessary. While Vantage encourages, through their hiring policies and by example, their employees to have active outside pursuits," she says, "when work needs to get done, it needs to get done and your personal life is put on hold."

However, says another, "We don't really have 'on the beach' time." One helpful soul explains, "Because associates have a lot of internal responsibilities (methodology development, research and writing, recruiting, marketing, etc.), it's unheard of to have absolutely nothing to do."

## Transparent - or invisible?

Unlike the great majority of consultancies, there are only two job titles at Vantage: associate and partner. Promotions, if you wish to call them such, are "not transparent." To be more accurate, they are nonexistent. "Promotions don't happen in terms of a new title," says one associate, but are a quiet matter of "more money, more responsibility and a greater degree of client contact." "Most times," says another, "the only real 'supervision' is a performance review. That means a lot of independence, but little guidance." This generates mixed reviews from employees.

On the positive side, says one insider, "we are less focused on titles than on just constantly pushing people to take on more and more challenging work." Another adds, "There is no up-or-out expectation. People are encouraged to stay as long as they like, assuming more and more responsibility based on experience and individual capability." A side effect of this is that "we don't have 'supervisors' per se – we work directly with partners in the firm." Other upshots mentioned by our sources are the "emphasis on managing your own career development and progress" and "freedom to work in your own fashion as long as you deliver against your deadlines," as well as a workplace "relatively devoid of typical office politics."

However, this lack of a transparent promotion system has its negatives as well. One person cites "no sense of progression (nowhere to be promoted)" and a "lack of formal processes to develop people." A colleague feels the "flat organizational structure where no transparent promotions take place can make working dynamics difficult if people aren't open and assertive with one another." A third agrees, "The unstructured environment can be challenging for people, especially those coming straight out of college or from rigidly structured firms."

## Community service

There's a fair amount of involvement with local philanthropy among Vantage employees, but it's not a matter of policy. "The firm does encourage community involvement," says one source. Another tells us there is "plenty of encouragement and willingness to support, but no sponsorship. As with everything at Vantage, if you feel strongly about something, you do it yourself." However, one person adds, "we're currently organizing a community service team to manage such activities, as there has been a lot of interest in this area."

## The advantage of Vantage

Rather than tell you how Vantage consultants feel about working there, we'll let a consultant there do it for us. One consultant summarizes, "Vantage is a fantastic place to work if you are self-driven and don't need a structured work environment to learn or be productive. There isn't anyone here to hold your hand – but if you raise your hand, your questions will always be answered."

# CONSULTING EMPLOYER DIRECTORY

# CALIFORNIA

**LECG**
2000 Powell St., Ste. 600
Emeryville, CA 94608
Phone: (510) 653-9800
Fax: (510) 653-9898
www.lecg.com

*Recruiting Coordinator*
Fax: (510) 653-9898

**PRTM**
1503 Grant Road, Suite 200
Mountain View, CA 94040
Phone: (650) 967-2900

*Attn: Recruiting*
Fax: (650) 967-6367
E-mail: uswest@prtm.com
Fax: (650) 967-6367
www.prtm.com

**Strategic Decisions Group**
2440 Sand Hill Road
Menlo Park, CA 94025
Phone: (650) 854-9000
Fax: (650) 854-6718
www.sdg.com

*Sydney Higa*
Recruiting Coordinator
2440 Sand Hill Road
Menlo Park, CA 94025
Fax: (650) 854-6718
E-mail: recruiter@sdg.com

# CONNECTICUT

**Gartner**
56 Top Gallant Road
Stamford, CT 06904
Phone: (203) 964-0096
www.gartner.com

*Employment Contact*
Human Resources
Fax: (203) 316-3445
E-mail: gartner@gartnercareers.com

**Mars & Company**
124 Mason Street
Greenwich, CT 06830
Phone: (203) 629-9292
Fax: (203) 629-9432
www.marsandco.com

*Francine Even*
124 Mason Street
Greenwich, CT 06830
Phone: (203) 629-9292
E-mail: recruiting@usg.marsandco.com

**Towers Perrin**
One Stamford Plaza
263 Tresser Blvd.
Stamford, CT 06089
Phone: (203) 326-5400
Fax: (203) 326-5499
www.towersperrin.com

*Employment Contact*
E-mail: careers.towers.com

# DISTRICT OF COLUMBIA

**Corporate Executive Board**
Suite 6000
Washington, DC 20006
Phone: (202) 777-5000
Fax: (202) 777-5100
www.executiveboard.com

*Recruiting Department*
2000 Pennsylvania Avenue, NW
Washington, DC 20006
Fax: (202) 777-5100
E-mail: jobs@executiveboard.com

**Watson Wyatt Worldwide**
1717 H Street, NW
Washington, DC 20006
Phone: (202) 715-7000
Fax: (202) 715-7700

www.watsonwyatt.com/careers/opportunities.asp

# GEORGIA

**Kurt Salmon Associates**
1355 Peachtree Street, NE
Suite 900
Atlanta, GA 30309
Phone: (404) 892-0321
Fax: (404) 898-9590
www.kurtsalmon.com

*Americas*
RecrNA@kurtsalmon.com

*Asia-Pacific*
RecrAPAC@kurtsalmon.com

*Europe*
RecrEU@kurtsalmon.com

# ILLINOIS

**Aon Consulting**
200 E. Randolph Street
Chicago, IL 60601
Phone: (800) 438-6487
Fax: (312) 381-6032
www.aon.com
jobsearch.aon.newjobs.com

**Braun Consulting**
20 W. Kinzie
Suite 1600
Chicago, IL 60610
Phone: (312) 984-7000
Fax: (312) 984-7033
www.braunconsult.com

*Experienced consultants:*
Phone:(888) 284-5621
Campus recruiting:
Phone: (888) 284-5628
www.braunconsult.com/careers

**DiamondCluster International Inc.**
Suite 3000
John Hancock Center
875 N. Michigan Avenue
Chicago, IL 60611
Phone: (312) 255-5000
Fax: (312) 255-6000
www.diamondcluster.com

*Employment Contact*
www.diamondcluster.com/careers

**Grant Thornton**
175 West Jackson Boulevard
Chicago, IL 60604
Phone: (312) 856-0200
Fax: (312) 861-1340
www.grantthornton.com
See job listings' specific e-mail
contacts.

**Hewitt Associates**
100 Half Day Road
Lincolnshire, IL 60069
Phone: (847) 295-5000
Fax: (847) 295-7634
www.hewitt.com
*Employment Contact*
was.hewitt.com/hewitt/careers/inde
x.htm

**Lexecon**
332 South Michigan Avenue
Chicago, IL 60604
Phone: (312) 322-0200
Fax: (312) 322-0218
www.lexecon.com

*Employment Contact*
Darlene Serrano
Human Resource Manager
Phone: (312) 322-0200
Fax: (312) 322-0218
E-mail:
chgo_recruiting@lexecon.com

**Navigant Consulting**
615 N. Wabash Avenue
Chicago, IL 60611
Phone: (312) 573-5600
Fax: (312) 573-5678
www.navigantconsulting.com

*Christine Bedalow*
Director of Recruiting
175 W. Jackson Blvd., Suite 500
Chicago, IL 60604
Phone: (312) 583-5700

**ZS Associates**
1800 Sherman Avenue
Suite 700
Evanston, IL 60201
Phone: (847) 492-3600
Fax: (847) 492-3409
www.zsassociates.com

www.zsassociates.com/careers/apply/co
ntactlist.html

# MASSACHSETTS

**Analysis Group**
111 Huntington Avenue
Tenth Floor
Boston, MA 02199
Phone: (617) 425-8000
Fax: (617) 425-8001
www.analysisgroup.com

www.analysisgroup.com/c_apply.htm
E-mail: recruiter@analysisgroup.com

**Bain & Company**
Two Copley Place
Boston, MA 02116
Phone: (617) 572-2000
Fax: (617) 572-2427
www.bain.com

*Employment Contact*
Online application:
www.bain.com/HCR/onlineapp/asp/app1.
asp

Recruiting contacts by location:
www.bain.com/bainweb/join/profiles_pla
ces/places.asp

**Boston Consulting Group**
Exchange Place
31st Floor
Boston, MA 02109
Phone: (617) 973-1200
Fax: (617) 973-1339
www.bcg.com

*Employment Contact*
www.bcg.com/careers/careers_splash.asp

**The Brattle Group**
Third Floor
44 Brattle Street
Cambridge, MA 02138
Phone: (617) 864-7900
Fax: (617) 864-1576
www.brattle.com

*Megan Dunn*
Recruiting Manager

**Charles River Associates**
John Hancock Tower
200 Clarendon Street, T-33
Boston, MA 02116-5092
Phone: (617) 425-3000
Fax: (617) 425-3132
www.crai.com

*Employment Contact - Boston*
Sara McQuarrie
Fax: (617) 425-3112
E-mail: hr@crai.com

*Employment Contact - DC office:*
Erica Scipio
Charles River Associates
1201 F Street N.W., Suite 700
Washington, DC 20004-1204
Fax: (202) 662-3910

**L.E.K. Consulting**
28 State Street
16th Floor
Boston, MA 02109
Phone: (617) 951-9500
Fax: (617) 951-9392
www.lek.com

*Employment Contact*
Carrie Brown
Phone: (617) 951-9500
Fax: (617) 951-9392
E-mail: boston_resumes@lek.com

**Monitor Group**
Two Canal Park
Cambridge, MA 02141
Phone: (617) 252-2000
Fax: (617) 252-2100
www.monitor.com

*Employment Contact*
http://www.monitor.com/cgi-
bin/iowa/careers
E-mail: Recruiting_us@monitor.com

**The Parthenon Group**
200 State Street
Boston, MA 02109
Phone: (617) 478-2550
Fax: (617) 478-2555
www.parthenon.com

*Employment Contact*
E-mail: recruiting@parthenon.com

**PRTM**
1050 Winter Street
Waltham, MA 02451
Phone: (781) 647-2800
Fax: (781) 647-2804
www.prtm.com

*Eastern U.S.:*
Attn: Recruiting
Fax: (781) 466-9853
E-mail: useast@prtm.com

**Putnam Associates**
25 Burlington Mall Road
Burlington, MA 01803
Phone: (781) 273-5480
Fax: (781) 273-5484
www.putassoc.com

*Erica J. Wines*
HR/Recruiting Coordinator
E-mail: careers@putassoc.com

# WASHINGTON, DC

**The Brattle Group**
Suite 800
1133 20th Street, NW
Washington, DC 20036
Phone: (202) 955-5050
Fax: (202) 955-5059

E-mail: recruiting@brattle.com
www.brattle.com/join/joinHome.html

# NEW YORK

**Accenture**
1345 Avenue of the Americas
New York, NY 10105
Phone: (917) 452-4400
www.accenture.com

*Employment Contact*
http://careers3.accenture.com/

**Buck Consultants**
1 Pennsylvania Plaza
New York, NY 10119-4798
Phone: (212) 330-1000
Fax: (212) 695-4184
www.buckconsultants.com

*Cathy Gushue*
Director of Human Resources
500 Plaza Drive
Secaucus, NJ 07096-1533
Phone: (201) 902-2465
www.buckconsultants.com/careers

E-mail: careers@buckconsultants.com

**Cap Gemini Ernst & Young**
Five Times Square
New York, NY 10036
Phone: (917) 934-8000
Fax: (917) 934-8001
www.cgey.com

*Employment Contact*
http://www.cgey.com/careers

**Deloitte Consulting**
1633 Broadway
35th Floor
New York, NY 10019
Phone: (212) 492-4500
Fax: (212) 492-4743
www.dc.com

*Employment Contact*
www.dc.com/careers

**First Manhattan Consulting Group**
90 Park Avenue
19th Floor
New York, NY 10016
Phone: (212) 557-0500
Fax: (212) 338-9296
www.fmcg.com

*Recruiting Coordinator*
90 Park Avenue
New York, NY 10016
Phone: (212) 455-9224
E-mail: recruit@fmcg.com

**Giuliani Partners**
5 Times Square
New York, NY 10036
Phone: (212) 931-7300
Fax: (212) 931-7310
www.giulianipartners.com

**IBM Business Consulting Services**
Route 100
Somers, NY 10589
www 1.ibm.com/services/bcs/index.html

*Employment Contact*
www-1.ibm.com/employment
Phone: (800) IBM-7080, ext. BCS

**Marakon Associates**
245 Park Avenue
44th Floor
New York, NY 10167
Phone: (212) 377-5000
Fax: (212) 377-6000
www.marakon.com

*Employment Contact*
All applicants should fill out a form at
/www.marakon.com/careers

**McKinsey & Company**
55 East 52nd Street
New York, NY 10022
Phone: (212) 446-7000
Fax: (212) 446-8575
www.mckinsey.com

*Employment Contact*
E-mail:
career_information@mckinsey.com

**Mercer Human Resource Consulting**
1166 Avenue of the Americas
New York, NY 10036
Phone: (212) 345-7000
Fax: (212) 345-7414
www.mercerHR.com

*Employment Contact*
See Joining Mercer at
www.mercerHR.com

**Mercer Management Consulting**
1166 Avenue of the Americas
32nd Floor
New York, NY 10036
Phone: (212) 345-8000
Fax: (212) 345-8075
www.mercermc.com

*Employment Contact*
E-mail: recruiting@mercermc.com

**Mercer Oliver Wyman**
99 Park Avenue
Fifth Floor
New York, NY 10016
Phone: (212) 541-8100
Fax: (212) 541-8957
www.merceroliverwyman.com

*U.S., Canada and Emerging Markets Recruiting*
E-mail: RecruitingNA@mow.com

*UK and Western European Recruiting*
E-mail: RecruitingWE@mow.com

*German and Central European Recruiting*
E-mail: RecruitingCE@mow.com

*All other recruiting*
E-mail: RecruitingOther@mow.com

**NERA**
50 Main Street
White Plains, NY 10606
Phone: (914) 448-4000
Fax: (914) 448-4040
www.nera.com

*U.S.*
NERA
50 Main Street
White Plains, NY 10606
Fax: (914) 448-4040
E-mail: recruitingteam@nera.com

*London and Brussels*
Recruitment
15 Stratford Place
London W1N 9AF
Fax: +44.20.7659.8501
E-mail: londonrecruitment@nera.com

**OC&C Strategy Consultants**
330 Seventh Avenue
11th Floor
New York, NY 10011
Phone: (212) 244-3550
Fax: (212) 244-1117
www.occstrategy.com

*U.S.*
E-mail: recruitment@occstrategy-usa.com

*London*
Katherine Day
OC&C Strategy Consultants
The OC&C Building
233 Shaftesbury Avenue
London WC2H 8EE
E-mail: Recruitment@occstrategy.com

*France*
Sophie Sliman
E-mail: contact@occstrategy.fr

**Roland Berger Strategy Consultants**
350 Park Avenue
30th Floor
New York, NY 10022
Phone: (212) 651-9680
Fax: (212) 756-8750
www.rolandberger.com

*Employment Contact*
www.rolandberger.com

**Stern Stewart & Company**
135 East 57th Street
New York, NY 10022
Phone: (212) 261-0600
Fax: (212) 581-6420
www.sternstewart.com

*Employment Contact*
E-mail: careers@sternstewart.com

# PENNSYLVANIA

**Hay Group**
The Wanamaker Building
100 Penn Square East
Philadelphia, PA 19107-3388
Phone: (215) 861-2000
Fax: (215) 861-2111
www.haygroup.com

www.haygroup.com/Careers/Overview.asp

# TEXAS

**A.T. Kearney**
5400 Legacy Drive
Plano, TX 75201
Phone: (972) 604-4600
Fax: (972) 543-7680
www.atkearney.com

*Employment Contact*
A.T. Kearney
222 West Adams Street
Chicago, Illinois 60606
Phone: (312) 648-0111
Numerous international hiring contacts;
check A.T. Kearney's web site for
regional information.

# VIRGINIA

**BearingPoint**
1676 International Drive
McLean, VA 22102
Phone: (703) 747-3000
Fax: (703) 747-8500
www.bearingpoint.com

*Employment Contact*
Sean Huurman
Director of Recruiting, America
E-mail:
us-consultrecops@bearingpoint.net

**Booz Allen Hamilton**
8283 Greensboro Drive
McLean, VA 22102
Phone: (703) 902-5000
Fax: (703) 902-3333
www.boozallen.com

*Employment Contact*
www.BoozAllen.com

**Dean & Company**
8065 Leesburg Pike, Ste. 500
Vienna, VA 22182-2733
Phone: (703) 506-3900
Fax: (703) 506-3905
www.deanco.com

E-mail: recruiting@dean.com

# ENGLAND

**PA Consulting Group**
123 Buckingham Palace Road
London, UK SW1W 9SR
Phone: +44 20 7730 9000
Fax: +44 20 7333 5050
www.paconsulting.com

*Americas*
Julie Davern
PA Consulting Group
315A Enterprise Drive
Plainsboro, NJ 08536
Fax: (609) 936 8811
E-mail: julie.davern@paconsulting.com

**Watson Wyatt Worldwide**
Watson House, London Road
Reigate, Surrey RH2
9PQ, England
Phone: +44 1737-241144
Fax: +44 1737-241496
www.watsonwyatt.com

www.watsonwyatt.com/careers/opportu
nities.asp

# GERMANY

**Droege & Comp.**
Poststrasse 5-6
40213 Dusseldorf
Germany
Phone: 49-211-86731-0
Fax: 49-211-86731-111
www.droege.de

*Droege & Comp., Inc.*
Attn: Recruiting
405 Lexington Ave.
35th Floor
New York, NY 10174
Phone: (212) 557-7616
Fax: (212) 577-6788
E-mail: recruiting@droegeusa.com

**Roland Berger Strategy Consultants**
Arabellastr. 33
81925 Munich
Germany
Phone: +49-89-92 30-0
Fax: +49-89-92 30-8202

*Employment Contact*
www.rolandberger.com

# ITALY

**Value Partners**
32 Via Leopardi
Milan 20123
Italy
Phone: +39 02-4854-81
Fax: +39 02-4800-9010
www.valuepartners.com

*Europe*
E-mail: recruitment@valuepartners.com

*South America*
E-mail: talita.onghero@valuepartners.com

# FRANCE

**Corporate Value Associates**
12 avenue Kléber
75116 Paris
France
Phone: +33 1 53 65 71 71
Fax: +33 1 53 65 71 99
www.corporate-value.com

*Paris*
E-mail: recruitfrance@corporate-
value.com
Phone: +33 1 53 65 71 87

*Boston*
E-mail: cvarecruitus@corporate-
value.com
Phone: (617) 267-5959

# CONSULTING RECRUITER DIRECTORY

## The Ford Group

Sandra D. Ford
CEO and Managing Director
The Ford Group, Inc.
295 East Swedesford Road #282
Wayne, PA 19087
(610) 296-5205
www.thefordgroup.com

The Ford Group, Inc. is a national boutique firm specializing in retained executive search for management consulting firms and leading corporations. Our clients include many of the world's premier organizations who retain us for our search and consulting expertise, as well as our ability to deliver timely, outstanding results.  The Ford Group offers several significant advantages by providing responsive, value-added services to our clients. Our firm seeks to form collaborative partnerships and strategic relationships with our clients based on mutual respect and outstanding client service.

# APPENDIX

# Industry Buzzwords

The consulting industry uses many buzzwords. Consultants easily lapse into their lingo while conversing with the layman, imposing panic on those who were unaware they even possess a "skill set" (those areas where you excel). Here is a short rundown of some of those words that consultants like to throw around:

**APD:** Advanced Professional Degree (e.g., JD, PhD, or MD).

**Application Service Provider (ASP):** A company that offers its clients online access to applications that would otherwise be located in their own computers.

**B2B:** Business-to-Business.

**B2C:** Business-to-Consumer.

**Balanced Scorecard:** A conceptual framework for translating an organization's vision into a set of performance indicators distributed among four perspectives: financial, customer, internal business processes, and learning and growth.

**Bananagram:** A graph showing profitability vs. relative market share. The graph shows that the higher the market share, the higher the profitability. (The typical measure of profitability for this graph is Return On Capital Employed, or "ROCE" [pronounced "roachy"].)

**BCG matrix:** A portfolio assessment tool developed by The Boston Consulting Group. Also called a growth/share matrix.

**Benchmarking:** Measuring a value, practice or other quantity (such as costs) against those of other companies in the industry.

**Blank slide:** Initial sketch on paper for a slide to be used in a case presentation (called blank because it does not include data until analysts input it).

**Brainteaser:** A consulting interview question in which the job seeker is asked to solve a logic problem.

**Boiling the ocean:** When a project team finds itself faced with an impossibly large amount of data.

**Business Process Re-engineering (BPR):** The process of reviewing a client's business processes, eliminating unneeded or "non-value-added" tasks, and then implementing the leaner, more efficient process.

**Case team:** Team working on a consulting project for a client; usually composed of one partner (or director), one consultant, and two or more analysts.

**Change management:** A service where the firm helps a company cope with a period of significant change (such as a merger, downsizing or restructuring).

**Consultancy:** A typically European term for "consulting firm," though the word has picked up currency in the United States.

**Core competencies:** The areas in which a company excels. Consultants believe a company should enter only those businesses that are part of its core competencies.

**Critical path:** A term from operations management theory. Every business process consists of a series of tasks. Some of these tasks are related to maintenance of the process or administrative and bookkeeping issues. Taken away, they do not directly impact the end result of the business process. If you eliminate these tasks, there remains the core set of tasks that must occur in order to produce the desired result. This is the critical path. In everyday consulting language, the term refers to only those work tasks that are most important at the time.

**Customer Relationship Management (CRM):** Term that refers to the data-gathering methods used to collect information about a client's customers. CRM usually focuses on sales force automation, customer service/call center, field service and marketing automation.

**DCF:** Discounted Cash Flow. The present value of a future cash flow.

**Deck:** A report detailing client issues and recommendations from the project team. Also known as a "deliverable."

**Drilldown:** Asking questions to gather more detail about a situation, usually from a high-level (big-picture) view.

**80/20 rule:** Getting 80 percent of the answer first in 20 percent of your time. The other 80 percent of your time might not be worth it. (A favorite of Bain chairperson Orit Gadiesh.)

**Engagement:** A consulting assignment received by a consulting firm; also called a "case" or "project."

**Enterprise Resource Planning (ERP):** Processes or software that help streamline departments or divisions of a company.

**Experience curve:** The principle that a company's cost declines as its production increases. One assumption used by consultants is that a company's costs decline by roughly 25 percent for every doubling in production (e.g., a company's 200th unit of a product costs 75 percent of the 100th unit's cost).

**Granularity:** Refers to the basic elements that make up a business problem. Imagine a handful of sand. At a high level, it is simply a handful of sand. At a granular level, it is bits of rock and shell matter reduced to fine granules over time by the ocean.

**Guesstimate:** A type of consulting interview question. Guesstimates require job seekers to make an educated estimate of something (often the size of the market for a particular product or service) using basic calculations.

**High-level view:** Also referred to as a "50,000-foot view." It describes a situation in general terms or as an overview of a situation. Also known as "helicoptering."

**Hoteling/Hot-desking:** A system used to assign space to consultants working on-site. Consultants move around so much that in some firms they are not assigned permanent offices — just a voice mail extension. Whenever they know they need to work on-site, they call up the office nearest them to request a desk.

**Hurdle rate:** A company's cost of capital. In general, if the return on an investment exceeds the hurdle rate, the company should make the investment.

**Implementation:** The process by which a consulting firm ensures that the advice it gives to a client company is enacted.

**Incubator:** A place or situation that encourages the formation and development of new companies by providing certain services (e.g., office space, Internet connections, support staff).

**Learning curve:** The rate at which a consultant acquires background information or industry knowledge needed for a case. A steep curve is a good thing.

**Letter of Intent (LOI)/Letter of Proposal (LOP):** A sales pitch to a potential client that lays out how and on what a consulting team will focus its efforts and what results the client should expect.

**NPV:** Net Present Value. The sum of a series of discounted cash flows. Used to assess the profitability for a client of making an investment or undertaking a project.

**O'Hare test:** A test used by interviewers to assess personality fit. "If I were stuck overnight with this person at O'Hare Airport, would I have fun?"

**On the beach:** The time between assignments, when consultants' work hours usually decline significantly. This expression originated at McKinsey.

**Out-of-the-box thinking:** Creativity.

**Outsourcing:** Hiring an outside vendor to perform a task normally performed within a company, often at a lower cost and with better results. Examples of processes commonly outsourced include payroll, data processing, recruitment, accounting and document processing.

**Pigeonholing:** Usually refers to a consultant's becoming overspecialized.

**Porter, Michael:** A founding principal of Monitor Group and the father of the consulting framework known as "Porter's Five Forces."

**Re-engineering:** A largely discredited fad of the early 1990s, which advocates a complete overhaul (and usually downsizing) of a company's strategies, operations and practices.

**Rightsizing:** Also known as "downsizing" — just a kinder, gentler term for restructuring the elements of a company. This is most often used in reference to headcount reductions but can apply to plants, processes, technology, financial elements and office locations.

**Scope creep:** When clients find themselves overly involved in tangential aspects of a project.

**Shareholder value:** The total net wealth of a company's stockholders. The primary goal of consultants in undertaking most engagements is to maximize shareholder value.

**Silo:** The tendency for a firm to emphasize vertical relationships within the organization at the expense of horizontal (interdepartmental, etc.) ones.

**Six-Sigma:** A process used by consultants to measure a company's performance. The term comes from the notion that a company's performance metric should never be more than six standard deviations (sigmas) from the ideal.

**Stakeholder:** A person who has a stake in the outcome of a particular situation. Most commonly, the stakeholders in a case are the shareholders, creditors, or employees.

**Supply chain:** The means and process of physically distributing goods to the consumer.

**Total Quality Management (TQM):** Management with the purpose of producing a product or service of the highest quality, with zero tolerance for defects.

**Up or out:** Promotion policy that requires consultants to leave a firm if not promoted within a certain period of time (usually two to three years). Also known as "sink or swim."

**Value-based management:** Consulting strategy whose ultimate goal is to increase shareholder value for the client.

**Value migration:** The flow of economic and shareholder value away from obsolete business models to new, more effective designs.

**Value-added:** Used to define a service or product in a marketplace that adds value to a preexisting product or way of doing things.

**Venture capital:** Any kind of equity-related financing.

**Work plan:** A schedule for completing a consulting engagement.

**Writing a deck:** Preparing slides for presentations to clients.

**White paper:** A report whose goal is to educate consumers on a major issue.

**White space opportunity:** An opportunity for a company to make money in an area in which it currently generates zero revenue (for example, launching a new product line, licensing an existing brand or technology or entering a new geographic market).

# Index of Firms

## Firms that are subsidiaries of larger companies

## Firms with major HR practices

## Public firms

## Firms with non-U.S. headquarters

## Firms with 10,000+ employees

## Firms with fewer than 1,000 employees

## Firms with fewer than 5 offices

## Firms with 50+ offices

# About the Author

## Marcy Lerner

Marcy Lerner is the vice president for content at Vault. She holds a BA in history from the University of Virginia and an MA in history from Yale University.

# How many consulting job boards have you visited lately?

## (Thought so.)

---

Use the Internet's most targeted job search tools for consulting professionals.

## Vault Consulting Job Board

The most comprehensive and convenient job board for consulting professionals. Target your search by area of consulting, function, and experience level, and find the job openings that you want. No surfing required.

## VaultMatch Resume Database

Vault takes match-making to the next level: post your resume and customize your search by area of consulting, experience and more. We'll match job listings with your interests and criteria and e-mail them directly to your inbox.

**V/\ULT**

> the most trusted name in career information™

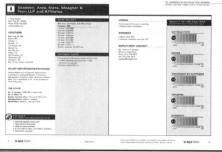